PENGUIN BOOKS

THE LIVING PRESIDENCY

Emmet John Hughes is a veteran of more than twenty years with *Time, Life, Fortune,* and *Newsweek.* He has been an adviser in four Presidential campaigns and, in 1953, served in the White House itself as an assistant to President Dwight D. Eisenhower. He is currently professor of politics at Rutgers University, where he teaches a course on the American Presidency. In addition to the present volume, Mr. Hughes is the author of *The Ordeal of Power, America the Vincible,* and other books.

D0594834

Also by the Author

THE CHURCH AND THE LIBERAL SOCIETY

REPORT FROM SPAIN

AMERICA THE VINCIBLE

THE ORDEAL OF POWER

THE
LIVING
PRESIDENCY

The Resources and Dilemmas of
the American Presidential Office

by EMMET JOHN HUGHES

PENGUIN BOOKS INC

Baltimore • Maryland

Penguin Books Inc
7110 Ambassador Road
Baltimore, Maryland 21207, U.S.A.

First published by Coward, McCann & Geoghegan, Inc., New York, 1973
Published by Penguin Books Inc, 1974

Printed in the United States of America

A portion of Chapter Four was published in somewhat different form
in the *Smithsonian,* in March and April, 1972.

All for Katherine
and a little for Caitlin

Contents

I have come across men of letters who have written history without taking part in public affairs, and politicians who have concerned themselves with producing events without thinking about them. I have observed that the first are always inclined to find general causes, whereas the second, living in the midst of disconnected daily facts, are prone to imagine that everything is attributable to particular incidents, and that the wires they pull are the same as those that move the world. It is to be presumed that both are equally deceived.

—ALEXIS DE TOCQUEVILLE

The Principal Powers of the President
as Stated in Article II of . . .

THE CONSTITUTION OF THE UNITED STATES
★　　　　　★　　　　　★

The executive Power shall be vested in a President of the United States. He shall hold his Office during the Term of four Years. . . .

The President shall be Commander in Chief of the Army and Navy of the United States, and of the Militia of the several States . . .; he may require the Opinion, in writing, of the principal Officer in each of the executive Departments . . . he shall have Power to grant Reprieves and Pardons. . . .

He shall have Power, by and with the Advice and Consent of the Senate, to make Treaties, provided two thirds of the Senators present concur; and he shall nominate, and by and with the Advice and Consent of the Senate, shall appoint Ambassadors, other public Ministers and Consuls, Judges of the Supreme Court, and all other Officers of the United States, whose Appointments are not herein otherwise provided for, and which shall be established by Law. . . .

He shall from time to time give to the Congress Information of the State of the Union, and recommend to their Consideration such Measures as he shall judge necessary and expedient; he may, on extraordinary Occasions, convene both Houses, or either of them . . .; he shall receive Ambassadors and other public Ministers; he shall take Care that the Laws be faithfully executed, and shall Commission all the Officers of the United States.

One

Some Thoughts by Way of Introduction: The Problem of the Presidency

Shall we have a King?

—JOHN JAY to GEORGE WASHINGTON, 1787

I believe that, as the Republic nears two centuries of age, a new inquiry into the American Presidency, and its living politics and its likely portents, still shares one thing in common with the venerable inquiry of John Jay. Now, as then, the questioning wonder over the role of the Chief Executive arises from dilemmas and doubts that belong to a particular time, and bespeak a special stress, in the life of the Republic. Now, as always, the scrutiny of the office has been spurred by specific concerns or immediate anxieties—or even mere personal experiences. And since these random spurs to thought shape the purpose and set the range of any study, they deserve to be briefly stated.

A few such particular provocations to this inquiry have been scattered over the past twenty years. The most vivid, though not the earliest, date from the year 1966—a trip around the globe and a quiet time for troubled reflection while flying through the skies between Saigon and London. This journey could be made, at that time, only with a sharp sense of the political presence of not one but two Chief Executives: the thirty-fifth and thirty-sixth Presidents, John Fitzgerald Kennedy and Lyndon Baines Johnson. For radically distinct as were the Presidential style and impact of the two men, they inspired equally serious questions about the office itself. The tragedy of Lyndon Johnson's Presidency did not require as proof, even as early as 1966, the visible evidence of the scene in Vietnam. While there did appear a new aspect to the sorrow of it all when one witnessed the crisp confidence of American soldiers in the field committed to an arena so alien and a cause so hopeless, there was no need to meet with American diplomats or talk with American generals in Saigon to sense the fatefulness of political decisions already made in Washington or foresee the inevitability of American disillusion with the war. Yet even a short visit to Vietnam quickened new awareness that the grave issues in such war-making went beyond debate about the conduct of American policy to doubt about the nature of the American Presidency. What sort of magistracy over the Republic could have authored and anointed such a conflict? What manner of self-deception could so grievously blur judgment and warp decision in the White House? And above all, would the verdict of history finally fall on one President and his counselors—or on the unbridled power of the Presidency itself?

The memory of John Kennedy's Presidency, as it lived at this same time and in this same Asia, commanded attention verging on astonishment for quite another cause: it struck me as an almost inscrutable matter of political mystery. This President now had been dead for almost three years. And this made the mystery: the remembering of his Presidency and the invoking of his name seemed more constant and reverent in Manila and Saigon and Singapore than in Washington or New York or Boston. The kind of homage felt and spoken, moreover, could claim the rare authenticity of being selfless and artless. This President had never even appeared in these lands. As President, he had neither given nor promised to these peoples any material things to enrich their lives or enlist their loyalties. There was no nation in all Southeast Asia that could indulgently grieve over his passing as the loss of its special benefactor. Nonetheless, a trust and a mourning of the dead President stayed absolutely alive in the minds of these absolute strangers—whether they were Prime Ministers or ordinary citizens, writers or illiterates, rich or poor. And from this surprising angle of vision upon the Presidency, there appeared other special questions. What qualities or circumstances enabled one man in the White House to excite a respect so personal and so profound? Were the tone and temper of a White House so appealing to the emotions of the wide world also those to arouse the convictions of the Republic? And above all, could a citizen patiently watching the Presidency come to see some of the magic elements in the hazy chemistry of Presidential leadership?

*   *   *

The mulling of such matters as these soon enough turned my thoughts back to a different and earlier time—with its own questions. This time was the spring of 1953, the first months of the thirty-fourth Presidency. And it was then that Dwight David Eisenhower had to weigh and define and state his nation's role in the world, and its view of Communism, in the sudden light of the death of Josef Stalin.

This was the only period when I knew close association and work with a President, for I was charged with the preparation of this Chief Executive's speeches and messages. In terms of foreign policy, the political season was at least mildly memorable for stirring Washington into feverish speculation over the future political life of the Soviet Union and anxious scanning of the probable pattern of Soviet-American relations. The nervousness of such a time impelled various voices in the White House, and indeed throughout the government, to urge some resounding Presidential proclamations, but of unclear substance and unresolved intent. As the din rose, the President and I had a number of rambling conversations about how —or whether—he should specifically address the moment. These talks came to their own logical end in the Oval Office late one March afternoon, as all of Eisenhower's thoughts seemed, suddenly and precisely, to crystallize. He paced the room in a wide arc, as always when he became animated and convinced, and he forcefully started speaking some thoughts that I have never forgotten. . . .

"Look, I am tired and I think everyone is tired," he said, "of just plain indictments of the Soviet regime. . . . Just *one* thing matters: What have *we* got to offer the world? What are *we* ready to do to improve the chances of peace? If we cannot say these things—A, B, C, D, E, F, G, just like that—then we really have nothing to give, except just another speech. . . .

"*Here* is what I would like to say," he pressed on. "The jet plane that roars over your head costs three-quarters of a million dollars.

This is more money than a man earning ten thousand dollars every year is going to make in his lifetime. What world can afford this sort of thing for long? We are in an armaments race. Where will it lead us? At worst, to atomic warfare. At best, to robbing every people and nation on earth of the fruits of their own toil.

"Now, there could be another road before us—the road of disarmament. What does this mean? It means for everybody in the world bread, butter, clothes, homes, hospitals, schools—all the good and necessary things for decent living. So let *this* be the choice we offer. . . . Let us talk straight: *no* double talk, *no* sophisticated political formulas, *no* slick propaganda devices. Let us spell it out, whatever *we* truly *offer*. . . .

"What do we say about the Soviet government?" he concluded. "The past speaks for itself. I am interested in the future. Both their government and ours now have new men in them. The slate is clean. Now let us begin talking to each other. And let us say what we've got to say so that every person on earth can understand it."

The Presidential speech that followed a few weeks later was called "The Chance for Peace," and it stayed faithful to those vigorous convictions proclaimed in the privacy of the Oval Office. Yet neither the spirit nor the substance of that address had much effect upon the actual conduct of the Republic's foreign policy over most of the next eight years. The passion of those Presidential avowals of early 1953—and their failure to be translated into actions—suggested still more elusive aspects of the office. Had many Presidents known even an occasion or two to reach toward such sanguine visions for the Republic and for the world? What lapses could make such a vision of political life fade to forgotten fantasy? And are the stalling causes more often due to the limits *upon* a President —or the limits *within* him?

A revealing Presidential incident that caused yet another kind of wondering was related to me in the spring of 1968. The last months of the Eisenhower Presidency and the last months of the Johnson Presidency could hardly have achieved a more dramatic contrast. While Eisenhower had managed to circle the globe and set the multitudes to cheering from Morocco to India, Johnson could manage to move about the Republic itself only with great caution, as the popular dissent over the Vietnam War raged and threatened. The hostility toward the proud Texan finally forced him to schedule appearances and speeches almost exclusively at Army or Air Force bases across the nation, on a carefully planned itinerary. On one such occasion in the Western part of the country, he had delivered his martial address, finished the official ceremonies, and proceeded toward the Presidential plane for his travel homeward to the White House, when a soldier in the official escort respectfully interrupted his movement. With understandable reticence, the soldier pointed and explained: "Sir . . . Mr. President . . . *your* plane is over there on the *other* side, sir." There ensued the briefest pause. And this President then responded with slow emphasis: "Son, I want to tell you something—just so you never forget. . . . *All* of them—those over here *and* those over there— are *my* planes."

The President who made this rather cheerless jest was soon to retire into a private world of righteous resentment. The descent of such a mood meant that there had been more history than humor behind his words—and still more questions. Did so surly an assertion of sovereignty speak only for one man in the White House at a time of rare political ordeal? Or did such bluntness betray a sense of power and possessiveness that the Presidency threatened to excite in all Chief Executives? And was there perhaps nothing so deceptive for any President as his thinking of any things as wholly *his,* other than the anxieties and aspirations of the people whose trust he must earn and hold?

There could be added to these mid-twentieth-century instances countless other provocative incidents, minor or memorable, in the modern history of the Presidency. Each tends to pose its own challenge to understanding the office. And I found my own inquiring thoughts particularly prodded by a couple of such earlier Presidential moments.

I chanced to read of Calvin Coolidge, toward the end of his Presidency, one day strolling Pennsylvania Avenue in Washington with a Senator as companion. As they neared the White House, the Senator asked with amiable facetiousness: "I wonder who lives there?" With half-serious drollness, the thirtieth President replied: "Nobody.

They just come and go." The questions suggested by this exchange were not hard to form. Was the essence of the great office really so shallow and banal? Did the Republic's Presidential process amount to merely a kind of mindlessly revolving door? And even as Presidents "come and go," was it not possible to examine and weigh both the intellectual baggage they brought with them and the political heritage they left behind?

I happened to read, too, a certain passage in the *Diary* of the eleventh President, James Knox Polk, from fourscore years earlier in the life of the Presidency. This tense and homely man, who clumsily but confidently spoke for the spirit of the Western frontier, was one of the rare Chief Executives to keep a daily record of his time in the White House. And the unembellished entry for Thursday, February 19, 1846, went thus:

> Saw company as usual until twelve o'clock today. Among others who called was the Rev. Mr. Dean, who had been many years a Christian missionary in China. He had with him a native Chinese man. . . . He spoke but little English . . . and appeared to be intelligent. On taking leave of him, and while shaking hands, he expressed in his own language, which was interpreted by Mr. Dean, that he had seen the King of this country, and said he would tell it to his countrymen when he got home. I told him through Mr. Dean there was no King in this country, but that he had seen a citizen who had been chosen by the people to manage the government for a limited time.[1]

It seemed to me fair to wonder whether this Chief Executive, whose own administration had been so assertive, ever meant to define the Presidency as so modest an exercise in "management." Did not the whole thrust of Presidential leadership depend on talents and skills of an order quite beyond managerial capacities? And was even the figurative notion of kingship in the White House so utterly unthinkable?

This last question might take the mind of any student of the Presidency back to the stressful and uncertain time just before the creation of the office in 1787. It was then that the most concerned of the 4,000,000 citizens throughout the states had come to realize that the fragile structure of the American Confederation could not truly guard life, liberty, and the pursuit of happiness. The signs of disorder and a sense of disarray were spreading through the newly freed colonies. George Washington was receiving grim reports from General Henry Knox of "faction and licentiousness" abroad in the land, while from John Jay came letters mourning that "the better kind of people" were already beginning to fear "the charms of liberty as imaginary and delusive." It was this contagion of fear that drove Jay to his nearly helpless, wholly remarkable asking of Washington: "Shall we have a King?" [2]

I suspect that all the history and all the irony of the American Presidency may start, as logically as anywhere, with John Jay's question. Of all the surprises awaiting any watchers of the Presidency over the next two centuries, there would be few to match this moment in 1787—scarcely more than four months before the Constitutional Convention in Philadelphia—when, among leaders of the rising against King George III, the issue was raised of the possible need to commit the promise of popular revolution to another regal institution. Asked of the man who would be the new Republic's first President, the question was posed, moreover, by the man who soon would be the nation's first Chief Justice. As they would judge and decree from this legal summit, John Jay and his successors—from the Marshalls and the Taneys to the Tafts and the Hugheses—would forever after have to think any such lurid speculation rather mad, for they would be gravely busy trying to define the powers of President and Congress with the precision of surgeons and the confidence of oracles. But the reigning mood of 1787 was the fretful confusion of the patriot, not the dauntless assurance of the jurist. And this hesitant spirit would last through the historic summer of the convention in Philadelphia, and all its conceiving and pondering of an office to be called the American Presidency—with no man present quite certain what the office meant, or threatened, or promised.

This sets the guiding purpose, then, of the present inquiry: to come to some better knowledge of whatever was there and then created.

II

PRESIDENCY. The greased pig in the field game of American politics.

—AMBROSE BIERCE, 1911

The author of *The Devil's Dictionary*, Ambrose Bierce, was the first commentator in American journalism to achieve a notable mixture of acidity and integrity. Quite often, too, he twirled his epigrams with a spin that seemed to insinuate more than one meaning. So it might appear with his sardonic view of the Presidency as the slippery prize-of-prizes teasing and eluding all but one of the political pack frantic in its chase. For the image could apply not only to those trying to win it, but also to those trying simply to define it.

From Founding Fathers to modern scholars, the study of the Presidency has remained strangely "greased" with doubt and ambiguity. When the delegates to the Philadelphia convention greeted the very first mention of a Chief Executive with awkward silence —and then proceeded to discuss the office with what James Madison called the "shyness of gentlemen"—the reticence was not surprising for the times. But some form of this "shyness" would last long enough to make most twentieth-century students of the Presidency sound as halting as its eighteenth-century makers. As one scholar forthrightly wrote in 1969: "The eminence of the institution . . . is matched only by the extraordinary neglect shown to it by political scientists. . . . There is an extraordinary dearth of students of the Presidency, although scholars ritually swear that the Presidency is where the action is before they go somewhere else to do their research." [3]

Why should this be so?

The lasting reasons provide some oblique insights. For the search of the "scientist" of politics tends to be a quest for indisputable data, measurable forces, and provable judgments. This very demand for precision essentially explains his "shyness" of the Presidency: the office refuses to qualify as an object of such fine scrutiny. Instead, it defies neat analysis in the most varied ways: by the character of its origins, its annals, its standards, its crises, and its decisions.

And yet each bar to its full understanding somehow gives a hint of its nature.

The Unconvincing Sources

The testimony about any Presidency can only appear meager, at any moment, by comparison with the glut of evidence from the other two branches of the national government. From the Congress there comes the deluge of data on committee hearings and floor debates and official votes. From the judiciary there comes the stream of the highest court's decisions, all mathematically divided, elaborately reasoned, and publicly explained. But where is there to be found any comparable evidence on the resolves—or defaults—of the Presidency? Instead, there comes a relatively thin flow of verifiable facts, more often than not carefully censored or calculated to prove Presidential wisdom, rather than to enrich public knowledge.

The obscuring of the sources does not require, moreover, such a design for deception as governed, for example, the progress of American intervention in Vietnam in the 1960's. In the twentieth century, the ordinary facts of Presidential life and power have conspired toward the same end. Thus, the steady expansion of the White House staff has made ever larger the number of Presidential advisers always protected from Congressional inquiry and often hidden from public view. At the same time, the mere speed of modern travel—as it facilitates a President's personal meetings with chiefs of state or field commanders or ambassadors anywhere on earth—tends to reduce sharply the number of matters that must be set down on paper. The record of the most historic encounters and decisions may thus become largely a matter of Presidential memory, usually safe from authoritative contradiction.*

No less inevitable is the fact that even those Presidents most given to candor commonly feel impelled to profess publicly what they dis-

---

* The sum of records and papers that all Presidents have left behind, at least since the 1920's, has been tolerated as one more exercise of Presidential discretion. What each has taken, left, or burned has usually been the final secret of his administration. Even so unreticent a President as Harry Truman prefaced nearly 1,100 pages of published memoirs with the warning "I have omitted certain material. Some of this material cannot be made available for many years, perhaps for many generations." 4

believe privately. Dwight David Eisenhower, for example, probably enjoyed and deserved a wider popular credibility than any modern President, but he could not have been presumed, therefore, always to be speaking his mind in public. To cite a rather innocuous instance, one scholar of the Presidency—asserting the importance and the pleasure supposedly found by most Chief Executives in the Presidential press conference—once cited as proof the words of Eisenhower: "As a matter of fact, I think this is a wonderful institution. . . . It does a lot of things for me personally." [5] As a matter of *unspoken* fact, Eisenhower resented the institution as an intrusion, a bore, and a burden, but he could hardly have been expected to announce this to the national press. Or to cite a more serious instance: Eisenhower never wholly gave up hope, during his eight years in office, that his Republican successor might be someone other than Vice President Richard Nixon. Throughout his Presidency, he variously described Nixon to friends or aides as "just not Presidential timber" or "a born loser." But he could not reasonably have been asked to advertise this opinion before the Republican Party or the American electorate.

Be they devious or forthright, then, all Presidents know the urge to keep somewhat inscrutable what they are doing, what they have done, and what they are thinking of doing. So far as this affects the attitude of other national politicians, it is generally accepted as a President's understandable desire to keep all his options at least partly open. So far as it affects the curiosity of the living citizen or the future historian, it is generally intended as a prudent attempt to keep all their eyes at least partly closed.

The Special Origins

All the masks worn and all the charades acted by the Republic's first thirty-seven Presidents may not have confounded observers any more than one elemental fact about the office: from its conception, it has behaved and evolved as a uniquely American creation. To cite one student's awareness of this: a distinguished European witness to American politics, Harold J. Laski, came from the University of London to the University of Indiana, just before the outbreak of World War II in 1939, to give a series of lectures on the American Presidency. The British scholar, whose close intellectual friends in America included Supreme Court Justices Oliver Wendell Holmes and Felix Frankfurter, talked of the office with sharp insight. And he stressed no matter more than this:

> The essence of the Presidency is the fact that it is an *American* institution, that it functions in an American environment, that it has been shaped by the forces of American history, that it must be judged by American criteria of its responses to American needs. . . .
>
> Whatever the intention of the founders, the history of the United States has molded it in ways they could not have foreseen. . . . There is no foreign institution with which, in any basic sense, it can be compared. . . . The President of the United States is both more and less than a king; he is, also, both more and less than a prime minister. The more carefully his office is studied, the more does its unique character appear.[6]

This discernment of the Presidency as a kind of splendid American aberration may have carried only one accent somewhat in error. Indeed, the Founding Fathers "could not have foreseen" the structure of the twentieth-century Presidency. But the singularly American character of whatever they were building probably had been its one quality intuitively sensed by many of them. So it was, at least, with the young and brilliant Alexander Hamilton. Exactly 140 years earlier, he had written, in January, 1799, to Lafayette: "I hold with Montesquieu that a government must be fitted to a nation, as much as a coat to the individual; and, consequently, what may be good at Philadelphia, may be bad at Paris, and ridiculous at Petersburg." [7] To this extent, the unique office could claim to be as much a product of art as of accident, as it would go on disconcerting its closest watchers.

And those disconcerted soon enough came to include the same shrewd British observer. In the autumn of 1946, not long after the end of World War II, Laski journeyed again from Great Britain to scan and report the American political scene. What he came to appraise, this time, was not the Presidency but a President. Of the Republic's thirty-third President, Harry S. Truman, Harold Laski wrote:

> The outstanding characteristic of the landscape is the absence of effective leadership. . . . President Truman . . . had never been trained to lead. He had never been accustomed to mobilize public opinion against a Congress which had taken the bit between its teeth. . . . [He] is a weak President because he has not the special kind of resolution which makes a strong President. He would like to be on good terms with everyone; he cannot make up his mind that a strong President must begin by realizing that much of his strength consists in his choice of enemies. . . .
>
> Under Mr. Truman no one quite knows whose hands have grasped the helm or for what port they propose to steer. . . . With a President who now, on economic matters, has no effective difference with the Republicans, the business man is, in fact, reinvested with the authority that he lost in 1932. . . . Mr. Hoover, so to say, is back in power. . . . A dead past sits triumphantly where, less than two years ago, the emerging future excited the hopes of the whole world.[8]

In the light of the next few years of American politics, a more mistaken picture of a President could not have come from a more talented portraitist. The American voter of the time, moreover, shared much of the judgment of the English scholar: the man in the White House—the poorly educated son of a Missouri mule trader—was a veteran of only such mottled political experience as his service to the corrupt Democratic machine of Kansas City, his contentious years in the Senate, and his few weeks in the nearly invisible role of Vice President. All such omens turned out to be, however, quite worthless. The "weak President" would fire both Harold Ickes and Henry Wallace from his Cabinet—along with General Douglas MacArthur from his wartime command in Korea. The Chief Executive who evoked an image of "Mr. Hoover . . . back in power" went on to be the President who would, at various times, lead the federal government to take control of the nation's railroad network, coal mines, and steel industry. In the realm of world affairs, this national leader lacking any "special kind of resolution" would preside over an audacious strategy of global anti-Communism. In the arena of national politics, this Chief Executive unable to "mobilize public opinion against a Congress" would gear his whole reelection campaign to an open assault upon the Republican-dominated, "do-nothing" Eightieth Congress. Finally, the candidate so anxious "to be on good terms with everyone" would march to his improbable victory in 1948 under the banner "Give 'em hell!" . . . . Yet even all this sufficed only for a spell to restrain most observers from rash and confident prophecies upon this peculiarly American magistracy.

The Hazy Criteria

What are the standards or measures for knowing the worth or the strength of any Presidency? Again, the contrast to the legislature and the judiciary emphasizes the problem. The Congress may be judged, perhaps imprecisely but rather graphically, by its laws, its leaders, its committees, its appropriations, its resolutions, its filibusters, or its negligences. The Supreme Court may be judged, of course, by its judgments. But where are the documented proofs of the Executive's ingenuity or folly?

Almost any President may personify the problem. To continue with Truman, for example, a prominent American scholar of the Presidency, Clinton Rossiter, talked back in 1956 to the Harold Laski of 1946 with the confident retort that "Harry S. Truman is a man whom history will delight to remember"; indeed, he appeared to have shown "a more clear-cut philosophy of Presidential power than any predecessor except Woodrow Wilson." [9] As a tribute from the mid-1950's, this seemed a fair correction to the disparagement of the mid-1940's. But by the mid-1960's the passage of one more decade found some students of the Truman Presidency examining it from still another perspective. They tended to doubt that an admirably "clear-cut philosophy" of power had dictated the dropping of the first atomic bombs upon Japan, and they tended to wonder whether some of the dramatic strokes against Communism—from the Truman Doctrine in the Middle East to the Korean War in the Far East—had not served less to guard America than to divide the world.

Yet there arises a difficulty more subtle than an inevitable variety of historical judgments upon men and events. The seemingly clear *criteria* for any judgment themselves have different meanings for different witnesses at different times. The political or intellectual isolation of the Presidency, for example, scarcely suggests a virtue or a strength of the office. A sensitive tribune of all the people cannot also be remote and aloof, and the disenchanted Presidential aides to Lyndon Johnson, when they later reflected on the failure of his leadership, found his proud isolation from criticism to have been a crucial cause. Yet the same mark of Presidential behavior has impressed others as being far from a curse: instead, it has suggested an independence of spirit, a resistance to clamor, and a steeliness of intent—all essential to Presidential initiative. Precisely in this sense, a student of the office as diligent as Woodrow Wilson— six years before he became the twenty-eighth President, to test his own teaching—could conclude: "It is the extraordinary isolation imposed upon the President by our system that makes the character and the opportunity of his office so extraordinary." [10]

As with one simple sign of Presidential life, so with almost all: each can be construed, understandably and plausibly, as either a strength or a weakness. The President who artfully excites the widest public support for his policies may also be deplored by his critics as the President who cravenly traffics in what Alexander Hamilton called "the little arts of popularity." The President who bends most limply before the will of the Congress may be hailed by his admirers as the President who heeds most scrupulously the restraints of the Constitution.

Since the birth of the Republic, one of the few firm facts of Presidential life has been the truth that a President, at all times, faces two constituencies: the living citizens and the future historians. The verdict from either source, however, may sharply contradict the other. The eighteenth and the twenty-ninth Presidents, Ulysses S. Grant and Warren G. Harding, are the only two Chief Executives to be categorically judged as failures by almost all American historians, but their administrations were celebrated by outpourings of popular support, respect, and affection. Even the historical assessment, moreover, may change almost any decade. In the case of a Wilson, the judgment of most thoughtful scholars first hailed him, before 1920, as the Republic's champion of human and national rights on the world stage; after 1920 and into the 1930's, the appraisal became suffused with the isolationist spirit of the times, and he became scorned as a clumsy idealist; with the advent of World War II, he was discovered to be, instead, an almost saintly prophet; and with the passage of a little more time, the scholarly suspicion returned that perhaps, after all, he had wretchedly blundered in a wondrous cause.

The Haphazard Events

The bursts of chance can raise or wreck all institutions: kingdoms and alliances, empires and churches. Most of these wear some saving armor, however, against the sudden stab of the grave event. A monarchy goes on by a law of inheritance, no matter the fate of one king, and a parliament goes on by a faith in debate, no matter the fate of one law. The American Presidency, too, has endured impressively, but behind a smaller shield against the slings and arrows of unexpected fortune. And its life has been from the beginning—in remarkable measure—a reign of chance.

The first American President, by the testimony of his Vice President, John Adams, may well have been spared calamity by a disease—not the President's but the people's. This came to pass in the spring of 1793, just as George Washington began his second term. The new Republic was being swept, and at times convulsed, with rejoicing over the French Revolution. It was a popular sort of festivity uninhibited by a general lack of knowledge of what actually was happening in France. While Jefferson was hailing the French upheaval as "the most sacred cause that ever man was engaged in," the Americans were cheering, from Boston salons to frontier cabins, the news that revolutionary France had declared war on England and Spain. The popular outcry made only more anguishing the diplomatic dilemma of the hour: by the treaty of 1778 with France, the new nation was committed to aid its European ally, specifically to defend French possessions in the Caribbean, with a navy that America did not possess. After meeting with his Cabinet to weigh the explosive situation, Washington decided not to be a Presidential prisoner of "commitment" in the West Indies—with an understanding of the better part of valor not to be shared, some 175 years later, by his successors and their sense of "commitment" in Southeast Asia. Accordingly, Washington issued, in April of 1793, the first Presidential declaration of neutrality.

The zealots of anti-monarchism, who were as impassioned as the crusaders of anti-Communism of an age to come, progressed quickly from rage to riot. As John Adams wrote of the ensuing hysteria in the streets of the capital city of Philadelphia, "ten thousand people . . . day after day threatened to drag Washington out of his house and effect a revolution in the government." [11] The mobs finally were dispelled not by speeches but by germs: a sudden outbreak of yellow fever sent some half of the city's 43,000 citizens either to death or to flight. By the view of Adams, the Republic escaped overturning by virtue of neither the government's power nor Washington's prestige: the day and the Presidency were simply saved by an epidemic.

The history of the Presidency in the twentieth century can also be read, at critical points, as a tale of weird hazard—at least, since September 14, 1901. On that date, the twenty-fifth President, William McKinley, died from the shots fired at him, a week earlier, by a crazed young anarchist. The Vice President succeeding him was the Theodore Roosevelt who would revel in the White House as his "bully pulpit." From that point in time, many a historian has dated the advent of the "modern" Presidency. And this transition indeed may have marked what one student of the Presidency, intending no grim pun, called "the triggering element" in all the evolution of the office.[12]

From that time, far into the twentieth century, the destiny of Presidents has followed, more than once, the trajectory of bullets. In February, 1933, a jobless bricklayer in Miami tried to assassinate Franklin Roosevelt, killed the mayor of Chicago—but narrowly missed the thirty-second President-elect. In November thirty years later, an assassin in Dallas did not miss and killed John Kennedy. And less than five years later, another gun in Los Angeles ended the life of Robert Kennedy, as he was campaigning to become the thirty-seventh President.

The fates of two Roosevelts and two Kennedys, over a span of time not very long in the Republic's life, make the guns sound as though they were firing questions as fast as bullets. If William McKinley had survived his wounds, who would eventually have been the national leader to find the "trigger" to the modern Presidency? If

Franklin Roosevelt had not been spared, when would a despairing people have come to know a New Deal by whatever name? If John Kennedy had not gone to Dallas in 1963, how many divisions of American soldiers, in the years to follow, would have gone to Vietnam? If Robert Kennedy in 1968 had not walked from a California auditorium through a kitchen exit to his death, where would Richard Nixon, a couple of years later, have been found strolling? By all such thin and terrible threads, the Presidency and its colossal power, at every instant, may dangle.

The Dark Decisions

The pulse of the life of the Presidency—and all that Woodrow Wilson meant by calling it "the vital place of action in the system" —moves by one rhythm: the making of decisions. To know a Presidency is to catch this rhythm. Yet there can be no secret to any Presidency so difficult to discover as the riddle of precisely how even one great decision came to be made.

The essence of the office decrees this. The true account of the making of a major policy in the White House requires an exhaustive knowledge of all things and all thoughts that conspired to influence a Chief Executive over a period of a few historic days or hours. But such perfect knowledge is impossible. Psychologically or historically, the sum of available evidence generally makes easier the analysis of the behavior of a mob than of a man. And the solitary authority of the man in the White House becomes a special sort of shroud—as one who served close to Lyndon Johnson later reflected:

> It is assumed that there is something called a "decision-making process" which can be charted in much the same fashion as the table of organization for a business corporation. . . . The fact is that a President makes his decisions as he wishes to make them, under conditions which he himself has established, and at times of his own determination. . . . Any student of the White House who believes that he is making a contribution to political thought when he analyzes the process is sadly mistaken.[13]

The climactic events of the Johnson Presidency gave strong supporting evidence to the truth of this judgment. On March

16, 1968, the President met with his staff, reviewed with them the military situation in Vietnam, and delivered *his* final judgment in these words: "Let's get one thing clear! I'm telling you now that I'm not going to stop the bombing. Now I don't want to hear any more about it. . . . I've heard every argument. I'm not going to stop it. Now is there anybody here who doesn't understand that?" * All those present who fully understood this had a considerable surprise awaiting them. A fortnight later—on March 31, 1968—the President appeared on national television to announce his decisions to (1) refuse to run for reelection and (2) halt the bombing of North Vietnam. There is no public record that anyone intimately involved quite came to "understand" the bridge that so swiftly spanned the distance between these two firm Presidential resolves.

To the history of the White House, such a sequence of events brings no novelty. With varying inflections, the same story has been told again and again. Franklin Roosevelt deliberately took delight in veiling his designs from his counselors. As one of them later wrote, without any rancor, Roosevelt "allowed no one to discover the governing principle" in his decision-making.[14] But neither strategy nor guile has been needed to cast long shadows in this area. As John Kennedy readily conceded, while he was in the White House: "The essence of ultimate decision remains impenetrable to the observer—often, indeed, to the decider himself." [15]

There was nothing at all casual, nor altogether mystical, in this judgment by Kennedy: it was based on long reflection and real uncertainty. Early in 1962, the historian Arthur M. Schlesinger asked a panel of historical and political scholars to rank all the Presidents from "great" to "failure," and he included in the panel the man in the White House who had written *Profiles in Courage.* The youthful President started to fill in his ballot, shortly stopped, and finally wrote the historian: "A year ago, I would have responded with confidence . . . but now I am not so sure. After being in the office for a year I feel that a good deal more study is required to make my judgment sufficiently informed. There is a tendency to mark the obvious names. I would like to subject those not so well known to a long scrutiny after I have left this office." And to the son of the historian then serving in his White House, Kennedy stated

* Reported in the New York *Times,* March 6, 1969.

the riddle of Presidential decision-making even more tersely: "How the hell can you tell? Only the President himself can know what his real pressures and his real alternatives are. If you don't know that, how can you judge performance?" [16]

This insight, too, was not new. Many a past President had spoken a like awareness—not egotistically, nor tremulously, but humbly. So it was in 1862 with the sixteenth President, Abraham Lincoln, when he talked to his Cabinet of how he then intended to proceed with the matter of emancipation of the slaves:

> I know very well that many others might, in this matter, as in others, do better than I can. . . . But . . . there is no way in which I can have any other man put where I am. I am here. I must do the best I can, and bear the responsibility of taking the course which I feel I ought to take.[17]

The intensely individual nature of this sovereignty may loom, then, as its first and abiding mark. Upon every President, this must impose all the tensions of knowing that indeed no "other man" can be "put where I am." And upon every student of the Presidency, this must force all the uncertainties of knowing that no other institution can be put in the place where it stands in history.

Two

The Idea of the Presidency

The Presidency is the most peculiar office in the world. There's never been one like it. . . . The longer I live, the more I am impressed with . . . our American Constitution. Read it and think about it. It's a plan, but not a strait jacket, flexible and short. Read it one hundred times, and you'll always find something new.[1]

—HARRY S. TRUMAN, 1959

There may be some wry interest in the fact that the two twentieth-century Presidents most sensitive to the constitutional origins of the Presidency—Woodrow Wilson and Harry Truman—also were, respectively, the only President of the age who had been a university president and the only President of the age who had never attended a university. It may be of still more interest that a time when almost any citizen of the Republic would have confidently named the Presidency as the most powerful office in the world of 1959, a former President, while not dissenting from the general opinion, would prefer to define it as "the most peculiar." And it should be of most interest that, whenever this former Chief Executive addressed students or teachers or journalists, he kept sending them back to 1787 to perceive what he was talking about. The advice was immensely practical. For all the unfolding paradoxes of the Presidency can only baffle the citizen who has never glimpsed the anomalous achievement of the Founding Fathers.

There were many things memorably "peculiar," in fact, about those eighteenth-century nation builders and the ways they went about their self-appointed business. They were, of course, presumptuous innovators. They had come together "for the sole and express purpose of revising the Articles of Confederation," and they proceeded to "revise" nothing and improvise everything. They were also, as a historic gathering, improbably youthful: five members were less than thirty years old, and Alexander Hamilton but little older; such articulate leaders as James Madison and Gouverneur Morris were in the middle of their thirties and James Wilson not much past forty; and only four of all fifty-five delegates had reached the age of sixty. As individuals, they included a vociferous few of the money-minded, who were anxious, in Madison's words, "to protect the minority of the opulent against the majority": one of their number, Charles Pinckney of South Carolina, argued for a property qualification for any President of at least $100,000. As a group, however, they were penny-poor. When the summer heat of 1787 brought snappish temper and political deadlock, Benjamin Franklin—at the age of eighty-one the most respected, after Washington, of all men present—proposed a soothing prayer to open all future sessions; but the motion lost, because the convention had no funds to pay a chaplain. And these architects of a free and open society firmly bound themselves by one notable vow: to keep their own deliberations completely secret.*

As the Convention's debates dragged on, from May 25 to September 17, 1787, there arose no problem that so distressed and divided the delegates as their approach to the office of the Presidency. The matter came close to alarming them. Through all his pre-convention correspondence with George Washington, Madison had conspicuously shied from the subject, confessing barely a month before the assembly in Philadelphia: "I have scarcely ventured as yet to form my own opinion either of the manner in which [the Executive] ought to be constituted or of the authorities with which it ought to be cloathed." [2] Writing his exuberant apologia for the new office in *The Federalist*, the following spring, Alexander Hamilton would concede: "There is hardly any part of the system which could have been attended with greater difficulty in the arrangement of it than

---

* The point was recalled by Professor Paul A. Freund (New York *Times*, June 25, 1971) apropos of the circulation of the Pentagon Papers on the Vietnam War. While recalling that the Senate debated in secret for its first five years, he also added: "I sometimes wonder irreverently whether we would have had a Constitution at all if the Convention had been reported by daily columnists."

this." [3] The course of convention argument on the subject, indeed, twisted and spiraled in ways as confounding to those present as to future historians.* In a single day's session, the Founding Fathers found themselves rambling from discussion of Presidential succession, to the Vice Presidential role, to treaty-making powers, to appointment powers, and on to a Presidential council. When they began repeating themselves too tiresomely, they referred all snarled issues to one of several convention committees—on Detail, on Style, or (most appropriately) on Postponed Matters and Unfinished Business.

The stammering of so many delegates followed not only from hesitations in political theory that they were weighing, but also from contradictions in political life that they were enduring. Quite simply, the spirit of 1787 was at war with the spirit of 1776. At the earlier date, a great many "truths" about a central sovereignty had seemed "self-evident," but a decade later, some of the more important of these seemed almost self-contradictory. The patriots' Articles of Confederation and Perpetual Union had needed only a few years to prove neither rational nor workable, much less perpetual: all too plainly, the freedom of a people could never be assured by the feebleness of their government. The leading citizens of the newly independent states thought they had seen almost frightening proof of this, the autumn before the Convention, when the debt-maddened farmers of Massachusetts had raised their staves and pitchforks behind Daniel Shays, had defied the courts and the laws of the commonwealth, and had driven even Washington to wonder whether "mankind when left to themselves are unfit for their own government." [5] From his post as American minister in Paris, Thomas Jefferson might shrug and philosophize in a letter to Madison that "a little rebellion now and then is a good thing." But this conveyed little solace to men trying to establish a new political order and structure. As the meeting in Philadelphia approached, and as Washington scanned the disarray of the states he had led toward fancied freedom, he wrote with rare passion: "I would wish anything and everything essayed . . . to avert the humiliating and

---

* As one historian of the Presidency who followed the tortuous progress of the incipient Presidency through Madison's *Notes* several times has frankly conceded: "I am still not sure" how a final consensus on the Executive power was reached.[4]

contemptible figure we are about to make in the annals of mankind." [6] In short, the Founding Fathers felt quite as much concern for an emergency as for posterity.

The person of Washington himself, as it towered in the eyes of the men assembled to "essay" a Constitution, served in a special way to dramatize their dilemma. For it forced the delegates to behold the political images of two leaders, facing opposite ways and exciting opposite emotions. The first was England's George III: the monarch who had shown them, so they believed, the peril and cost of a single man's power, when too commanding and capricious. He had been the very spur to revolution. But the second was this Virginian hero: the patrician soldier who had shown them the strength and worth of a single man's leadership, through all the years when the rebel American cause had veered, again and again, toward disaster. He had been the very savior of revolution. What cogent lesson on the prudent forms of personal sovereignty, then, could be learned from the contradictory testimony of these two principal witnesses to the birth of the nation? It was almost as if the images of king and patriot had been graven on two coins, one to be clasped in either fist of each delegate, as he was dared to wager which one was weighted with a clearer and safer portent.

In this atmosphere, the most basic political premises seemed at hopeless odds. A faith in man collided with a distrust of the people. For most delegates, the citizenry at large may have been "endowed by their Creator" with some "unalienable rights," but He had left His work carelessly unfinished, by failing to bless them with much unmistakable wisdom. From this there followed the doubt as to which carried the greater threat to the liberty and prosperity of men: a rabble within one state or a sovereign over all states? When this question was restated in terms of the division of powers among the branches of a new national government, the answer of Madison would be to resolve the conflict by the singular device of institutionalizing it, as he would clinically explain in the famous formula: "Ambition must be made to counteract ambition." Freely translated, this could be read as a political command to the executive and the legislative branches: fight fairly, openly—and forever. Yet even this much tolerance of executive power could not easily be conceded by rebels against the Crown whose political instincts were attuned to the idea that "sovereignty and legislative power are identical." [7] Such an equation might seem preposterous to twentieth-century Americans, driven to frequent wonder whether Congress could sensibly conduct its own affairs, much less the Republic's. But the concept was natural enough for eighteenth-century Americans who had been driven to revolt by royal mandates and colonial governors.

The attack upon these fears of an independent Presidency was led by James Wilson and Gouverneur Morris of Pennsylvania. In an ingenious parliamentary tour de force, they mingled lessons from the colonial past and prospects for the national future. At one moment, they were reminding the delegates of the spells of cowardly irresponsibility that had been displayed by the Continental Congress and many of the states' legislatures. The next moment or the next debate, Wilson was defining the requisites for any effective Executive as "energy, dispatch, and responsibility," and Morris, with his vision of "a large extent of Country," was appealing for an Executive "with sufficient vigor to pervade every part of it." Most prophetically of all, there was Wilson in almost any session, audaciously depicting the future President as "the man of the people," and there was Morris foreseeing explicitly that the "Great and the wealthy" would "in the course of things . . . necessarily compose the Legislative body," thus demanding an Executive armed to stand as "the guardian of the people, even of the lower classes, ags. Legislative tyranny." [8] And there was Morris, finally, compressing all his thoughts into the kind of aphorism most appreciated by any parliamentarian: "This Magistrate is not the King, but the prime-minister. The people are the King." [9]

The clash over these sweeping ideas rang through all debates over the specific powers and limits of the Presidency. With regard to the constitutional formula for relations between the Executive and the legislature, for example, the divided delegates fought vigorously on at least three signal issues. *First:* on the matter of the very election of a President, they were keenly aware that no less than eight of the thirteen states chose their chief executive by vote of the legislature, while Pennsylvania had a collective executive council of twelve from whom a "president" was chosen. This tradition found voice in the urging of Roger Sherman of Connecticut that the national legislature appoint any future President to ensure "making him absolutely dependent on that body." [10] A majority of the delegates voted no less than five times for this Congressional power before the opposition finally prevailed. *Second:* both Madison and Morris had to argue strenuously on behalf of a President's power to appoint ambassadors, ministers, and judges. With seeming logic, Morris pointed out that if the Executive can be safely trusted with the command of the army, there should be little reason to dread his authority over these offices. Yet this power of appointment remained wholly with the Senate, until the final fortnight of the Convention, only at that late stage to be reduced to the right of "advice and consent." *Third:* as originally set forth in the Virginia Plan, a Presidential veto power over legislative action was to be exercisable only through "a council of revision" in which the Chief Executive would sit with "a convenient number of the National Judiciary." Only after two and a half months had passed did the Committee on Detail return from one of its obscure sessions to gain the Convention's approval of a personal veto power. And it seems safe to assume that no delegate voting affirmatively ever imagined that, less than fifty years later, a self-appointed tribune like the seventh President, Andrew Jackson, would be brandishing this power in a way designed to make the Presidency, as never before, the hope of the people at large.

The discussion of the war-making power produced no formidable confrontations but two interventions by Madison that later generations would have reason to remember. With respect to the Congress' defined authority, the power to "make" war was amended at Madison's urging to the power to "declare" war—with the object (according to Madison's *Notes*) of "leaving to the Executive the power to repel sudden attacks." Lest this suggest great faith in Presidential discretion in this area, however, Madison intervened a month later to urge that two-thirds of the Senate be empowered to make treaties of peace "without the concurrence of the President." As Madison's reasoning went: "The President . . . would necessarily derive so much power and importance from a state of war that he might be tempted, if authorized, to impede a treaty of peace." [11]

Throughout all the talk of a Presidency, there was no question that brought forth such a cascade of irreconcilable notions as the issue of a President's term of office and right to reelection. Here, the colonial precedents offered almost no help. The Articles of Confederation had provided for a "president" who was merely a chairman and who could hold office for only one out of any three years. Among the states, a total of ten limited their chief executives to one-year terms, but the steadier political experience of New York, with its three-year term, had impressed many of the Founding Fathers. In their gropings, the delegates discussed almost all formulas within reason—some with, and some without, bans on reelection. A Virginia delegate urged "seven years at least," while a Delaware delegate favored a three-year term with reeligibility for a maximum of nine years. A delegate from South Carolina argued against "a frequency of the elections" because the states of South Carolina and Georgia "were too distant to send electors often." [12] After many circular debates and referrals to committees, the constitutional formula was finally settled on only in the closing days of the Convention.* By then, the delegates had had ample chance to prove their talents for colorful metaphors on the whole subject of Presidential selection. At one point, George Mason of Virginia— who would refuse, despite his old friendship with Washington, to sign the Constitution—declared that "it would be as unnatural" to allow the people to choose a President "as it would to refer a trial of colours to a blind man." And to this and like remarks, Gouverneur Morris offered the retort: "If the Legislature elect . . . it will be like the election of a pope by a conclave of cardinals." [14]

There were differences no less apparent in the Founding Fathers' division over a matter as crucial as the choice between a single or a plural executive power. When James Wilson on June 1 first had the temerity to urge a single executive, Madison dryly recorded for his *Notes* the "ensuing" of "a general pause." Of the various alternatives proposed, none was more intriguing than the call by George Mason for an executive "invested in three persons, one chosen from the northern, one from the middle, and one from the Southern States"—on the grounds that these three wise men would "bring with them, into office, a more perfect and extensive

---

* From Paris, Jefferson wrote both John Adams and James Madison his great "dislike" for Presidential reelection, warning Madison: "Experience concurs with reason in concluding that the first magistrate will always be re-elected if the constitution permits it. He is then an officer for life." [13]

Knowledge of the real Interests of this great Union." [15] While the delegates rather soon accepted the principle of a one-man executive, there persisted to the end some stubborn advocacy of an institutionalized council around the President. Even in the Convention's last days, Benjamin Franklin contended that the delegates "seemed . . . too much to fear cabals," and the unappeasable Mason finally exclaimed: "We [are] about to try an experiment on which the most despotic governments had never ventured. The Grand Signor himself had his Divan." [16]

Against this background, the fight over ratification of the Constitution came to center on the fears already voiced over the Presidency-to-be. The cry of Patrick Henry that it amounted to an "awful squint toward monarchy" found warning echoes throughout the thirteen states. The necessary approval by nine states did not come until June, 1788, and even then, New Hampshire had voted support by only 57 to 47 and Washington's own Virginia by only 89 to 79. Nor could fears so widespread be dismissed altogether as the hysteria of critics whom Hamilton chastised for propagating a "parade of imaginary horribles." [17] Within the secret convention, in fact, Hamilton himself had delivered a five-hour appeal for a replica of the British system as "the best in the world," and the delegates from Maryland insisted that no less than twenty of the fifty-five delegates privately favored some structure along monarchic lines. In the North, then, New York's Governor George Clinton could plausibly rally the Constitution's foes with his philippics insisting that "this President" did not "essentially differ from the king of Great Britain." In the South, the man who would be the Republic's fifth President, James Monroe, joined Patrick Henry with the alarm over any future President: "Once he is elected, he may be elected forever." And the defenders of the Constitution in North Carolina had to answer broadside charges that "the pope of Rome might be elected president." [18]

All forensics of the day aside, the heart of the matter was essentially what would prove vexing for two centuries to come. Like so much that was crucial at the Philadelphia conclave, the historic wording of the first sentence of Article II had been determined only days before the Convention's end. The last-minute work of the Committee of Style and the facile pen of Gouverneur Morris, the sentence read simply: *"The executive power shall be vested in a President of the United States."*

In all the annals of politics, there may never have been written a critical proposition more direct in sound and more cryptic in substance. Beyond decreeing a single executive, the words specified nothing. Unlike the first sentence of Article II on the Congress, there here appeared no precise or limiting reference to "Powers *herein granted*." Instead, there was very little plainly given, very little clearly withheld. As a summation of all the labyrinthine debates of the Convention, this did not define: it deferred. With a truly "peculiar" restraint—or spectacular shrewdness—the Founding Fathers thus left the Presidency, their most special creation, to be shaped by the live touch of history. And this could fairly be called their forever memorable gamble.

There were some among them who appeared well aware of this—or so goes at least one appropriate story. After the close of the Convention, Benjamin Franklin returned to his Philadelphia lodgings to face one final question. It came from his landlady, politely asking: "Well, Mr. Franklin, what have you given us, a republic or a monarchy?" And Franklin answered with his characterestic realism: "A republic—if you can keep it." [19]

II

Every vital question of state will be merged in the question, "Who will be the next President?"

—ALEXANDER HAMILTON

In that season gray with doubt, when the Republic was being born, there were many distinguished patriots and ordinary citizens who found all clouds dispelled by the sunburst genius of young Alexander Hamilton. He seemed to break through all uncertainties to make clear, by irresistible reason and rhetoric, the terms of the Constitution and the powers of its Executive. The work of Hamilton was a marvel of intelligence and persuasion, as he wrote and orated, through a strident time, to induce the states—and especially his

and John Jay's New York—to give final assent to the Constitution.*
A brilliant advocate and a bruising adversary, Hamilton was the
first, and possibly the most gifted, of a rare and valuable breed of
national leader who would serve the Republic: the politically committed man with a mind as strong as his will, his wits as keen
as his ambitions. Nor did he have to wait upon posterity for his
recognition. At the age of thirty, he was the most trusted counselor
of Washington, some twenty-five years his elder, and his patron
honored him for "judgment intuitively great." Neither patron nor
friend, Thomas Jefferson nonetheless acknowledged him to be the
"Colossus of the Federalists." A European statesman not easy to
awe, Talleyrand, linked Hamilton with Fox and Napoleon as the
age's three supreme figures. And as a political prophet, he would
command special respect from the sages of distant generations. He
not only had the boldness to urge the thirteen states to "think con-
tinentally," and he not only caught a vision of America as no bu-
colic democracy but a commercial giant. He also deserved the
admiration of historians, who could say of him, some 175 years
later: "To Hamilton the enormous expansion of the power of the
Presidency by the mid-twentieth century would have been less a
surprise than a vindication of his notions of the need for administrative power, energy, and efficiency." [20]

These Hamiltonian notions were challenging and exciting wherever they appeared: in his letters, in his speeches, and in his essays
in *The Federalist*. A born polemicist, Hamilton enlisted John Jay
and James Madison to share the prodigious labor of producing,
within little more than six months, *The Federalist*'s eighty-five articles on behalf of the new Constitution. The result was both a classic exercise in political propaganda and one of the most sophisticated studies of the Presidency ever written. With his every
exhortation in the name of the office, Hamilton showed a true instinct for its creative power, as he used, again and again, one word
to cite its political essence: "energy." This was the heart of his plea:

* To New Yorkers of the later twentieth century, the climax of the heated debates of 1788 strike an interesting note. For all the skill of Hamilton and Jay in
leading the Federalists urging ratification, the opposition led by Governor George
Clinton stayed strong enough to lose the final vote by only a margin of three out
of fifty-seven. And Hamilton and Jay gained even this precarious victory only
with the threat that, should the Assembly fail to ratify, New York City would
secede from the state and join the greater Union.

"Energy in the Executive is a leading character in the definition of good government." [21] Through all writings and addresses, he struck this word like a drum, as though the insistent beat would summon the people's awareness of the need for a Presidency to command "all the requisites to *energy*." [22] Whenever calm analysis seemed not enough to persuade, Hamilton turned to grand augury, as he foretold the time sure to come in American life "when every vital question of state will be merged in the question, 'Who will be the next President?' " [23] No other advocate of the American Presidency, peering out of the late eighteenth century, saw so far ahead with so shrewd a guess.

Yet precisely this marked a lack in the whole Hamiltonian perception: he *was* guessing—or pretending or parrying—through most of what he spoke and wrote. Nor was this true merely because all the analysis in *The Federalist* could only be, of course, a brave attempt to explain an office that did not yet exist. There were other limits to the light he could shed. As a pamphleteer of the hour, he often pressed his case with more vigor than candor. And as a seer into the American future, he shared the special fortune needed by most political prophets to perpetuate their memories—the luck of being right for the wrong reasons.

Perhaps it was fitting that this statesman, whom all future Presidents would have reason to thank for much of their power, should also seem a kind of father to many of them by virtue of his mastery of a Chief Executive's skill in proclaiming one thing while planning another. This apostle of Presidential power preached no message more insistently than the disarming idea that a stingy Constitution actually had endowed the President with prerogatives both modest and innocent. As for the Presidential power of appointment, Hamilton measured it as betraying "evidently a great inferiority . . . to that of the British king"; indeed, the appointive power of even the Governor of New York "must, in practice, be greatly superior." [24] As for the President's authority as Commander in Chief, Hamilton professed to find this, too, comparatively puny: the President suffered a position "much inferior" to any British monarch, with a role possibly even dwarfed by the "larger powers" of the governors of Massachusetts and New Hampshire.[25]

Although the shape of such argument was obviously warped to

fit the polemical need of the time, there appears something unforget-tably incongruous in this political prophet's easy shrug, and avowed serenity, over a President's military command. For this would be the power with which James Polk, the eleventh President, would force war with Mexico to give Congress its initial lesson in how a President can fight first and consult later. This would be the power, too, that the sixteenth President, Abraham Lincoln, would choose —the device of a military order—to change the life of the Republic with his Emancipation Proclamation. And this would be the power by which Lyndon Johnson, the thirty-sixth Chief Executive, would preside over the tragedy of Vietnam, to prove how a President can lead not the Congress alone, but all the people, to war first and weep later.

Across the whole world of Hamilton's political thought, more-over, there fell the shadow of his fear and distrust of the mass of the people, whom he viewed as "a great Beast." Among the Found-ing Fathers, he stood not at all alone, of course, when he damned with such definitions. The delegates to the Constitutional Conven-tion nodded approvingly to more than a few warnings against the "turbulence and folly" of democracy, and a majority of them took little exception to a speech by Hamilton reminding them: "Take mankind in general, they are vicious." [26] This indicates the al-most bizarre nature of Hamilton's clairvoyance about the Presi-dency. Much as the institutional result might vindicate or delight him, he could only have been appalled by the political causes. For any concept of a President as the tribune of the people would have stirred him to another decrying of the democratic fantasies that he found so mortal to ancient Athens and ancient Rome. The majesty of *his* Presidency was to rise from the bold manipulation of federal powers, not the vulgar mandate of popular votes. A Hamilton trans-ported to the twentieth century would have acclaimed the "energy" of the Presidencies of Theodore Roosevelt and Woodrow Wilson and Franklin Roosevelt. But a Hamilton informed of their methods —all their uses of partisan propaganda, public theatrics, and elec-toral stratagems—would again profess only scorn for such leaders with "talents for low intrigue." [27] And this contempt for political devices so insidiously popular made it easy, though not fair, for a

Jefferson to deplore Hamilton himself as "not only a monarchist, but for a monarchy bottomed on corruption." [28]

The epithet of Jefferson may be enough to suggest that Hamilton had not, after all, indisputably clarified what "the executive power" so vaguely "vested" by the Constitution truly meant. The new Republic had to have, obviously, some kind of head, leader, and symbol. The initially nameless *he* could not claim a throne, wear a crown, or wave a scepter. But what, then, should he wield, and by what title? The memory of centralized power in London had so stained the colonial title of Governor that four of the revolutionary states had preferred to call their chief executives mere *Presidents*. To patriots wanting to be forever rid of kings and governors, the office of a President sounded tolerably safe in name. But beyond the name, it yet remained for a man—and for many men—to give it living meaning.

III

The eyes of Argus are upon me.

—GEORGE WASHINGTON

What Alexander Hamilton brought to the making of the Presidency with his intellect and his words, George Washington brought with his life and his acts. After him, all Chief Executives would be attended and aided by a growing company of precedents. Only Washington started with nothing—except the grave awareness that all words, gestures, rituals, and policies would swiftly fill in the blank spaces left by the Founding Fathers. The astonishing achievement of this First Citizen was twofold. As President for eight years, he made the office tolerably workable. But as a man—before that—he had made the office itself possible.

Throughout the Philadelphia Convention, all the ingenuity and eloquence of Morris or Wilson or Hamilton or Madison had led the delegates to envision a Presidency not nearly so persuasively as the quiet force of the sight of General Washington presiding from his armchair. His image that initially had challenged all delegates—

some with their spoken dread of, some with their secret desire for, monarchic forms—finally helped steady their thoughts and allay their fears. As one delegate to the Convention would later write to a relative: *"Entre Nous,* I do [not] believe they [the Executive powers] would have been so great, had not many of the members cast their eyes toward General Washington as President; and shaped their Ideas of the Powers to be given a President, by their opinions of his Virtue." [29] Through all the constitutional history of the Republic, there might appear no paradox more striking than this: the whole studied and written design for government—a free government avowedly of laws and not of men—critically turned, from the outset, upon faith in one man.

There was another particular way in which the man suited the elusive nature of the office: the patriot general rose before his contemporaries—and remained for his historians—something of a mystery himself. The Yankee secretary and aide who served him for years, Tobias Lear, reminisced about him with almost as much puzzlement as respect. A bit ruefully, he noted that the most "intimate acquaintance" with the General-President, far from bringing great enlightenment, "sometimes led one to think him more than a man." [30] The man in the portraits of Gilbert Stuart—a figure at least six feet tall, with massive head, wide and deepset eyes, protruding nose, and jutting chin—stands imposing in scale but mysterious in spirit, as if velvet and lace were not the ordinary dress of the day but a personal costume for a private masque. For all the volumes of papers he left behind, and their scanning by generations of scholars, he has stayed probably more obscure and enigmatic than any man to take his place.

The personal life of this aristocratic revolutionary always has read like an almost unbroken study in anomaly. A citizen rightly honored as a father to his country, he knew no such fortune as a husband: he was sterile and childless. Uniquely gifted, among all Americans of his time, to rouse and hold the trust and confidence of a revolutionary rabble or a distraught people, he found his own life shadowed by repeated spells of dark depression—a man haunted by what Jefferson called his "gloomy apprehensions." An author and a speaker of as many phrases as would ever be remembered of any President, he had no schooling beyond the age of fourteen, and he labored painfully, for many years, to avoid doing outright violence to language. As President, he somehow misled history into remembering him as one of the Republic's leaders most drawn and attached to Europe, almost as if he were an expatriate English country squire; but his eye and mind were directed toward the Western frontier more intently, in fact, than any President before Andrew Jackson. And of all Presidents who left lasting marks on the office, Washington alone, far from aggressively seeking it, had honestly dreaded it as "an ocean of difficulties." As he had written, not long before he would take his first oath: "My movements to the chair of government will be accompanied by feelings not unlike those of a culprit who is going to the place of his execution." [31]

There seemed to prevail in his public life, too, a pattern of persistent contradictions. He was a leader devoid of all serious personal vanity, but he had enough taste for official pomp to enjoy traveling in a handsome coach drawn by six horses or on a white steed with leopard-skin housing. He distrusted the role of personality in the Republic's politics, especially the excessive hopes of citizens in the magic of personal leadership. Yet no American President, perhaps ever, would so change the life of the Republic, not by intellectual command or political daring, but by a matchless force of personality. During all the labors of the Constitutional Convention, for example, even though he would prove so decisive a presence, he had played almost no role in the debates, saving his one speech till the assembly's very end. But when he would long to retire at the end of his first Presidential term, the emotional appeal to him by Jefferson spoke the practical truth: "North and South will hang together, if they have you to hang on." [32]

The inauguration of Washington, and of the Presidency itself, was marked by almost equal measures of idolatry and irony—even beyond the need of the first President to borrow an additional 100 pounds from his principal creditor to pay his way from Mount Vernon to the capital city of New York. To begin with, the first chosen representatives of the new Republic could not have got their official business off to a more languid start. The Electoral College's unanimous vote for Washington had been taken on February 4, 1789; but a quorum of both Houses of Congress, required for opening the ballots, could not be persuaded to reach New York even by the end of March, and not until April 14 could the Secretary of the Congress bear the official news to Mount Vernon, there to be answered with Washington's promise to serve as President with "an honest zeal." By then, the waiting period had lasted long enough to make the first President groan over "the stupor or listlessness" of the men supposedly launching the Republic on its course.[33]

There was nothing listless, however, about the outpourings of people, from cities and villages, who cheered and followed the first President on his eight-day journey to New York, by carriage and on horseback. The lusty display resembled a triumphal Roman procession, and the popular celebrations of his birthday, indeed, would soon drive one critical journal to complain: "Even Cincinnatus received no adulations of this kind." [34] The continuous relays of mounted guards of honor at his side sent up clouds of dust thick enough to hide from him the countryside, while the saluting guns and soaring bouquets and tolling bells followed his path through Maryland and Pennsylvania and New Jersey. From Elizabethtown Point, a luxurious barge, mainly moved by oars and escorted by a colorful naval parade, bore the head of the new Republic to the foot of Wall Street on Manhattan Island—through the singing of some new words to the music of "God Save the King":

> . . . Joy to our native land,
> Let every heart expand,
> For Washington's at hand,
> With glory crowned.

The melody carried warning of a dispute to beset the inauguration itself. For the House and the Senate soon were snarled in argument over simply what to call the first President. With grandiloquence, Vice President John Adams argued: "What will the common people of foreign countries, what will the sailors and soldiers say" when constrained to use no phrase more splendid than merely "George Washington, the President of the United States? They will despise him." Accordingly, Adams called for the designation of "His Most Benign Highness." A Senate committee—setting a precedent for verbosity to be respected by many of its heirs—contrived a more elaborate title: "His Highness the President of the United

States of America and Protector of the Rights of the Same." [35] Only after much acrimony was the royalist verbiage abandoned, with the hope that future citizens would not "despise" so plebeian a title as President of the United States.

Throughout this confused overture to the first Presidency, Washington kept his sure poise and balance. In all his public demeanor, he behaved quite like the Washington who—in all his private correspondence—favored no adjective so much as "sensible," by way of compliment to any person or action. At the same time, he may well have been fortified by the religious spirit—or the sense of fatalism—that was the most striking mark of his brief First Inaugural. Therein, he directed all thoughts to the "Almighty Being who . . . presides in the Council of nations," or to "the Great Author of every public and private good," or to "the Invisible Hand which conducts the affairs of men." Whatever the precise meaning of these supplications, their ardent faith sharply contrasted with his candid skepticism toward all the recent gushing of popular support. For he distrusted it as any sure source of strength for the Presidency, as he wrote to one fellow Virginian:

> I fear if the issue of public measures should not correspond with their [the public's] sanguine expectations, they will turn the extravagant (and I may say undue) praises which they are heaping upon me at this moment, into equally extravagant (though I will fondly hope unmerited) censures. So much is expected, so many untoward circumstances may intervene. . . .[36]

And this might be read as a profoundly "sensible" caution—for all his Presidential heirs—to be braced for the hazards of public opinion.

The turbulent eight years of Washington's Presidency abounded, of course, in creative acts and suggestive hints that no successor ever could wholly forget or ignore. From the issuance of a national currency to the pattern of Congressional relations, the bases of republican government were moved into place. Like all who would follow him, he grieved that his critics "continually aimed" at him their "arrows of malevolence." [37] When first he personally reported to Congress on the state of the new nation, he was assailed for the presumption of "a Speech from the Throne"—but the precedent endured. When he traveled through New England or the Southern states, so that Americans might simply see how a President looked, he was denounced again for monarchic manners—but the Presidency profited. He even anticipated his successors' more rancorous sentiments about Congressional trespassing into the realms of foreign policy. He personally sat with the Senate, through two tedious sessions, to gain "advice and consent" for a treaty with the Creek Indians. The experience sufficed to teach him that consultation with the Senate did not move with the dispatch of Revolutionary War councils with his generals: when he finally left the Senate chamber with his treaty, he was overheard to vow that he would "be damned if he ever went there again!" And he slammed the door, indeed, against his or any other President's ever thereafter personally coming to share in such Senate debate.

Perhaps most worth remembrance, however, were Washington's very first hours and days as President, for he largely gave them over to a matter that would test all his successors: the watching of the gates and the doors all around his office. Now as always, the crucial question was: how open should they be—to what people and to what ideas? The Presidency was but two days old when Washington announced in the newspapers that he would receive "visits of compliment" only at an appointed hour on two days a week. The news instantly set an ultrarepublican Senator from the western part of Pennsylvania, William Maclay, to raging that "for him to be seen only in public on stated times, like an eastern Lama, would be . . . offensive." [38] Although such vehement protesters could not be appeased, Washington finally settled on two occasions when any citizen in decent attire—without introduction or prearrangement—could call upon his President, while a third occasion of a weekly dinner would be reserved for a rotating group of invited officials and their families. Before so deciding, however, he had written Madison and Hamilton and Adams and Jay for their counsel on all aspects of Presidential protocol—down to the detail of whether he might occasionally escape for a quiet tea with a friend. But his serious concern was the avoidance of "an ostentatious show of mimicry of sovereignty." While he needed a private and protected time for work, he showed an almost uncanny sense of the abiding peril of

Presidential isolation. Accordingly, he vowed to keep open "the avenues to useful information from the many," lest he risk becoming "more dependent on that of the few." [39]

A decade after he began the making of all his precedents, Washington found himself where he had always wished to be—as he wrote Lafayette, "on the banks of the Potomac, and under the shadow of my own vine and my own fig-tree." [40] There, in the very last month of his century, he died quite suddenly. And without excessive emotion, his first Secretary of State, Thomas Jefferson, looked back upon his Presidency and concluded:

> His person was fine. . . . His mind was great and powerful without being of the very first order; his penetration strong, though not so acute as that of a Newton, Bacon, or Locke; and as far as he saw, no judgment was ever sounder. It was slow in operation, being little aided by invention or imagination, but sure in conclusion. . . .
>
> Perhaps the strongest feature in his character was prudence, never acting until every circumstance, every consideration, was maturely weighed. . . . His integrity was most pure, his justice the most inflexible I have ever known.[41]

There would rarely be written a more concise reminder, for any future President, of certain qualities he would most need to have and to prove.

I V

> American democracy has revived the oldest political institution of the race: the elective kingship.
>
> —HENRY JONES FORD, 1898

All worry over what the Founding Fathers had wrought, with their creation of the Presidency, was not dispelled by even the combined force of Hamilton's forensic labor and Washington's heroic labor. The cynics and alarmists persisted. To Washington, they seemed outrageously to slander him, with their charges of regal pretensions and ambitions. To Hamilton, these critics of Presidential power were inventing their flimsy fears in "the regions of fiction." And as he went on, half sighing and half snarling, to defend the President: "He has been shown to us with the diadem sparkling on his brow and the imperial purple flowing in his train. . . . The images of Asiatic despotism and voluptuousness have scarcely been wanting to crown the exaggerated scene." [42]

With his blend of reason and ridicule, Hamilton won the debate, but he never killed the dread. This was the lingering fear, decade after decade, that some sort of monarch had hid in the suit of the President. By the 1830's, when Andrew Jackson dared to be the first President to appeal to the people over the head of Congress, the Whigs cried out against "King Andrew I," flagellating him, in the vituperative fashion of the time, as "a detestable, ignorant, reckless, vain, and malignant tyrant." [43] In 1848 a more detached sort of distrust was voiced, when the Swiss people went about drafting their own new constitution: they followed aspects of the American example, but they shunned a presidency in favor of an executive council, from obvious fear of a president's power. In the same year, as the vigorous Presidency of James Polk was ending, a quietly serious Senator from Maryland named Reverdy Johnson, warning the chamber against an "overshadowing" Presidency, spoke the most direct of answers to the assurances of Hamilton: "It may yet be that a diadem may sparkle on the brow of an American President." [44]

All notions of royalty in the White House, moreover, have not come from critics alone. A half century after the caution of the Maryland Senator, the Pennsylvania editor Henry Jones Ford, who has been called the scholarly herald of the twentieth-century Presidency, published his glowing appreciation of the leadership of the Chief Executive. "In the Presidential office as it has been constituted since Jackson's time," Ford rejoiced, "American democracy has revived the oldest political institution of the race, the elective kingship. It is all there: the precognition of the notables, and the tumultuous choice of the freeman, only conformed to modern conditions." [45]

Beneath all the spirited argument on the subject, the enduring question about the man in the White House has not been, of course, any superficially ceremonial issue of precious gems on his forehead or regal names for his office. It has been the profoundly practical matter of the power and the purpose of the Presidency, their true range and their right limit. Inevitably, such an issue has excited the most varied emotions in so large a Republic. For it is the kind of queston likely enough to make any one citizen feel and sound of two minds—as was the case, in fact, with the mind of Woodrow Wilson.

There was no other of the nation's first thirty-seven Presidents who spent so much time trying to describe the office before he filled it. The pre-Presidential inquiry by Wilson notably included two books, published more than twenty years apart: *Congressional Government* in 1885 and *Constitutional Government in the United States* in 1908. The two famous studies were not only impressive, but also irreconcilable. The first saw the Presidency in terms of its political eclipse in the decades following the Civil War, and Wilson concluded: "The actual form of our present government is simply a scheme of congressional supremacy. . . . Congress [is] the dominant, nay, the irresistible, power of the federal system. . . . The President . . . [is] the first official of a carefully graded and impartially regulated civil service system . . . and his duties call rather for training than for constructive genius." [46] But the second Wilsonian assessment saw the office—albeit without so stating—in terms of the boisterous Presidency of Theodore Roosevelt, during the years following the Spanish-American War. And Wilson now perceived the real nature of a President to be this:

> His is the only national voice in affairs. Let him once win the admiration and confidence of the country, and no other single force can withstand him. . . . His office is anything he has the sagacity and force to make it. . . . The President is at liberty, both in law and conscience, to be as big a man as he can. [47]

There was nothing absurd in either one of these views of the White House. Each reasonably reflected its time. In the span of years between the leadership of a general like Grant and the leadership of a colonel like Roosevelt, after all, the rank of the Presidency itself had known a spectacular climb. But the political sum of the two Wilsonian verdicts added little to the confident judgment of the ordinary citizen conscientiously concerned about his Presidents, about what they should be given, and about what they should be denied.

The old question of John Jay thus has seemed still to hover in new form. *Do* we have a king, and, whatever we call him, what is his size? Should we pity him as the dwarf of Wilson I or fear him as the giant of Wilson II? And what is the right orbit for the sweep of his power: *with* the people, *through* the people, or *above* the people? And beside the Congress, around the Congress, or despite the Congress?

There is every reason to believe that the wondering about such matters will go on as long as the Presidency—perhaps even longer.

Three

The Mystery of the Presidency

> Government is not fundamentally either an office of laws or men but of imponderables behind both of them.
>
> —WILLIAM BENNET MUNRO

There sometimes occurs, as one scans the political life of any republic, a thought worth exploring because it seems, for a teasing moment, so quixotic. Occasionally, the notion may even enlighten, rather than merely bemuse. Such a conceit might suggest that the Western world has known only two extraordinary, enduring, and sovereign offices vaguely similar in their authority over people, their complexity of labor, and their subtlety of prerogative. These two improbably comparable ministries would be the Presidency of the American Republic and the Papacy of the Catholic Church.

Such a suggestion in no way confirms the eighteenth century fears of North Carolinians who foresaw "a very serious danger" of a Roman Pope becoming an American President. Nor is it meant to give equal offense to Baptists in Texas and papists in Tuscany. The parallel may be mildly provocative, but not slightly subversive, for the saving distinctions rise high. Quite obviously, there appears an impressive political difference between a Pope's sovereignty over a few score Roman acres and a President's sovereignty over a half of the American continent. There can be fancied no resemblance, in role or ritual, between Rome's College of Cardinals and America's Electoral College, and the celebrations of victory at the end of a Presidential campaign, varied and colorful as they have been on most election nights, have never been known to include the skyward spiral of a column of white smoke from the

Capitol dome. And the lyrical ways to quicken the emotions of the faithful remain distinct in each community: the thrill felt by most Americans when a President's appearance summons the salute of "Hail to the Chief" bears no great resemblance to the mood evoked by a Gregorian chant.

Through decades of patriotic American rhetoric, moreover, there has not been heard more than the predictable amount of reverence for the Republic as the One, Holy, and Apostolic Democracy. Once Thomas Jefferson referred carelessly to the Founding Fathers as "demi-gods," but he soon recanted. As for the infinite comfort afforded by the dream of personal infallibility, this has been—in the Roman case—no less than a stated doctrine. But the same has been —in the American case—no more than a private and unspoken conviction clutched by a few Presidents who have slipped it, like a charm, under their White House pillows, to bring the sleep of a peace unruffled by uncertainty, after a long day of possibly irretrievable blunders.

There remains some reason, nonetheless, to mention the Presidency and the Papacy in the same breath and under the specific terms: authority, complexity, and subtlety.* Other than the men in these two offices, there reigns no Western chief of state or head of church whose actions and words, alliances and anathemas, can circle or change the world in a way almost erasing the frontiers of nations. Conceivably, only an unchallenged leader of a united Islam might dare so much. Nor does there live another sovereign whose inescapable tasks are so immense in variety and so impossible to finish. The Roman Pontiff who must be forever a pastor, a statesman, a theologian, a patron, an administrator, and a symbol finds his match in the American President who must serve always as an executive, a politician, a legislator, a benefactor, a commander in chief—and a symbol. There would seem to be, too, no other august offices whose sovereigns so frequently display an odd talent for startling their own constituents. Around the middle years of the twentieth century, the surprise that an unpretentious Harry Truman

* The mention has been made, parenthetically, at least once before, by James Bryce in *The American Commonwealth*, first published in England in 1888. Opening his long-remembered chapter on "Why Great Men Are Not Chosen Presidents," Bryce measured the Presidency as "this great office, the greatest in the world, unless we except the Papacy." [1]

proved to be for his political community—expecting neither firm leadership nor bold ventures—roughly anticipated the astonishment that an unpretentious John XXIII would shortly visit upon his religious community.

In the light of even such loose analogies, a more general thought about the very nature of the Presidency may not appear wholly extravagant. Perhaps all the sweep of Presidential leadership becomes more visible and sensible when looked upon as a political mystery rather than a political institution. And all the trial of the Presidency may come to be seen less as a naked play of powers than as an obscure play of paradoxes.

There is less imagery than accuracy, I believe, in such a view of the life of the White House. The word "institution" connotes the fixed or the inherited or the prescribed, by birth or custom or law. But never in its history has the American Presidency behaved so obediently. To speak of the office as a *mystery,* moreover, is not to voice awe or give homage: it is only to observe a political fact that, as the dictionary says, "arouses wonder by being difficult to understand or solve." * This does not sound like too romantic or sentimental a description of the place of a President in the American system.

All semantics aside, the notion of mystery can hardly offend any reader of the story of the whole Western world. All of this history's truly world-changing events have been, of course, matters of the sort to "arouse wonder" and "difficult to understand." So it was with the fifteenth century's Renaissance Man, born and reared in—of all places—the brutish chaos of the city-states of Italy. So it was with the nineteenth century's appearance of Industrial Man, skilled and trained to make—of all places—an island in the North Sea, without great size or resources, the imperial and commercial wonder of its age. So it was, also, with the eighteenth-century gathering of fifty-five American citizens in—of all places—the city of Philadelphia, there to prepare the most ingenious and ambiguous charter for Political Man ever written. And no one of

* *The American Heritage Dictionary* goes on to explain that the roots of the word go back to late Latin *misterium,* only a variant of *ministerium.* As the latter means simply "service," the definition would surely be rejected by no American President.

these occurrences, of course, made simple sense: it only made serious history.

The witnesses to the Presidential mystery, however, need not be summoned from times or places so remote. The heart of the matter becomes clear enough from a scattering of remarks, over a few years, by the first President to be born in the twentieth century. From 1956 onward, John Kennedy pressed his campaign for the White House with a zest befitting the youngest man ever to seek and to win it. In the embattled process—more precisely, in January, 1960—the Kennedy who was still a Senator told the National Press Club in Washington what he thought a President should be:

> In the challenging, revolutionary Sixties, the American Presidency will demand more than ringing manifestoes issued from the rear of the battle. It will demand that the President place himself in the very thick of the fight. . . .
> He must above all be the Chief Executive in every sense of the word. He must be prepared to exercise the fullest powers of his office—all that are specified and some that are not. . . . He must re-open the channels of communication between the world of thought and the seat of power. . . . [For] the President is alone, at the top.[2]

The address of the youthful candidate was much applauded. And among its telling passages were those in which the candidate of 1960 reached back to the professor of 1906 to repeat Woodrow Wilson's assurance that a President was splendidly free to be as big a man as he wished.

Between this first buoyant appraisal of the Presidency by John Kennedy and his last such commentary, there intervened enough troubles to give pause, as well as maturity, to even a less intelligent Chief Executive. Despite the narrowness of his margin of victory in the 1960 election, he went on to deliver an Inaugural Address breathing no fear and some fire, as he saluted the coming to power of not only a new administration, but also a new generation. Through the less than thousand Presidential days thereafter left to him, he fought his way through the many snares set to test and to trip him: the tedious wrestling with the Congress in Washington and the nasty sparring with Nikita Khrushchev in Vienna, the floundering into the Bay of Pigs in Cuba and the trespassing toward disaster in Vietnam, the beating down of prices in America's steel industry and the bluffing back of Soviet missiles from the Caribbean.

The Kennedy thus seasoned finally wrote, only four months before his murder, a few pages to introduce a small book by his closest White House aide, Theodore C. Sorensen, entitled *Decision-Making in the White House*. Here the accents and inflections sounded strikingly different from those of only three years before. Now neither "the very thick of the fight" nor the sovereign command from "the top" seemed altogether true pictures of a President's arena or his power. The man in the White House described his office, instead, as "formidable" and "exposed." Joining all his Presidential forebears, he sighed that "no one in the country is more assailed by divergent advice and clamorous counsel." Cautioning all his Presidential successors, he warned: "There will always be the dark and tangled stretches in the decision-making process." But throughout these last formal notes he left, briskly etching the Presidency, the one quality and word he stressed most was: "mysterious." [3]

As for what he found so cryptic, he probably had given the clearest hint on a particularly festive occasion during his second year as President. By this time, he had come to realize that neither the command of the President nor the consensus of the Republic gave irresistible force to any edict that an unruly world preferred to ignore. By then, too, he had become acquainted with the uncertainty of the wisdom trumpeted by Presidential counselors. He had come to understand also that the more than 2,000,000 souls in the executive bureaucracy—all presumably at the service of the President—often had somewhat less interest in his salvation than in their own. All too aware of his own swift instruction in such facts of Presidential life, he presided over an unprecedented White House reception, in the spring of 1962, for guests quite remote from all politics. This was a gathering of forty-nine winners of the Nobel Prize. Among the honored, there were poets and physicians, playwrights and mathematicians, lawmakers and peace-makers. And the young President addressed to them the revealing tribute: "I think this is the most extraordinary collection of human talent, of human knowledge, that has ever been gathered at the White House

—with the possible exception of when Thomas Jefferson dined [here] alone." [4]

This salute from one President to another, over the arc of a century and a half, celebrated something constant in the office itself. From the White House of Jefferson to the White House of Kennedy, of course, there was no outward measure of the office that had not wildly grown: the array of precedents, the legion of advisers, the size of the Republic to be governed, and the greatness of the world role to be filled. Yet one decisive thing had changed not at all: the need for any President—at the final critical moment—to stand, think, and act alone.

II

THE EXECUTIVE POWER SHALL BE VESTED IN A PRESIDENT OF THE UNITED STATES. In modern parlance, this phrase was to prove a "joker." [5]

—CHARLES C. THACH, JR.,
The Creation of the Presidency

The First Inaugural's reference to "the Invisible Hand" on all great public affairs alluded to providential matters, of course, but the words of Washington could as well have applied to the more mundane business of Presidential powers. The sometimes exasperating and sometimes exciting uncertainty of these powers has been remarked upon, with sorrow or with pleasure, by President after President. What Wilson cheered as the chance for each President "to be as big a man as he can"; what Truman called "a plan, but not a strait jacket"; what Kennedy sensed as "the dark and tangled stretches" in decision-making—all these have been but changing Presidential metaphors for a lasting fact. The essential truth has followed from what the author of *The Creation of the Presidency* perceived to be the "joker" of the Constitution's cloudy grant of power. By this grant, the living exercise of Presidential leadership would forever mean each President's own handling of the "wild card" dealt by the Founding Fathers. And the political worth of the "joker" would always depend upon why, when, and how it is played.

The abiding paradoxes of Presidential history, and all its anomalies and surprises, thus have been something more than the chances of fate or the caprices of Presidents. They have been true birthmarks of the office—the very terms of its creation. Boldly loose and free, these terms mock and deny all rigid theories about Presidential office and life. This is why the most seemingly plausible propositions so often have been found to be only rough guesses or unwise wagers. And a few such usually unquestioned propositions call for a little inspection. . . . .

The Immensity of Authority

There would appear no quality of the Presidency so impossible to deny as its massive power, over all the world of nations, and the relentless growth of this power, through most of the twentieth century. Yet the appearance must somewhat dazzle and deceive, for the most vehement dissents have come, in fact, from the Presidents themselves, a surprising number of whom have felt less empowered than imprisoned by their office. The cries and complaints to this effect have not issued, moreover, only from such aggrandizing Chief Executives as a Theodore Roosevelt or a Woodrow Wilson or a Franklin Roosevelt. The Presidential testimony to a power shortage in the White House can be taken from quite different witnesses, set apart much too far in time to compare notes or match arguments. And two such Presidents, a full century distant from each other, would be James K. Polk and Harry S. Truman.

The resemblance so striking between the President of the 1840's and the President of the 1940's tends to pose some challenge to any unqualified theory of an irresistible evolution in the Presidency. The two men were remarkably akin politically: both raised in border states, both far more versed in the ways of a legislator than an executive, and both the dedicated servants of other Presidents—Andrew Jackson and Franklin Roosevelt—who truly presided over their political careers. The rough profiles of the characters of the two Presidents, moreover, would be hard to distinguish. A respectful student of Polk's Presidency has termed him "an honest, conscientious, and limited man" who was "devoid of all personal magnetism," a man whose "range of interests also was remarkably limited" and with strikingly "few . . . intellectual contacts" beyond the gates of the White House.[6] An admirer of Truman would have conceded the same. By the measure of political promise or forecast, the approach of both men to the Presidency invited much the same skepticism: when the 1844 Democratic Convention in Baltimore chose the first "dark horse" in the Republic's history, the derisive Whigs asked, "Who is James K. Polk?"; and a like sort of question was echoed, not derisively but anxiously, a hundred years later, when Roosevelt's death made of Truman a President. Among all Presidential elections, moreover, the victory of Polk in 1844 over the magnetic and compelling Henry Clay may well have been the only precedent for the memorable improbability of Truman's 1948 triumph over the presumed-to-be next President, Thomas E. Dewey.

Both Presidencies were highlighted by the matching ways in which each man went about making nonsense of the omens and fools of his prophets. A relentless will for work kept both Presidents striving beyond all normal limit to their labors: the daily routine of Polk at his desk ended only when sheer exhaustion stopped him.* Beyond this, both men were equally ready to evade or to ignore Congress, on any matter from federal patronage to international war. The Congress of May, 1846, that humbly recognized "a state of war is existing by act of the Republic of Mexico"—a state of affairs wholly shaped by Polk's plans—made easy and natural, by any historical scanning, the meekness of House and Senate in June, 1950, when they readily accepted the *fait accompli* of American military action in Korea. In full attire as Commanders in Chief, both Presidents either deplored or dismissed their less-than-loyal generals in the field: as with Polk and his generals, Winfield Scott and Zachary Taylor, so with Truman and his general, Douglas MacArthur. Most impressively of all: the grand commitments by Truman to the world role of twentieth-century America, from France to Taiwan, were scarcely more bold than the nineteenth-

* Of all the "unusual qualities" to be ascribed to Truman by his admiring Secretary of State, Dean Acheson, "the first of these" was "the priceless gift of vitality." In Acheson's words: "Mr. Truman could work, reading and absorbing endless papers, and at times play, until well past midnight and be up at six o'clock walking deserted streets with hardy Secret Service men. . . . He slept . . . never worrying, because he could not stay awake long enough to do so." [7]

century resolves by Polk to set the Oregon boundary, take the California terrain, and extend the Republic's sovereignty over another half million square miles. And not completely content with this, Polk entered serious negotiations with Spain "to purchase the island of Cuba" in a "profoundly confidential" encounter—a scheme whose success might have spared John Kennedy two ordeals.[8]

The sum of this should indicate the "energy" of two Presidents who never could be considered soft or whining. Both were, instead, strong and stubborn. As one historian has written of the earlier President, so it could be bluntly said of both Chief Executives: "What Polk went for, he fetched." [9]

The toughness, decisiveness, and tenacity of these two Presidents are the qualities that give special credibility to laments upon their office which, spoken by men of less steel, might be misread as confessions of weakness. For Polk and Truman shared—as they did so many intuitions and attitudes—a common regret that a President lacked the power to inspire or impel the doing of those things that he most deeply believed must be done. There is no stridence in the tone of the *Diary* of James K. Polk during his Presidency, but the sorrow of frustration sighs like a wind through all its political seasons. Alternately startled or enraged by members of Congress who "constantly deceive me," Polk had to conclude grimly: "I am almost ready at some times to conclude that all men are selfish, and that there is no reliance to be placed in any of the human race." [10] And at just about the same time in the next century, Harry Truman would nod back and concur: "I sit here all day trying to persuade people to do the things they ought to have sense enough to do without my persuading them. . . . That's all the powers of the President amount to." [11]

A fondness for hyperbole—a quickness to exaggerate both afflictions and attainments—has long been an occupational hazard for all Chief Executives. From this addiction, neither a Polk nor a Truman could be wholly immune. But the complaints so similar, from times so separate and from leaders so aggressive, might make any future President wonder a bit whether historical rumor could be trusted to tell him the whole truth of his real power.

The Mastery of Congress

For at least two generations, a critical test of any President's leadership has seemed to be the skill of the Chief Executive to act effectively as the nation's Chief Legislator. A Woodrow Wilson would be first the master, but finally the victim of Congress. A Warren Harding would be its creature, a Calvin Coolidge its comfort, a Herbert Hoover its companion. From World War I till the Great Depression, when Franklin Roosevelt both inspired and tormented Congress, the power of the Presidency faltered. And all such facts of modern Presidential life would seem sure signs of an often decisive connection between the citizen's allegiance and the Congress's deference to the same President.

Yet the Presidential story did not respect such logic in the decade after World War II—as the political fortunes of a Dwight Eisenhower plainly showed. Since the drowsy days of Calvin Coolidge a generation earlier, the White House had been home for no President so courtly toward the prerogatives of Congress nor so unruffled by its rebuffs. From 1952 to 1960 the two terms of the former general's Presidency were governed—or inhibited—by his conscious resolve to correct an imbalance between the proper powers of the Congress and the Executive which he imagined to date from the 1930's. In this spirit, the abstention of an Eisenhower was to be offered as a kind of Presidential atonement for the acquisitiveness of a Roosevelt.

From the first year of his Presidency, Eisenhower observed this passive role toward Capitol Hill. Upon the sudden death in 1953 of the Senate majority leader, Robert Taft, the probable but not inevitable successor was William Knowland, a California Senator certain to oppose the President on major issues both national and foreign. But the prospect of such Senatorial hostility distracted this President not at all from his larger purpose, and he sternly enjoined his Cabinet: "This Administration has absolutely no personal choice for new Majority Leader. *We* are not going to get into *their* business." [12] Thereafter, the reward for such restraint on the part of the Republican President became, slowly but inevitably, the ascendancy of the Senate's Democratic leader, Lyndon Johnson—never a man to stand back from a political vacuum. The legislative result was a leadership from the White House that could claim no more than two or three victories in the eight years of the Eisenhower Presidency.

The pertinent political fact was that all such weakness in the Congressional arena evidently did nothing to diminish Eisenhower's strength in the popular arena. As the closest counselor of Lyndon Johnson later remarked upon those years of Democratic domination of Congress: "The one thing that the Democratic leadership, for all its unquestioned superiority in political tactics, could not do was to make a serious dent in the prestige of Dwight D. Eisenhower." And this same Democratic observer of the not-very-militant former general in the White House went on to concede that this accommodating Chief Executive, by pure force of personal popularity, "as a constitutional monarch . . . could have had a lifetime job." [13]

The regime of Eisenhower thus dramatized another curious truth about power in the White House: under certain political circumstances, there could occur a virtual divorce between the impact of a President and the impact of his Presidency. Obviously, the mood and instincts of the people at this particular time found both response and assurance in the presence and manners of Eisenhower—as a healer rather than a leader, a man of virtue rather than vision. Yet his remarkable capture of public support and faith came about without any subtle design or contrived effort or rhetorical skill. With an almost casual indifference to such artifice, he won and held all the public confidence that a Woodrow Wilson or a Lyndon Johnson craved so deeply and pursued so painfully. And the glow of this conquest by the *man* in the White House stayed quite unshadowed by any retreats or surrenders on Capitol Hill.

The Special Reign over Foreign Affairs

A kind of law of Presidential life, sometimes imagined to be almost beyond amendment by circumstance, recognizes a far stronger force of Presidential leadership in foreign affairs than in domestic affairs. A President appears, indeed, a freer man to impose his will in the larger arena. He enjoys this relative freedom for reasons not only constitutional but also practical. His sources of information are matchless (even when they are wrong); his command of weapons is total (even though it is alarming); and his patriotism of purpose constrains any critics (even when they are right). When this Caesarian figure must fight in the arena of domestic policy, however, he shrinks to more commonplace size, as he finds himself encircled and goaded by a continent of hungry constituencies—all equally ready to beseech, use, abuse, ignore, or defy him. And so great has looked this political distance between these two arenas that the White House has seemed to many a home for the uneasy coexistence of "the two Presidencies." [14]

Even this general insight can occasionally mislead a citizen, however, as dangerously beguile a President. Harry Truman was merely stating the reality as he saw it, for example, when he once flatly said: "I make American foreign policy." [15] Such an assertion by any twentieth-century President might be largely correct, so far as it went. But it did not go far enough. After the Republic's foreign policy has been *"made,"* what happens *next?* More explicitly, after the world or nation, ally or foe, reacts to the policy "made" in America, what then does a President choose to reply or command? And these questions suggest a couple of immediate qualifications to any extravagant vision of Presidential omnipotence in world affairs.

In the first place, the impact of Presidential power upon the world of nations does not follow from its traditional existence, of course, but from its practical exercise. Majestic as this authority may seem, the power, as delivered to each President, arrives with no self-firing mechanism. More often than not, the success of Presidential action depends far less on the caliber of his military weapons than on the clarity of his political aims. As proof, there should be needed no more evidence than the remarkable contrast between decisions and actions of John Kennedy over a short span of time in so small a sphere as the Caribbean Sea. On a scene far from being the most troubled or crucial in the world, this one President—conscientiously served by the same set of advisers and evidently inspired by the same set of objectives—could lead the nation through two scarcely believable crises: the fiasco of the invasion of Cuba and the defiance of the Soviet Union's adventure in nuclear missiles for Cuba. There intervened only eighteen months between the same President's failure to shake the government of an impoverished island people and his ability to confront the world's second nuclear giant. In that year and a half, there had occurred no important changes whatsoever in the arsenal of Presidential weapons or the range of Presidential purposes. Nothing had changed but the more thoughtful appraisal—and the more resourceful use—of the powers at hand.

In the second place, a President at no time is any more wholly free of the past than he is completely lord of the present. The heritage can be heavy. The origins and strategies of the longest war in the Republic's history, the conflict in Indochina, weaved their way like vines through no less than five Presidencies, from Truman to Nixon. Of all documents found in the Pentagon Papers recording the tragedy, there are few more painfully naïve than a memorandum of May 23, 1961, from Vice President Lyndon Johnson to President John Kennedy, upon the Vice President's return from a visit to Saigon. There he had saluted as "the Winston Churchill of Asia" South Vietnam's President Ngo Dinh Diem—whose overthrow thirty months later, encouraged by American policy, would also bring his assassination. In the Washington of 1961, the Vice President called for the "joining" of "the battle against Communism" in Asia, lest "the vast Pacific becomes a Red Sea." Even at this pitch of fervor, however, he conceded the possibility of a future moment when the nation might have to choose "whether we commit major United States forces" or "cut our losses and withdraw." To that ultimate question, he offered the answer: *"We must remain master in this decision."* [16] But this was not an interpretation: it was simply an incantation.

The dream of such "mastery" implied that all Indochina would hold its breath, as well as its fire, until the American President had finished carefully computing the precise point at which American involvement would become unbearably costly. But the point of no-reward had long since been passed—somewhere, somehow, along the trail back to 1950, when the gift of great quantities of military equipment to the French colonial armies (by the word of the Pentagon study) already had "directly involved" America and "set" the course of its policy.[17] More than a decade later, there had come the critical change, barely visible but nearly irreversible, from what the Department of Defense scholars described as the "limited-risk gamble" of the Eisenhower Presidency to the "broad commitment" of the Kennedy Presidency. Thereafter, "the dilemma of the

U.S. involvement dating from the Kennedy era" was the riddle of how to use "only limited means to achieve excessive ends." [18] And this incongruity became the legacy of still two more Presidents.

Any historical vision of rather severe Presidential authority over foreign affairs, moreover, has found dramatic contradiction in the climactic events in two of the more turbulent Presidencies of the twentieth century. These dismal last days in power belonged to Woodrow Wilson in 1920 and to Lyndon Johnson, almost exactly fifty years later. And there is a cold sort of light shed by the trials of both men.

The sadness of the end of Wilson's Presidential life almost blurs its lesson. Physically and politically paralyzed for the last year and a half of his Presidency, and the last four years of his life, this was the Wilson who possibly had excelled all predecessors in both the intellectual preparation he brought to the office and the political achievements of his first term in it. This was the Wilson, too, who earlier had learned so well, as governor of New Jersey, the pragmatic details of partisan patronage, political maneuver, and legislative bargaining. Despite this intricate instruction, however, he devoted his last days in power, not to any realistic dealings with his enemies on Capitol Hill—banded and sworn to destroy his dream of world peace—but to an evangelical tour of the Western states, exhorting all citizens to believe that "this great nation," by ratifying the Treaty of Versailles and entering the League of Nations, would find itself sublimely ascending to "those heights upon which there rests nothing but the pure light of the justice of God." [19] After the gods had seemed to join the Senators in deserting him, Wilson huddled in his invalid's chair and warmed himself, through this winter of his Presidency, with the confidence that the voters of 1920, as they spurned the Republican candidacy of Warren Gamaliel Harding, would pronounce a "great and solemn referendum" confirming the rightness of his own cause. But when some 25,000,000 ballots had been counted, of course, Wilson found his last hopes buried beneath a Harding plurality of 7,000,000. In the path of deities and legislators, the people, too, had followed and turned deaf.

This President lived on another three years in Washington, finally to leave the capital one of the most poignant vignettes in the history of the office. In his spacious home on S Street, he became a man bent in frame and broken in spirit. The Armistice Day of 1923 was the fifth anniversary of the victory to which he had led the Republic in World War I. To mark the occasion, he was wheeled to the steps before his home; he there managed, with help, to stand upright; and he spoke to the crowd come to pay their respect:

> I am not one of those that have the least anxiety about the triumph of the principles I have stood for. I have seen fools resist Providence before, and I have seen their destruction, as will come upon these again—utter destruction and contempt. That we shall prevail is as sure as that God reigns.[20]

With this farewell curse upon his infidel successors, Wilson left the Presidential scene forever, and he was dead within less than a hundred days.

A half century after the Armistice of 1918, President Lyndon Johnson surrendered his White House under political and emotional terms that were strikingly similar. He bore no such physical scars as Wilson, and he publicly voiced no such personal venom. But for the rest, the two retreats from Presidential power followed much the same route. What Versailles had done to Wilson, Vietnam had done to Johnson. Each Chief Executive had anointed a Presidential policy as a sacred cause. For both men, to compromise such a cause was to contaminate it. For the first President to negotiate with a Henry Cabot Lodge seemed as unthinkable as for the second to negotiate with a Ho Chi Minh. Each called upon the Republic, accordingly, to support its President not merely as a matter of political judgment but as a recognition of "moral commitment." Both came to regard all vocal dissenters from their *ex cathedra* definitions of national doctrine as apostates or heretics. And as each left behind him the loud chorus of his critics, he heard all the din as giving no hint of his own error, but only a sign of his own valor.

The ultimate irony reached beyond their parallel fortunes. These were the only two Presidents of their century (with the possible exception of Herbert Hoover) to feel at their backs, as they departed from the White House, such icy blasts of popular dislike and distrust. But the storms had not blown up in that one of "the two

Presidencies"—the arena of national politics—where the man so often seems so besieged and vulnerable. Both times, they had risen in the realm of foreign affairs, where the grand powers of any President are supposed to let him stand most tall and feel most safe.

The Critical Role of Public Opinion

Beyond all tricks of history and all quirks of Presidents, there would appear to be one unchallengeable truth: the dependence of Presidential authority on popular support. Indeed, the destinies of Wilson and Johnson themselves can be read as clear signs of this. And the judgments of all historians of the Presidency concur that the loss of the people's trust is the one mortal disaster from which there can be no real recovery.

Indisputable as this may be, however, a reminder to a President on the fateful point serves him about as helpfully as a memorandum on the need for continuing to draw breath. To be sure, no President in the middle of the twentieth century could reasonably repeat the complaint of James A. Garfield that the nation's Chief Executive was "the last person in the world to know what the people really want and think." [21] By the 1950's the problem had taken on a wholly modern shape, but not necessarily one more encouraging. The President by this date found himself informed by—or enmeshed in—an almost endless flow of ticker tape registering the more-or-less exact and up-to-the-month "quotations" on public beliefs and doubts and worries, all affecting the political value or "cost" of almost every imaginable issue, from Law-and-Order to Ban-the-Bomb. But when the exhaustive data have been fully compiled and charted, the sum has often looked like a guide to Presidential decision not much more reliable than the average Wall Street counsel on economic investment.

There may be more than figurative resemblance, in fact, to the two types of augury. On the occasion when J. P. Morgan was asked by a young man for some oracular advice on the course of the stock market, he candidly replied: "It fluctuates, my boy—it just fluctuates." So, too, with the movements of public opinion. For although the graphs and reports on popular mood and taste are usually clear, a vast amount of what they so clearly report is itself both ambivalent and mercurial.

The ambiguity starts with the most popularly cherished concepts of the Presidential office itself. Thus, a full generation of surveys conducted since the 1930's by the American Institute of Public Opinion has unmistakably reflected two unchanging popular attitudes toward the Presidency: (1) the American people respect and want the "strong" leadership that requires an untimid use of Presidential powers; and (2) the American people distrust and fear an aggressive leadership that threatens an unbridled use of Presidential powers.* In a historical sense, this struggle of the people with themselves to define an ideal Presidency may be appreciated as a kind of extension of the same debates that once troubled the Founding Fathers. But in a practical sense, from the viewpoint of a twentieth-century President, this has meant that the most sophisticated statistics, as they register the divided will of the people, yield more questions than answers.

Again and again, the careful weighing of public opinion has revealed, more than all else, a steadfast contradiction between avowed theory and desired reality. In the year 1944, for example, a nationwide sampling of the electorate reported 57 percent in favor of a constitutional amendment restricting any President to two terms in the White House, *and* the voters in the same year proceeded to call Franklin Roosevelt to a fourth term by a margin of more than 3,500,000 ballots. In the year 1959—and eight years after passage of the Twenty-second Amendment—an equally confounding sort of popular conversation could be overheard. Almost two-thirds (64 percent) of the polled electorate renewed their approval of the ban on the third term; *and* 58 percent of the same voters also wished a chance to vote for President Dwight Eisenhower, if only he would run for a third term.[23]

---

* To note but one characteristic instance: following Truman's inheritance of the Presidency, a survey by the American Institute in April, 1945, inquired whether the citizen viewed as "good" or "bad" the general prospect that "Congress will [now] have more importance and power than it had under Roosevelt." The popular approval was overwhelming: 65 percent rejoiced and only 16 percent demurred. But after the new President and Congress had sparred only a few months, the same survey inquired into any feeling that the President might "take a stronger stand" in order "to get Congress to carry out his recommendations." The verdict was now equally vehement in reverse: 52 percent favored "stronger" executive action, with only 21 percent dissenting.[22]

There has been something equally disconcerting, for the man in the White House, about the most regular index of public opinion taken since the 1930's: the uncomplicated question of approval or disapproval of a President's performance in office. For much the greater part of the time, a clear majority of the electorate, with often stoic indifference to circumstances in the nation or the world, has approved the Presidential conduct of the Republic's business. On this continuing chart of public approbation, the score of the embattled Roosevelt never dipped below 50 percent; the trusted Eisenhower only once fell to a low of 49 percent; and the comparatively unformed Presidency of Kennedy enjoyed a popular approval ranging from 69 percent to a low of 57 percent of the voters. The course of this graph for Harry S. Truman was a study unto itself. Soon after entering the White House, when he was least known, he commanded an unprecedented 87 percent rating in national approval; after some time in office, he broke another precedent, with a spectacular lack of popular support, down to a meager 23 percent; and the national election of 1948 gave the definitive retort to this reckoning.[24]

When the Chief Executive has turned to popular polls not for any general appraisal, but for specific sentiment on an immediate problem, the search has seemed as tortuous and the landmarks as blurred —above all, in the sphere of foreign affairs. The citizens of China, so traditionally inscrutable to the citizens of America, for example, could only find American attitudes toward Communist China, through the 1960's, quite unbelievably inscrutable. By the records of one nationwide poll, a survey in 1964 showed only 10 percent tolerating or approving Communist China's entry into the United Nations, with an overwhelming 73 percent opposed. By 1971 almost one-half (48 percent) of all Americans were giving their approval, while barely one-quarter (27 percent) clung to their opposition.[25] The interval between these radically different judgments, moreover, had been the years of the Vietnam War, whose need and whose cost were ascribed by a large part of the American electorate to Communist China's leadership of the international conspiracy to turn the Pacific Ocean into "a Red Sea." * At the

* Any peculiarity in this "swing" in popular opinion was simultaneously surpassed by the even more incongruous evolution of official Republican doctrine on

same time, a no less extreme change had been observed in the citizenry's view of the Vietnam War itself. In mid-1965 the question of whether the Republic had "made a mistake" in "sending troops to fight in Vietnam" found only 24 percent perceiving a "mistake," with 61 percent approving the action. By mid-1971 there had been achieved "a complete reversal of opinion," with a new 61 percent now regretting the decision.[26]

For all Presidents, the trouble with any such information is not that it is really incomprehensible, of course, but that it is essentially irrelevant to the urgent matter of making decisions. It gives postmortem facts to men busy with prepartum politics. And the volatile nature of all such reports can be seen in the positive rewards, according to opinion polls, enjoyed by any President who has managed a clear-cut disaster in international relations. In 1960 the shooting down of an American U-2 plane on its spying mission over the Soviet Union—followed by the White House's elaborate and futile misrepresentation of the incident—sent the popular esteem for President Eisenhower climbing by some 6 percent. In 1961, the disaster of the Bay of Pigs—followed by President Kennedy's full acceptance of responsibility for the folly—sent his popularity into an even steeper ascent of some 10 percent.[27]

A President scanning with the mysterious ways of public opinion might find some sort of lesson in the contrast between the reactions to these abrupt Presidential misfortunes and the responses to the prolonged ordeals of Woodrow Wilson and Lyndon Johnson. The blunders of Eisenhower and Kennedy followed a careless decision or a reckless impulse—not a policy protracted in time or debate or sacrifice. As such, they could excite sudden sympathy and brisk forgiveness. But the less fortunate Presidents became identified with unyielding policies that were lengthily deliberated, persistently argued, and stubbornly pursued. As such, they provoked gradual impatience and eventual intolerance. But a Chief Executive can find nothing pragmatically instructive in these distinct popular judg-

---

the subject. Through most of the 1950s, Henry Cabot Lodge, as President Eisenhower's Ambassador to the United Nations, tenaciously fought against any UN recognition of Communist China as a "reward for aggression"—in Korea. In 1971—after a decade of war in Vietnam—he counseled, as President Nixon's chairman of a commission to review Chinese relations, the wisdom of widening contacts with China, so that there might come an end to that country's "self-isolation."

ments, lest it be an ironic encouragement to make major mistakes only with dazzling speed. And the public verdicts of both kinds have never come forth from a poll or a computer in time to caution or inspire any President in the wise wielding of his powers.

III

> He must see what he sees with the eyes of the multitude upon whose shoulders he stands.[28]
>
> —HAROLD J. LASKI,
> *The American Presidency*

The image of the man in the White House, as seen by Laski, may suggest a weird sort of Presidential contortion. But the metaphor was not muddled. It incisively stated what this witness saw above all else: the abiding incongruity of the Presidency.

A President repelled by any notion of his office as ungainly or untidy might be tempted, of course, to impose some symmetry upon it by imagining and invoking inflexible laws of politics or unmistakable lessons from history. The search for the magic of such logic, however, could produce only a study in the absurd—above all, as so hapless a President might try to apply literally to the present some Presidential parallels from the past. As he coveted the popular affection of an Eisenhower, he would be impelled to a mimicry of leadership by abdicating his role as Chief Legislator and promising Congress never to "interfere" in "their" affairs. As he remembered the suffering of a Wilson, he would shun all energetic efforts or designs for world peace, as explosive hazards to his own political security. And as he feared any crises within the Republic so plaguing as the decay of cities or the spread of poverty, he would ease tension by diverting the public mind to some foreign challenge—preferably, a crisis met in a manner clumsy enough to assure embarrassment before the world, hence acclaim throughout the nation.

The recital of such fatuities is not itself absurd. Despite its extravagance, it warns watchers of the White House against all sweeping propositions and summary definitions which, by facile analogy or theory, would take the office out of its ever-changing context, and its ever-elusive place, in the Republic's history. There may be, I suspect, but one immutable fact of Presidential life: there are *no* immutable patterns to describe it, no invincible strategies to govern it. For throughout its existence, again and again, the smoothest generalizations about it have broken against the rough edge of an event or under the hard fist of a man.

None of this is so eccentric or capricious as it might sound. The essential political reality may have been best stated not by any President but by a Supreme Court Justice. "The life of the law," Oliver Wendell Holmes insisted, "has not been logic; it has been experience." Years later, Holmes pressed again (in *Lochner v. New York*) the same historical point, as profoundly true of the Presidency as the judiciary: "General propositions do not decide concrete cases. The decision will depend on a judgment or intuition more subtle than any articulate major premise."

The American jurist here cast in legal language much the same discernment with which his good friend, the British scholar, had studied the odd posture of the President, who must be at once *above* and *within* the people. Both men were echoing, too, something of Walter Bagehot's understanding that any democratic statesman must be "an uncommon man of common opinions." [29] Each of these insights suggested the awesome range of the values that the President must try to reconcile, the loyalties he must try to hold, the conflicts he must try to narrow, the issues he must try to illuminate, and the strategies he must try to blend.

If these things be true, as I believe, this President—any President—finds himself commanded to perform an almost interminable series of conjuring acts to control the ceaseless contradictions of Presidential life. He must proudly cherish and profess political principles—yet sometimes pursue his greater purposes unslowed by lesser scruples. He must summon his people to be with him—yet stand above, not squat beside them. He must question his own wisdom and judgment—but not too severely. He must hear the opinions and heed the powers of others—but not too abjectly. He must appease the doubts of the critic and assuage the hurts of the adversary—sometimes. He must ignore their views and achieve their defeat—sometimes. He must be aggressive without being contentious, decisive without being arrogant, and compassionate without being confused. He must respect ideas—without fancying them substitutes for acts. He must respect action—without unharnessing it from reason. He must respect words—without becoming intoxicated with his own. He must have a sense of purpose inspiring him to magnify the trivial event to serve his distant aim—and to grasp the thorniest crisis as if it were the merest nettle. He must be pragmatic, calculating, and earthbound—and still know when to spurn the arithmetic of expediency for the act of brave imagination, the sublime gamble with no hope other than the boldness of his vision.

There never has been, and there never could be, a constant compass or a sovereign logic to set the way to meet an array of challenges so anomalous. For all Presidents, as for the first President, the forbidding prospect has had to present "an ocean of difficulties." And the art of its brave navigation and safe passage is the heart of the mystery.

Four

The Man in the White House

The process of election affords a moral certainty, that the office of President . . . will be [by] a constant probability . . . filled by characters pre-eminent for ability and virtue.

—ALEXANDER HAMILTON [1]

The public lives of nearly twoscore American Presidents have persuaded many historians to agree that Hamilton's optimism has been vindicated. The majority of men in the White House have displayed, especially through times of stress, both steadiness of purpose and skill in politics. At the same time, no wholly dishonorable or cruel or corrupt citizen has ever been able to capture the office. Beyond this, a Harold Laski could judge no fewer than eleven Presidents to have been "extraordinary men." [2] Specifically comparing American Presidents and British Prime Ministers, over the years from 1789 to 1945, he found that a count of the outstanding national leaders from the American Revolution to the New Deal—and from the younger Pitt to Winston Churchill—ended in an Anglo-American tie. To match Pitt, Peel, Palmerston, Disraeli, Gladstone, Lloyd George, and Churchill, there were Washington, Jefferson, Jackson, Lincoln, Theodore Roosevelt, Wilson, and Franklin Roosevelt.[3] By this reckoning, the office of President had enjoyed better fortune than any modern political invention of the Western world.

So favorable a judgment found Hamilton to be right once again, however, for the wrong reasons. Actually, the very sincerity of Hamilton's prophecy might be doubted. More shrewdly than most Founding Fathers, he knew that "ability" and "virtue" in a political leader were qualities so distinct and separate that both could only rarely be expected to abound in the same person. Quite aside from such realism, Hamilton would have been appalled by the "process of election" elevating the great majority of Presidents. The suffrage itself was, for him, a highly privileged affair: the 4,000,000 Americans of his day included some 700,000 slaves, and the millions of votes of their descendants did not figure in his calculations of the future, any more than the equally alien idea of women presuming to go to the polls. The notion of political parties, with all their contention and divisiveness, was wholly repugnant to him. So also would have been even a hint of the stridence and sophistry of a twentieth-century national campaign. And the prospect of such a wild democratic folk dance as a Presidential nominating convention, with its confetti and parades and cabals, could have sent him fleeing back to his birthplace in the British West Indies, where the natives behaved more predictably and complaisantly.

Such distaste for the tricks and frills of the "process of selection" has been not at all peculiar, of course, to a Hamilton, or to his eighteenth century, or to his conservative tradition. In modern Presidential politics—and from liberal voices, too—the process has brought laments and sighs. In 1968, for example, the Democratic Senator who dared challenge his Democratic President over the Vietnam War, Senator Eugene McCarthy of Minnesota, seemed a lusty campaigner as he entered various primary elections, aroused the Republic's youth, and deplored most political artifices. In fact, however, he deplored nothing quite so fully as the tormenting path that led toward the White House, lest it be the hugeness of the powers he saw amassed there. Even before this became clear—from his personal passivity at the 1968 Democratic Convention—the Senator had repeatedly philosophized to his advisers: "Power is best exercised by those who are sought out by the people. . . . And the seeking of me as a candidate came like the dew in the night. It was rather gentle . . . but there were signs in the morning that something had happened during the night, and so here we are." [4] These very phrases came from the text of his nominating speech for Adlai Stevenson eight years earlier, in 1960, and still another eight years before, Stevenson himself had gingerly accepted his own nomination for the Presidency in 1952 as "a cup" that he had prayed might "pass" from him. The verbal elegance of both men adorned the same political reticence. Beneath their Democratic skins, the two candidates shared the aristocratic aversion of a Hamilton to partisan brawling for high office. So feeling and so acting, they forgot one of the very few apparent laws of Presidential campaigns: after George Washington, no memorable national leader has reached the White House who has not fought hard, even harshly, to arrive there.

Since the rowdy politics of Andrew Jackson's day, the Presidential convention in particular has been no hospitable place for candidates who spoke of the Presidency in terms of nocturnal dew or sacrificial wine. It has demanded the coarser language of ambition, fervor, and combat. Inevitably, this kind of nominating convention has offended countless critics, esthetically and politically, with its many absurdities: its hollow orations and incantations, its tedious rituals and protocols, its shabby haggling and bargaining.

These critics sometimes have failed to weigh, perhaps, how the trials imposed on all candidates can also rudely instruct them, as a prelude to sterner tests to come. To turn ordeal into triumph, a candidate must have a steely will for power and its hazards, and this may not be poor preparation for a President who will have to act—more than once—by the bracing reminder of Thoreau that "a man sits as many risks as he runs." The victorious campaigner must also learn the unwisdom of simple answers to complex questions—for there is no *simple* way to enlist the support of hundreds or thousands of convention delegates from all regions of the Republic. In the process, the candidate has been taught the cost of hasty and reckless words in public. He has been made to learn the arts, as well as the limits, of compromise, and the courtship of an unfriendly state delegation can be excellent practice for confrontation with a hostile Congressional faction. He has had to struggle, too, to rally and unite antagonistic forces in a political coalition, and this may alert him a little for the more intricate Presidential labor of shaping alliances of nations. He has been exposed, moreover, to endless demeaning encounters with both men and groups for whom he has no true respect, but only real need. This imposes a test of endurance, with a smell of humanity, not at all inappropriate for a President so soon to be attended by advisers so unctuous, and prerogatives so numerous, as to leave little room in the spirit for a memory of humility. All these experiences can toughen and ready a President-elect. For the first fact that he must face upon entering the White House has always been the unsettling knowledge that he begins work with at least 40 percent of the citizens of the Republic believing that he is the wrong man for the office.

Along with this welcome awaiting all new Chief Executives, the men persevering so far might be expected to share a few other common experiences, traits, or origins. From enough such data, a student of the Presidency, in an age devoted to statistics, might hope to trace a kind of group profile of Chief Executives. He might hope to glean some facts more enlightening, for example, than the revelation that the median age of Presidents entering the White House, from the eighteenth through the twentieth centuries, has stayed in the range of fifty-four to fifty-five years, with no greater variance. Yet the sifting of all such calculations seems to yield but a few nuggets of mild interest.

By origin and by heritage, the Presidents indeed have observed a few imprecise patterns. A total of nineteen, more than half of them, have been born in the three states of Virginia, Ohio, and New York, and an identical number have had the same states as their places of residence when inaugurated. Only five have not been born in the East (Hoover, Truman, Eisenhower, Johnson, and Nixon). All of these belong to the twentieth century, and this suggests that the White House, too, has gone West. In ancestral terms, all but five have traced their heraldry to the British Isles, with the more or less Teutonic exceptions being Martin Van Buren, Theodore and Franklin Roosevelt, Herbert Hoover, and Dwight Eisenhower. A like inclination has marked their religious inheritance. More than one-half—another total of nineteen—have worshiped in the Episcopalian, Presbyterian, or Methodist churches. And all of them have professed allegiance to some specific church, except for three: Thomas Jefferson, Abraham Lincoln, and Andrew Johnson—a by no means unimpressive representation for the unorthodox.

By way of more personal background, the American President has been born to a large family, the number of children averaging seven and Benjamin Harrison surpassing all, with twelve brothers and sisters. No Chief Executive has been an only child, and two-thirds of them have been the eldest child or son. Neither the occupations nor the interests of their fathers have seemed predestining. By far the majority, a total of twenty-one, were engaged in some form of agriculture, and only nine had had any contact with either national or state politics. As for the future Presidents' own education, there were thirteen—more than a third—who found no bar to their ambitions in their lack of a college degree. Once transported to the White House, they proved notably inferior in fertility to their forebears: they sired an average of but half as many children as their fathers, while six had none at all.

The arithmetic of Presidential trivia does cast a few doubts, however, on some conventional wisdom about the office itself. For all candidates pursuing "the greased pig," any advantage of political party has been only cyclical and inconsistent: both the Republican and the Democratic parties have won the chase fifteen times. To an American people generally certain of their devotion to the arts of peace, there may be some surprise in the fact that eleven, or nearly a third, of their Presidents since 1789 had previously served as generals. As for the presumed value of prior executive experience, this would appear to be a notion logically sensible but politically irrelevant. Among the ten men in the White House evidently best trained and prepared by this standard, only three would later be judged to have been effective executives in the White House.* Finally, there appears little support for the popular assumption that the Vice Presidency generally serves a politician as a starting point only toward obscurity or retirement. In fact, no less than a dozen Vice Presidents have lived to find themselves Presidents. And by this accounting, there would seem no more promising way to reach the White House than through this particularly gloomy passage.

The vague sum of all these calculations rather suits the perverse nature of the office. It decrees nothing indisputable and assures nothing predictable. The number of distinguished American Presidents over the decades may indeed have matched the number of distinguished British Prime Ministers. But there emerges little in the

* The ten most rich in administrative experience would be: James Monroe, Martin Van Buren, Andrew Johnson, Rutherford Hayes, Theodore Roosevelt, Grover Cleveland, William Howard Taft, Calvin Coolidge, Herbert Hoover, and Franklin Roosevelt.

process of their selection to suggest how the fittest survived or how they acquired their distinction. And the inescapable inference would seem to be that—with the preparing of Presidents—the shortest line between two points may be, more often than not, a zigzag.

II

Away with the cant of "measures, not men!"—the idle supposition that it is the harness and not the horses that draw the chariot along.[5]
—PRIME MINISTER GEORGE CANNING (1770–1827)

Headstrong and heedless of a Canning, a pair of confident British observers of the American Presidency, though separated by half a century, have offered almost identical descriptions of the role and labor of any Chief Executive. In the 1880's, James Bryce explained in *The American Commonwealth:*

> A President need not be a man of brilliant intellectual gifts. . . . Eloquence . . . imagination, profundity of thought or extent of knowledge . . . are not necessary for the due discharge in ordinary times of the duties of his post. . . . Four-fifths of his work is the same in kind as that which devolves on the chairman of a commercial company or the manager of a railway, the work of choosing good subordinates . . . and taking a sound practical view of such administrative questions as require his decision.[6]

The analogy chosen by Bryce seemed to have some strange appeal, as late as the 1930's, to a learned compatriot. For the historian Philip Guedalla also concluded: "The true history of the United States is the history of transportation . . . in which the names of railroad presidents are more significant than those of Presidents of the United States." [7]

There is a certain fascination—and some enlightenment—to be found in misjudgments of such magnitude. To begin with: even were it true that "four-fifths" of Presidential labor has been indistinguishable from the role of "the manager of a railway," the proposition would prove very little. The remaining "one-fifth"—saved from the time-consuming drudgery of routine administration—could afford all hours needed for the few irrevocable decisions, or the few memorable initiatives, that give historic meaning to any Presidency. In fact, any portrait of the nation's Chief Executive as essentially a "manager," requiring only a "sound practical" knack for office routine, conveys little more than a caricature of leadership in the White House. There are reasons to argue, indeed, that, out of all the talents and capacities of a President, there may be none less important than his administrative skill. There is no quality easier for a President, surely, to find and to hire in other men, and the Presidents most masterful politically have included those most careless administratively. As the distinguished constitutional scholar Edward S. Corwin once alluded to two of these Presidents:

> Not only Lincoln's temperament, but his entire lack of previous administrative experience and the Western attitude that no elaborate bureaucratic machinery was needed must have contributed to [disorder]. . . . His frontiersman's conceptions of the requirements of sound administration were no less naïve than Jackson's, whose record as a spoilsman he far surpassed.[8]

There has been no other of the thirty-seven Presidents, moreover, whose range of experience with "sound practical" matters surpassed the record of Herbert Hoover when he entered the White House in 1928. The ensuing Executive leadership did not accidentally fail: a good part of its failure could be ascribed to precisely the background supposed so specially to endow this President. Or as one of his acid critics looked back after 1932 and concluded: "Mr. Hoover was never President of the United States; he was four years Chairman of the Board." [9]

Over the generations, there have persisted perhaps few illusions about the Republic's leadership so popular and so false as the idea that the world of business and the world of politics respect quite similar rules for power and success. Instead, there is virtually no place in the business realm for the untidy, unpredictable, and unending give-and-take of compromises behind almost all serious decisions in the political realm. Nor does anything in the life of the most powerful business executive prepare him for the most recurrent encounter in the life of a President—the collision with an organized opposition ready and armed to challenge or rebuff him. And for just these reasons, the political careers of distinguished businessmen in the executive branch have been marked by neither much joy nor great success.

Such general contrasts between leadership in the private sector and in the public sector imply many more specific distinctions. These are sharp enough to indicate a few more unique marks of the Presidency itself. And any Chief Executive in the White House could invite all other chief executives in the land to consider them —at least ten such revealing differences:

\# The forces of history and mythology, beloved tradition and cherished folklore, attend and exalt the White House as no other office in the Republic. This alone sets the place apart from the directors' boardrooms or the presidential suites of United States Steel, United Airlines, or United Fruit. For the officers of such enterprises are not and could not be leaders who live in the shadows, or govern by the memories, of famous predecessors; who hear a national anthem or a Marine Band honor their every appearance; who read in the national press, every day, their household name, their family routine, their political fortune, their world influence, their personal victories and their personal vicissitudes; and who may watch on national television, any night they wish, their own prerecorded orations to the Republic, or to the world, on any cause from flood control in the Middle West to arms control in the Middle East. There are no merchants or bankers, no managers or manufacturers —even at the dizziest heights of power above the marketplaces of the nation—who must test their sobriety, every day, by savoring so much heady wine.

\# On the more prosaic level of Presidential work, the administrative chores of this executive bear little similarity to those of any other. If he could be said ever to confront a board of directors, for example, this body would be his Cabinet. But few heads of great corporations even have dreamed of the luxury of presiding over a board so obligingly docile as the President's Cabinet. Under Franklin Roosevelt, Secretary of War Henry Stimson captured in one phrase the sense of frustration shared by generations of Cabinet members, when he confided to his diary, after one Cabinet meeting, the mood of almost any such gathering: "The same old two and sixpence, no earthly good." [10] This particular President was notorious for the elaborate and deliberate ways in which he ignored Cabinet members, delegated overlapping powers, authorized imprecise missions, and exasperated rival subordinates. It was his studied intent, of course, to keep them at bay, as well as at odds. Some years later, a Budget Director who had served the New Deal—a man with traditional views on rational administrative practice—conceded: "I'd say that Roosevelt must have been one of the greatest geniuses as an administrator that ever lived. What we couldn't appreciate at the time was the fact that he was a real *artist* in government." [11] The estimate was largely true of this Chief Executive. But the "artistry" of such methods would hardly have excited widespread admiration at General Motors or Standard Oil.

The aspirations of great leadership—along with all the accepted criteria for success or failure—are wholly different for the man in the White House and any other executive. For most American Presidents, even the less visionary among them, there have been few concerns more nagging than the distant judgment by history. But the opinions of posterity arouse no comparable interest in the realm of private business or finance. For like reasons, there has never been a Presidential State of the Union message rendering an annual account of political profit and loss audited like a corporation's statement of earnings. Because there can be no such meticulous short-term reckoning, a President with his eye on the far horizon may dare to shrug a little—as could no presiding officer of a great industry—and join in the easy confession of a Harry Truman: "There are probably a million people in this country who could do the presidential job better than I, but I've got the job and I'm doing the very best I can." [12]

In an inexorable way, never true of inherited power in the private sector, the powers of the Presidency have a tendency to be historically cumulative. For all the cycles in the sharing of power among the branches of the federal government, there has appeared a steady progression in one respect. Each aggressive President has reached back—over the heads of the meekest who came before him—to pick up from the point where the last aggressive President left off. Thus did a Franklin Roosevelt effectively ignore three Presidents

directly preceding him, to act as if he were the immediate successor to a Woodrow Wilson and a Theodore Roosevelt. Over the generations, this habit has seemed almost to assure the size of the Presidential inheritance, as Edward S. Corwin perceived, since the "precedents established" by the most forceful Presidents "are available to less gifted successors." [13] Or, as Henry Jones Ford explained in the late nineteenth century, even after Presidential power had been "bent and held down," by Congress or by circumstance, the repeatedly proved fact was that "its springs were unbroken, and it sprang up unhurt." [14]

\# In a vulnerable way, never true of any other private or public office in the Republic, the powers of the Presidency can be snarled, at any time, by uncontrollable forces in the nation or unforeseeable events in the world. Within the country, there is more wish than truth, for example, in any image of the modern President as the wise and knowing guardian of the national economy and general prosperity. Most Presidents possess neither confidence nor sophistication in these areas, and no President since the 1920's, in fact, has made serious pretense to such personal knowledge. Beyond the shores of the Republic, the prediction, much less the direction, of affairs becomes still more unsure. The wrecking of great Presidential designs does not require anything convulsive or cataclysmic, shaking the globe. An assassination in Sarajevo or a massacre in Warsaw, the rise of a wall in Berlin or the fall of a cabinet in Paris, an election of Socialists in Santiago or a revolt of generals in Saigon—any of these may suffice to refute a President's assumptions, deflect his policies, or even cloud his chances for reelection. And no other American chief executive can boast or complain of living so dangerously.

\# The President is identified with the very life of his vast community, as is no other leader, even of the Republic's greatest corporate empire. In the economic sector, the officer presiding over the most imposing monopoly or conglomerate may be discredited and dismissed, and the result could be the enterprise's more swift and certain prospering. In the political realm, however, there can be no such divorce of the President, short of the wholly improbable event of impeachment. Politically and symbolically, the President and the Republic are one—so closely tied that it is scarcely possible for either to gain and the other to lose, or for either to be wounded without the other being scarred. Under the Constitution, of course, the length of the contract is limited, but its bonds are almost indissoluble—until the next Presidential election.

\# The pressure of time is a special stress of the Presidency, in more than one oppressive way. The tension does not date merely from the vast expansion of Presidential responsibility in the twentieth century: the *Diary* of Polk groans almost monotonously over White House days leaving him "almost prostrated by fatigue." [15] Apart from the more obvious official claims upon his time, the President must face an incomparable host of popular demands, often as petty as they are persistent. For the people have come to look to him, as to no other individual, for resounding opinions on all matters from geopolitics to pornography; for exhorting messages to all gatherings and conventions, from bankers to teamsters; and for appearances in all forums for all occasions, to cheer his favorite athletes or to salute his returning astronauts. And to make complete this conspiracy against his time and his patience, the Constitution and its Twenty-second Amendment, setting the span of Presidential life, have put him—from the moment of his oath of office—in a historic race against the clock. In short, "the category of time," as one observer of this race has remarked, "is more important to the President of the United States than to any other political leader in the world." [16]

\# Partly to meet these pressures—and partly for no higher reason than to please Presidents—the Oval Office enjoys the protection of such a ring of services and servants as shields no other place in all the Republic. In the words of one former Presidential adviser:

> The White House is an ideal cloak for intrigue, pomposity, and ambition. . . . The institution provides camouflage for all that is petty and nasty in human beings, and enables a clown or a knave to pose as Galahad and be treated with deference.[17]

Such a vignette may be too severely drawn, but there is no denying the world of resources at the Chief Executive's command. There is no limiting of the number of his aides and retainers. There is no accounting for his privileged funds. There is no forgetting—as Presidents are fond of doing—that the Secret Service, which they ritually lament as an invasion of their privacy, serves no less as a guarantee of their privacy. As for the realm of big business or high finance, of course, an occasional executive suite enjoys the protection of its own regiment of sentinels and sycophants. But there is no titan of industry or commerce who can hope to match the deployment of guards around the American President. He can only envy it.

As if by way of atonement for his peculiar executive privileges, denied all powerful citizens in the private sector, the political life of the President gravely depends on one critical test that they are spared: the enlistment of public confidence. Somehow, he must find his own sure footing—somewhere—on the terrain of "that queer, shifting, labyrinthine amalgam we call public opinion." [18] By the mid-twentieth century the "eyes of Argus" that Washington had felt upon him had come more to resemble the stare and scrutiny of millions of citizens who see themselves as "stockholders" with rightful "shares" in any Presidency. By vote or by trust, they claim a personal "investment" in their national leadership. Depending on the greatness of their political hopes—or the size of their financial contributions—they await return or reward in varying measures, but *all* expect *something*. And there can be found, nowhere in the Republic's society, another constituency so huge, so clamorous, and so capricious.

The authority and success of any President's answer to this constituency ultimately depend, I believe, on the most elusive of all these matters: the quality and the force of Presidential *style*.* Nowhere more than here does a dramatic distance open to separate the role of a President and the role of James Bryce's "chairman of a commercial company." Such a company must concern itself, indeed, with mass media, public relations, and popular responses. Yet these are not in any direct or intimate sense problems *of* "the chairman": their nature does not revolve around *his* character, and their solution involves popular appreciation of a product, not a person.

The challenge to an American President, however, has far less to do with the devices of Madison Avenue than with the doctrines of

---

* "*Style* . . . the way in which something is said or done. . . . The combination of distinctive features of . . . expression, execution, or performance. . . . A quality of imagination and individuality expressed in one's actions and tastes" (*The American Heritage Dictionary*).

James Madison. For by the terms of the Founding Fathers, along with the amendments wrought through history, the person of the President is wholly inseparable from his administration's policies, purposes, and results. As the people judge them, so they judge him. Without him, there *is* no "product" of his Presidency to take to the political marketplace: indeed, one of the important unwritten powers of his office is the deciding of *what* to produce, by law or act or word. Within the federal government, the executive branch does not, by abstract authority, firmly hold its own balance in the shifting division of powers shared with the Congress and the Court: it is *his* weight that adjusts the scales. And throughout the Republic, it is not the preachment or promise of a faceless administration that carries to all states, communities, and citizens. Whether it stammers or enthralls, the only living voice is *his*.

A distressed but keen perception of all this was written early in 1931. This was a time, of course, when the Great Depression was deepening, the spirit of the people faltering, and the prestige of the Presidency withering. The most prominent Republican journalist of the day, William Allen White, had watched the regime of Herbert Hoover stumble through two years of promises and procrastinations. And White might have seemed to be sending a direct retort to James Bryce, a half century in the past, as he wrote to a friend:

> From forty to sixty percent of the Presidential office is not in administration but in morals, political and spiritual leadership. . . . As President of the Nation and servant of God, he has much more to do than to run a desk as the head of the greatest corporation in the world. He has to guide a people in the greatest adventure ever undertaken on the planet.[19]

The words may have struck too strong a messianic note. Yet this could not be remarkable, at a time when millions of Americans without work or hope were wondering who might appear, or what might happen, quickly enough to save them. And the focusing of so much of their own emotion—and the pressing of so much of their own burden—upon one office and one man conclusively measured the everlasting difference between any President of the United States and any president of the Union Pacific.

III

The executive power shall be vested in a single person. His style shall be "the President of the United States."

—COMMITTEE OF DETAIL,
Philadelphia Convention, 1787

The Founding Fathers' eighteenth-century use of the word "style" might be fancied to be one of their more sly symbolic acts. The language of the Committee of Detail was edited into its constitutional form by Gouverneur Morris, but the power that Morris exercised in this final wording derived from his chairmanship of another committee, which was itself called the Committee of *Style*. And by the hindsight of history, these usages of one word might be imagined subtle clarifications of the ambiguous text of Article II, with its invitation—delivered anew to each President as explicitly as his oath—to weigh and use his grant of power according to his own sense of right action.

There is no fantasy to the fact that the substance of the Constitution left a political void that could only be filled by the *style* of the President. And any twentieth-century student of the Presidency, possibly assuming that the theatrics of Presidential life owe their inspiration to the age of television, need merely glance back to the time of the first President, presiding over "the Washington court." Upon that "court," years after Washington's death, John Adams looked back and wrote his nasty but shrewd eulogy:

If he was not the greatest President he was the best Actor of the Presidency we have ever had. His Address to the States when he left the Army: his solemn Leave taken of Congress. . . . his Farewell Address to the People when he resigned his Presidency. These were all in a strain of Shakespearean and Garrickal excellence in Dramatic Exhibitions.[20]

So constant have been these displays of drama, enlivening all strong Presidential leadership, that what Adams wrote of Washington has been said, with either a smile or a sneer, about any aggressive Chief Executive ever since. The flair of certain presidents for "Dramatic Exhibitions" has been emphasized, moreover, by its contrast to the performance by other men in the White House wholly at a loss for such talent. Indeed, the first transfer of Presidential power provided a sudden study in this difference between Executive temperaments, as well as a forewarning of the abrupt transitions to be witnessed by all future generations. A Martin Van Buren following an Andrew Jackson, an Andrew Johnson following an Abraham Lincoln, a William Howard Taft following a Theodore Roosevelt, a Warren Harding following a Woodrow Wilson, a Dwight Eisenhower following a Harry Truman—each of these, in his own individual way, reflected something of the alternative styles of Presidential leadership first foreshadowed by a John Adams called to take the place of a George Washington. By the understatement of one historian, the first President was "a tough act to follow." [21] But the distinction between the two men—the martial hero and the portly intellectual—struck deeper than this. And its sharpness could be guessed from the time in 1790 when Vice President Adams had exploded to Benjamin Rush: "The history of our Revolution will be one continued lie. . . . The essence of the whole will be that Dr. Franklin's electrical rod smote the earth and out sprang George Washington." [22]

As such acidity almost assured, the official life of the second President amounted to what has been called "a full agenda of woe." Barely succeeding to the Father of His Country by the margin of three electoral votes, Adams suffered the taunt of being a "three-vote President" from the start, and, at the end of his one term, his bitterness over Thomas Jefferson's victory in 1800 drove him to shun his successor's inauguration. Through his years in office, he displayed admirable qualities of intelligence and tenacity, above all in keeping the young nation from involvement in the conflict between England and France. A man of singular talent and insight, he would be judged by Vernon Parrington to be possibly "the most notable political thinker . . . among American statesmen." But he was, unfortunately, other things, too: arrogant, cranky, aloof, vain, and secretive. With this character, he managed to alienate both Jeffersonians and Hamiltonians, the Congress and the public alike. This confident and cerebral Chief Executive lacked, in short, all saving sense of Presidential style. And when he retired to the life of a Massachusetts farmer, he confessed with glum candor: "Some sin to me unknown involved me in politics." [23]

*   *   *

A quite similar sort of drama in Presidential succession was re-enacted a little more than a century later. The protagonists now were the Republic's twenty-sixth and twenty-seventh Presidents, Theodore Roosevelt and William Howard Taft. In this instance, of course, Taft came to the White House as Roosevelt's insistently chosen successor. But this would only edge with painful irony the radical conflict between each man's ideas of *how* a President should act and lead.

In the headlong process of staking his claim to being the first modern President, Theodore Roosevelt played his role with the zest of a crusader and the glee of a boy. After Ohio's Republican boss, Mark Hanna, issued his famous lament on "that damned cowboy" gaining entry to the White House, Roosevelt happily took the sneer as a cue and proceeded to give the Presidency what one scholar of the office later called "the absorbing drama of a Western movie." [24] The act was no affectation. Back in 1884, Roosevelt had written a friend that, once he put on his special cowboy suit, complete with revolver and rifle, "I feel able to face anything." [25] Or as a relative, fully aware of his love of center stage, once commented: "When Theodore attends a wedding, he wants to be the bride, and when he attends a funeral he wants to be the corpse." [26] The tireless display of such enthusiasm drove another observer to see him as "an interesting combination of St. Vitus and St. Paul." [27] But what mattered was that his use of drama was no mere indulgence: it had impact. In the words of Archie Butt, his military aide: "One never gets away from Mr. Roosevelt's personality. . . . When he comes into a room and stands as he always does for one second before doing something characteristic, he electrifies the company." [28]

Over the years, the process of "electrification" relied upon a rare talent for both words and gestures to convey his Presidential message. With seemingly effortless ease, he coined phrases and slogans, from "muckraker" and "lunatic fringe" to "square deal" and—most characteristic of all—"my hat is in the ring." Traveling with as much studied purpose as he talked, he was the first Chief Executive to use the Presidential junket for its publicity value. In 1907 he made a trip down the Mississippi River, to provide a lively backdrop for announcing a White House conference on conservation of natural resources. The following year he became the first President to travel beyond the nation's borders, with his visit to the site of the new Panama Canal. All these were but token signs of his aggressive belief in the President's role as "a steward of the people," under historic command not to view the Constitution as "a strait-jacket cunningly fashioned to strangle growth" and not to preen himself on "the negative merit of keeping his talents undamaged in a napkin." [29]

For all his reforming thrusts on the national scene, from breaking trusts to planning conservation, the style of TR's leadership became most vivid and uninhibited in foreign affairs—whether he was negotiating for the Panama Canal Zone, which earned the Republic the distrust of Latin America for decades, or mediating the Russo-Japanese conflict, which earned him the Nobel Peace Prize. In all major decisions on world policy, he acted with an impartially divided disdain for both his Cabinet and his Congress. As he once said of the former: "I took Panama without consulting the Cabinet. A council of war never fights, and in a crisis the duty of a leader is to lead." [30] When in 1906 he sent his Secretary of War, William Howard Taft, to restore order to Cuba's anarchic affairs, he told Taft bluntly: "I should not dream of asking the permission of Congress. . . . It is for the enormous interest of this government to strengthen and give independence to the Executive in dealing with foreign powers." [31] But the most dramatic and effective Rooseveltian performance on the world scene came with his dispatch of the battle fleet—all sixteen battleships and 12,000 men—on their 1907–1909 world cruise to impress all nations, especially Japan. By all contemporary judgments, the impact of the fleet upon the great powers was altogether as electrifying as this President's entry into a drawing room, and he later viewed the stroke as "the most important service that I rendered to peace." [32] The exact manner in which he rendered this "service," moreover, had to be almost as significant as the action itself. The plan for the global display of power provoked immediate opposition from Congress, finally mounting to a threat to refuse funds for the grandiose operation. Unruffled, Roosevelt replied that this would matter not at all: he already had funds enough to move the fleet from its Atlantic bases to the Pacific, and if members of Congress chose to leave the battleships there, the decision to strip the East's defenses would, of course, be theirs. How could a mere Senator combat such a Rough Rider?

Whatever the failings of this Roosevelt, with his occasional compromises and his frequent pretenses, the Republic has known few Presidents who proved so convincingly the greater importance of style than statute. Throughout his tenure, he kept exciting many to marvel—and some to wince—at what one newspaper summarized as "the scrapes he gets into, the scrapes he gets out of—the things he attempts—accomplishes—demolishes—his appointments and his disappointments . . . his assumptions, presumptions, omnisciences, and deficiencies." More tersely, William Allen White concluded: "If he was a freak, God and the times needed one." [33] By his own standards, in any case, he had ample reason to write in 1909 to his son: "I have been a full President right up to the end." [34] And the pride—like the style—followed from the unabashed Presidential pleasure that he confessed: "I have thoroughly enjoyed it, for it is fine to feel one's hand guiding great machinery." [35]

The William Howard Taft who followed him, thanks to TR's lingering touch on the "great machinery," proved to be—by the measure of Presidential style—the retort incarnate. If Roosevelt had loomed as the frustrated general, almost lusting for combat, Taft clearly was the frustrated judge, ever longing for quiet. And the two men could only end by being as hopelessly at odds as their dreams.

While the Taft Presidency was not without its recorded victories, from advocacy of the federal income tax to the prosecution of twice as many antitrust suits as had been pressed by the Roosevelt administration, the future Chief Justice never ceased, as he once wrote, to "feel just a bit like a fish out of water" through all his White House years.[36] Or as he had told his wife back in 1906, while campaigning as a member of the Roosevelt Cabinet: "Politics, when I am in it, makes me sick." [37] And he practiced his adversion as President, explaining to Archie Butt: "I have made up my mind . . . that I will not play a part for popularity. . . . I cannot be spectacular." [38] With so stubborn an unconcern for popular support of Presidential purpose, it is not surprising that he could write, toward the end of his term, an almost coldly candid description of his own regime: "It is a very humdrum, uninteresting administration, and it does not attract the attention or enthusiasm of anybody." [39] Rather loftily indifferent to the press and impervious to his critics, he conceded to the military aide who had served both Presidents that "of course Roosevelt would have come back at" the critics, "but I cannot do things that way." With complacence, he consoled himself: "By and by the people will see who is right and who is wrong." [40] Nor could anyone close at hand persuade him of the political meaninglessness of popular appreciation of a President deferred until the "by and by."

The true want was exactly sensed by Secretary of War Henry Stimson. As his Cabinet aide said of him, apropos of one particularly vacillating encounter with Congress, "he would not strike out from the shoulder," but left Stimson to feel "as if I were taking his fist and trying to drive it forward for him." [41] In spirit, the same problem had driven Roosevelt, during Taft's first campaign for office, to cry out: "Do not *answer* Bryan; *attack* him!" But this appeal was as lost upon Taft as TR's exhortation to "treat the political audience as one coming, not to see an etching, but a poster." [42]

The contrast in styles between Taft and Roosevelt led inexorably to the anguishing conflict of the two Presidents in 1912. With unthoughtful enthusiasm, Roosevelt had told Taft in 1908: "I have always said you would be the greatest President, bar only Washington and Lincoln." As a prophet, TR had foreseen everything but the essential: how a Taft would *act* as President. When the final break came, Taft openly wept and exclaimed, with pained disbelief: "Roosevelt was my closest friend." And when the rupture became formal with Roosevelt's rebellious Progressive candidacy, the Republican leader Chauncey M. Depew promptly spoke the political obituary for both men: "The only question now is which corpse gets the most flowers." [43] As it turned out, Roosevelt got 600,000 more votes than his protégé-foe, but the two together had contrived to give the election to Woodrow Wilson with a million and a quarter fewer popular votes than his divided opponents.

The delayed political postscript for Taft—at once happy and revealing—came with his service as Chief Justice from 1921 to 1930. Long ago, in 1900, he had written his brother of his love for the bench: "Perhaps it is the comfort and dignity and power without worry I like." [44] No President could ever have defined his enjoyment of the White House, of course, as the pleasure of "power without worry." As a fretful President prone to laziness, sleeping too much and eating too much, Taft had betrayed the size of his worry in the size of his waist, but as a confident Chief Justice he worked hard and controlled his weight. "I love judges, and I love courts," he once had said. "They are my ideals, that typify on earth what we shall meet hereafter in heaven under a just God." [45] A serious man of such temper and style who had had to live at 1600 Pennsylvania Avenue—groping through the imponderables of Presidential decision, searching for logic and despairing of intuition—could have felt only that he had been somehow sent to the wrong address and the wrong life. So, indeed, he wrote in 1925, after four restoring years on the Supreme Court: "The truth is that in my present life I don't remember that I ever was President." [46]

*   *   *

Through most of the years while William Howard Taft was distinguishing himself on the highest bench, the Republic's twenty-ninth and thirtieth Presidents, Warren Gamaliel Harding and Calvin Coolidge, together gave an instructive eight-year lesson on an easily neglected aspect of Presidential style. These two Chief Executives could hardly have appeared more different: Harding congenitally warm and gregarious and trusting, Coolidge calculatedly cool and reserved and shrewd. Both men nonetheless shared a notion of the Presidency as an office that should be dignified and detached, uncombative and unpolemical—altogether the reverse of the style of either the Roosevelt now dead or the Roosevelt to come. So believing, each man, by the very slackness of his grasp on power, behaved in the White House quite as the nation liked and expected. And so behaving, they served to remind all political historians again that the style of any President, its aptness and its popularity, could not be prescribed by fixed formula: it could only be judged by the prevailing mood of the people at a particular time.

With Harding, the Presidency took on exactly the tone wanted by the nation—after eight years of Wilson. It was typical of the embittered Wilson, after his vain fight for his treaty and his League, to mock Harding as "the bungalow mind," and it is true that a Babbitt-like quality in Harding seemed almost to have been celebrated by Sinclair Lewis' publication of *Main Street* soon after Harding became President. But the popular longing of 1920 was for a return to the lazy peace of Main Street. A relaxed and kindly Harding offered a near-perfect relief to the rigid and doctrinaire Wilson. It was true that Harding tirelessly "bloviated"—as he described his own ornate rhetoric—with speeches about patriotic virtue that were barren of political content. But as F. Scott Fitzgerald noted: "It was characteristic of the Jazz Age that it had no interest in politics at all." It would be hard to insist, therefore, that such an age had the wrong President. When Harding suddenly died on a speaking tour in California, after but two and a half years in office, the procession by train bearing the President's body back to Washington was wept over by mourners across the land, with an outpouring of grief that the New York *Times* called "the most remarkable demonstration in American history of affection, respect, and reverence for the dead." [47] Shortly thereafter, a more surprising eulogy came from Harold J. Laski, carrying on his voluminous correspondence with Oliver Wendell Holmes: "I was very moved by Harding's death. . . . I thought him mediocre in ability but with a real and generous goodwill to his fellowmen, a quality I am still sentimental enough to think important." [48]

With Coolidge, the White House took on exactly the air needed by the nation—after its years with Harding. Again, the prevailing temper of the times echoed in the Holmes-Laski correspondence, now with the American Justice writing his English friend: "While I don't expect anything very astonishing from [Coolidge], I don't *want* anything very astonishing." [49] The President obliged, throughout his five years. In the memory of one member of the permanent White House staff, as he later wrote, "no other President in my time ever slept so much." [50] When this Chief Executive once was asked how he got his exercise, he replied: "Having my picture taken." [51]

In a sense, he might have answered the same if asked how he projected his Presidency. He raised passivity to nearly the level of strategy. "If you see ten troubles coming down the road," he observed, "you can be sure that nine will run into the ditch before they reach you and you have to battle with only one." [52] In a very short time, it would be hard to believe that a President could flatly declare, "This is a business country . . . and it wants a business government." [53] But much the same euphoric sentiment was shared in the Coolidge years even by a Lincoln Steffens and a Walter Lippmann, with the latter avowing as late as 1928 that "the activities of business" impressed him as "more novel, more daring, and in general more revolutionary than the theories of the progressives." [54] *
And there was yet another, more positive way that Coolidge suited and served his time. The scandals of the Harding regime—Teapot Dome, the Veterans' Bureau, and the Department of Justice—did not erupt until after Harding's death, bringing on what the favorite folk humorist of the time, Will Rogers, called the "great morality panic of 1924." But with Coolidge in the White House—a model of personal rectitude who could be dubbed a "Puritan in Babylon"—the Presidency itself was spared public scandal and popular distrust. Thus a Republican administration that, in a different time and with different luck, would have been hounded from office actually suffered not at all: a Coolidge at once so clean and cool easily won election in his own right, when a trusting and shrugging electorate gave him almost twice as many votes as his Democratic challenger.†

*   *   *

The Harding-Coolidge era would ever after seem a strange, almost vacant prelude to the most harrowing modern test of Presidential leadership. There were vastly more than Coolidge's "ten troubles," of course, fast coming down the road of the Republic. They arrived with the Great Depression, an ordeal matched in the Republic's history by the Civil War alone. For a nation as for a man, the time of searing crisis can become the time of enlighten-

* The faith in business throughout the 1920's could also be measured by the feebleness of organized labor: from a 1920 peak of 5,000,000 members, the enrollment in the AFL fell to 3,400,000 by 1929.

† In the 1924 election, less than one half of all eligible voters bothered to go to the polls.

ing self-discovery. So it was now: the meeting and surviving of the Great Depression dramatized, as never before or since, the fateful meaning of the style of Presidents. And the drama was achieved by two Presidents successively facing the same historic test with their memorably different political ways and manners—Herbert Hoover and Franklin Roosevelt.

The Presidential fate of Hoover followed twists of irony almost too extreme for political fiction. Few Presidents in office stayed so religiously loyal to their political and economic convictions, beyond all reach of contradicting circumstance or tempting expedience; and few would force themselves, as well as their country, to pay so great a price for their fidelity. When he entered the White House in 1929, Hoover had long been hailed as the masterful technician of twentieth-century economy and technology. By the time he made his farewell Presidential drive down Pennsylvania Avenue in 1933 he had been denounced as a kind of co-conspirator in the worst economic debacle in American history.

But the ironies had deeper roots in his past. This man whom the angry jobless of the Great Depression would bitterly honor, by christening their shacks and slums Hoovervilles, had been years earlier the humanitarian hero of relief and reconstruction, during and after World War I, who had moved thankful Europeans to name many a Hooverstrasse to the memory of his charity. From World War I, he had emerged—rather like General Dwight Eisenhower after World War II—as a national figure above ordinary politics, without known partisanship, and courted as a future leader by Democrats and Republicans alike.* As the nation of 1920 was leaving world conflict behind and looking toward national prosperity ahead, an Assistant Secretary of the Navy in the Wilson administration had written excitedly to a friend in Europe, envisioning the Hoover of the future: "He certainly is a wonder, and I wish we could make him President of the United States. There could not be a better one." And the Democrat with this ardent hope was young Franklin Roosevelt.[55]

There was a pathos to go with the folly after 1928. Much of it

---

* Before eventually declaring his Republican allegiance, the first electoral victories ever won by Hoover had been registered in the 1920 *Democratic* primaries in New Hampshire and Michigan.

was to be found in prophecies and promises of Hoover so far from reality as to suggest the utterances less of an economist than of an exorcist. These had started when this Secretary of Commerce under Calvin Coolidge´ had celebrated his Presidential nomination in 1928 with the public assurance that the nation stood "nearer to the final triumph over poverty than ever before in the history of any land." The decade soon to begin would mark, instead, the first time since 1789 when a greater number of people chose to leave the Republic than to enter it. By the time of the 1932 campaign the statistics of life were vastly more persuasive than the speeches of candidates: the nation's industrial production had fallen to barely one-half its 1929 level, and 12,000,000 citizens were without jobs. The start of Hoover's campaign presaged its end: he went back to his native Iowa for his opening speech, there to be greeted by a couple of thousand farmers marching through the streets of Des Moines under banners of derision proclaiming: "In Hoover We Trusted—Now We Are Busted." [56] And to his own political helplessness in this crisis, Hoover himself would later add in his *Memoirs* the pained, still-uncomprehending postscript:

> I was convinced that efficient, honest administration of the vast machine of the Federal government would appeal to all citizens. I have since learned that efficient government does not interest the people as much as dramatics.[57]

How had this "guardian of the people" worked and responded, looked and sounded, during his four years in the White House? They had been years as striking for greatness of industry as for absence of insight. Almost ascetically, the style of this leadership seemed dictated by a firmness uncompromised by compassion. This was a White House for working, not for weeping. This President was no Coolidge, regularly napping each afternoon. Hoover struggled through eighteen-hour days until "so tired that every bone in my body aches." After the pain of such work, all public or partisan outcries against a "do-nothing" President could provoke only an unspeakably bitter resentment.[58]

Understandable though this was, the ultimate cause of the general unhappiness had to be a Presidential misunderstanding. The hours that he spent at his desk asserting his operational control over "the vast machine of the Federal government" satisfied no need or call of citizens who cared only to know where "the vast machine" was leading them, not how smoothly its engines were running. But the orthodoxy of Hoover's social and economic ideas had little patience, and no answer, for heretical questions about individual need and federal aid. Accordingly, he could offer two prescriptions, for example, for the national response to the drought of 1930: first, he approved a Congressional appropriation of $45,-000,000 to save the livestock of Arkansas; and second, he opposed any outright grant of $25,000,000 to aid the farmers and families affected, since such governmental relief "would have injured the spiritual responses of the American people." [59] Under such a definition of the "spiritual" needs of citizens, all who had begged for federal help could only envy the happier lot of incorruptible cattle.

Through all this practicing of his economic theology, this President moved or weaved with an almost tragic lack of humor, warmth, or confidence—except in his own rightness. Back in 1919, at the Versailles Conference, John Maynard Keynes—amid all the criticisms of the treaty that he had written in *The Economic Consequences of the Peace*—had singled out Hoover for his sense of "reality, knowledge, magnanimity, and disinterestedness." Yet even then Keynes had seen the man to look like an "exhausted prizefighter," pursuing the best of intentions with "his habitual air of weary Titan." [60] This became the very "air" of his Presidential leadership. A veteran of the administrative staff in the White House, who had seen many Presidents pass through, later remembered of Hoover that he "never laughed aloud" but "always had a frown on his face." In communications with his staff, he observed a chill courtesy, avoiding either rebuke or debate, since he felt "a man should not become embroiled with his inferior." [61] In communications with the press, he nervously kept his distance, for he was angered or confounded by almost any criticism. In communications with the people as a whole, he could display neither flexibility nor force: he found the struggle with words difficult, as he labored over his own texts in longhand, and his hazy homilies left the public bored and impatient.

Yet these Presidential ways often seemed to reflect not so much missing talents as controlling habits. He doggedly repeated his refusal to exhort or to excite the nation: "This is not a showman's job"; or, "I can't be a Theodore Roosevelt." [62] Years after his Presidential ordeal was over—but while the dream of its renewal lived on with him—Hoover sneered at Democratic leadership as merely comprising "men chosen by election for oratorical triumphs." [63] This disdain for Presidents who could move the people seemed almost a matter of perverse principle, and he once bluntly said: "I have never liked the clamor of crowds. . . . The crowd is credulous, it destroys, it hates, and it dreams—but it never builds." [64]

There does not appear to have crossed Hoover's mind the question of how a President could govern the "crowd" of the American Republic if they stayed incredulous toward him. Obviously, he had never heard the first President described as "the best Actor" in the role. Nor could he have remembered the pointed sense of Washington's own aphorism: "The truth is the people must *feel* before they will *see*." Instead, the thirty-first President distrusted and denied any suggestion that a critical part of his task was to make the people "feel" anything in particular. Or as William Allen White wrote of him—as well as of all Presidents—shortly before this Chief Executive surrendered the power he had never brandished:

> President Hoover is a great executive, a splendid desk man. But he cannot dramatize his leadership. A democracy cannot follow a leader unless he is dramatized. A man to be a hero must not content himself with heroic virtues and anonymous action. He must talk and explain as he acts—drama.[65]

This particular Presidential tragedy had to rise from deep within the man. In this Chief Executive there appeared no deceit, no greed, no selfishness, no rascality, no sloth. When he spoke, he betrayed none of the eloquent arrogance of a Woodrow Wilson, and when he acted, he showed none of the elaborate deceptiveness of a Lyndon Johnson. At the same time, he wholly lacked a Wilson's mature perception of Presidential leadership or a Johnson's honest passion for populist reform. These were clues to the whole trouble. What proved so fatal to this Presidency was, quite simply, what was *not* present. Hoover had no more caused the country's economic agony, of course, than he had prevented it. Rather, he had first watched it, then parried it, next lectured it, and finally excused it. At no time in the process, however, did the event become *his*. As he had not provoked it, so, too, he never seized it. And ultimately, he could see himself standing in relation to the terrible crisis only in terms of his innocence or his absence.

*   *   *

Less than a fortnight after Franklin Roosevelt's inauguration in March, 1933, William Allen White was writing to the historian Allan Nevins: "My feeling about Roosevelt [is] that it is not so much what he does as the way he does it. The people will forgive mistakes. They will not forgive inaction, debate, cowardice, dilettante hesitation, splitting hairs." [66] The journalist's judgment on Roosevelt was as shrewd as his lament over Hoover. Already FDR had given the nation, immediately upon his nomination, a clear sign of his sense of the *way* to do things, politically and dramatically. Discarding the venerable ritual of all previous Presidential nominees—frozen in a pose of silence, until formally advised of their selection some weeks later—he had flown to the Democratic Convention in Chicago to become the first Presidential nominee ever to deliver a speech of acceptance in person. No man to miss such a chance for an "oratorical triumph," he left the delegates happy and hoarse from cheering his vow: "I pledge you, I pledge myself, to a *new deal* for the American people." And while his future biographers might debate the merits of many programs of the legislative "deal" over which he presided until 1945, all would have to agree that the Presidency itself, after him, could never be quite the same.

The Presidential style of Roosevelt was neither impulsive nor unrehearsed, for he and his counselors shared an almost joyous sense of political theater. "No cosmic dramatist," Robert E. Sherwood acknowledged long after, "could possibly devise a better entrance for a new President—or a new Dictator, or a new Messiah —than that accorded to Franklin Delano Roosevelt. . . . Herbert Hoover was, in the parlance of vaudeville, 'a good act to follow.'

Roosevelt rode in a wheelchair instead of on a white horse, but the roll of drums and the thunderclaps which attended him were positively Wagnerian." [67] The political setting was perfect, indeed, for letting a President loose. "The whole country is with him, just so he does something," as Will Rogers said. "If he burned down the capitol, we would cheer and say, 'Well, we at least got a fire started anyhow.' " [68]

This sort of franchise for leadership could not be wasted on a Roosevelt. He took due note of it with one declaration in his First Inaugural of a deceptively innocent sound: "Our Constitution is so simple and practical that it is possible always to meet extraordinary needs by changes in emphasis and arrangement without loss of essential form." In plainer words, this President was ready at once to reach for "the joker" in the "deck" of constitutional powers and to play the card—for all its worth and in his own way. And any historian must be tempted to imagine the Franklin Roosevelt of 1933, as he sat at his inauguration in his wheelchair, discreetly winking and silently thanking the Gouverneur Morris of 1787, as he had hobbled about the Philadelphia Convention on his one leg.

The contrasts between the two Presidents of 1933, however, did not follow wholly predictable lines: as always around the White House, the unlikely anomalies intruded. A Roosevelt who had often journeyed to Europe in his youth remained, all his life, surprisingly unsophisticated about European history and diplomacy; * a Hoover who had directed great enterprises of engineering and mining on four continents developed no full vision of an American world policy; but the untutored Roosevelt helped the Republic defend and lead the Western world. A Hoover almost coldly cerebral, as well as philosophically positive about all social and political issues of his Presidential days, shunned the counsel or the company of "intellectuals," but a Roosevelt who had never tried to impress Harvard University with grades above "the gentleman's C" would summon an unprecedented "brain trust" of advisers to his Washington. A Hoover who had climbed to wealth and power from a background more modest than any President since Andrew John-

* It was a reflection of the temper of the times, as much as of Roosevelt's immediate interests, that his First Inaugural devoted only one paragraph to foreign affairs.

son—a President whose father had been a blacksmith and who was orphaned at the age of nine—had become, as President, the stony symbol of American conservatism. And a Roosevelt, who had known only a life of relative affluence and indulgence, attended through his youth by governesses and tutors, would grow into the lively hero of American liberalism.

To reassure and to rally "the credulous crowd" so distrusted by Hoover, FDR reached for the readiest weapons—his own words— with the cry that "the only thing we have to fear is fear itself." An aphorism that was more a sound than a thought, it nonetheless was spoken with a zest that exhilarated the same millions of Americans who would have discarded it, were it murmured by a Hoover, as one more reason to suspect their President of mindless euphoria. Along with the soar of slogans and the series of "fireside chats" to the nation, Roosevelt courted and mastered the press that had left Hoover estranged. The New York *Times'* Arthur Krock judged him to be the shrewdest reader and critic of newspapers he had ever seen in the Oval Office. And the editor of *Editor and Publisher* summed up his impact upon even the most jaded of White House reporters: "If Mr. Roosevelt fails the craft, by any false word or deed, he will break a hundred hearts that have not actually palpitated for any political figure in many a year." [69]

But the apparent political magic was not wrought by words alone: quite as swiftly, there came the astonishing array of New Deal legislative proposals that sent the Seventy-third Congress into ninety-nine days of frenzy without precedent.* The headline writers could barely keep pace with the lawmakers: the AAA subsidies to farmers and the NIRA codes for business, relief for the unemployed and loans for the homeowners, the safeguards of "Truth of Securities" and the promises of the Tennessee Valley Authority. Amid this display of Congressional fireworks, there were some Senators who fretted over the long-range implications of such a carnival of Presidential initiatives. To these legislators, worrying over remote constitutional consequences, the man who would become Roosevelt's closest of all counselors, Harry Hopkins, once snapped

---

* The stunning sequence began with an emergency banking bill dispatched with such speed that it was never properly printed: rushed to Capitol Hill in some half-dozen typewritten texts, bearing penciled notes and corrections, it passed the House of Representatives by acclamation in less than forty minutes.

the retort: "People don't eat 'in the long run,' Senator. They eat every day." [70]

The words of Hopkins caught the spirit of relentless pragmatism, the passion for ceaseless improvisation, which was the activist answer of Roosevelt to the shackling orthodoxy of Hoover. As Roosevelt confessed his zeal for experiment to Daniel C. Roper, his Secretary of Commerce and old friend from the Wilson years: "Let's concentrate upon one thing—save the people and the nation. And if we have to change our minds twice every day to accomplish that end, we should do it." [71] He told the White House press corps, too, that he fully intended to play the Presidential role like a football quarterback, unburdened by any rigid game plan, since "future plays will depend on how the next one works." [72] This was the kind of talk that long since had driven Hoover, with a rare flash of wit, to call his successor a "chameleon on plaid." [73] And it impelled H. L. Mencken to report of Roosevelt: "If he became convinced tomorrow that coming out for cannibalism would get him the votes he so sorely needs, he would begin fattening a missionary in the White House backyard come Wednesday." [74]

Both the exuberance of FDR and the exasperation of his critics celebrated, with exactly opposite feelings, the driving force of the New Deal: at its heart, as Richard Hofstadter later observed, "there was not a philosophy but a temperament." [75] Once asked by a reporter to state his philosophy, Roosevelt jauntily described himself as "a Christian and a Democrat—that's all." [76] Such nonchalance only increased the torment of his opponents. They might hope to refute an obnoxious "philosophy," dissecting it from premise to conclusion, but how should they duel with an insidious "temperament"? The White House had known aggressive reformers before, of course, but never one so wholeheartedly indifferent to political theories, economic formulas, or intellectual systems.

This President's central purpose was not to conceive and prescribe a national program, but to quicken and sustain a national mood. So aspiring, he could presume, on the occasion of his renomination in 1936, to raise a toast to his own first term: "Better the occasional faults of a Government that lives in a spirit of charity than the constant omissions of a Government frozen in the ice of its own indifference." By virtue of this confident self-absolution

—and the popular readiness to believe in the goodwill behind the rite—FDR could go on practicing his political artistry, feeling free to shift speed or change course, swerve or careen, without breaking loose from the trust of most of the electorate. As William Allen White had written after Roosevelt's triumph in the 1934 Congressional elections: "He has been all but crowned by the people." [77] And the old question of John Jay, at such a time, seemed to echo faintly from afar.

In the long view of the Republic's history, the audacity and inventiveness of this Presidential style made possible something far more important than the political success of one President: it made possible the survival of the two-party system of government. For even as FDR was being attacked for subverting the system—by his manipulative use of either mass media or federal largesse—he was, in fact, saving it. The economic crisis at the end of the 1920's had driven not merely the impoverished and the jobless, but also a legion of liberals and intellectuals, to despair of a political solution. Like their lineal descendants in the 1960's, the most impassioned liberal critics—from John Dewey and Stephen Vincent Benét to Reinhold Niebuhr and Lewis Mumford—had pronounced the death of the "old politics." These anxious watchers of the Presidency, wishing a plague on both national parties, saw the Democratic Party itself as nothing more than "the demagogic face of Republicanism." [78] Yet—by 1939—Harold Laski could survey the state of the Republic and salute the Roosevelt who, as he wrote, "has gone for the big things; he had dramatized the issues upon which men know their lives to depend." As he went on to say, FDR had summoned the people to feel and to share "the emotions of a drama in which each spectator felt himself associated with the fortunes of the actors involved." [79]

This achievement might be judged this President's greatest service: the holding of the wide American audience, to witness and to believe the repertoire of policies and programs that a versatile democracy could perform—even in a theater that seemed afire. There was no undue arrogance in Roosevelt's boast to Orson Welles that they were the two best actors in the nation. For the histrionic talent of this thirty-second President provided a fair match for the "Shakespearean" skill of the first man to walk the same stage.

I V

> He is so eminently our representative man, that, when he speaks, it
> seems as if the people were listening to their own thinking aloud.
> —JAMES RUSSELL LOWELL,
> *Essay on Lincoln*

A look at the styles of a few men in the White House might easily
bring despair to all students of the Presidency seeking a science,
rather than recognizing an art. The problem has brought as much
mental anguish to Presidents as to scholars—even to Presidents as
temperamentally different, for example, as a William Howard Taft
and a Lyndon Baines Johnson. Quite as Taft conceded—or boasted
—his inability to "play a part for popularity," so Lyndon Johnson,
at the end of his third year in office, described his own popular
standing, half proudly and half plaintively: "They'll say about me
I knock the ball over the fence—but they don't like the way he
stands at the plate." [80]

The heart of the matter is neither so superficial nor so perverse.
What shapes and makes an effective Presidential style? There can be
no compact instructions, of course, or perfect prescriptions. But this
is ultimately a question of not designs, but insights—not stratagems,
but senses. And there appear certain specific *senses* of political life
whose presence or absence set the tone and decide the force of all
Presidential leadership. Thus:

A Sense of Confidence

The American President probably may make a public display of
almost any mood or emotion, from rage to grief, with no harm to
his leadership so grave as a show of hesitation. His citizens may
be largely aware, though not expertly informed, of the imponderables and uncertainties that precede every major act or policy. But
they look and listen to him to learn not his doubts, but his decisions.

The confidence that enlivens and strengthens a President is no
superficial optimism. It is a deep sense of trust both in himself and
in the nation. The Republic can progress nowhere, if he lacks faith
in either. With different Presidents, this confidence has been borne
with various airs, and it has assured in different ways. A direct meet-

ing of such contrasts came in 1960, when Dwight David Eisenhower, the oldest President to live in the White House, gave over his powers to John Kennedy, the youngest of all men elected to the office. With Eisenhower, the maturity and the experience of the man had so affected the nation, through eight years, that he could claim a popular trust unmatched by any other President of the twentieth century. With Kennedy, the youth and the vitality of the man excited quite another kind of confidence, with a vision to "get America moving again" in brave new directions. The brief blaze of hopes marking the New Frontier was not ignited by lavish promises or grandiose programs, moreover, but by what one aide of the young President has fairly described as Kennedy's gift for "raising people's *confidence* about their own capacities and about the country's." [81]

The most historically memorable display of this gift had come a quarter century earlier, of course, with FDR's leadership through the Great Depression. As Alfred Kazin once made the point incisively:

> It is bizarre that Roosevelt's personal air should now make the Thirties seem an age of *confidence,* but it does and it did. . . . Roosevelt's assurance was not only extraordinary, but because of the obvious impress of his personality . . . a presence so definite yet unplaceable, like Napoleon's, that it has become a historical truism without becoming less of a historical mystery.[82]

A Sense of Proportion

Without some such disciplining sense, the most confident Presidents would have habitually blundered beyond the bounds of political reason—as the boldest, indeed, have occasionally done. By its nature, the avoidance of excess and extravagance—alike in promises and programs, words and laws—most often is a virtue not instantly visible. But its absence can be glaring and damning. All national leaders profess to realize that the political value of their currency—and their credibility—can be dangerously depreciated by the inflationary practices of promising too much, exhorting too much, legislating too much, or simply talking too much. The commonplace truth, however, often goes unobserved. In the case of a Presidential aspirant like Senator Hubert Humphrey, for example, a chronic failing was noted, many years before his 1968 candidacy, by Adlai Stevenson's diagnosis of the Senator as "a politician with more solutions than there are problems." After defeating Senator Humphrey in 1968, President Richard Nixon went on to show a surprisingly similar fondness for hyperbole—as when his 1971 State of the Union message hailed his own proposals for federal reorganization as a "New American Revolution" or when he saluted the return of American astronauts from their moonflight as providing mankind with "the greatest week in the history of the world since the creation." The political trouble with such excess can be serious, for the lack of a fitting sense of proportion suggests some want of a firm sense of value. And by way of contrast to these instances, two Presidents as dissimilar as Eisenhower and Kennedy nonetheless shared a common resolve to shun extravagance in explaining their acts and their attitudes, whether in political campaigns or press conferences.*

The Presidential loss of a sense of proportion has marked, moreover, at least three of the least happy moments known in the White House in the twentieth century—all afflicting, strangely, three of its most skillful politicians. With Woodrow Wilson, the headlong evangelism with which he hailed the Treaty of Versailles as reflecting "the pure light of the justice of God," along with his disdain for any impure bargains with Senate leaders, brought on the misery of his last Presidential months. With Franklin Roosevelt, the landslide victory of 1936 intoxicated him enough to send to Capitol Hill his snarled scheme for "packing" the Supreme Court. And with Lyndon Johnson, a near defiance of all sense of proportion was required for him to compare the support of Saigon with the saving

---

* The propensity of Richard Nixon for superlatives appears throughout his autobiographical *Six Crises*. As Professor James David Barber has commented, the pitch of this self-examination is set at an almost strident level by such phrases as "the most scarring personal crisis of my life . . . the most exciting day of my life . . . the greatest moment in my life . . . the longest, hardest, most intensive campaign in American history . . . the greatest test of my life . . . the worst experience of my life . . . nothing could match it . . . an utter flop . . . the supreme tragedy." (Cf. *The Presidential Character*, Englewood Cliffs, N.J., Prentice-Hall, 1972.)

of West Berlin or to equate the values and the purposes of the Vietnam War and World War II.

A Sense of Drama

While it may take various forms of expression, this Presidential art, not always but most often, has found its spark in a combativeness as ready to join a conflict as to cheer a consensus. Like so many aspects of the Presidency, this adversary stance of the Chief Executive has been less a matter of the personal willfulness of successive Presidents than a consequence of the deliberate decisions of the Constitutional Convention. Ever since James Madison's fifty-first *Federalist* paper urged "the necessary partition of power," all forceful Presidents have had to live with—and act on—the predetermined clash of interest between the executive and legislative branches. This is not a matter of truculence or bravado. "Dull government can only endure," as Harold Laski observed, "when government is unimportant"—that is, during a Coolidge era when enough of the citizenry could believe that "dullness is the same as soundness." [83] But a truly *important* Presidency has never failed to raise the noise and dust of combat.

By the standard of this serious sense of political drama, the Presidencies of the twentieth century may readily be compared. There could be no quicker measure of the distance between the Republican Presidencies of Theodore Roosevelt and Dwight Eisenhower, for example, than this: whereas Roosevelt rejoiced in the office as his "bully pulpit" from which to preach and yell, Eisenhower found no national leaders more repugnant than those whom he decried as the "desk pounders," always ready to exhort or to excoriate. Among modern Democratic Presidents, the appreciation of the uses of confrontation has been much more keen. Woodrow Wilson revived the custom of Presidential appearances before Congress, which had lapsed since Jefferson's time, and as one historian has noted: "He literally dramatized the Presidential message to Congress." [84] Franklin Roosevelt looked far beyond Capitol Hill, of course, to mock and dare, as his chosen enemies, the nation's "economic royalists," and while he assailed them as a host of the unscrupulous rich, he retained them like a band of unemployed actors—all for casting in his drama of the duel between Wall Street and Pennsylvania Avenue. Harry S. Truman fought toward his improbable victory in the 1948 Presidential campaign by taking on the role of the Republic's prosecutor of "the do-nothing Eightieth Congress." An editor who interviewed Truman on the eve of that campaign later reported: "I had never before seen such an example of faith, serenity, and atomic belligerency in any one human being." [85] And precisely these qualities often have reassured the citizenry, over the decades, that their Presidency was alive, well, and militant in Washington.

A Sense of Timing

Without some sure instinct for pace and rhythm, even those Presidents most gifted in "Dramatic Exhibitions" might soon enough become not popular heroes, but national bores. There have been modern Presidents—notably, the two Roosevelts—with an unusually astute sense of when to thrust and when to parry. But none has surpassed the sixteenth President, Abraham Lincoln, in this most subtle political intuition.

The classic display of this gift of Lincoln came, slowly and deliberately, with the Emancipation Proclamation. For month after month following his election and the South's secession, he had been forced to weigh no less than four unsettling but related problems: his own attainment of the Presidency with less than 40 percent of the popular vote; his need to keep the slaveholding border states loyal to the Union; the threat of English recognition of the Confederacy; and the lack of an auspicious military moment for making any bold political move. Through this painful interim—until after the Battle of Antietam—Lincoln resolutely deferred action, as he explained to one friend: "I can see emancipation coming; whoever can wait for it will see it; whoever stands in its way will be run over." [86] Meanwhile, he exasperated the zealots who besieged him, including one delegation of church leaders whom he failed to pacify with the wry warning that a premature proclamation might be as meaningless as the Pope's bull against the comet. He did not tell them that the draft of their longed-for statement already had been written and rested on his desk. By the time of the proclamation's final release in September of 1862, Lincoln had gained not only such critical goals as keeping the border states from rebellion and rallying British opinion to the cause of anti-slavery. In the words of historians some generations later, he also had "lifted the Civil War to the dignity of a crusade." [87] He had known, in short, how to wait. And the example would instruct any future President on how best, at times, to lead.

A Sense of Constancy

It is one thing for the man in the White House to seem to revise his political itinerary, from time to time, but it is quite another thing for him to seem to revise his political identity. With no necessary loss of popular trust, he may vary his methods, but *he* must not appear to vary or to waver. A Washington or a Jefferson, like an Abraham Lincoln or a Franklin Roosevelt, knew the critical distinction between changing course and changing conscience.

Of all modern Presidents, probably none perceived this so poorly as Lyndon Johnson. The very rhetoric of his administration, with its inconsistent appeals and variable inflections, evolved as a study in dissonance. Like a creature of mercurial moods, he could address his audience—either an elite gathering or the whole nation—and sound, by swift turns, belligerent or benign, diffuse or trenchant, vulgar or lofty. Toward the end of his Presidency, the New York *Times* correspondent covering his White House, Max Frankel, reported a single episode that might be taken as an epitome of his regime:

> Not long ago at a White House meeting with influential publishers, Mr. Johnson was asked why he would not halt the bombing of North Vietnam. His response was no mere argument of his case. For fifteen minutes, reports a close observer of the President, "there stood Saint Francis of Assisi, bathed in light beneath his halo," pouring out a passionate confession of his yearning for peace and a vivid account of the diligence of his search. The room was rapt.
>
> Through several more questions the mood prevailed until there came the predictable inquiry: If all that is so, perhaps it is true, as some suggest, that the President is not really hitting the enemy as hard as he should? And suddenly, as if in full regalia, there stood the

Commander in Chief, ticking off the target lists, the clipped statistics of damage done and the promise of the further pressures planned. Again, the room was rapt.

Here, as he does so often, Mr. Johnson had shown his determination to be Everyman's President. But, to his critics, he seemed simply to be trying to be all things to all men.[88]

By the nature of the Presidency, such an exercise cannot for long succeed. The office is a place to be filled, both constitutionally and psychologically, by one man, not several men. And the wearing of many faces by the President cannot bring to pass the joining of many factions in the Republic. Or as Washington had explained to a friend in 1779: "To please everybody is impossible; were I to undertake it, I should probably please nobody." [89]

A Sense of Humanity

All the stories, like all the styles, of the Presidents seem to argue unmistakably that no artfulness of strategy can compensate for a chillness of spirit. As with a President's sense of confidence, so also with this faculty—at once to be directed toward himself, with humility and humor, and toward the people, with warmth and compassion. Without some clear sign of such qualities, the craftiest expedients have stayed tedious and vain.

The telling instances abound. When a Lincoln had to try to heal the first great schism in the Republic's history, he warned—in the last speech of his life—against any punitive theory of Reconstruction based on the idea of treating the states that had seceded as foreign, occupied territory. Any such plausible notion he called "merely pernicious abstraction." When a Hoover faced the nation's second great schism, however, he imagined that it could be papered over with just such an "abstraction"—in the form of his own economic theory.

There is an incalculable price to be paid by any Presidency that gives the appearance of comprehending—or caring—not quite enough. And the knowing and heartening kind of communion that is possible, between the President and the people, was described long ago by James Russell Lowell, in a few sentences of his *Essay on Lincoln:*

> In the public utterances of President Lincoln is a certain tone of familiar dignity, which . . . is perhaps the most difficult attainment of mere *style*.
>
> There must be something essentially noble in an elective ruler who can descend to the level of confidential ease without forfeiting respect. . . . No higher compliment was ever paid to a nation than the simple confidence, the fireside plainness, with which Mr. Lincoln always addresses himself to the reason of the American people. . . . He never appeals to any vulgar sentiment, he never alludes to the humbleness of his origin; it probably never occurred to him, indeed, that there was anything higher to start from than manhood; and he put himself on a level with those he addressed, not by going down to them, but only by taking it for granted that they had brains and would come up to a common ground of reason. . . .
>
> Homely, dispassionate, showing all the rough-edged process of his thought as it goes along . . . with an honest kind of every-day logic, he is so eminently our representative man, that, when he speaks, it seems as if the people were listening to their own thinking aloud.[90]

The Presidents of a century later, whenever they heard any popular questioning of their humanity or their credibility, could usefully question themselves by honestly wondering whether their voices sounded much like this voice.

The sum of these six senses of Presidential style might be called a sense of history. There is nothing banal or vague about this: a great many Presidents have pathetically lacked it, and a great part of its meaning is as explicit as a sense of humor. Without this last, there can hardly be any true perspective on sudden events, political life, or one's own Presidential self. Such humor was a mark, for example, of the political grace of John Kennedy. With him, it was shaped by detachment and sharpened in irony. He privately described the Washington, where he had spent so much of his short life, as "a city of southern efficiency and northern charm." [91] The whimsy bespoke wisdom in any man confronting the moderately terrifying federal establishment. And when the first volume of Dwight

Eisenhower's Presidential memoirs was published, he told Arthur Schlesinger, Jr., with a like insight: "Apparently Ike never did anything wrong. When we come to writing the memoirs of this administration, we'll do it differently." [92]

A sense of humor less taut and more broad enlivened the Presidency of Franklin Roosevelt, whom Kennedy so much admired. As much as all else, Roosevelt's sense of history inspired him to tease and to test his opponents, almost mischievously. A splendid instance of this occurred in 1938, when he was nervously invited by the Daughters of the American Revolution to address their convention, and he shrewdly accepted. A confrontation between FDR and the DAR then could only be strained. But when Roosevelt rose and saluted the Daughters as "fellow immigrants," the tension cracked, and the President proceeded to say:

It so happens, through no fault of my own, that I am descended from a number of people who came over on the *Mayflower*. More than that, every one of my ancestors on both sides . . . every single one of them, without exception, was in this land in 1776. And there was only one Tory among them. The text is this: Remember, remember always, that all of us, and you and I especially, are descended from immigrants and revolutionists.[93]

Such a sense of both humor and history calls to mind the uncommon definition of the word "style." This is the particular part of a sundial which, according to the dictionary, "projects a shadow used as an indicator." And its function is, of course, to tell time.

The metaphor fits. The Presidency also depends on, and responds to, the political climate all around it. So doing, it "projects" and it "indicates," marking and measuring all the surrounding atmosphere. If the man who is President is a national leader both purposeful and persuasive, he catches the strongest light about him, so that witnesses of even dim vision can glimpse it. He then calls the people to see and to know the true time that it is in the day and the history of the nation. And he thus becomes the style of the Republic.

Five

The Gates of the White House

Things get very lonely in Washington sometimes. The real voice of the great people of America sometimes sounds faint and distant in that strange city.[1]

—WOODROW WILSON

The iron gates and fences encircling the offices, gardens, and lawns of the White House probably trace the most critical dividing line in the political life of the Republic—a kind of American frontier that never vanishes. With regard to the state of the Presidency, there may be no fact more decisive than the moral and intellectual baggage that each new President carries across this border. Has he known what to bring and what to leave behind? For the long labor of the unknown decisions to challenge him, does he arrive with anything like clarity of purpose and flexibility of method? Or are his purposes fragile, instead, and his methods rigid? . . . And with regard to the state of the Union, there may be no question more vital than the freedom of passage—for ideas and beliefs and emotions—moving both ways past these same bars. Are the citizens able to get through, so that their hopes and hesitations alike are sensed and known? And is the President able to speak back, with words that enlighten and acts that encourage? Or do the voices of each sound to the other all too "faint and distant" for mutual trust and common cause?

There have been only occasional moments in the life of the Presidency when such questions might be answered with certainty. Indeed, it seems hard to be sure whether the long history of the office has tended to swing these White House gates more open or more closed. Thus it may be easy—but is it true?—to depict the Presidency as having evolved from relative simplicity, not too remote from the ordinary citizen, toward incomparable isolation, much too removed by pride and protocol from the national life. Obviously, the President of the mid-twentieth century has found himself ringed with people and things awaiting only his command to attend or amuse: any one of a personal staff of scores of men and women stands ready to satisfy his immediate taste for food or drink, limousines or helicopters, Senators or ambassadors, movies or symphonies, absolute privacy or loud company, solitary walks or military reviews, voyage by battleship or travel by golf-cart. Any list of such available indulgences implies a palatial sort of world apart, scarcely like Presidential life before World War I. Then a William McKinley could hope to direct the whole executive branch through a modest staff of eight or ten aides. In the 1880's a Grover Cleveland might reasonably be expected to answer personally most phone calls to the White House, when so few of the capital's inhabitants even owned the revolutionary instrument. Still earlier, there seemed nothing remarkable to a Lincoln or a Polk when the White House might be invaded any day by hordes of nameless handshakers or office seekers, wandering in from the streets to see *their* President in *their* White House. And all such nineteenth-century ways inspired a James Bryce to depict Presidential life in *The American Commonwealth* as admirably open and unpretentious:

> The social relations of an American President to his people are eminently refreshing. . . . There is no servility, no fictitious self-abasement on the part of the citizens. . . . The curiosity of the visitors who throng the White House on reception days is sometimes too familiar; but . . . Presidents have now more reason to complain of the persecutions they endure from an incessantly observant journalism. . . . The spirit of equality which rules the country has sunk too deep into every American nature for [the President] to expect to be addressed with bated breath and whispering reverence. He has no military guard, no chamberlains or grooms-in-waiting; his everyday life is simple. . . . He is surrounded by no such pomp and enforces no such etiquette as that which belongs to the governors even of second-class English colonies. . . .[2]

Yet the political meaning of the gates to the White House—and what they keep out and what they let in—cannot be defined by these habits of social life. The crowds of strangers around Lincoln or Polk may have tested the patience of any President of the era; but they had not come to test or to question his policy, and throughout the Presidency, a tolerance for strange people has had little to do with a receptiveness to strange ideas. A President like Polk, even as he jostled and sparred with beggars of money and seekers of office, found himself so chained to his desk by work that he lived an almost recluse life. He made few public appearances, gave almost no public addresses, and enjoyed no intellectual associations beyond the company of Washington's more commanding politicians. As for such travel about the country as even the first President had deemed essential, so that the citizenry might glimpse their Chief Executive, Polk could grieve to his *Diary* in the summer of 1848 that "I have not been three miles from the President's mansion" in more than a year. After almost a year and a half in the White House, he had escaped Washington for but one day—a visit to Mount Vernon—and he ruefully observed: "My long confinement has considerably enfeebled me." [3]

As for the confinement of modern Presidents, this has taken altogether other forms and enfeebled in other ways, of course, than the physical restrictions that oppressed James Polk. There have arisen barriers of mind and spirit that have kept Presidents sealed in their own prisons of thought, even as they have traveled without restraint across their nation or around their world. And to match the contrast between appearance and reality in the regime of Polk, there may be no more striking twentieth-century example than the Presidency of Lyndon Johnson.

By the measure of both political instincts and personal habits, the Johnson years in the White House gave the impression of a regime open to popular view, almost vulgarly, and sensitive to public opinion, almost feverishly. Both to watch and to reach the people beyond the White House gates, there had never been a Presidency more fully equipped or obsessed with all pertinent devices of modern technology, partly because Lyndon Johnson surpassed all Presidents in the delight and assurance he found in all such gadgets. These included not one but three television screens in the Oval Office; a battery of telephones at arm's reach, scattered through the White House in all possible drawers or nooks; and a cluster of loudspeakers for his bulletproof limousine, so his voice could carry to crowds whom he exhorted from as far as fifty yards away. These were but the technical signs, moreover, of his genuine eagerness for intimate contact with his constituency. Until his last year in office, he rejoiced in the campaign swings or speaking tours that gave his hands the chance to "press the flesh," as he said, of throngs surging to greet or clutch him. He sought to talk to them, too, in the most popular and earthy language, and after Presidential surgery, what could be more natural for such a Chief Executive than to invite the nation to view his abdominal scar? All the while, he never ceased striving to prove to all around him the fullness and the freshness of his information on the mood of the nation—as computed by the public opinion polls filling both his pockets and his thoughts.

Yet all these outward signs of an alert and attentive White House were essentially as meaningless as a President's aimless chatter, a century earlier, with total strangers strolling the mansion corridors. For all its gregarious bluster, this President's administration proved thoroughly addicted to secretive politics and devious policy. It sought to hide from public view, till the last moment, the least historic appointments to national office—almost as assiduously as it plotted to conceal the all-too-historic development of its foreign policy in Southeast Asia. Constricted rather than emancipated by three decades of experience on Capitol Hill, Lyndon Johnson appeared never to surrender the myth that the business of the Republic and of all nations could be transacted as he had presided over the business of the Senate: by back-room compacts and under-the-table bargains. So obvious became his Presidency's practice of subterfuge that the White House press corps circulated the jest that no administration in memory had so heartily believed that the shortest distance between two political points always had to be a tunnel. Or as this President's closest counselor for years, Bill Moyers, later explained, after his own disillusion and resignation: "The real problem with Lyndon Johnson is that *he* probably believes about ninety percent of what he reads or *hears*. So he finds it perfectly natural to expect the *people* to believe about 90% of what he *says*." [4]

With the lines of communication between the President and the people so blocked in both directions, the depressing result brought back, once more, the haunting memory of Woodrow Wilson's last year in office. Like many national leaders trapped by popular distrust, both Presidents came to act and speak as though a steady escalation of rhetoric might raise the siege and restore the faith. Exhorting his citizens on his last Presidential travels, Wilson had dared profess to believing: "The hearts of men like Clemenceau and Lloyd George and Orlando beat with the people of the world." [5] Visiting his soldiers in Vietnam, Johnson had dared confess his plainer dream: "Come back home with that coonskin on the wall!" The accents were different, but the fantasy was the same—a holy grail within reach of a people brave enough to believe. The eventual price for such grand self-delusion could only be a capital city and a White House perceived to be thus:

> The social-political atmosphere of Washington [was] one of bleak and chill austerity suffused and envenomed by hatred . . . that seemed to poison and blight every human relationship.
>
> The White House was isolated. It had no relation with the Capitol or the local resident and official community. Its great iron gates were closed and chained and locked. . . . It was in a void apart. . . . It all made for . . . bitterness and a general sense of frustration and un-happiness.[6]

These notes on the beleaguered White House of 1919 could have applied quite as accurately to the President who left the White House in 1969. Even the more sympathetic judgments upon both these men have sounded, on occasion, plaintively alike. Among the first thoughtful chroniclers of the Wilson years, Frederick Lewis Allen sadly concluded: "He had given all he had to the cause, and it had not been enough." [7] Among the first reflective historians of the Johnson years, Lyndon Johnson closed his own memoirs with the true enough words: "I had given it everything that was in me." [8] But a prideful dedication to personal duty could spare neither President the consequences of a willful deafness to public mood. And whenever any Chief Executive, similarly impaired and introverted, has shown this same self-conscious sense of sovereignty, he has revealed himself to be something of the very kind of "monocrat" whom Thomas Jefferson most had feared.

After the grace of humility, there would seem to be no saving quality that a President may lose more swiftly, upon entering the White House, than a sense of perspective. The loss may be illustrated by one personal incident from the Johnson years. Late in his second term, as the critical clamor over the Vietnam War kept insolently rising, the ever more resentful thirty-sixth President found himself particularly nettled by the criticisms of a friend who, like the President, had devoted his public life to the Democratic Party. Summoning his friend to a private evening of exhortation at the White House, the President, with his fondness for statistical proofs, aimed his appeal thus: "How can a Democrat like you speak out this way? Look at the *number* of things I have done . . . the laws passed in this last Congress . . . the millions— the billions—of dollars appropriated for every decent cause . . . education and housing and welfare . . . all the executive actions to help the poor and the blacks. And despite this, all you can speak of, and complain about, is *Vietnam!*" After suffering a long monologue in this vein, the guest felt spurred to answer. "Mr. President," he said softly, "what do you think would be the place in history of Abraham Lincoln if he had been right and wise about everything—*except* the Civil War?" [9] After this, the Presidential courtship ended in a couple of moments.

The price of lost perspective has not fallen alone, of course, on Democratic Presidents dreaming of world unity or Vietnam victory. In the half century between Wilson and Johnson, there appeared no example of this lapse so painful as the sight of Herbert Hoover trying to explain to the Republic the Great Crash and the Great Depression. Barely two months after the debacle of October, 1929, Hoover was boasting to Congress that the White House had "re-established confidence," [10] and the empty sound of all such forecasts made Will Rogers laugh somewhat nervously: "We are the first nation in the history of the world to go to the poorhouse in an automobile." [11] But this President saved his most impressive display of insensitivity for the summer of 1932, when he ordered out Regular Army troops to drive off the ragged army of 25,000 needy and jobless veterans who had marched to Washington for help as the Bonus Expeditionary Force. Taunted for his action by crowds during the 1932 Presidential campaign, Hoover had finally snapped: "Thank God you still have a government in Washington that knows how to quell a mob." [12] Even before the stress of the campaign had begun, he had insisted to the press that the veterans' ranks had been largely populated by Communists, ex-convicts, and hoodlums. And this judgment had provoked the novelist Sherwood Anderson to write an open letter that might have been addressed—under any date—to any White House trying to close its ears against the sound of dissenters, always so easy to condemn as unlawful or unwashed:

> I am wondering, Mr. President, if men like you, men now high in our public life, captains of industry, financiers—the kind of men who seem always to be closest now to our public men—I am wondering if all of you are not nowadays too much separated from the actuality of life. Everything has been very highly organized and centralized in America. Perhaps you have been organized and centralized out of our common lives.[13]

The truth would appear to be that the life of the White House has required neither great crises in national policy nor great schisms in public opinion to seduce almost any President toward retreat into "a void apart." On any basis for judgment—be it personal awareness or national leadership or common sense—each President of the twentieth century has found some way to ignore political reality long enough to impel any future historian to begin at least one incredulous question with the cry: *How could he have . . . ?* To this, there appear no exceptions. How *could* so shrewd and pragmatic a leader as Theodore Roosevelt not have seen in 1912 that the splintering of Republican votes almost assured a Democratic victory? . . . How *could* a Warren Harding, after spending most of his life in partisan politics and eight years in the United States Senate, have ingenuously chosen as his chief counselors men who were parasites and scavengers? . . . How *could* a Calvin Coolidge, a reasonably educated man who had held public office almost all his adult life, have been so disdainful of national leadership that he could insist: "If the Federal Government should go out of existence, the common run of people would not detect the difference in the affairs of their daily life for a considerable length of time"? [14]. . . . How *could* so gifted a national leader as Franklin Roosevelt have cared not at all to instruct himself in political philosophy or economic theory—or bothered not at all to prepare Vice President Harry Truman for possible succession after his own twelve years in the White House? *. . . How *could* so practical a politician as Harry S. Truman have minimized the popular fear of Communist espionage, or defied the Congress with vetoes over-ridden no less than twelve times, or ended his Presidential days imagining that Vice President Alben Barkley (at the age of seventy-four and under the anathema of organized labor) might be his successor in 1953? Or how *could* this President so sensitive to his-tory—almost fifteen years after the holocaust of Hiroshima—have answered a university student's questioning of his decision to drop the atomic bomb, with these words: "That was not any decision that you had to worry about. It was just the same as getting a bigger gun than the other fellow had to win a war and that's what it was used for. Nothing else but an artillery weapon." [15]

In the case of Dwight Eisenhower, there appeared, at least to his critics, all too many instances when he remained aloof, serene in a sanctuary of his own, beyond the clash of living politics. He seemed so in his shunning of any confrontation with Senator Joseph McCarthy, his deference to the strategies of Secretary of State John Foster Dulles, and his indifference to the advances of Soviet tech-nology and weaponry. Even apart from such debatable decisions-not-to-decide, Eisenhower viewed the Republic's whole political life with a kind of detachment implying that the gates of *his* White House placed him, properly and peacefully, in a world apart. Per-haps he never betrayed this sentiment more plainly than in a press conference after the Congressional elections of 1958. In those elec-tions the President's party had suffered a rout. And as his exchange with the press proceeded:

> *Question:* What do you think was the primary reason? . . . Was it local issues or perhaps disenchantment with the Admin-istration . . . ?

---

* During the eighty-two days when Truman was Vice President, Roosevelt was in the capital less than a month, and the two met only twice by appointment. Truman later estimated that he saw FDR only eight times during the year before Roosevelt's death.

Answer: Disenchantment with what?

Question: With the Administration.

Answer: Well, so far as I know, I have never varied in my basic convictions as to the functions of the Federal Government in our country and . . . the great, broad, middle-of-the-road that the United States should be following. I have preached this as loudly as I could for six years. . . . After four years of that kind of teaching, the United States did give me, after all, a majority of I think well over 9 million votes. . . .

Now, here, only two years later, there is a complete reversal; and yet I do not see where there is anything that these people consciously want the Administration to do differently. And, if I am wrong, I'd like to know what it is. . . . If they want me to do anything else, I don't know exactly what it is.[16]

The homely and casual phrases—"I do not see" and "I'd like to know"—could have been spoken by any President whose composure rather easily withstands either new mandates or sudden rebukes from the citizenry. To many Presidents of both national parties—and of quite disparate philosophies and talents—the lure of some form of righteous isolation has proved, sooner or later, too consoling to resist. In the late 1940's, the Republicans aimed their taunt at the man in the White House with a political pun better than most: "To err is Truman." To the historian of the office, however, the quip was excessively personal. For to err has been abidingly Presidential.

II

Are you sure that you fixed your eyes on
A goal beyond the politician's ken?
Have you the will to reach the far horizon
Where rest the hopes of men?

—ROBERT E. SHERWOOD, 1933

The poetical questions addressed to Franklin Roosevelt in 1933, on the eve of his first oath of office, sounded much like the nervous questions that any citizen of the Republic, even in less critical times, might wish to ask of any President first entering the White House. They imply another important truth, moreover, about the frontier marked by the White House gates. This is a line cutting clean through the life of the chosen leader himself: as he has crossed it, he has been expected to become, at least in part, such a person as he has never been before, and for better or worse, he has almost always seemed to change, but in ways rarely expected. In the case of Franklin Roosevelt, the skeptical poet would shortly become one of this President's devoted counselors, but he was initially an observer of little faith, who added the sardonic refrain to mark the departure of Herbert Hoover and the arrival of something unknown:

> Plodding feet
> Tramp—tramp
> The Grand Old Party's
> Breaking camp.
> Blare of bugles
> Din—din
> The New Deal is moving in. . . .

People from the selling game, the preaching game, the drugs game,
The fixing game, the teaching game, and every other mugg's game—
They've all come to Washington, from regions widely scattered
To watch a fellow take an oath—as if it really mattered.[17]

What historical difference would be made by the new political sounds of 1933? No one then knew, with any conviction. The liberal *New Republic* had derided the whole 1932 Presidential contest as "an obscene spectacle," and Walter Lippmann had dismissed any vision of Rooseveltian liberalism with the unhesitant verdict: "The notion . . . that Wall Street fears him is preposterous. Wall Street thinks he is too dry, not that he is too radical." [18] At the moment such a judgment was not so preposterous as it soon would seem. There as yet existed (as later would be hard to remember) no working alliance between organized labor and the New Deal, and union workers so disliked the conduct of labor disputes by the National Recovery Administration that, even in 1935, they still described the

NRA as the "National Run Around." * On a more reflective level, moreover, Harold Laski had written Justice Holmes, promptly after the 1932 election, that the Roosevelt who had just fought "a second-rate campaign, evasive and timid" looked like "a pill to cure an earthquake," and Holmes had agreed that if he had had a vote, "it would have been for Hoover," since the new President appeared nothing more than "a good fellow with rather a soft edge." [19] Only thirteen months later Laski was exulting to his American friend that his "admiration for Roosevelt" had soared to such heights that now "America excites us all as never in my lifetime." [20]

The refusal to be an obedient creature of Presidential prophets was no special distinction of Franklin Roosevelt. Again and again, long before the New Deal, the men entering the Oval Office had acted as if their first pleasure were to confound oracles. At the outset of each new administration, too, there has always been that momentary hesistant pause when those most concerned suddenly feel most uncertain about what is to happen next. Thus, a century before Robert Sherwood put his doubts in rhyme, Daniel Webster had struck the same moody note, as he anticipated the arrival of Andrew Jackson in Washington:

> Nobody knows what he will do when he does
>   come. . . .
> My opinion is
> That when he comes he will bring a breeze
>   with him
> Which way it will blow, I cannot tell. . . .[21]

In this instance, the final surprise was no delight, for the "reign" of "King Andrew I" confirmed the darkest fears in the Whig soul of the Senator from Massachusetts.

Over the span of history, the more progressive spirits in American society have enjoyed the more pleasant surprises from the Presidency. This fact is not in itself surprising, since the relative audacity of any Chief Executive can hardly be guessed until he has

---

* The New York *Times* of February 3, 1935, headlined the news, for example: LABOR UNIONS BREAK WITH THE NEW DEAL. The report described William Green and other AFL leaders as "almost in despair" over the policies of "an unsympathetic administration."

had his chance to touch the unique powers within his reach, while the abiding Whig attitude toward the office can only be jarred by such assertiveness. With Woodrow Wilson, for example, there appeared very little in the earlier life and thought of the scholarly professor and the supple governor from New Jersey to forewarn of the major initiatives of the New Freedom. During some thirty years, Wilson's recorded views of the Presidency had varied with what he easily observed rather than what he emphatically believed. He was almost forty years old when he published his biography *George Washington*, and this shallow study revealed less about the first President than about the author who would be the twenty-eighth. His appraisals were stiffly conservative; his view of Washington's Presidency showed little insight into the office; and he found Thomas Jefferson so democratically disoriented by "demagogues and philosophers" that "the strain of French philosophy [had] . . . weakened and permeated his thought." [22] As for practical politics, Wilson's march toward the Presidency had started with his commitment to lead the Democratic Party back to "the conservative principles which it once represented"; his first major stride toward the White House came with his pledge to old-line New Jersey leaders that, as governor, he would never "set about fighting or breaking down the Democratic organization"; and the cabal of conservative Democrats from Wall Street, whose support sped him on his way, chose to be represented in their dealings with him by the agile George Harvey who would next appear on the national stage as a principal architect of the nomination of Warren Harding in 1920.[23]

Although most modern Republican Presidents have conceived the role of Chief Executive more narrowly, they also have sometimes managed to make Presidential augury a treacherous exercise. The case of Theodore Roosevelt was obviously a special one: greatly as he contributed to setting the pace and style of the modern Presidency, there had been few watchers of the White House who had wasted any time before the fact even considering such a possibility, and there is little reason to believe that anything but McKinley's assassination would have given him the chance to change so much. A half century later, Dwight Eisenhower could be said, for reasons quite his own, to have filled the office in ways quite his own. While he shunned most acts that might have been called adventurous or astonishing, of course, neither Republicans nor Democrats, nor supporters nor detractors, could have foreseen with great accuracy his prevailing Presidential manner. Years before his election, a group of leading Democrats had dreamed of nominating him as *their* candidate in 1948, with as much enthusiasm as Thomas E. Dewey and Henry Cabot Lodge pressed the Republican nomination on him in 1952. And months after his election, he jested with Senator Robert A. Taft over the fiction, so helpful to his nomination, that his political philosophy had ever been more liberal than the Ohio Senator's.

There were few marks of Eisenhower's Presidency more apparent, indeed, than the man's refusal to behave as a predictable product of the political times, or the personal experiences, through which he had grown to the size of world leader and national hero. His spectacular rise to fame—from an unknown colonel in Louisiana to the victorious commander of allied armies in World War II— wholly occurred by the will and under the Presidency of Franklin Roosevelt. Yet this did nothing whatsoever to color or inspire Eisenhower's view of the Presidency itself; on the contrary, he came to the White House to preside over a Presidential regime that conveyed the general look—and the specific intent—of a deliberate retort to a Roosevelt's leadership. In all matters political, the two men could scarcely have been more unalike. Where Roosevelt had rejoiced in power, Eisenhower was suspicious of it. Where Roosevelt had tightly clutched all useful prerogatives and constantly tested all loyal subordinates, Eisenhower fingered his authority hesitantly and directed his staff slackly. Where Roosevelt had sought to arouse the Congress, Eisenhower sought to assuage it. Where Roosevelt had always behaved as an impassioned Democrat, Eisenhower commonly acted like a bored Republican. Where Roosevelt trusted nothing in political life so much as his own judgments and intuitions, Eisenhower relied on nothing so confidently as a Cabinet consensus, a special commission, or a study group. And where Roosevelt saw the Presidency as a chance to goad and prod the sluggish processes of government toward the new and the unknown, Eisenhower saw the Presidency as a command to respect and encourage the sovereign processes of government to safeguard the old and the proved. In Eisenhower, these attitudes did not derive—as with Hoover—from some complex structure of orthodox politics and economics. They amounted to neither more nor less than the way he *felt*. And no man, perhaps including himself, could have predicted precisely how he would react to Presidential power, until after the two had met.*

There appears something about spontaneous Presidential behavior even more remarkable than the fallibility of its prophets, however, and this is the fragility of each Chief Executive's own pre-Presidential avowals and commitments. Again and again, the longest-standing professions of political faith have been abandoned so unexpectedly as to suggest that the practical conduct of a President may disconcert no one more than the President. Indeed, the elusive nature of the office seems to find further proof in the fact that men who have spent decades of struggle to reach it sometimes seem rather soon to have only a vagrant notion of what they should do with it. Or in the patronizing but also knowing opinion of Lyndon Johnson:

> As discerning and perceptive as the American people are, I believe that very few of them have ever been able to grasp what transpired in the minds and hearts of the thirty-seven men who have served them in the Presidency. The recognition of unrelenting responsibility reminds me of the truth of a statement I heard my father repeat many times: "Son, you will never understand what it is to be a father until you *are* a father." [24]

Whether the Presidential awakening has come from the impact of "unrelenting responsibility"—or from the incense of almost unimaginable authority—the historical result has been the same. The most innovative and effective Presidents, from the start of the Republic, have been those most ready, at any propitious moment, to break

* After the thirty-seventh President, Richard Nixon, had been in office more than a year, I asked a man who had known and worked with him intimately for almost a quarter of a century if he could assuredly state any of this President's immutable convictions. "Yes, I think there are clearly two," he replied. "He really is a fiscal conservative who believes in balanced budgets. And he has built his political life on a kind of anti-Communism he will never temper." After three years in office, of course, Mr. Nixon was on his way to Peking to reestablish serious dialogue with Communist China, and the programmed deficit of his Presidency was on its way toward $90 billion.

their own unbreakable commandments of the past. The tradition may be traced at least back to Thomas Jefferson. This Founding Father had let pass no chance, from the outset of Washington's administration, to assail the Federalists for stretching the Constitution. But the third year of his own administration brought the astonishing opportunity to purchase from Napoleonic France the whole Louisiana Territory of more than 800,000 square miles for the sum of $12,000,000, and the third President found such a bargain well worth the sacrifice of scruples over a Constitution that conferred no federal right whatsoever to buy new territory or create new states. As for any charge of a loose and carefree reading of sacred political writ, Jefferson loftily explained, after his departure from the White House: "To lose our country by a scrupulous adherence to the written law, would be to lose the law itself . . . thus absurdly sacrificing the end of the means." [25] And not even Hamilton could have said it better.

The sequence was quite the same with Lincoln. As a Whig Congressman, he had been much given to echoing Jefferson's fulminations against the centralizing tendencies of Federalists. Deploring the heretical ways of Democrats, he had vowed: "Were I President, I should desire the legislation of the country to rest with Congress, uninfluenced by the Executive in its origin or progress, and undisturbed by the veto unless in very special and clear cases." [26] But when Lincoln became President, he felt free enough of these strictures of his own to become what so circumspect a scholar as Edward S. Corwin would later call "a dictator even exceeding the Roman model"—as he ignored his Congress and brandished his power to recognize a state of civil war, call up the militia, impose a blockade, increase the Army and the Navy beyond statutory limits, spend millions without legal appropriations, emancipate the slaves, and suspend habeas corpus.[27] For all such acts, Lincoln offered the disarming rationale: "Was it possible to lose the nation and yet preserve the Constitution? By general law, life and limb must be protected, yet often a limb must be amputated to save a life, but a life is never wisely given to save a limb." [28] This may have been both plausible and inescapable, of course, but Whig Congressman Lincoln had seen the Constitution as no such dispensable "limb" when he had assailed Democratic President Polk's use of his war powers to press the conflict with Mexico: "Allow the President to invade a neighboring nation whenever he shall deem it necessary . . . and you allow him to make war at pleasure." [29]

With respect to Franklin Roosevelt, he surely stood unsurpassed among Presidents in his readiness to "think anew" and "act anew," with true Lincolnian pragmatism, regardless of the laws he had favored during the last Congressional session or the speeches he had made during the last Presidential campaign. On one occasion, not long after his first election, he was annoyed enough by reminders of his 1932 campaign rhetoric—quite reminiscent of the early economic theories of Woodrow Wilson—to direct his chief speech writer, Samuel I. Rosenman, to restudy a particularly embarrassing address given in Pittsburgh, with the hope that past text might somehow be reconciled to present policy. After careful perusal of the speech, Rosenman returned with the forthright counsel: "Mr. President, the only thing you can say about that 1932 speech is to deny categorically that you ever made it."

As most Presidents have found it relatively easy to put from their minds all Pittsburghs in their pasts, they also have shown skill in fooling most prophets in one more disconcerting way. In the case of almost every Presidency, the vigor of its action—or the caution of its conduct—has borne virtually no relation to the size of its mandate. In 1800–1801, the election ended in the 73 to 73 electoral tie between Thomas Jefferson and Aaron Burr, with John Adams' 65 votes close behind. Only twice in the following 168 years would the electoral plurality be narrower than Jefferson's margin over Adams, and the choice between Jefferson and Burr stayed deadlocked in the House of Representatives through thirty-five ballots, before a few Federalists, weary of backing Burr to block Jefferson, finally cast blank ballots. In his First Inaugural, Jefferson briefly genuflected to the partisan realities, with his benign statement: "We are all Federalists, we are all Republicans." Aside from a few such rhetorical pauses, however, he proceeded to conduct his Presidential business as though thoroughly confident that an indissoluble majority of the electorate stood ready to follow wherever he led. . . . In 1860, the Lincoln who would arrogate to himself such unprecedented power began his progress toward the White House with a victory, at the deeply divided Republican Convention in Chicago, which his biographer, Lord Charnwood, understandably called "the most surprising nomination ever made in America." [30] From there, he proceeded to campaign for another victory that he won with the support of only 39.9 percent of the electorate. . . . And in 1913, Woodrow Wilson began a first Presidential term that many historians have viewed as the most creative four-year display of Presidential leadership in the Republic's history. Yet he had taken office with the popular support of a million and a quarter fewer citizens than had voted for his two Republican opponents. . . . As studies in contrast, there have followed such impressive electoral triumphs as Warren Harding's 1920 plurality of 7,000,000 votes—an avalanche for the age—and the landslide victories of Dwight Eisenhower in 1952 and 1956. No Presidents could have asked for more resounding popular mandates. But no two Presidents of the twentieth century more resignedly left both their party and their country roughly where they first had found them, undisturbed and unchanged.

Thus, almost all conventional signs and omens of any Presidency —the substantial mandates, the solemn promises, or the plausible prophecies—have appeared to avail little and to foretell less. For this, the sovereign cause has not been some spasm of unreason that seizes each new President promptly upon his passage through the White House gates. Instead, it appears a matter firmly dictated by the very nature of the work he has come to undertake.

A President comes to the Oval Office, above all else, to make decisions. To do this, he must feel, lunge, and sometimes claw his way through those "stretches" of Presidential life that even the ebullient John Kennedy quickly found to be "dark and tangled." He cannot enter this thicket with any map or survey for he cannot know in advance the dilemmas to be raised or the questions to be asked. To anticipate the unknown, a President neither avoids nor accomplishes much by striving to make up a theory. But to face the unavoidable, he has to do—ultimately—what is harder. He must make up his mind.

III

The Presidency of the United States carries with it a responsibility so personal as to be without parallel. . . . No one can make decisions for [the President]. No one can know all the processes and stages of his thinking. . . . Even those closest to him . . . never know all the reasons why he does certain things and why he comes to certain conclusions.[31]

—HARRY S. TRUMAN

Almost all Presidents have sighed with Truman over their own half-blind groping toward conclusions on the graver matters pressed upon them. A William Howard Taft, who would have liked to discover a steady and impersonal logic for all Presidential business, nonetheless once listened unbelievingly to an aide presuming to inform him on "the machinery of government," and he later laughed to a friend, "You know, *he* really thinks it *is* machinery."[32] A Woodrow Wilson, who would have liked to propound scholarly theorems for Presidential decision-making, instead explained: "Governments are what politicians make them. . . . Government is not a body of blind forces [but] a body of men . . . not a machine but a living thing. It falls, not under the theory of the universe, but under the theory of organic life. It is accountable to Darwin, not to Newton."[33] And a Richard Nixon, who might have preferred to believe that the executive branch could be run like a law firm, once impatiently listened to an adviser assess government in terms of "the appropriate mechanism," and he responded with a recollection of an East European official who years before had shown him with pride a splendidly modern steel mill under efficient management, but then had confessed: "It's not hard to find men who understand machinery. Our trouble is that we don't have enough men who understand men."[34]

Such testimony notwithstanding, there has persisted, alike among students and practitioners of government, a deadlocked argument over what might be called a choice between "the Man" and "the Structure" as the decisive element in Presidential performance. On occasion, the same President has even appeared to speak for both sides of the debate. Thus, President Nixon would seem to have forgotten the wisdom of his Communist guide when he fervently embraced the recommendations of his Advisory Council on Executive Organization. After a two-year study the council's 1970 report of more than 400 pages inspired the thirty-seventh President to key his 1971 State of the Union message to a restructuring of Cabinet departments which, so he professed, would help to speed nothing less than "a New American Revolution." The Presidential advisory group encouraging such a vision boasted far more experience in business than in government, and its chairman's favorite maxim was that "organization *is* policy," a precept that he saw as a political translation of Sigmund Freud's axiom that "anatomy is destiny." [35] Most veterans of White House service, however, have found that, the more closely they have observed a President, the less mechanical—and the more profoundly personal—has appeared the whole process by which he makes his decisions. In the words of Theodore C. Sorensen: "To be preoccupied with form and structure—to ascribe to their reform and reorganization a capacity to end bad decisions—is often to overlook the more dynamic and fluid forces on which Presidential decisions are based." [36]

Quite literally, these decisive "fluid forces" may be almost anything from a President's gastric juices or adrenal glands to pernicious signs of inflation in the American economy or suspicious Soviet troop movements in Middle Europe. To gauge or to discipline such miscellaneous matters, there are no perfected bureaucratic barometers, of course. And at least initially, therefore, the making of historic or hazardous decisions has been, and must be, a matter far less of *procedures* than of *perceptions*.

There are a couple of these basic perceptions that have become —or so I have come to believe—possibly more important than most others. To be specific:

A President needs the perception to sense, as well as candor to admit, the profound difference between information and vision— between a massing of facts and a mastery of judgment. It is a common and careless popular inclination, which no President has ever vigorously discouraged, to imagine that because the Chief Executive may know "more" about a critical question, he must also know "best." Or as Lyndon Johnson avowed in his memoirs: "I always remembered my father's advice: 'A man's judgment on any subject is only as good as his information.' " From such legitimate but limited truth, however, this President appeared to make the extreme inference that the volume of his data assured the virtue of his decisions. Accordingly, he went on to cite, as a principal cause of "conflict" with Congress, the Executive's superior (because larger) "information," thanks to the "number of experts and statisticians available" to it.[38]

Some trials of earlier Presidents also suggest the span that can separate information from vision within the White House. In the case of a Herbert Hoover, he almost dazzled associates like his Secretary of State, Henry Stimson, with his grasp of data and detail. As Stimson saluted him: "He has the greatest capacity for assimilating and organizing information of any man I ever knew." And as Bernard Baruch agreed: "To Hoover's brain, facts are water to a sponge." [39] Unfortunately, the same figure of speech applied to Hoover's lack of firm strategy in trying to rally popular confidence against the onset of the Great Depression. In the case of such a Warren Harding, there was no need for wracking crisis, of course, to bring on a spell of agonizing irresolution. For him, the very abundance of facts before him only made matters worse, as he honestly confessed: "I listen to one side and they seem right, and then . . . I talk to the other side and they seem just as right, and there I am where I started . . . God, what a job!" [40]

If the Presidential process of decision-making is to be reasonably pure—and free from self-deceptions—the Chief Executive needs a still larger perception to acknowledge, alike to the public and to himself, two related truths. First, the weight of evidence favoring one major decision against another is often dismayingly slight. But second, he almost invariably has several alternatives among which (almost arbitrarily) to choose. With any President, the chances are that he contemplates neither truth with pleasure. It is always easier to pretend that the wisdom of a policy has been overwhelmingly, not narrowly, dictated by all "facts" gathered from all sources of "information." And it is also easier, at all times, to contend that the justice of a chosen course has been so demonstrably proved that *no* reasonable alternative exists—especially in the realm of foreign affairs, whenever the honor or the safety of the Republic can be invoked as the test from which none dare flinch.

Yet few political decisions of real life are at all of this order of clarity or immutability, as shown by almost every international crisis or issue since the Second World War. The chain of such situations—each with at least two realistic alternatives—may readily be traced as far back as the American decision to introduce Japan to the dread force of nuclear weapons: there was no inexorable logic ruthlessly leaving President Harry Truman "no other choice," and there are citizens in all civilized nations who have come to wish that he had made another. So it was, too, with West German rearmament: there were those who would have preferred to build a NATO alliance without remilitarization so swiftly after demilitarization along the Rhine. So it was with the Truman Doctrine's military embrace of Turkey and Greece: there were those to argue that action so close to the Soviet Union could only harden Soviet distrust of the West and quicken the pace of Soviet rearmament. So it was with both the successful American airlift breaking the Soviet blockade of Berlin in 1949 and the absence of American air cover for the abortive invasion of Cuba in 1961: each case offered obvious options to have done more, or less, or nothing. So it was with the military objectives of the Korean War: they could have been declared to have been accomplished either by securing the original border with North Korea or by establishing a defensive line across the Korean peninsula's narrow waist, rather than the brash drive northward to the Yalu River and the Chinese border. And so it was, of course, with the steadily climbing commitments to Indochina by no less than five successive Presidents. There emerges nothing more clearly, throughout the once-secret Pentagon Papers, than the opportunities of President after President to cite one source of intelligence or another, one kind of counsel or another, to give an air of reasonableness to any policy of his own choosing. And ultimately, it was the minds of Presidents—not the gates of the White House—that closed.

These are a few of the unalterably personal qualities in any President's decision, and yet, even they do not—alone and of themselves—wholly *make* his decision or his policy. For this, the most self-assured or self-sufficient of Presidents still require some supporting "structure" and functioning "organization." Even in this lofty political arena, an opinion is not a decision, and a pronouncement is not a policy. Shortly before Harry Truman turned over his White House to Dwight Eisenhower, he murmured a wry prophecy. "He'll sit right here and he'll say, 'Do this, do that,' " Truman warned, "and nothing will happen. Poor Ike. It won't be a bit like the Army. He'll find it very frustrating." [41] While the forecast may have been mildly malicious, the personal jibe conveyed a general truth. Each serious Presidential decision—far from being an instantly incarnate fact—must reach back for reasons and reach ahead for results. The sovereign verdict therefore entails not one act, but three acts: the acquiring of knowledge, the forming of judgment, and the executing of decision. Of these, the second marks what Harry Truman perceived to be the central "responsibility so personal" as to be "without parallel": the man's choice, by his own mind and his own will. But this—without the first—can mean no more than a political superstition, based on nothing verifiable, and —without the third—it can promise no more than a political incantation, geared to nothing attainable. As inexorably as a geometric triangle, a creative and effective Presidential policy must observe all three aspects of decision. And the want of any one of them can leave only something wholly different and deformed.

*   *   *

All Presidents of the Republic have come to perceive, either certainly or cloudily, that two of their more awesome challenges are really one: the defining of personal decisions, largely within the walls of the Oval Office, and the detecting of popular persuasions, wholly beyond the gates of the White House. For both tasks, each Chief Executive traditionally has looked for help to two sources of information and inspiration. These are both complementary and competitive. And they are his personal staff and his official Cabinet.

The essential purpose and character of a White House staff—both the services it usually performs and the criticisms it usually provokes —may be dated from the famous Kitchen Cabinet assembled by the Republic's seventh President, Andrew Jackson. As if anticipating the needs of most of his successors, Jackson turned to a coterie of personal advisers because he could not find "the necessary standards of selflessness and candor" in the politicians in his Cabinet. [42] One member of this Cabinet, Secretary of the Treasury William Duane —as if anticipating *his* successors—darkly deplored the Presidential inner group as "an influence, at Washington, unknown to the Constitution and to the country." [43] Undeterred, Jackson proceeded to rely especially upon two talented journalists, Amos Kendall and Francis Preston Blair. A contemporary described the former in terms applicable to any influential counselor in the White House a century or more later: "He is supposed to be the moving spring of the whole administration: the thinker, planner, and doer, but it is all in the dark. Documents are issued of an excellence which prevents their being attributed to persons who take the responsibility of them. . . . Work is done, of goblin extent and with goblin speed, which makes men look about them with a superstitious wonder." On Capitol Hill, the "wonder" was rancorously voiced in the House by a Congressman who assailed the same Presidential aide as "the President's *thinking* machine, and his *writing* machine—ay, and his *lying* machine! . . . Man of all work— nothing was well done without the aid of his diabolical genius." [44] All this foreshadowed with reasonable accuracy the Presidential use and the Congressional abuse of a Wilson's Edward House, a Roosevelt's Harry Hopkins, an Eisenhower's Sherman Adams, a Kennedy's McGeorge Bundy, or a Nixon's Henry Kissinger.

The numerical growth of the President's staff, however, has been an institutional phenomenon of the middle part of the twentieth century. Quantitatively, there had been little early warning of what was to come. Thomas Jefferson entering the White House in 1801 had charge of one messenger and an occasional secretary; three-quarters of a century later, Ulysses S. Grant had two professional staff members; and Woodrow Wilson worked his way through World War I with seven aides. In 1939, there was nothing unreasonable in the question posed by Franklin Roosevelt's Committee on Administrative Management, led by Louis Brownlow: "Where . . . can there be found an executive in any way comparable upon whom so much petty work is thrown?" [45] Following World War II, the steep upward curve of popular pressures and demands upon the White House could almost be charted by the headlong increases in the cost and size of the Presidential staff. Even after great expansion under Roosevelt, the White House staff's 1947 appropriations amounted to less than $850,000, but by 1970 they hovered around $3,900,000; and for all the Executive Office of the President, the 1947 cost of some $5,000,000 had become by 1970 a $38,000,000 bill. For the office of the Vice President alone, the budget for the 1971 fiscal year called for more than $1,000,000 to support "special functions" and "clerical assistance"—a sum considerably more than funds for all the White House staff less than twenty-five years before. As for the number of employees, the staff of the White House alone totaled almost 550 in 1970, while the 1971 budget additionally called for more than 600 employees in the Bureau of the Budget, more than 50 for the President's Council of Economic Advisers, and more than 70 for his National Security Council. And while this growth quickened, decade after decade, one Presidential candidate after another ritualistically vowed to reverse the trend promptly after his election.

The trend could hardly have been different, of course, for the crucial role of the Presidential staff has come to be to serve as the Chief Executive's eyes, ears, and—occasionally—tongue. More precisely, it serves as his liaison in three different directions: with the executive branch, with the Congress, and with the mass media. In all three areas, it is counted and called upon to perform functions of infinite variety: to save time, to gather data, to verify rumor, to screen visitors, to answer mail, to prepare messages, to draft speeches, to schedule trips, to prod departments, to coax Congress, to court journalists, to recommend appointments, to summarize news, to smother scandal, to baffle opponents, to cheer followers— all in all, to keep the President and the world beyond the White House gates on speaking terms both cordial and trustful.

The staff that each President brings into the White House almost always has suggested a good deal about his personal tastes and habits. Beginning with recruitment, each modern President has tended to go his own way. Franklin Roosevelt found his men mainly in government or journalism. Truman relied even more on veteran public servants. Eisenhower looked to the business world for as much as a third of his staff. Kennedy preferred governmental agencies and universities, gathering two-thirds of his people from them.[46]

The Presidents' uses of their staffs, too, have varied as radically as Presidential temperaments, and the cases of Roosevelt and

Eisenhower again illuminate by contrast. As Louis Brownlow once wrote, Roosevelt liked to "both encourage and cultivate chaos up to a certain point above which he was the Boss," [47] and he enjoyed the administrative quiver of what Arthur Schlesinger, Jr., called "the agony below." To feel this was to sense that his hand was on the pulse of governmental action. But Eisenhower wanted no part of this political sport, which he viewed as a childish diversion and an operational danger. He sought, instead, a sense of security from a staff system directed by Assistant to the President Sherman Adams and envisioned as a civilian replica of orderly military procedure. To fit his administrative style, Roosevelt preferred his staff to be versatile generalists, broad in both expertise and perspective and hardy enough to wrangle and compete with one another. Instead, Eisenhower veered toward authoritative specialists, varied in experience, distinct in competence, and mannerly enough to keep out of one another's way. Roosevelt saw the White House staff as *his* staff —an extension of himself. Eisenhower saw it as any general's (or any President's) official guard—a protection of himself.

Each of these President's approaches to his staff conformed to his particular view of the proper nature of communication between the White House and the wide public. To Eisenhower, this communication should be discreet, distant, and cool: he scanned the press carelessly and indifferently, he regarded most journalists as impudent inquisitors, he disliked public speeches and political rallies, and he distrusted reports or polls of public opinion. For this President, his office's dignity also implied its privacy, and to be "a President of all the people" one also had to be a President somewhat *above* the people. To Roosevelt, the communications of a President had to be quite the reverse: lively, intimate, and open. He read a half dozen newspapers daily and avidly, delighted in public appearances and addresses, and observed public opinion with a fascination extending to snippets of gossip. Far from discerning much dignity in privacy, he practiced an almost promiscuous curiosity. He not only expected his staff to keep him fully apprized of events and trends, great and small, but also exhorted his friends, his relatives, their wives, and (above all) his own wife to keep him fully informed about his staff. His ears cocked and his nostrils sniffing, he typically urged a leader of Democratic women: "Pay no attention to what people are saying in Washington. They are the last persons in the country to listen to." Or as he once told Rexford Tugwell: "Go and see what's happening. See the end product of what we are doing. Talk to people. Get the wind in your nose." [48] And his staff was supposed to be following this scent all their days.

For modern Presidents of all temperaments, however, there have been practical and insistent reasons for a steadily larger White House staff. As the federal government has been called to deal with social and economic problems ever more complex, it has had to plan and direct action on fronts far broader than the traditional authorities of particular departments or agencies on the Cabinet level; any massive campaign on such matters as urban renewal, medical insurance, welfare assistance, educational aid, or pollution control has demanded the kind of generalship that no one department can provide, and there has been nowhere to turn but to the President's own Executive Office. All this further enlarges another function of any White House staff: the oversight of existing programs, so that their review and revision may make them tolerably responsive to the original intent of the Chief Executive or the Congress. The cumulative and often confused nature of all such activities, moreover, creates an atmosphere of potentially creative ambiguity —a situation wherein competing or even conflicting methods and purposes can, by their very friction, spark new ideas for new actions. Even a President without a Roosevelt's fondness for capricious experiment can sense that a little asymmetry may be more stimulating than too much rigidity. This is precisely what Louis Brownlow meant when he wrote about his 1939 study of administrative management some years afterward: "I am happy to say that I did succeed in keeping out of the Report any organization chart of any kind, type, character or description whatsoever." [49]

Imposing as are these managerial duties of a President's staff, the primary role of his closest counselors has remained essentially personal. For they—or perhaps only one or two among them—may find ways to relieve his often chilling sense of being utterly alone. To all Presidents, this aloneness has commonly seemed the bleakest part of a Presidential life in which almost all association with other humans, even mere conversation, becomes tainted with the uncandid and the devious—as each encounter threatens to betray some other person's selfish seeking, another faction's sly probing, or another nation's hostile designing. A President's longing for some respite from this may have been described most forthrightly one day early in 1941, in a White House dialogue between Franklin Roosevelt and the head of the Republican Party, Wendell Willkie, whom Roosevelt had defeated in the election of the previous November. The meeting occurred the day before the first inaugural of a third Presidential term in the Republic's history, and it also marked the eve of a journey to Great Britain that Willkie had volunteered to make in support of American foreign policy. In the course of their talk, the President remarked that Willkie should meet with his closest aide, Harry Hopkins, who then happened to be in London. As Robert E. Sherwood later reported, Willkie did not like the suggestion and asked: "Why do you keep Hopkins so close to you? You surely must realize that people distrust him, and they resent his influence." And Roosevelt replied—speaking, in a sense, for all Presidents:

> I can understand that you wonder why I need that half-man around me.* But—some day you may well be sitting here where I am now as President of the United States. And when you are, you'll be looking at that door over there and knowing that practically everybody who walks through it wants something out of you. You'll learn what a lonely job this is, and you'll discover the need for somebody like Harry Hopkins, who asks for nothing except to serve you.[50]

It happens that, on the occasion of Sherwood's own first meeting with Hopkins more than two years earlier, he had confessed to his diary that the President's confidant seemed "a profoundly shrewd and faintly ominous man." Yet when he later looked back upon the role of Hopkins in the White House, Sherwood appreciated it as the most sensitive service for which a President might hope: "Hopkins made it his job, he made it his religion, to find out just what it was that Roosevelt really wanted and then to see to it that neither hell nor high water, nor even possible vacillations by Roosevelt himself, blocked its achievement." [51]

Unfortunately, a Roosevelt-Hopkins relationship—with its qualities of "selflessness and candor" so valued by Andrew Jackson—has been an exception to the rule of the more common kind of bonds

---

* The harsh reference was to Hopkins' physical frailty and wraithlike appearance.

between President and staff. Only a President of confidence and conviction can welcome the advice of counselors of independence, with *their* convictions. Quite often, there is very little that is "self-less" bravely displayed on either side. And over the decades, the resulting relationship has tended to be flawed in at least three ways:

\# The Presidental staff often lacks the serious political experience to serve the Chief Executive in other than personal terms. It is almost a commonplace of life in the executive branch for any newly elected President quickly to find himself in the middle of a polemic without end: the White House staff deplores the administrative bureaucracy as "unresponsive," and the veterans of departments and agencies deplore the new President's staff as "indecisive." The odds are reasonably good that both sides are partly right but that the argument will be continuing unabated four or eight years later. For this, the President may have no one to blame more than himself, if he has built his staff around men who are congenial rather than sophisticated. It seems a pertinent fact, in any case, that during the thirty years following the executive branch reorganization of 1939, some 170 professional aides moved in and out of the White House; and of this number, less than 10 percent—a total of only 15—had some previous experience as politicians.[52]

\# The Presidential staff has been prone to be, almost inevitably, less concerned with Presidential conscience than with Presidential comfort. In the White House, the rewards for complacence and conformity can seem irresistible. By comparison with most Presidents, for example, Harry Truman appeared more tolerant of dissent than most. Yet when a staff member once half-seriously proposed the President's retaining an adversary "no-man" to question and challenge Presidential decisions—even though any such aide might last but six months—Truman replied with fine frankness: "Six *months?* I wouldn't have him around six *minutes!*"[53] The majority of Presidents, of course, have never even heard so heretical a suggestion. In the late years of the Eisenhower Presidency, the White House staff's solicitude prescribed as a primary communal task the suppression of news that might (in the favored phrase of the time) "upset the old man." And in the closing months of the Johnson Presidency, the Chief Executive basked in the assurance of his closest advisers that the frequent slandering of Presidents like Lincoln and Wilson and Roosevelt could be read as proof that the angry attacks upon *his* foreign policy merely assured that *he* too—by the slow but sure reckoning of history—was destined for greatness.

In the specially sheltered world within the White House gates, the line between decent solicitude and dreary sycophancy has always seemed hard to draw and hold. The most intimate of Woodrow Wilson's counselors, Colonel Edward M. House, had little reason to fawn. Yet even at a time when he was cramming his own diary with criticisms of Wilson, he could write directly to his President: "I do not put it too strongly when I say you are the one hope left to this torn and distracted world. Without your leadership, God alone knows how long we will wander in the darkness." [54] The staff of almost any President has been eager to serve him such heady brew. And the essence of the problem may have been caught, quite unintentionally, by a misprint in the New York *Times* in a story dated May 1, 1970. The story reported President Richard Nixon's speech of the previous night, which had announced the American invasion of Cambodia. It quoted the President as explaining his decision to be one that had been reached only "after full consultation with the National Security Council, Ambassador Bunker, General Abrams and my other *admirers.*" Such a slip of the tongue toward truth, of course, should have originated in the White House.

\# The Presidential staff, far from combating all forces that conspire toward a President's isolation, more often than not have to struggle against its own tendency to share his sense of remoteness from the world beyond the official gates. In this spirit, the "passion for anonymity," which has been supposed to attest the proper loyalty and humility of a Presidential aide, may be more likely to take the form of a passion for immunity.* By the rules of "executive privilege," the President's principal counselors on national or international affairs cannot be called to testify upon their policies before any inquiring Congressional committee. Thus spared the ordeals of mere Secretaries of State, Defense, or Treasury, the more

---

* Within a year of the Brownlow Committee's call for a "passion for anonymity," Harold Laski (*The American Presidency*, p. 261) was cautioning: "If it is intended to mean that they should deliberately screen themselves from the public view, I believe that the end called for is not attainable, and possibly not even desirable. A dictatorship can afford, is even built upon, the *éminence grise.* . . . But, in a democracy, I suggest that the more we know of the men who actually assist in the shaping of policy, the more honest that policy is likely to be."

powerful Presidential aides may almost be forgiven their private notion of living charmed and protected lives. Only such a sense of confidence could have permitted, for example, the declaration by Lyndon Johnson's chief foreign policy adviser, McGeorge Bundy, writing in January, 1967:

> One of the greatest contributions of our last two Presidents has been their insistent habit inside the government of reviewing established policies to test their continuing validity. . . . Both of them have continuously understood what both professors and bureaucrats too easily forget—that the most admired plans and policies, whether freshly minted in the imagination or sanctified by long establishment, are no better than their demonstrable relation to the American interest.[55]

As the chief White House architect of American policy in Vietnam, at the time of these assertions, this White House aide effectively proved, in a few words, that an authoritative member of the staff can be as unperceptive as a President about a national policy's "demonstrable relation to the American interest." And when White House counselors applaud their President for an "insistent" capacity for self-criticism, the President can hardly be expected to doubt such intellectual virtue in himself.

The staff of the White House thus has managed to be something of a paradox itself, alongside all other paradoxes of the Presidency. Where it should be utterly invaluable, it may be nearly insidious. When it should make a President frown, it may prefer to make him laugh. And while its essential role is to keep a President awake and alert, the easier course, always, is to let him drowse.

*   *   *

The role and the history of the Presidential Cabinet, too, have largely been both predictable and unreassuring. Like so much else in Presidential life, this fact also can be at least partly traced to some historic hesitancy on the part of the Founding Fathers. A Cabinet to advise the President is not authorized or even mentioned by the articles of the Constitution. Less than a month before the Philadelphia convention finished its deliberations, however, Gouverneur Morris still was proposing a council of state, and less than a fortnight before the final text was sealed, Benjamin Franklin kept insisting that such a council "would not only be a check on a bad President but be a relief to a good one." [56] But such concepts finally vanished along with all notions of a collective executive. When the Committee on Style had done with these proposals, all that remained was the vague authorization of the President to "require the Opinion, in writing, of the principal Officer in each of the executive Departments, upon any Subject relating to the Duties of their respective Offices."

In Western political theory, the idea of an advisory council to help a sovereign make decisions has had a venerable tradition, which scholars have traced back to the *Politics* of Aristotle and his observation: "It is already the practice of kings to make themselves many eyes and ears and hands and feet." In American political practice, however, the Presidential Cabinet increasingly has seemed to qualify—and rather clumsily—only in the last respect of the Aristotelian definition. In fact, the hope for a higher place in the American system began waning as early as 1787, when Alexander Hamilton directly disputed Franklin's vision with the argument that an empowered council supposedly serving any Chief Executive could only prove to be either "a clog upon his good intentions" or "a cloak to conceal his faults." [57]

The lasting political limbo in which the Cabinet would largely live did not, however, become instantly apparent. As the first Secretary of the Treasury the irrepressible Hamilton himself took an office that Congress had intended as an extension of its own fiscal authority and converted it into a citadel of Executive power allowing him often to behave like the first President's Prime Minister. At the same time, early political usage began to supply what constitutional language had omitted. The Congress initially authorized only the Departments of State, War, and Treasury, along with an Attorney General's office; but the heads of these departments by 1791 began occasionally convening for a sort of collective review and judgment (although it was an omen of the far future that the President somehow managed not to attend the first such recorded meeting). By 1793 James Madison was applying the word "Cabinet" to these conferences, and a decade later, the term was used in the *Marbury v. Madison* decision by Chief Justice John Marshall. Even after another four decades, a President as unawed by his advisers as James Polk still religiously held weekly Cabinet meetings, at which as many as five hours might be spent in debate on one message to Congress, and a majority vote usually prevailed on matters as grave as the Mexican War and the Oregon boundary.[58] Along the way, moreover, the promise and prestige of the Cabinet had been enhanced by the fact that—for all the twenty-eight years between the regimes of John Adams and Andrew Jackson—the man in the White House consistently had been a former Secretary of State. Indeed, a Pennsylvania conclave of Jackson supporters in the 1824 campaign could raise the cry: "This artificial system of cabinet succession to the presidency is little less dangerous and anti-Republican than the hereditary monarchies of Europe." [59]

Any such menace or eminence of the Cabinet, however, tended to erode steadily from Jackson's day onward—at a speed usually measurable (with the exception of Polk) by the strength of the President. A singular anomaly also came to characterize the relations of President and Cabinet: even though the Presidential power to remove executive officers remained in such serious dispute as to bring turmoil to the regimes of both Andrew Jackson and Andrew Johnson—and the question was not definitely settled until the 1926 case of *Myers v. United States*—the Chief Executive's right to ignore his Cabinet altogether was an uncontested privilege more and more regularly indulged. In the spirit that made Andrew Jackson prefer the intimacy of a "Kitchen Cabinet" to the formality of his "official family," he also refused to submit issues to Cabinet vote, as he bluntly explained: "I have accustomed myself to receive with respect the opinions of others, but always take the responsibility of deciding for myself." [60]

The meeting of all great crises in the history of the Republic, from the Civil War through the Great Depression, found the President handling his Cabinet in this Jacksonian manner. With Lincoln—after the Battle of Antietam provided the military occasion he had sought for his Emancipation Proclamation—he addressed his assembled Cabinet in the famous words recorded in the diary of Secretary of the Treasury Salmon P. Chase: "I have got you together to hear what I have written down. I do not wish your advice about the main matter—for that I have determined for myself." [61] With Wilson and World War I, there occurred no consultation whatsoever with his Cabinet over either the 1915 sinking of the *Lusitania,* or his 1916 invitation to all belligerents to state their war aims, or his 1917 call upon Congress for a declaration of war, and even after the Republic had been at war for almost a year, one department head described a typical meeting: "Nothing talked of at Cabinet that would interest a nation, a family, or a child. No talk of the war." [62] And with Franklin Roosevelt, the prevailing Presidential behavior was summarized by his spirited Secretary of the Interior, Harold Ickes:

> The cold fact is that on important matters we are seldom called upon for advice. We never discuss exhaustively any policy of government or question of political strategy. The President makes all of his own decisions. . . . Our Cabinet meetings are pleasant affairs, but we only skim the surface of routine affairs. [63]

For all the consistency of the Cabinet's dependence on the Chief Executive's methods and whims, however, the capacity and the temper of particular Cabinets have widely varied. In general, they have offered variations on either one of two basic models: the Lincolnian Cabinet, chosen essentially for political usefulness, or the Wilsonian Cabinet, assembled largely for intellectual congeniality. On the whole, the first type has proved far more effective than the second. In the case of Lincoln, it was characteristic that he invited into the Cabinet two of his defeated political rivals, Salmon P. Chase and William H. Seward. The result was one of the most competent and influential Cabinets in the nation's history. In the case of Wilson, the predisposition of the President called for "minds that would travel along with his own." The result here was assessed by his Secretary of the Treasury, William G. McAdoo:

> The weak point of the Wilson Cabinet, it seemed to me, was . . . in the matter of political prestige. Most of its members were unknown to the country, and were without political experience or following. From the beginning I saw clearly that the Cabinet would be unable to give the President the effective support which he needed to meet the strenuous opposition that was certain to confront the Administration. [64]

With the rare exception of such a Cabinet as Lincoln's, in short, the institution has done strikingly little to enable the President to see more clearly, or influence more effectively, the wide arena of national politics. It has been slackly used, moreover, for one purpose that would seem most natural: the improvement of Presidential liaison with Congress. From the Civil War to the eve of World War II—from Lincoln's first administration in 1861 to Roosevelt's second administration in 1940—a total of 308 Cabinet positions were filled. The statistics over this span of time reflect a remarkable disregard of the Cabinet for thoughtfully planned political ends. Of the 308 appointees, for example, only 81 had known any previous service in either the House or the Senate, and during this period of eighty years, only 25 men came directly into the Cabinet from either legislative chamber. As for broader political representation, in terms of the states of the Union, the record was no more impressive—with a total of 105 of the 308 posts being filled by nominees from only six states. In the light of this rather confounding history of the Cabinet, politically and administratively, it becomes understandable that a pragmatic President-elect like John Kennedy, shortly before his inauguration in 1961, would turn to a close adviser and pose the serious question: "Just what the hell good does a Cabinet *do,* anyway?" [65]

A reasonable basis for this question would be the obvious fact that the Presidential Cabinet does—and means—so much less than the British Cabinet. Most critically, the American officer, unlike his counterpart in Great Britain, not only finds himself without a parliamentary seat, but also, with the rarest exceptions, commands no personal base of political power from which either to help or to harass a President. Indeed, the contrast of this weakness with the strength of eminent leaders in the legislature partly explains why Presidents have been able to lure so few of the latter into their Cabinets. Quite often, the leaders of a President's party in Congress can bring to bear on White House decisions more influence than any cabal of Cabinet officers. Even in the realm of foreign affairs, the Secretary of State, although he looms as a *primus inter pares* within the Cabinet, may deliver a major speech or advocate an important policy with less effect and consequence than a chairman of the Senate Foreign Relations Committee, and the seniority and prestige of this chairman often lead him, over a period of a decade and more, to view Secretaries of State as mere transient officials who can cause little lasting trouble. As a result, such figures in

Congress may talk—and talk back—to a President with more sense of assurance and equality than any member of his Cabinet.

The selection of the American Cabinet, again unlike its British counterpart, normally proceeds with no concern at all for encouraging a coherent sense of collective responsibility (as may even occasionally inspire House or Senate). From the outset, the department heads well may personally know neither one another nor the President summoning them. This does not entirely ill suit the nature of their work: they are not called to stand on some common ground, but to administer a bureaucratic principality, subject to overriding policies, largely dictated by the White House. Under these circumstances, neither the individual performance nor the indignant resignation of one member of the Cabinet is likely to make much difference to Presidential will or policy. Nor does one official in this group necessarily even feel affected by the offenses or derelictions of a colleague, who may at least occasionally embarrass a President. The strange Presidency of Warren Harding sufficiently illustrated this. Three members of his Cabinet were deeply implicated in the outrageous oil scandals. Yet not only did two members of the same Cabinet—Secretary of State Charles Evans Hughes and Secretary of Commerce Herbert Hoover—stay unsullied and unharmed, but one went on to be Chief Justice, the other to be President. And all the political while, both innocent men found it perfectly natural to act as if the spectacular malfeasance of their Cabinet colleagues had taken place on some remote and nameless planet.

While each Cabinet officer lives largely in a realm of his own, moreover, both the President and the more powerful voices from the private sector feel entirely free to carry on—with little heed of all the Cabinet—their own direct and extensive dialogues on all national issues. To leaders of business or labor, the accessibility of a President—far more readily presumed than the availability of a British Prime Minister—encourages them to take their appeals on important matters not to any Cabinet department but to the White House. And a President tends to respond in kind: a leading financier may command more of his respect and attention than his Secretary of the Treasury, and the president of a leading university may influence his educational policies more than any concerned member of his administration.

Despite all these traditional contrasts to a parliamentary Cabinet, however, the vast growth of the federal role in national life since World War II might have been expected almost certainly to compel a new reliance by any President upon the counsel and work of his Cabinet. In 1940, a student of the Presidency as shrewd as Harold Laski foresaw exactly this:

> If, as I conceive, the Presidency, in the future, is to be of more and not less importance . . . the question of the advice upon which the President can rely becomes clearly an urgent matter. The wider the range of his functions . . . the more, obviously enough, he must delegate. . . . [This] means firstly a more important type of Cabinet officer. . . . It would be no more than a return to historic precedent, since the quality of the Cabinets up to Jackson's day was far higher than it has been at any time since that period. . . . [The President] needs far more men of real standing. . . . I think myself that this means a Cabinet of men who are themselves of approximately presidential quality.[66]

For one political moment almost thirty years later, Richard Nixon indeed seemed striving to fulfill this prophecy, not long after his election, when he went to the unprecedented extreme of introducing his newly appointed Cabinet to the people on national television.* But he had served less than half a term in the White House when the officials acclaimed so recently had become lost in an unprecedented obscurity; the Department of State exercised less command over decisions of foreign policy than at any time since the 1930's, and the transfer of power from Cabinet officers to White House aides appeared more drastic than ever in the memory of any Congressman or bureaucrat.

What had happened to so logically certain a prospect? The answer reveals a good deal about life in the Cabinet. And it throws a little more light into the Oval Office itself.

The members of the "official family" of the Cabinet have stayed political dependents, as devoid of constitutional or personal power as Vice Presidents and with lesser title, narrower duty, and feebler

* The Washington *Post* noted in a lead editorial (March 17, 1970): "In the beginning . . . in the pre-inaugural days . . . you could get the idea that all Mr. Nixon would be wanting in the way of White House staff was a couple of fellows to take phone calls from members of the Cabinet. The *Cabinet*—that, to use youth's favorite barbarism, was where it was going to be at."

hope. To unite such a disarmed group, there has appeared no bond more firm or familiar than recital of the cliché "I have only one client—the President." This helpless spirit has prevailed: the last Cabinet member to rise above such sophistry, as an avowed matter of principle, William Jennings Bryan, submitted his resignation in the year 1916. Since then, the atmosphere of acquiescence has left the Cabinet almost uncomprehending of the faculty that James Reston of the New York *Times* in 1970 described as "the hard but essential challenge of thoughtful minds." As Reston went on to add: "Among the minor tragedies in Washington in the last generation has been the triumph of good manners over honest convictions . . . the polite conspiracy of silence that has tended to prevail in the last quarter of the century." [67]

Rather than dispatch Cabinet officers to make their independent reconnaissance of the world beyond the White House gates, moreover, the Presidents have been more disposed to tame them as servants and train them as apologists. Here, a range of Presidential emotions including suspicion, pride, and secretiveness has evidently come into play. Long ago, even a President as unfearful as James Polk could conclude, after years of observance of Secretary of State James Buchanan's tedious maneuverings: "No candidate for the Presidency ought ever to remain in the Cabinet. He is an unsafe adviser." [68] The more modern control of department heads, however, has extended even to the flow of routine governmental news—with the White House of Eisenhower and Kennedy and Johnson and Nixon insisting that almost any noteworthy event be made known to the world, not as the result of the work of any Secretary so much as a sign of the sagacity of "the administration." And perhaps the most sophisticated variation of this technique appeared with the official sponsoring and advertising of dissenters—as a kind of Presidentially licensed "devil's advocates"—within an administration. During the tortuous private debate over Vietnam policy within the Johnson administration, for example, this role was filled by a highly articulate Undersecretary of State, George Ball. As it was subsequently explained by a White House aide and witness, George Reedy:

> Strangely enough, an official devil's advocate is more likely to solidify the thinking of the President . . . than it is to make the

President pause. During President Johnson's administration I watched George Ball play the role. . . . The Cabinet would meet and there would be an overwhelming report from [Secretary of Defense] Robert McNamara, another overwhelming report from [Secretary of State] Dean Rusk, another overwhelming report from [the White House's own] McGeorge Bundy. Then five minutes would be set aside for George Ball to deliver his dissent. The others . . . because they expected him to dissent . . . automatically discounted whatever he said. This strengthened them in their own convictions because the Cabinet members could quite honestly say, "We heard both sides of this issue discussed." . . . They heard it with wax in their ears.[69]

Another burden to the institutional life of the Cabinet has been the recurrent faith of Presidents that certain departments—usually, Treasury or Commerce or Defense—need and invite the technical expertise and administrative talent of men of outstanding success in the world of business and finance. Almost always, however, these men have become accustomed to institutions—as James Bryce failed to sense—whose lines of authority are direct and not devious, and whose yardsticks of success are quantitative and not elusive. In such alien experience, there occurs almost nothing to help their initiation into government. Historically, they have entered the Cabinet to take on the role of an Andrew Mellon presiding over the Treasury Department, under Calvin Coolidge, or a Charles Wilson presiding over the Defense Department, under Dwight Eisenhower. And with rarely an exception, they only have proved anew the judgment of so dedicated a Republican leader as Senator Henry Cabot Lodge, observing in the year 1910: "The businessman dealing with a large political question is really a painful sight." [70]

Aside from all issues of individual skill or personal courage, the Cabinet lacks—finally—the character and structure to make it a sensible private forum for the debating of broad policy or profound decision. The men who assemble for a Cabinet meeting are no more versatile veterans of national politics, usually, than they are subtle students of political philosophy. Each man has received his office and title for particular and unrelated reasons. He either has achieved special distinction in a certain administrative area, or made a special contribution to the last national campaign, or won the special confidence of powerful forces in the private sector, or shown a special influence on certain factions on Capitol Hill, or enjoyed a special association with the President or his chosen counselors. These are understandable political credentials. But they bring little or nothing to any governmental council supposed to be deliberative or creative.

Nor can a President impose constructive unity on such a body, merely by wishing or imagining it. There is no doubt that Dwight Eisenhower wanted and exhorted his Cabinet to be as reflective and authoritative as a military council. To many political students and political journalists, therefore, his Cabinet seemed to acquire a respectable importance for two reasons: he frequently called it to meet, and he frequently urged it to decide. But these were merely signs of his personal fondness for a theoretical process that never came to political life. There is not one noteworthy resolve of the Eisenhower Presidency—from the refusal to put the moral authority of the Executive behind the Supreme Court order for school integration to the refusal to follow the call of the Joint Chiefs of Staff for military intervention in Indochina—that could possibly be ascribed to the deliberations of his Cabinet. As the agenda for any weekly meeting of Eisenhower's Cabinet repeatedly showed, a miscellany of unrelated topics of current political interests does not impose coherence on a group of officials bound together by nothing more than their affinity for the same administration and their assembly in the same room. Instead, such a gathering can scarcely escape the disquieting knowledge of how little they have to say seriously to one another . . . a Secretary of State counseling on a critical labor dispute, a Secretary of Agriculture appraising a lucrative military contract, a Secretary of Defense analyzing a public education policy, or a Secretary of Transportation criticizing a nuclear arms treaty.

For all these reasons, the Presidential Cabinet, not unlike the White House staff, has generally rendered service of uncertain value. At many times and under many Presidents, there have appeared Cabinet members whose industry could not have been greater and whose dedication could not have been firmer. Yet they have known only the rather dim honor of short struggle in a kind of twilight zone of national politics—the arena of undeclared and unresolved conflict between public policies and private interests, between the new administration and the old bureaucracy, and between the dreams of the Executive and the doubts of the Congress. There have appeared, too, such occasional figures in the Cabinet, exerting such impressive influence upon their Presidents, as Secretary of State Dean Acheson, with Harry Truman, or Secretary of State John Foster Dulles, with Dwight Eisenhower. Yet these have been singularly personal relationships, based upon the kind of confidence and intimacy that could be neither dispersed among their colleagues nor bequeathed to their successors.

The historical pattern has been essentially as old as the Presidency. Shortly after he had left the White House, Thomas Jefferson wrote to a correspondent in France about his pride in the harmony of his Cabinet. And his satisfaction probably revealed more than he meant to convey:

> There never arose, during the whole time, an instance of an unpleasant thought or word between the members. . . . Yet, able and amicable as the members were, I am not certain this would have been the case had each possessed equal and independent powers. . . . But the power of decision in the President left no object for internal dissension, and external intrigue was stifled in embryo by the knowledge which incendiaries possessed, that no division they could foment would change the course of the executive power.[71]

The Cabinet has therefore stayed through most of the Republic's history an accommodating creature, rather than an enlightening creation, of the President. Each President always has paid a special price, moreover, for the particular kind of political peerage he chooses to elevate. If he prefers to bestow titles on party creditors, he cannot expect also to turn to them as political counselors. If he summons those who excite regional pride or personify factional power, he cannot enlist them also to help him define national purpose. If he wants only the company of the personally loyal and the ideologically congenial, he can hardly dispatch them as persuasive propagandists to the political unbelievers. If he desires the arts of men intelligent enough to make converts, he must also welcome into his entourage men independent enough to make criticisms.

With his official Cabinet as with his personal staff, he must choose between knights-at-court who insulate him and those who inform him. And the less abrasive breed has been his more frequent preference.

I V

If he rightly interpret the national thought and boldly insist upon it, he is irresistible; and the country never feels the zest of action so much as when its President is of such insight and calibre. . . . A President whom it trusts cannot only lead it, but form it to his own views.[72]

—WOODROW WILSON, 1908

A peculiar anomaly of Wilson's Presidency was his theoretical sensitivity—and his practical insensitivity—to the treacherous waves of public opinion. Long before his time in the White House, he wrote on no subject with more discernment, and even during his Presidential years, he could insist that he cared to know "what they are talking about around quiet firesides" across the nation, far more than "what they are talking about in the cloakrooms of Congress." [73] But there emerged little in his Presidential practice that corresponded to this humble preachment. His confidence in his own oratorical powers persuaded him to address the Congress in person more often than any previous Chief Executive, but he shunned the personal contact with the press that might have helped to make *him* a much more understandable and appealing figure "around quiet firesides." The ritual of a Presidential address to a respectfully attentive Congress presented a rather reassuring contrast with the risk of encounter with a naggingly inquisitive press. He could apply none of the art of a Theodore Roosevelt in using the press to project issues and dramatize positions. Instead, Wilson withdrew from reporters much the way he shied, throughout his career, from any men or forums too likely to question or to contradict him, and after the nation entered World War I, he discontinued altogether the press conferences that he had always disliked. And all such fretful reticence finally led him to a far less sanguine vision of "irresistible" Presidential leadership readily attuned to "the national thought"—as he himself sighed:

> The little things count quite as much as the big in this strange business of leading opinion and securing action. . . . The President is a superior kind of slave, and must content himself with the reflection that the *kind* is superior.[74]

Neither the contradictions spoken nor the frustrations felt by a Wilson were peculiar to his Presidency, of course. From the beginning of the Republic, the men in the White House almost always have found the labor of "leading opinion" to be at best a "strange business," and their tension with the press has seemed like a Presidential twinge as old as the office itself. The first President believed in all forms of free speech as ardently as any patriot of his time, but Washington anticipated all distraught successors with his decrying of the storm of "newspaper abuse" so damaging to "the government and the officers of it" that "it will be impossible, I conceive, for any men living to manage the helm or to keep the machine together." [75] The learned Jefferson exalted freedom of the press as "one of the great bulwarks of liberty," but he also found the press so full of "falsehoods and errors" that "the man who never looks into a newspaper is better informed than he who reads them." [76] Some 150 years later, Dwight Eisenhower practiced the counsel of Jefferson by scanning newspapers only occasionally, with scarcely disguised disdain, and by urging Cabinet and staff to observe the same distrust. Yet he could earnestly vow in public: "I . . . will die for the freedom of the press." [77]

This prevailing Presidential attitude has not been a case of perversity or hypocrisy. Instead, it simply attests to the fact that there probably exists no relationship in Presidential life more ambiguous in its rules, more unsure in its workings, and more serious in its consequences than the encounter with the national press—written or broadcast or televised. For no other relationship is so likely at once to nettle, probe, and reveal a Presidency—above all, a particular President's own personal gift for the larger dialogue with the people in which he must both talk and hear, at once enlighten and be enlightened.

This political meeting takes place, as it were, at the very gates of the White House—as well as at the doors to every important office of the executive branch. In an elementary sense, the press is striving to get *in,* in order to discover and recount a President's most important and guarded acts and attitudes, and the President is striving to get *out,* in order to affect the judgment and deserve the trust that will determine his life in office and his place in history. Such a relationship is—essentially and rightly—adversary. By the willfulness of neither but by the nature of both, each has a different constituency, an independent perspective, and a separate purpose. Nonetheless, the two are linked together in a certain inescapable intimacy. Each profoundly needs the other, and neither can effectively act without some civil contact and some open communion. The results of an absolutely hostile relationship could only be inconceivable: a mute President and an ignorant press. Nor does this mutual need entail a compromise of integrity. In the lawcourt, there exists a naturally adversary relationship between prosecution and defense, but both sides must be represented—for the judicial process to work. And in the public forum, the need is not much different: both the Chief Executive and the national press must be present and heard—for the Presidential process to work.

The process makes each side struggle in ways both awkward and ambiguous. On the side of the press, the professional task appears nearly a contradiction in terms. The journalist seeks to explore deeply, without offending fatally. He hopes to unveil important truths, without betraying important sources. Ultimately, he strives to convey a wholly true portrait of a Presidency—without wholly alienating the man portrayed. On the side of the President, the duality of purpose can be even more graphically stated. The executive branch annually spends tens of millions of dollars to achieve the tightest secrecy in certain areas. And it spends even more millions to assure, in other areas, the widest publicity.

The high cost of executive secrecy, in dollars and in labor, measures the modern Presidency's anxiety to filter the flow of news for its own ends. Shortly before World War II, the first legal basis for executive secrecy was set by general orders of the War and Navy departments, followed by a 1940 executive order from Franklin Roosevelt applying only to military intelligence. In the early 1950's, a Truman order embracing nonmilitary matters was followed in 1953 by an Eisenhower order (No. 10501) so broad as to become known as "the bible of security stamping." By 1962 a House Committee on Government Operations reported that "more than a million government employees" had authority to impose security restrictions on "all kinds of documents." [78] By 1971 an authoritative witness before a House subcommittee testified that the files of the Department of Defense alone contained some 20,000,000 classified documents. In 1972 the General Accounting Office estimated the annual cost of the executive branch's secrecy vigilance as falling in the range of $60,000,000 to $80,000,000. [79]

The investment in executive publicity, meanwhile, has climbed far higher. By the word of the Bureau of the Budget, the cost of departmental public relations activities for the fiscal year 1970–1971 came to a total of $164,000,000. [80] This sum included as its largest item the $37,000,000 spent by the Department of Defense alone. It excluded altogether the cost of White House operations, however, where more than fifty employees made up the largest public relations staff at the Presidential level in the nation's history. And from these figures, it might reasonably be guessed that the executive branch, for all its elaborate apparatus for secrecy, was spending some three times as much upon the arts of publicity.*

Aside from larger questions of the true national interest, the intensity of these related strivings for both secrecy and publicity pose a practical question to any President: are they relevant and effective enough to warrant such lavish investments? Probably for any President, but surely for any Chief Executive with confident purpose—as resolved as a Theodore Roosevelt to be "full President right up to the end"—such an anxious reliance on the censor's or the publicist's strategy of half-truths seems a waste both extravagant and demeaning. The impact of official, self-serving publicity is limited at best. Most such publicity strikes the press as suspect or offensive, and any responsible Washington journalist has come to regard the mimeograph machine of almost any federal office as an official lie dispenser. At the same time, the Chief Executive who speaks for himself, either to invite credit or to accept

---

* Without doubt, these figures from *official* sources are almost absurdly conservative. Serious analysts have estimated that the Pentagon spending alone—on news, propaganda, and secrecy—runs into billions of dollars each year. (For example, cf. Richard J. Barnet, *Roots of War* [New York, Atheneum, 1972].)

blame, alone can wield the most disarming of weapons: simple candor. The eventual consequences of secrecy as a pervasive policy, moreover, can only be damaging to the whole executive branch. The price is paid, sooner or later, in political currency of several kinds. Although such a policy may thwart a few inquisitive observers, it is certain to protect many more incompetent officials, who are privileged to hide their personal folly in the guise of Presidential policy. It inevitably narrows the area for responsible public discussion and debate, and for this, the President ultimately may suffer more than his critics.* It no less surely drives the national press toward a mood of resentful hostility, and an atmosphere so poisoned can spread general disbelief of the word of the government on any subject. And all these are but fresh reminders of the essential truth long ago expressed by James Madison, some years after his own experience in the White House: "A popular government, without popular information, or the means of acquiring it, is but a Prologue to a Farce or a Tragedy; or perhaps both." [81]

While all the more traditional artifices eventually may harm or fail, however, there are Presidential counselors who hope—and Presidential critics who fear—that the advent of television has given any Chief Executive a new and decisive advantage in his encounter with the press. It might seem that no more favorable medium could be devised to allow a President to carry his cause beyond the White House gates to the farthest reaches of the Republic. Through this medium, the Chief Executive may look more persuasive, open, and intimate than in any other—even though he has been able to set the stage and prepare the drama to his own calculated design. He can command at his chosen hour a wider audience than anyone else in the nation. And the very nature of the medium allows one man to summon attention in a way that no group can hope to match, for how can a legislature collectively answer the Chief Executive, or how can an opposition party collectively refute him, on the television screen?

All this is plausible—but, as a proof of new Presidential power,

* One notable such instance involved the Bay of Pigs operation in 1961, when the New York *Times* refrained from publishing the details of its prior knowledge of the planned invasion. After the fact, John Kennedy remarked to the editors of the *Times* that they, he, and the country would probably have been better off if they had not practiced such self-restraint.

far from certain. There are other and contrary factors at work. In the first place, the nature of television has meant that the kind of "bully pulpit" so enjoyed by a Theodore Roosevelt can now be found in places far from the White House grounds. It can be heard on city streets, thronged with antiwar demonstrators; or distant battlefields, littered with a war's casualties; or Capitol Hill, excited by public hearings called to expose a war's follies. As the Presidency gains new exposure, so also do such very different scenes as these. In the second place, there has appeared no convincing evidence that even the most rehearsed actors on the medium—including the men in the White House—can foresee or control the final, popular effect of even its most sophisticated use. Indeed, the fact would seem to be that television "exposes" in two quite distinct senses: it exposes its user to the opportunity to talk and look as he wishes, but it also exposes him to the risk of being heard and viewed—and judged—by millions of citizens as *they* wish and believe. In this sort of double exposure, the advantage has not appeared to fall automatically to the President. The first two Chief Executives to have enjoyed the uses of television for full Presidential terms have been Lyndon Johnson and Richard Nixon. As for the first, he found the White House command of the medium so far from widening the "sale" of his policies that he became the only modern President to surrender the White House under the pressure of a massive display of public distrust. And as for the second, he has spent his political career, both before and during his White House years, struggling with no dilemma more obstinate than the haziness of his televised personality and the half-trust of his avowed followers.*

The sum of these facts carries one warning lesson. In the critical

* Reporting on the troubled White House of early 1968, Max Frankel vividly depicted the failure of mass media to help solve the problems of leadership plaguing Lyndon Johnson:

"His voice glides from elegant whisper to raucous boom through every human emotion, abhorrence to zeal. . . . It is projected by a giant hulk of a man whose very size has long been a formidable weapon in human relations. The glints and glares of deep-set eyes illustrate every message. . . . Huge hands cut the air and clear a path for the coordinated assault. Up close, the whole being is invariably impressive and, magnified by the aura of the Presidency of the United States, often overwhelming.

"Yet from every side there comes the persistent cry . . . that the voice does not ring true, that the medium dissipates the message, that this dominant and domineering figure, . . . surrounded by every symbol and gadget of power, fails to move and inspire the nation." (*New York Times Magazine,* January 7, 1968.)

encounter with the media, there can be no real victory for any President won by a campaign essentially based on either distrust or deceit. What truly is at stake is not a narrow exercise in public relations but a broad display of popular leadership. And the abiding need for public confidence suggests the wisdom of treating the press not as a natural enemy, but as a skeptical, yet potential, ally. This precarious alliance—like public confidence itself—cannot be sustained by tiresomely clever stratagems or evasions. The requisite is the Presidential *presence:* all the visible acts and the audible words that make *him* believable and believed. For these, there can be no artful substitutes. Such is the very essence of the Presidential system: the tone is set—and the truth, if it is to be said, must be spoken—from the top. No President can call on others, as if they were character witnesses, to prove his credibility or his integrity. He alone can stand above the venerable American traditions of suspicion of government, fear of power, and distaste for politicians. And no person and no policy, no propaganda and no charade, can take the place of the one thing vital to all else: the *word* of this *man.*

The decade of the 1960's provided more than enough testimony on the matter. This was a time when the American people stumbled toward a political disenchantment of a kind rare in the Republic's history: they were shaken in their faith in the American Presidency. They had cause. The litany of official lies seemed longest in the realm of foreign affairs, where the Presidential voice usually speaks with least interruption or contradiction. The falsehoods were as varied as they were crude: the 1960 U-2 spy plane shot down over the Soviet Union, originally dismissed by the White House as a venture in collecting weather data; the invasion of the Bay of Pigs, initially discounted as a spontaneous adventure by Cuban exiles; the dispatch of marines to the Dominican Republic, allegedly dictated by the simple need to save imperiled Americans; and the seemingly interminable secrecy and subterfuge shrouding military interventions, false year after false year, in Vietnam, Laos, and Cambodia. As one serious student of the Republic's foreign policy wrote in the spring of 1971: "The Government has been caught out in enough deceptions, even on the most important issues, to raise strong doubts in the minds of most informed Americans about the value of the official word." [82]. . . And the gaudy power of television, during this same decade, finally proved of no help to the Presidency in allaying those doubts, or masking its own policies, or glorifying its own purposes.

All this has hardly left the President helpless, however, for any honest and creative effort to arouse popular faith and following. When the secretive ways and synthetic devices are forsworn, there remain to him—as to no other citizen of the Republic—a wealth of resources for not merely informing, but profoundly and properly influencing, the public mind. At a particular moment, the White House's degree of success may depend, of course, on matters as variable and unpredictable as a people's mood or a President's charm. But at all times, there appear three factors most vital to his impact on national opinion:

Patient preparation. A perceptive President has never forgotten the need to help the people to be ready—intellectually and emotionally—to listen and respond to the new. In any Chief Executive, this demands restraint and intuition. The alternative is government-by-surprise, which mistakes brisk improvisation for brave innovation. No two modern Presidents sensed this more keenly than the two Roosevelts. In the case of the first, he knew in 1903 that he wanted new legislation to regulate railroad rates; he waited until after his impressive 1904 victory to begin arousing popular support and pressure; and he steadfastly stumped the country for a year and a half until Congress in 1906 passed the Hepburn Act. In the case of the second Roosevelt, exactly thirty years later, he knew in 1933 the need for social security legislation; he first tried the subject in 1934 on a meeting of business editors and followed this with a generalized message to Congress on broad goals; he carefully paced his fireside chats and public speeches on the subject, while establishing a commission to study the program and delaying direct pressure on Congress to enact it; and by the summer of 1935 he had what he wanted.

Political discrimination. Neither the press, the Congress, nor the public can for long sustain its own excitement, even once aroused, over a great many issues at one time. In any year, with any session of Congress, or at any press conference, the President must decide what matters most and there focus his own words and his listeners' thoughts. At his best, Wilson could do this masterfully. And at his worst, he could forget it altogether.

The essential truth here is almost as old as the Republic. When a dismayed supporter of Thomas Jefferson wrote this President to convey his distress over how little the administration of his choice had actually accomplished, Jefferson had this to say, by way of reply:

> I am sensible how far I fall short of effecting all the reformation which reason would suggest, and experience approve, were I free to do whatever I thought best, but when we reflect how difficult it is to move or to infect the great machine of society, how impossible to advance the notions of a whole people suddenly to ideal right, we see the wisdom of Solon's remark that no more good must be attempted than the nation can bear.[83]

Personal persuasion. It is a familiar fact of White House life that an hour's appeal by the highest White House aide may not slightly budge a stubborn Senator, whereas a few moments alone with a President can wholly convert him. The same law applies to a much larger audience: there can be no volume of prepared texts to match the force of the Chief Executive in person before his press conference or public audience. For Franklin Roosevelt, the press conference challenged and excited him as what he called "a special art all by itself." And a description by Leo C. Rosten of Roosevelt's dexterity in the art suggests how all men in the White House might hope to direct their dealings with the press:

> At his first meeting with the newspapermen, on March 8, 1933, Mr. Roosevelt announced that the correspondents would be free to ask direct oral questions. The President's advisers had warned him against oral questioning as an unnecessary and hazardous procedure. . . .
>
> When the questioning began, the full virtuosity of the new Chief Executive was demonstrated. . . . His answers were swift, positive, illuminating. He had exact information at his fingertips. . . . He was lavish in his confidences and "background information." He was informal, communicative, gay. When he evaded a question, it was done frankly. He was thoroughly at ease. . . .
>
> The correspondents were exhilarated. Mr. Roosevelt's first inter-

view with the reporters of the capital ended in a spontaneous outburst of applause, a phenomenon unprecedented in White House annals. One of the oldest and most respected correspondents in Washington . . . called it "the most amazing performance the White House has ever seen." [84] *

A final aspect to the whole encounter with the national media is of far greater moment than the stirring of applause or appreciation for the President. For there is more to this meeting than the Chief Executive's recognition of the people's *right* to know. He has to recognize, no less, his own *need* to know. The meeting is never a monologue: it is the President's rare chance to learn what he should hear, as well as to speak what he may wish. Even though Wilson failed to remember in the end this was what he understood: around the White House, indeed, "things get very lonely," and "the real voice" of the Republic can barely be heard in the "strange city" of Washington. And this particular encounter—unlike any Cabinet session, unlike any staff meeting, and unlike any Congressional conference—affords some chance for the most sheltered of Presidents to catch some echo of a nation's talk "around quiet firesides."

For any President, this is a unique chance. Here—as nowhere else in his official life—he can regularly meet with reasonably informed citizens who owe him nothing. Here—as nowhere else—he can hear questions and statements conceived not to please him but to prick him. Here—alone—he may be driven by unfawning interrogation to go back, once more, and scan anew an old premise or doubt anew an old assumption. So provoked, a President may imagine only critics and enemies before him. A few may be nothing more, of course. But a larger number can effectively be his allies against the threat he has most to fear: his own confident isolation.

---

* A striking study in contrast can be found in Woodrow Wilson's first press conference. While he began by appealing for the help and confidence of the correspondents, his manner was so aloof that even a sympathetic reporter found it "suspicious, reserved, a little resentful." The result was that he "utterly failed to get across to those men anything except that this was very distasteful to him; and they, on their part, resented it very, very seriously. They came out of that conference almost cursing, indignant." All this reflected the spirit of the *obiter dicta* that Wilson in 1912 had issued to another press gathering: "You gentlemen must learn sooner or later that you must take me at my word." (Cited by Barber, *Presidential Character, op cit.*, pp. 59–60.)

In the last analysis, all this becomes a test not so much of a President's ingenuity in popular promotion as of his capacity for private reflection. Of all twentieth-century Presidents, probably those who were both most comfortable and most persuasive with the press were three: Theodore Roosevelt, Franklin Roosevelt, and John Kennedy. And it would appear no coincidence that the same three Chief Executives stood forth, too, as those most receptive to new ideas from the world beyond the White House gates.

The central paradox of this dialogue between a people and their President is the fact that its sensible end is not at all a perfect agreement. Even though a President's ability to act depends critically on his popular support, the wisdom and the courage of his action depend on his being much more than a mere creature of his following. The tension set by these two needs may measure the supreme stress of the office. At any time in the Republic's history, to know the popular will can be crucial, but to obey it could be catastrophic. And the gray expanse between these political truths marks the political no-man's-land where each President appraises his people, sets his purposes, confronts himself, and invites history's distant judgment.

Or as Theodore Roosevelt recalled, some time after he had left his White House:

> People used to say of me that I was an astonishingly good politician and divined what the people were going to think. This really was not an accurate way of stating the case. I did not "divine" how the people were going to think; I simply made up my mind what they ought to think, and then did my best to get them to think it.[85]

And to a President who chooses to act in this spirit, the gates of the White House can look like no prison, no palace, no barrier at all.

Six

The Restraint of Presidential Power

GLENDOWER: I can call spirits from the vasty deep.
HOTSPUR: Why, so can I, or so can any man. But will they
           come when you do call for them?

—King Henry IV

The Shakespearean dialogue went to the heart of the political quandary of the American President—or so, at least, it once was said by John F. Kennedy. The caution of even a medieval warrior with the élan of Hotspur sounded, even to a Chief Executive with the verve of Kennedy, as the most apt reminder that the Presidential power to act never can be wholly headlong and free. Like all thoughtful predecessors in the White House, this President saw the ultimate test of his leadership as turning on one question: who answers, and what happens, when the Presidential "call" goes out to "the vasty deep" of American political life? Will the people care, the Congress stir, or even the bureaucracy obey? And if there be no answer but a sullen silence, what comes next: a new speech, a new statute, a new Cabinet, a new policy—or a new President? . . . On still another occasion, the same President voiced more bluntly his sense of constraint and confinement in office. With the onset of the Cuban missile crisis in the autumn of 1962, he held one particularly exhausting conference with Congressional leaders on alternative plans for countering the Soviet Union's thrust. The meeting proved a moil of contradictory counsel. And when it was through, as he described the babel to a close friend and counselor, he burst forth: "They can have this ———— job. There is no joy in it." [1]

The jeremiads of Presidents have echoed through all generations of the Republic, of course, as if each man in the White House sooner or later saw himself striving as pitifully as Sisyphus, condemned to pushing his huge stone up his hopelessly high hill in Hades. Some of the loudest cries have come, as might be expected, from some of the weakest Presidents: a Hoover calling the office "a compound hell" [2] or a Grant confessing that "I never wanted to get out of a place as much as I did to get out of the Presidency." [3] The laments of the more assertive Presidents, however, have not sounded too different. Although Harry Truman was the immediate heir to Presidential powers vastly enhanced throughout the Roosevelt years, he wrote in his *Memoirs:* "The pressures and the complexities of the Presidency have grown to a state where they are almost too much for one man to endure." [4] Decades before Truman—and before the "complexities" of life in the White House had multiplied to modern number—Woodrow Wilson warned with biting irony: "Men of ordinary physique and discretion cannot be Presidents and live, if the strain be not somehow relieved. We shall be obliged to be picking our chief magistrate from among wise and prudent athletes—a small class." [5] Even though James Polk had been a fair match for Truman in political confidence, he recorded in his *Diary* in February, 1849, his almost sardonic sense of the office: "I am heartily rejoiced that my term is so near its close. I will soon cease to be a servant and will become a sovereign." [6] And even though Thomas Jefferson had shown himself a rare master of the Congress, with all its formidable challenge to the Presidency, he confessed in a letter to James Monroe in 1809: "Five weeks more will relieve me from a drudgery to which I am no longer equal." [7]

The monotony of laments so alike, from Presidents so unalike, suggests a possibility of common cause: a distress borne not by one kind of leadership but by all kinds, and a strain felt not only in the age of the nuclear bomb but also in the age of the wagon train. A cynical student of the office might diagnose the unremitting complaints as symptoms of occupational disease—a case of at least mild paranoia, passed in contagious succession from President to President. It is true enough that a number of Chief Executives have proved a large capacity for self-pity. But it is truer still that all of them, from the most venturesome to the most reticent, have shared one disconcerting experience: the discovery of the limits and restraints—decreed by law, by history, and by circumstance—that sometimes can blur their clearest designs or dull their sharpest purposes.

To any President, the array of these restraints occasionally appears almost overpowering, so infinite is their variety. In time, they stretch from the resolutions of the Constitutional Convention to the resolutions of the last session of Congress. In nature, they are legal and institutional, social and economic, practical and psychological. And in history, they mark those treacherous changes whereby new and great powers somehow also manage to become new and great burdens.

The most obvious restrictions, though by no means the most frustrating, follow from the written and unwritten law of the Republic as reflected in the Constitution, the prerogatives and enactments of Congress, and the rulings of the Supreme Court. By decree of the Founding Fathers, Congress was invested with certain powers explicit enough, at least theoretically, to balk a President on nearly every front—from raising an army to making a peace, from naming his ambassadors to paying his bills. The drastic power of impeachment has proved to be, except for the sad case of Andrew Johnson in 1868, the "mere scarecrow" that Thomas Jefferson forecast. But there has been nothing lifeless about the power of the House of Representatives to dominate the budgetary process, or the right of two-thirds of both Houses to override a Presidential veto, or the authority of the Senate to reject (by simple majority) a President's appointments or to repudiate (by a vote of one-third plus one) his international treaties. By the basic law of the Republic, moreover, the very process of amending the Constitution was made essentially a Congressional monopoly. As Harry Truman sensed from his inability to fight the Twenty-second Amendment's ban on a third term, which he viewed as a direct assault on his office, an amendment approved by two-thirds of both Houses wholly bypasses the White House on its way to ratification by the states, and there is no way for a President to invoke the same process to rebuff or restrict the Congress.

The decisive limit imposed on the Presidency by the Founding

Fathers, however, was the matter of time. The fixed four-year term of office has set the pace of the office in ways even beyond their foreseeing. From this rhythm, there has followed the special pressure on the President to get great deeds quickly done, be it for their own sake or for his own reelection. This pressure brings a perspective on history and a sense of urgency in the White House that find no match elsewhere in the national government. The justices of the Supreme Court enjoy an altogether different outlook, as they weigh matters before them with the serenity and patience of men snug in life tenure. The ranks of the federal bureaucracy, too, include thousands of public servants who have served several Presidents with detachment and who look forward with confidence to surviving several more. And whereas a British Prime Minister like Gladstone could seriously influence his nation's political life for some thirty years, the Constitution countenances such enduring power not for any President, of course, but only for those senior oligarchs of Congress who well may be his most implacable foes. Perhaps more than all else, this radically different sense of time decrees both the political and emotional distances between the White House and Capitol Hill. For as Lyndon Johnson wrote in his memoirs about both branches of government:

> The President and the Congress run on separate clocks. . . . Consequently, the Presidency is geared to force decisions and actions. . . . In contrast . . . a careful Congressman can make a home for life on Capitol Hill. While the President must live with crises and deadlines, a Congressman can cultivate the art of delay and refrain from commitment.[8]

The authors of the Constitution thus added one more political paradox to the long list they contrived. The Senator from any state has time to spend and time to spare. Neither Senate nor House can be dissolved by the Executive. It is thereby assured that legislators may ponder and decide at leisure. And only the President of all the United States must hurry.

To the broad prescriptions of the Founding Fathers, the Congresses of successive generations have insistently added specific restraints of their own. As a rule, any significant grant of authority to the Executive has been hedged with explicit or implicit restrictions, such as a Presidential accounting at specified times, on the exact use of powers conferred. Most often, too, Congressional appropriations are made with binding details elaborately devised to hold to a minimum the exercise of Executive discretion. And the Presidential power of appointment to offices within the executive branch has repeatedly been limited, not only by the venerable practice of Senatorial courtesy, but also by statutory requirements on the personal qualifications, as well as the party affiliations, of appointees to specific agencies and commissions.

By comparison with Congressional practices, the rulings of the Supreme Court, perhaps surprisingly, have ventured relatively little into the President's political terrain. "For most practical purposes," Clinton Rossiter judged, "the President may act as if the Supreme Court did not exist." [9] This has proved most conspicuously true in times of military crisis: even when Abraham Lincoln and Woodrow Wilson and Franklin Roosevelt were stretching their powers as Commander in Chief to the utmost, the Court shied from any direct challenge, lest it find itself presuming to define the overwhelming exigencies of national "emergency" in stultifying legal abstractions. During such tense periods, the Justices have been as readily inclined as Senators and Congressmen to salute, without murmur, the flag over the White House.

Nonetheless, ever since Thomas Jefferson decried the "twistifications" of Chief Justice John Marshall—whom he also dubbed a "gloomy malignity"—almost all Presidents have stayed uneasily conscious of the quiescent power of the Court to find new occasions to question Presidential policy. The modern Presidency has discovered that such jarring encounters may even come in two quite distinct ways. The more familiar instances have followed from rulings that struck down important laws or acts of the Chief Executive. Among the more famous of these have been the 1935 decision (*Schechter Bros. v. U.S.*) forcing Roosevelt to dismantle the National Recovery Administration and the 1952 decision (*Youngstown Sheet and Tube Co. v. Sawyer*) compelling Truman to lift the federal seizure of the steel mills. Yet this sort of rebuff probably troubled Roosevelt or Truman no more than a wholly different kind of Court initiative upset Dwight Eisenhower two years later. When the Supreme Court presided over by Chief Justice Earl Warren in 1954 ordered an end to school segregation, it was not nullifying any Presidential or Congressional act: instead, the Court was filling a legal and political vacuum created by the inaction of the executive and legislative branches. As a result, this particular President had thrust upon him by the Court the executive responsibility for a new national policy that he had neither defined nor desired. To enforce this policy, moreover, he would eventually have to order the dispatch of federal troops to Little Rock, Arkansas—"a Constitutional duty," as Sherman Adams later wrote, "which was the most repugnant to him of all his acts in his eight years in the White House." [10] All in all, the event served to remind any President that an untimid Supreme Court could find more than one way to make a President change course.*

Beyond Court rulings and Congressional enactments, and beyond the federal government itself, the Constitution and laws of the Republic confront the President with the ramified challenge of the whole federal system—all its fifty independent state sovereignties, all politically proud but economically poor. This is the kind of slanted challenge that at once refuses and demands. For the line between a President's authority and a state's autonomy strikes many a Chief Executive as a frontier guarded on only one side: he can trespass nowhere into the realm of the state's reserved rights and powers, but the state can trespass deep into the realm of his policies and his resources. In economic terms, the states can press their demands, singly or regionally, for farm subsidies or school aid, for metropolitan transport or rural conservation, for special benefits for local unemployed or special contracts for local industry, for saving sheep from drought or saving cities from blight. In political terms, these constitutionally secure sovereignties—as well as the greater cities within them—can become like feudal estates, whose governors and mayors must be treated by even a President, especially in a national election year, with as much tact and deference as foreign dignitaries. These local barons and earls have found ways, all the while, to complicate the President's own foreign policy—by passing anti-

---

* Only the previous July, Eisenhower had told a Presidential press conference: "I can't imagine any set of circumstances that would ever induce me to send Federal troops . . . into any area to enforce the orders of a Federal court." (New York *Times,* July 18, 1957.)

alien laws, by urging immigration quotas, by snubbing foreign dignitaries, by exciting ethnic minorities, or by demanding tariff walls. And all these pressures can drain no resource of the White House so much as the one most precious of all: the President's time to get his own work done.

II

The Constitution was contrived by the hands of men who had their fingers crossed.[11]

—PENDLETON HERRING

The history of the Presidency often seems to hint that the Founding Fathers' ambivalence of mind has somehow lived on through the generations to direct—and to divide—the political forces shaping the office. For at every great turning, these forces have seemed to be of two minds, one pledged to give and the other sworn to retrieve, all in the same motion. Even as the office has swollen in size and might, there has been much in the process that has appeared—at least to the men in the White House—to suffocate as well as liberate. And so most Presidents have tended to squint uncertainly at the armory of their political weapons as a stock of double-edged swords.

The growth of the Republic from a cluster of Atlantic states into a global power, for example, eventually impelled Presidential responsibility to grow to comparable greatness. This is a rough truth accepted by all students of the Presidency ever since Alexis de Tocqueville explained: "It is generally in its relations with foreign powers that the Executive power of a nation has the chance to exert its skill and its strength." [12] And yet the axiom cannot be read to mean that the President's freedom of action has risen on a steady graph, smoothly soaring with the nation's quickening world involvement.

To go back somewhat in time, the Republic was more than a hundred years old, and already grown to the size of a continent, when the turn of the century found John Hay, Secretary of State to both Presidents McKinley and Roosevelt, complaining: "A treaty entering the Senate is like a bull going into the arena. No one can say just how or when the fatal blow will fall. But one thing is certain—it will never leave the arena alive." [13] More acidly, John Hay's friend Henry Adams wrote of the statesman's ordeal: "The Secretary of State exists only to recognize the existence of a world which Congress repudiates whenever it can." [14] Despite the exaggeration of such laments, they serve as reminders that the sheer size of American power in the world brought no guarantee of the grander authority of a McKinley as compared with a Jefferson or a Polk. Nor did the full martial entry of the nation on the international scene, with World War I, give the President any full franchise to lead the Republic where he would. Quite apart from the fate of Woodrow Wilson himself, for example, the advocacy of participation in the World Court by the next four Presidents— Harding, Coolidge, Hoover, and Roosevelt—availed nothing in the face of the opposition of a Senate Foreign Relations Committee stubbornly led by a Henry Cabot Lodge or a William Borah or a Hiram Johnson or a David Walsh.

To move ahead in time, the advent of the nuclear age did not automatically increase a President's range or ease of choices in times of international crisis. A glance at the arena of the Caribbean alone proves as much. At the start of the century, when Hay and Adams were deploring the lack of Executive authority in foreign affairs, McKinley had just completed the acquisition of Puerto Rico. By 1903 Roosevelt was conspiring to foment Panamanian revolution, disdaining the wrath of Latin American opinion, and gaining the wanted terrain in the spirit of his subsequent boast: "I took the Canal Zone, and let Congress debate, and while the debate goes on, the canal does so also." [15] Some sixty years later, John Kennedy could execute no such spectacular strokes nor invoke such simplistic formulas. No matter how softly he spoke, he could not brandish a nuclear weapon like a Rooseveltian "big stick." And the results were the clumsy scheme for the Cuban invasion of 1961 and the tortuous confrontation over Soviet missile sites in 1962.

The vast enlargement of a President's power to do good or harm throughout the world, in short, has not made the exercise of this power more comfortable nor the thrust of his leadership more decisive. Instead, the command of such might, by him and by the nation, can complicate and confuse. For as any President makes decisions in the nuclear age, he finds that many old and helpful distinctions have been erased. He cannot draw a firm line between limited action and catastrophic adventure, for some other nuclear nation may not bow to his sense of the difference. He cannot draw a sure line between personal judgment and expert opinion, for his own reasoned conclusion more than ever must rely on the technical knowledge of specialists. He cannot draw a prudent line between hasty retorts and considered decisions, because the speed of communications—and missiles—can demand the promptest of answers.* He cannot draw a convenient line between the nation's affairs and the world's affairs, for such a line has virtually lost all political meaning. He cannot try to appeal to domestic opinion while he tries to ignore foreign opinion, for the two are in constant communion. He cannot view his possible power to pacify divided regions of the earth as an unqualified blessing, for their sudden plunge toward war can be construed, however unjustly, as his unqualified failure. He cannot see the immensity of his military resources as a shield for either his own foreign policy or his own political life—as Lyndon Johnson learned by 1968. And he cannot face the most basic domestic problems without awareness of their impact upon the most immediate foreign problems—whether the matter be production costs upsetting trade balances with Germany and Japan, or the struggle over civil rights troubling relations with African nations, or the cost of scientific education threatening future military parity with the Soviet Union.

Within the traditional sphere of domestic policy, however, the question might reasonably be asked: has not the rise of the President's power fully matched the growth of the Republic's economy into the industrial wonder of the twentieth century? Both by Congressional statute and popular demand, the President has in-

* The time perspective appears again. In 1846 the news of the first fighting in the War with Mexico took a fortnight to reach President Polk, and the sheer necessity to act in the field, in an age of such communications, left the Chief Executive free to ponder problems of longer range than tomorrow's military tactics. In 1962, after the first photographic evidence of the deployment of Soviet missiles in Cuba, there followed public criticism that the President was not awakened in the middle of the night to scan the pictures, rather than wait until the early morning.

deed become the appointed overseer of the well-being of a continent. In the course of a generation, and with rather few restraints, he has found himself empowered to set profits, close banks, suspend securities, smash trusts, fix quotas, postpone strikes, spur productivity, relieve disaster, encourage commerce, control inflation, combat panic, and avoid depression. All this would appear more than enough to make an Andrew Jackson—the first self-styled people's tribune resolved to fight privileged interests—gape with envy.

But the total effect of even such grand investitures on Presidential life cannot be gauged quite so simply. As in the world, so in the nation, there recurs a frustrating equation: to possess greater powers to confront greater problems at greater risk does not assure a political gain. Once again, the same forces and events for which a President is made *responsible* also threaten to be those in which he is made *vulnerable*. The predatory appetites and intractable conflicts of the often ravenously free enterprise system, which the President is commissioned to control or reconcile, obviously cannot be made to vanish or retreat by proclamation. To be posted as guardian of the people's prosperity amounts to a mandate to deal personally with all these interests and groups, corporations and unions, factions and lobbies—all in the name of the general good. But a President might be forgiven for viewing it as a dubious sort of prerogative to have to grapple with such a host of private powers from Texas oilfields to Michigan assembly lines and from Seattle union halls to Pittsburgh boardrooms. For at the next national election, *they* will sit among the final judges, of course, on the equity or generosity with which *their* President has treated *them*.

The sheer zest with which the private sector often duels with the public authority of the President enlivened one noteworthy clash in 1952. On the eve of a potentially crippling steel strike, President Truman issued Executive Order No. 10340 directing government seizure of the steel mills, and he set forth the reasons for his drastic action in an address to the nation. The following night, the president of the Inland Steel Company, Clarence Randall, went on nationwide radio and television to deliver a rebuttal that expressed with rare public candor the private sentiments of major industrial leaders whenever they feel beset by a President·

*   *   *

I am here to make answer on behalf of the steel industry to charges flung over these microphones last night. . . . I am a plain citizen. He was the President of the United States.

Happily we still live in a country where a private citizen may look the President in the eye and tell him that he was wrong, but actually it is not the President of the United States to whom I make answer.

It is Harry S. Truman, the man, who last night so far transgressed his oath of office, so far abused the power which is temporarily his, that he must now stand and take it.

I shall not let my deep respect for the office which he holds stop me from denouncing his shocking distortions of fact. . . .

He has seized the steel plants of the nation, the private property of one million people. . . . For whom has he done this? Let no American be misled. This evil deed, without precedent in American history, discharges a political debt to the C.I.O. Phil Murray now gives Harry S. Truman a receipt marked "paid in full.". . .

I . . . tonight call upon Americans everywhere to take up the challenge the President threw down last night.[16]

This particular "challenge" to the Presidency was carried by the steel companies to the Supreme Court. While the nine Justices filed seven opinions, with only the three dissenters joining in a common judgment, the majority ruling (*Youngstown Sheet and Tube Co. v. Sawyer*) went against the President. The defeat came to him, moreover, against the background of the Korean War and his appeal, for the sake of American armies in combat, to avoid any breakdown in steel production. There followed a strike of more than fifty days and a settlement allowing a substantial increase in steel prices which, as Mr. Truman later wrote, "I approved . . . with a reluctant heart, for I was convinced that it was wrong." [17] Quite understandably, there were witnesses to this whole episode who thought Truman himself wrong in his constitutional notion of Presidential prerogative, and these critics included a majority of the Congress. But whatever the delicacies of the constitutional argument, the end of the affair—which came twenty years after FDR had first set leaders of industry to decrying the advent of Presidential economic dictatorship—proved how vigorously the same leaders could rise, fight, and rout a President on ground of his own choosing.

Neither the resilience of giant industry nor the truculence of great unions, however, has had to wait for the drama of direct jousts with the President to prove that they can thwart him. All the while that the colonial economy grew into a continental colossus, and left far behind all Jeffersonian dreams of agrarian paradise, the same dynamics of industrial growth that drew the executive branch more and more into the marketplace also substantially altered—and potentially fortified—the power of the Congress to assert *its* independence. This came about in two related ways. In the first place, the constitutional right of the private citizen to petition Congress became magnified into the collective right of massive organizations—farmers or bankers, miners or teachers, industrialists or doctors—to petition, besiege, or overwhelm Congress with lobbies and campaigns on every public issue from health insurance and public education to excise taxes and freight rates. The variety of these pressures has not only presented Senators and Representatives with a galaxy of special constituencies either to court or to claim. It has also provided a constant competition with the White House for the attention and action of the Congress.* In the second place, the economic and geographic growth of the Republic transformed Congress into a body representing a continent rather than a country, at least in the European sense. And beyond even the intent of the Founding Fathers, this has made ever more natural and certain the disposition of members of Congress to speak out for sectional interests, rather than stand up for Presidential policies.

These twisting trends have done particularly much to set the style —and lower the voice—of Presidents of a conservative temper. As they have observed the usually easy affinity of legislative leaders and business leaders, the more prudential Presidents have sniffed the peril that an aggressive challenge to either almost invites a coun-

* It has often been observed by historians that the first long period of Presidential faltering before Congress, through the years between Jefferson and Jackson, was marked by the Presidency's lack of many political resources available to the twentieth-century Presidency, such as: an organized national party, an effective personal staff, a popular electoral mandate, and all the resources of mass media to appeal over the heads of Congress to the citizenry. But it has been less observed that the early Presidents were, at the same time, unchallenged by masses of organized citizens clamoring for Congressional attention from Senators and Representatives who would need their financial and organizational support at the next election.

terattack from the other. It is scarcely a coincidence that all modern conservative Presidents have therefore shown an equal deference toward both. Thus, the Harding who was the genial creature of "the Ohio gang," as well as the nation's labyrinthine oil interests, did not wait even for his election to assure the Congress of his dedication to the "revival of party government as distinguished from personal government." So also with the Coolidge who could anoint the economic life of the 1920's with the blessing: "The man who builds a factory builds a temple" and "the man who works there worships there." [18] Such a President would be equally ready to avow: "I have never felt that it was my duty to attempt to coerce senators or representatives, or to take reprisals. The people sent them to Washington. . . . I avoided almost entirely a personal opposition." [19] And so it had to be, too, with the Eisenhower whose awe of business success inspired the recruitment for his Cabinet of magnates, devoid of all political experience, from the worlds of coal and shipping and soap and banking and motors. He also had to be the President blandly turning aside from the harsher conflicts in Senate or House as "strictly *their* business."

Whatever their varying political temperaments, however, all modern Presidents have shared the sense of yet another way in which the nature of the office oddly contrives, at one and the same time, both to strengthen and to strain. This particular problem follows from nothing less than the American people's cherished image of their Presidency—the unique hope with which the citizenry beholds this office, alone in all the apparatus of government. There may be no more needful popular act of faith addressed to any national leader in the world—or at least the world of more or less democratic societies—than the eager readiness of Americans to believe in each new President's goodness and wiseness. By the more extravagant premises of this belief, he is expected to be both the robed incarnation of the past and the armored prophet of the future: the spiritual descendant of the Founding Fathers fully trained and prepared for the age of laser beams and space platforms. As for the more mundane present, he must be presumed, by this vision, to know all things and to like all good things: monetary problems and military strategy, baseball standings and Boy Scouts, moon landings and movie heroes. All such flights of faith suggest, as Clinton Rossiter once wrote, that "the final greatness" of the Presidency may lie in its character as "not just an office of incredible power but a breeding ground of indestructible myth." [20] And what grander dimension could be added to the office—apparently?

Yet the appearance may deceive. Myths in politics are never invulnerable. They can be almost as easily destroyed as the man made to wear them. And the full force of such popular fantasies can press upon a President impossible demands. Vis-à-vis any Congress, he is expected to behave as a pure kind of conscience of the nation—if only because Capitol Hill seems an unlikely place for conscience to abide. Vis-à-vis any crisis, he may be expected by the credulous to play God—if only because there exists a larger consensus on who is the President than on who is the Creator. Vis-à-vis the world, he may well be expected simultaneously to preserve the globe's peace and disperse the nation's enemies, thereby advancing —at once pacifically and belligerently—toward the ideal human estate: a world where America alone commands the military might to dictate the moral equality of all peoples. Such popular conceits are extortionate enough to have driven all Presidents and Presidential candidates since World War II to leaven even their campaign rhetoric with self-protective promises to promise not too much. No precaution could be more sensible. For even during a rare spell of slackened public demand, the President is seen—and judged—as *both* the leader and the symbol of the Republic. There immediately follows from this yet another contradiction: the first role is activist and militant, while the second is static and benign. Irreconcilable as they are, they prescribe the cardinal myth that a President can and should be both *in* political life and *above* political life. And the persistence of this kind of "indestructive myth" must belong among the trials, rather than the trophies, of the Presidential office.*

There is a final trick that the history of the Republic forever

---

* Only three years out of office, William Howard Taft delivered a set of three lectures on the Presidency in 1915, at the University of Virginia. Among the most understandable of his laments, he had this to say: "The President so fully represents the party that secures political power by its promises to the people, and the whole government is so identified in the minds of the people with his personality, that they make him responsible for all the sins of omission and of commission of society at large. This would be ludicrous if it did not have sometimes serious results. The President cannot make clouds to rain, he cannot make the corn to grow. . . ." (*The Presidency* [New York, Charles Scribner's Sons, 1916], pp. 47–48).

plays upon the Presidency almost, as it were, without thinking about it, and it is no less insidious for being obvious. On the eve of his inauguration, a newly elected President is given to contemplating the legacy of the Presidential past as a matter of unmatched prestige; on the morning following, he is certain soon to be thinking of it in terms of unwanted precedents. For he quickly discovers that the hand of the past, in the White House, is not at all dead but all too alive. And it goes on writing an oppressive number of things: a law now impossible for anyone to veto, a deficit mathematically impossible to erase, a subsidy politically impossible to slash, an agency too entrenched to eliminate, a welfare program too popular to reverse, a depressed stock market beyond quick revival, or a careless foreign alliance beyond instant renunciation. Such are a few of the shackling souvenirs likely to be left behind by any President's immediate predecessors. The intelligent gathering and disposing of them will take time—a great deal of time . . . perhaps as much as four years . . . and then. . . .

The discovering and facing of all such matters can be enough to make almost any newly elected President suddenly wonder—as he first goes through the drawers of the desk in the Oval Office—whether he really should have coveted so long his chance for so close a look at the motley memorabilia of sovereignty.

III

I now predict that no President of the United States of either party will ever again be reelected.[21]

—*Polk: The Diary of a President,* 1847

The routine labors of one of the most conscientious of Presidents, James Polk, provide insight into both the life in his executive mansion and the life of the White House nearly a century later. Polk described himself understandably enough as "the hardest-working man in the country," [22] for his chores ranged almost absurdly from grand enterprises to tedious trivia. This President somehow found time for debate with military officials over the better kind of mules for campaigns in the War with Mexico; for two evenings every week devoted to the traditional open house for "members of Congress, strangers, and others"; [23] or for personal direction of two or three departments of his government, when their heads fled the humid summers in Washington. All the while, he delegated as little power as possible, for he had confidence in almost no member of his Cabinet, including his mercurial Secretary of State, James Buchanan. As for a White House staff, his *Diary* refers again and again merely to "my private secretary." With so few resources at his call, he nonetheless at the outset of his administration told the historian George Bancroft, his Secretary of the Navy, the "four great measures" he envisioned as the goals of his administration: a reduced tariff, an independent treasury, the settlement of the Oregon boundary, and the acquisition of California. For all his loss of time on menial matters, and despite his constant fatigue, Polk left the Presidency with all four purposes fulfilled. In the process of adding more than a half million square miles to the Republic's territory, he left an endowment surpassed only by Jefferson's purchase of the Louisiana Territory. All this was remarkable, indeed. The only flaw in the record is the fact that faster than any other ex-President— within fifteen weeks—Polk was dead.

Exactly ninety years later, the stresses of Presidential life were much different—perhaps. During Franklin Roosevelt's first term, the elaborate structure of executive departments would have amazed a Polk, of course. He probably would have been even more awed by the army of lawyers, economists, and intellectuals marching on Washington through those years to become the "brain trust" of this intensely personal Presidency. Nonetheless, Roosevelt scanned this large disarray of talent and concluded, quite sensibly, that the Presidency itself needed more assistance and coherence. From this awareness came his establishment of the Committee on Administrative Management under the chairmanship of Louis Brownlow. The scholarly committee's report at the start of 1937 opened with a terse sentence whose appeal linked the age of Polk and the age of FDR: "The President needs help." Or as Roosevelt argued in his covering message to Congress on the committee's conclusions: "It is humanly impossible, under the system which we have, for [the President] fully to carry out his Constitu-

tional duty as Chief Executive, because he is overwhelmed. . . ." [24]
With Congress' characteristic lethargy in such matters, it took two
years to approve a much modified version of the Brownlow proposals. There followed in September of 1939 Roosevelt's Executive
Order No. 8248 creating the Executive Office, which included the
Bureau of the Budget and a small but precedent-setting corps of
White House executive assistants and administrative experts. And
modest though this appears, there have been many students of the
Presidency who believe that Order No. 8248 narrowly averted a
paralysis of Executive leadership and a breakdown of the government.

While the immediate needs may have been met, however, the
years ahead soon made clear that the broad problem was far
from solved: instead, its nature had been changed in a way posing
new problems. The innovations of FDR heralded the institutionali-
zation of the Presidency and of the Executive Office—under a
President who indulged his own restless disregard for conventional
institutions or orderly communications. This was no tidy legacy to
leave. By the time of Roosevelt's death, the new Presidential controls over the ever-growing bureaucracy had been in force five years.
But the small degree of comfort which they allowed his successor in
the Oval Office may be judged from Harry Truman's later re-
membrances:

> Within the first months I discovered that being a President is like
> riding a tiger. A man has to keep on riding or be swallowed. . . . A
> President is either constantly on top of events or . . . events will soon
> be on top of him. I never felt I could let up for a single moment.[25]

And with that unconscious bow to the memory of James Polk, it
would plainly appear that—no matter how many things had been
amplified and organized in the interval—Harry Truman had picked
up the President's administrative burden only to find it weighing
much the same as a hundred years before.

None of this is to deny that the President of the mid-twentieth
century has been counseled, consoled, and protected in ways un-
imagined by a Polk. Nor is it merely to sketch one more instance
where the concentration of powers in the White House seems

swiftly followed by their complication. All this is by way of reminder that the sprawl of a vast federal bureaucracy, far from reinforcing a President, more probably threatens to engulf him. For such are this bureaucracy's formidable size and independent disposition that it can loom as an almost autonomous fourth branch of the government.

There was no modern President who felt, at various times, either more alarm or more amusement over this than Franklin Roosevelt. He was the first of the Presidents, after all, to contend in peacetime with such a modern bureaucracy. And this is what he had to say of some of the citadels of power around him:

> The treasury is so large and far-flung and ingrained in its practices that I find it is almost impossible to get the action and results I want. . . . But the Treasury is not to be compared with the State Department. You should go through the experience of trying to get any changes in the thinking, policy and action of the career diplomats and then you'd know what a real problem was. But the Treasury and the State Department put together are nothing compared with the Na-a-vy. The admirals are really something to cope with, and I should know. To change anything in the Na-a-vy is like punching a feather bed. . . .[26]

A curious kind of bipartisanship has come to characterize most laments, as well as misunderstandings, over the role of the federal bureaucracy. While Roosevelt was deploring a problem which the myriad agencies of the New Deal itself had done much to aggravate, the generation after the Roosevelt Presidency became habituated to Republican campaign orators' incessant use of the word "bureaucracy" as if it were the longest obscenity in the language. The inference of such rhetoric has always been that the federal administrative octopus was far more likely to strangle the innocent citizen thousands of miles from Washington, rather than the man in the White House actually caught in its tentacles. Such an image of the bureaucracy has encouraged the bipartisan confusion: the Republican administrations have contended that a basically liberal bureaucracy constantly threatens to discredit their conservative programs, while the Democratic administrations have insisted that a stubbornly conservative bureaucracy persistently manages to blunt their courageous initiatives. All such fulminations rise from the single, false notion that the basic concerns of Presidential policy and the federal bureaucracy are properly and happily identical. Accordingly, even so sophisticated an observer of Washington life as McGeorge Bundy, after years of service in the White House of both John Kennedy and Lyndon Johnson, could complain that "Cabinet officers are special pleaders" and "should run their part of the government for the Administration—not run to the Administration for the interests of their part of the government." The fitting retort to this was given by Mr. Harold Seidman, a veteran of service in the Bureau of the Budget during the same years when Mr. Bundy was in the White House: "One might as well echo Professor Henry Higgins's plaint in *My Fair Lady,* 'Why can't a woman be more like a man?' " * [27]

There are several reasons for not expecting any such political transvestism. These reasons do not indict either the Presidential office as presumptuous or the "fourth branch" as insubordinate. They simply explain the distance separating the two—under an overcast of mutual suspicion scarcely possible to break through:

First: the relentless growth of the executive branch has made equally difficult either serious intellectual exchange or effective Presidential control. To cite but a few statistics from the longer sweep of national history, the first Presidency administered a total of nine federal programs; by the time of the thirty-seventh President there existed 1,400 federal grant-in-aid programs, and no one in the federal establishment dared even guess how many programs in all were operative.[28] In the year 1816, the first year for which the figures are known, the entire executive branch numbered 4,479; by the early 1960's, the comparable figures were some 2,500,000

* Almost a generation before the New Deal sped the federal establishment on the way to its modern size and power, William Howard Taft could describe its underlying independence of temper thus: "There are in the civil service in Washington chiefs of divisions and assistant chiefs of bureaus who have been there for decades. They are loyal to the government and especially beholden to any one President. They are as important in the army of civil servants as the old noncommissioned officers are in a military force. They have far greater experience than the heads of their departments and bureaus who change every presidential term. Their lifelong fidelity and efficiency are not rewarded by notices in headlines. They have true philosophy, and are content with small salaries, permanent tenure, the consciousness of duty well done, and the flattering dependence upon them that their immediate superiors feel" (*The Presidency, op. cit.,* pp. 69–70).

civilian employees and nearly 3,000,000 military.[29] Within a more modern time span, Woodrow Wilson in 1914 submitted to the Senate a total of 3,418 nominations for civil and military offices, and in 1958, Dwight Eisenhower submitted a total of 59,079.[30] The 1930 federal budget amounted to $3.3 billion, with a $700,-000,000 surplus, and the 1972 budget came to about $230 billion —a total some seventy times larger reached in just over forty years. These figures suffice to suggest the size of the task defying any President who seeks to impress his personality on such a governmental population. "To speak of the Federal bureaucracy as if it were a homogeneous entity," as Harold Seidman has written, "is obviously most misleading. About the only thing that some Federal employees have in common is that they are paid by the U.S. Treasury." [31] And the President who dreads this legion of careerists, as a conspiracy bent on his embarrassment or his frustration, fails to perceive the realities as completely as the President who wastes dreams on a vision of mobilizing them in an army eager to do battle for his own political success.

Second: across all the political landscape of this fourth and most populous branch, there stretches a chain of traditional citadels defended like forts against any Presidential incursion. "Every once in a while one gets the view down here in Washington," Senator Hubert Humphrey once remarked, "that the respective departments are members of the United Nations, and that each has a separate sovereignty." [32] But beyond the departments, over which a President may at least assign a member of his Cabinet and his assistants, there extends the long list of fiercely independent agencies and bureaus and commissions. Even when Congress in 1939 gave Franklin Roosevelt limited power to reorganize the executive branch, there were no less than nineteen agencies, like the Civil Service Commission, that he was forbidden to touch. When the National Security Council was created in 1947, the action could be suspected of being less an effort to aid the President as Commander in Chief than an attempt by a Republican Congress to trespass into an area where his authority has been supposedly unique: the Congress both named the officials to belong to the NSC and forbade the designation of any additional members without the advice and consent of the Senate.[33] In addition to the important regulatory commissions, whose structure has been decreed by Congress, a body such as the Joint Chiefs of Staff, by virtue of the prestige and experience of its members, can make its own case on critical defense issues, either forthrightly with Congress or surreptitiously through the press. And no agency of the federal government excelled the Federal Bureau of Investigation under J. Edgar Hoover, of course, in its secretive and separatist ways. Surpassing even most senior members of Congress in official length of stay, Mr. Hoover saw too many Presidents arrive and depart to be intimidated by any one of them, nor did he bother to conceal his feelings from those whom he distrusted or disliked. In 1971, a scholarly analysis of federal statistics gathering, commissioned by the Commission on Federal Statistics, found the FBI to offer a conspicuous example of what it called "bureaucratic pathology." The general pattern was described as the sustained practice of "autonomy seeking, obfuscation and suspicion . . . to counter the penetration of a bureau's affairs by 'outsiders.' " [34] To this mentality, of course, no "outsiders" might present so great a threat as Presidents of the United States, who alone *could,* if they were so bold, change both habits and men. And the steadfast reluctance of Chief Executives to act in any such fashion has shown how hard it sometimes can be for them to be masters in their own executive house.

Third: it is an ironic fact that, even as the executive establishment has grown too big for him to know and to manage, the President has become—with like speed—more and more dependent on it. As the sweep of his own duties has dramatically increased, the claims on his time have become more various, the need for special expertise has become more constant, and the dealings with Congress have become ever more intricate. All this has made more urgent the need to assign and to delegate authority. But—confidently—to whom? In the process of expediting decisions, each substantial delegation of power itself demands yet another decision, so that the President has to take as much care with the important men around him as with the important issues. This almost endless testing and retesting of a President's judgment long ago impelled Theodore Roosevelt to write to his son Kermit, back in 1907, some thoughts that would trouble the minds of all twentieth-century Presidents:

*   *   *

The truth is that I have a great number of tasks to do, and that except in a very few of them, either the best men I can get have weak streaks in them, or the conditions under which I work are so faulty that to accomplish even a moderate amount of good is exceedingly difficult. In other words the great majority of the instruments with which I work have each some big flaw. I have to endeavor to bear down as lightly as possible on the flaw and get the best results I can in spite of it.[35]

Fourth: the evolution of the federal bureaucracy has taken on one final form as distressing as all else to a Chief Executive—the network of the unspoken but unbreakable alliances between powerful forces within the executive branch and major factions in the Congress. More often than not, these bonds tend to stretch on to embrace those special interests of the private sector whose lobbying camps are never pitched very far from Capitol Hill. Again, this signifies no malicious conspiracy against the White House, but a natural current in federal life that moves, by the drift and direction of its own concerns, against the President's powers and desires.

The ceaseless activity of these forums for special pleading within the executive—but so close to the legislature—sometimes sounds like an echo of a political time easily forgotten, before the Constitution itself. Under the Second Continental Congress, the role of the executive, insofar as it existed, was filled by *ad hoc* committees. Each new problem gave birth to a new committee, until these bodies numbered more than a hundred, and the prestigious John Adams supposedly served on as many as ninety of them.[36] These were the embryonic methods and the scattered powers that were gathered by the Constitutional Convention in order to create a coherent executive authority. But a nostalgia for this politically primitive past would seem almost to have lived on in the spirits of countless bureaucrats staffing the offices of the executive branch. In any case, there persists an alert sense of common cause that binds the appropriate committee or subcommittee in the Congress with its matching agency or division in the bureaucracy. And no President ever has been able wholly to prevent these ties from affecting debate over all laws on all issues—from mine safety to farm acreage, from housing programs to depreciation allowances, from fiscal policy to military strategy.

All these dilemmas belong to the labyrinthine maze through which a President must find his way in order to have his way. In the rather bleak words of an official study of executive management in the mid-1960's:

> Under the present system, the President can exert only minimal influence over the selection, supervision, motivation and evaluation of the thousands of key career executives on whom he must depend for effective execution of his policies.*

A few years earlier, John Kennedy had often made the same point in not altogether happy jest. When he heard some suggestion for a new federal program, he would dryly respond: "That's a good idea. Now let's see if we can get the government to accept it." But he found nothing funny in a discovery about bureaucratic habits that he stumbled on at the peak of the 1962 crisis over Soviet missiles in Cuba. A message from Nikita Khrushchev then proposed a withdrawal of the Soviet weapons in exchange for a removal of American missiles from Turkey. The President had ordered that removal a year and a half previously. And the message from Moscow was needed to advise him that, over the intervening eighteen months, nothing had happened in Washington.

A life of dueling with the federal bureaucracy has taxed the humor of all modern Presidents. None bore the ordeal better than Franklin Roosevelt. As he could find time to write in a 1939 memorandum to his Director of the Bureau of the Budget:

> I agree with the Secretary of the Interior. Please have it carried out so that fur-bearing animals remain in the Department of the Interior.
> You might find out if any Alaska bears are still supervised by (a) War Department (b) Department of Agriculture (c) Department of Commerce. They have all had jurisdiction over Alaska bears in the past and many embarrassing situations have been created by the

* Committee for Economic Development, "Improving Executive Management in the Federal Government," July 2, 1964.

mating of a bear belonging to one Department with a bear belonging to another Department.

F. D. R.

P.S. I don't think the Navy is involved but it may be. Check the Coast Guard. You never can tell! [37]

*   *   *

The command over a slippery bureaucracy is but one of several prerogatives of the President so dubious as to leave most Chief Executives rather unsure whether to laugh or to groan. Depending on the taste and temperament of each President, these hollow honors may include, for example, the greater part of his formal functions as chief of state, which look so glamorous and are so onerous. The entertainment of visiting monarchs and premiers may generally be expected to afford about as much delight as an unbroken evening of television commercials, and the welcome extended to the dignitaries of necessitous allied nations usually contains as much honest joy as the sentiment of any family household receiving a sudden visit from its most indigent relative. But these are minor nuisances compared to two major powers that can bring almost any man in the White House more pain than pleasure. And these are the President's related roles as the leader of his political party and the dispenser of federal patronage.

The obvious fact that a President stands at the head of his party does not assure him any obvious help in his striving to be personally effective *as* President. On the contrary: there is no record of any President reporting that his life in the White House had been strengthened or simplified by his power as party leader. It is true that Harry Truman stressed this role as one of what he called the "six jobs" of any President.* But Truman—alone of all twentieth-century Presidents—had no significant professional base outside the partisan politics that had filled his whole life. As he said of himself with splendid bluntness: "I was raised a politician and went from precinct to President." [38] And even this dedicated partisan almost had to order his own 1948 nomination by his beloved Democratic Party, defying a party consensus that he was doomed to the defeat that never came.

* The other five were those usually cited: Chief Executive, Chief Legislator, Chief Diplomat, Chief of State, and Commander in Chief.

The most popular and persuasive of modern Presidents have lived more at war than at peace with their own parties. With Theodore Roosevelt, the disenchantment with the Republicans under his own chosen successor exploded into the fury of the Bull Moose rebellion of 1912. With Woodrow Wilson—seduced by his own notions of British parliamentary politics and party responsibility—the disenchantment came by a different route: his imprudent appeal in the 1918 election for a Democratic victory to ratify his personal leadership started the eclipse of his political power. With Franklin Roosevelt, a President as happily partisan as any man ever in the White House nonetheless—by his abortive Supreme Court reform plan in 1937 and his futile attempt to purge hostile Democrats in 1938—helped seal an alliance between Southern Democrats and Republicans that would endure for several Presidencies to come. And even Dwight Eisenhower, who was never charged with daring adventurism in partisan politics, so despaired at times of the GOP's reactionary pull toward the past that he thought and talked of the possible need to form a third party.*

Why should there recur such tensions between a President and his own party? Or why should a national party tend to drain, rather than sustain, its own leader in the White House? As the modern Presidency has evolved, a few historical causes have become fairly clear.

The hold of a President on his party has tended to lessen rather than grow as the party, like the nation and the economy, has come to reach from Maine to California. "Let's remember," Eisenhower once explained, "that there are no national parties in the United States. There are . . . state parties." [40] Or as any modern Democratic President might pose the problem somewhat differently: let us remember that we are not a very cohesive alliance—but Southern conservatives and Northern liberals, racist Americans and black Americans, Texas millionaires and New England intellectuals. In either the Republican or Democratic traditions, these divisions im-

* It may suffice to recall but one sign of the Republican atmosphere that so exasperated Eisenhower. During the 1958 Congressional elections, after Eisenhower had been in office for six years, the chairman of the Republican Congressional Campaign Committee, Representative Richard M. Simpson of Pennsylvania, took the occasion to make public his conservative distaste for the President's "modern Republicanism"—by urging GOP candidates for the House to "make known" any "disagreement with the President's policies." [39]

pose upon the President an endless labor of appeasement, so that he often finds the business of healing conflicts within his own party as complex as the work of soothing factions within his own executive branch.

The task was not always so intricate. By the long view of the Republic's history, Andrew Jackson stands forth as the first aggressive partisan of all the Presidents. As his two terms neared their end in 1836, Jackson was not only able to impose on a restive Democratic Convention Vice President Martin Van Buren as his personally chosen successor. He also could force the Vice Presidential nomination of a Richard M. Johnson, whose most arresting distinction was the candor with which he acknowledged a black mistress who had borne him two daughters. And ever since those furiously partisan days in the White House, the progressive slackening of a President's power to rule his party by edict may be judged by imagining the chance of any twentieth-century President trying to duplicate Jackson's audacity.

Perhaps more seriously the essential character of the two national parties, as amalgams of quite divergent philosophies, makes either an uncertain instrument to serve a coherent and decisive Presidential program. At critical times, indeed, it has seemed that the difference between the two parties means less than the distance between the Executive and the legislature, and at such times, when Senators or Representatives must choose between loyalty to their party or to their branch, the second allegiance often prevails. To see the case again from the perspective of the early Republic: James Polk was a sufficiently ardent Jacksonian Democrat to be known as "Young Hickory." He had served in the House of Representatives for seven successive terms and as Speaker for two years. He was a serious enough party loyalist, moreover, to become the first President to give official recognition to political parties in his inaugural address. Yet for all this—and barely a decade after "Old Hickory" had left the White House—Polk was telling his *Diary* of his woes as a party leader that future Presidents would understand all too well:

The truth is that the next Presidential election has divided the Democratic party in Congress into factions, each adhering to their favourites, and the effect is . . . to paralyze and defeat all my measures. In the Senate three or four Democrats who may dissent from the body of the party can defeat any measure. . . . Mr. [John C.] Calhoun can carry with him that many votes, and I now consider him the most mischievous man in the Senate to my administration. The people must be made to understand this state of things. With a nominal majority in each house, I am in truth in a minority in each.[41]

Finally, these particular signs of conflict point to the larger truth that the urgent interests of the Presidency and of the party are neither identical nor necessarily harmonious. Thus, it is inevitable that the personal reflection of any President often must turn on *his* prospective place in history, but it would be inconceivable for any party to pretend that *its* collective soul was fired by such a distant purpose. The most familiar clichés of modern Presidential rhetoric indicate this disparity of interests and ideals. Two Presidents as unalike as Dwight Eisenhower and Lyndon Johnson nonetheless echoed each other's public hope and resolve to be "President of *all* the people." Such pious aspiration has nothing in common with the competitive and combative mentality of a political party. The voice of a President may also quiver with some genuine feeling when he proclaims his supreme concern to be "not the next election but the next generation." But his party reverses such an order of preference: nothing matters more than the imminent mandate. At the same time, a harsh sort of law governs the relative intensity of conflict between a President and his party: the more positive his own political philosophy, the more negative the response of a party anxious to blur issues and avoid schisms. A Harding or a Coolidge could be relaxed partisans, therefore, since they had no personal convictions troublesome enough to vex their followers. But both the Republican Roosevelt and the Democratic Roosevelt had to pay the political price for their abrasive principles.

The unease of the President as party leader tends to become most unpleasant when he must function as the Republic's supreme purveyor of patronage. Here, an odd irony dates from the Constitutional Convention itself. The Founding Fathers abhorred all notions of political parties, of course, and they were spared any clear glimpse of the shape of partisan politics to come. But they entertained, with mixed emotions, an exaggerated vision of the future impact of Presidential patronage. Thus, James Madison's *Notes* on the convention reported the mildly cynical insistence of Gouverneur Morris that an effective Presidency needed a generous supply of "loaves and fishes" to enable the Chief Executive to "bribe the Demagogues." [42] At the same time, James Monroe sharpened his arguments against ratification of the Constitution, during the Virginia Convention of 1788, with warnings against the peril of the President's powers of appointment:

> Will not the influence of the President himself have great weight in his re-election? The variety of the offices at his disposal will acquire him the favor and attachment of those who aspire after them. . . . Members of the different branches of government . . . will esteem him, because they will be acquainted with him, live in the same town with him, and often dine with him. This familiar and frequent intercourse will secure him great influence. I presume that when once he is elected, he may be elected forever.[43]

All such forecasts on federal patronage, approving or forbidding, have proved rather wildly inflated. To be sure, some of the early Presidents—Thomas Jefferson quite as much as Andrew Jackson—put their appointive powers to systematic political use, and a Grant and a Harding allowed themselves to be used for the enrichment of their associates. But these were scarcely instances of historic consequence to the enlarging of Presidential power toward and through the twentieth century.

The fact is that this particular prerogative of the Presidency has turned out to be usually puny in effect, generally distasteful to Chief Executives, and frequently damaging to their serious purposes. Ever since the Pendleton Civil Service Act of 1883, the number of political appointments available to any President has kept steadily declining. When the Republican Party returned to power in 1952, after twenty years of exile from the White House, the GOP leaders suffered a kind of cultural shock with their unhappy discovery of the small number of political posts to dispense as spoils. But this arithmetic aside, the self-defeating nature of Presidential patronage had been noted a couple of generations earlier, with William Howard Taft's pithy lament that every White House appointment fatefully produces "nine enemies and one ingrate." As Taft went on to grieve, when he lectured on the Presidency a few years after leaving the office: "I cannot exaggerate the waste of the President's time and the consumption of his nervous vitality involved in congressional intercession as to local appointments." [44] Decades before Taft or the extension of civil service, moreover, Lincoln had confessed: "It is not the rebellion that is killing me, but the Pepperton post office." [45] And the earliest direct retort to Monroe's dread of a President "elected forever" had been issued by Polk, with his prediction that "no President" would "ever again be re-elected"—precisely because of the dilemma of patronage. In the mordant words of "Young Hickory":

> The patronage of the government will destroy the popularity of any President. . . . In every appointment which the President makes he disappoints half a dozen. . . . I sincerely wish that I had no offices to bestow. I cannot gratify all who apply, and it is certain from my experience that the dispensation of the public patronage is a weakening operation.[46]

The final phrase of Polk may be read to cover a multitude of stresses. By the judgment of almost any of the Republic's thirty-seven Presidents, "a weakening operation" truly describes at least some facet of *all* historic changes in their office: its involvement in the wide world and in the continental economy; its collision with the private sector and the federal bureaucracy; and its eminence in partisanship and patronage. Somehow, all these grants or gifts of power left it to seem as hard as ever, rather than any easier, for a President to "call" those elusive "spirits from the vasty deep."

IV

> Oh, if I could only be President and Congress too for just ten minutes! [47]
>
> —THEODORE ROOSEVELT

*   *   *

Although the authors of the Constitution misjudged some political matters, and never dreamed of others, that would shape the life of the Republic, there was one strategy wherein their aim was particularly true: the locking of the Executive and the legislature in lasting conflict. Among their final degrees, none was more firm than their denial to the Chief Executive of any power to affect the choice or the career of legislators. No problem was left more clouded than the question of how a President might bring his leadership to bear on Congress. And not even the ordinary citizen—with his constitutionally specified right to petition Congress—was left so emptyhanded as his President, trying to reach out to the legislature.

The design of the Founding Fathers was candid and calculated. As Hamilton stressed in one apologia in *The Federalist,* they were resolved to create something more formidable than "a mere parchment delineation of the boundaries" between the two branches.[48] To this end, they chose to rely on the less noble instincts in man, since they strongly suspected these to make up his greater part. After insisting that "ambition must be made to counteract ambition," Madison went on to deride any retort that such a prescription reflected poorly on human nature, asking bluntly: "What is government itself, but the greatest of all reflections on human nature?" [49] And during the convention debates, Gouverneur Morris had stated the Constitution's intent even more explicitly: "One interest must be opposed to another interest. Vices as they exist, must be turned against each other." [50] All their fears of the transcendent power of either Presidency or Congress, in short, made *their* ambition a near obsession. And they impressively succeeded.

Through Presidency after Presidency, the desired dissonance has risen, often thunderously. As the first President to use his popular appeal as a lash on Congress, Andrew Jackson heard himself vilified in language so harsh that Senator Daniel Webster's railing against him seemed mild for the times: "A Briareus sits in the centre of our system, and with his hundred hands touches everything, controls everything." [51] A few years later James Polk met his first serious rebuff while still in his first year in the White House, when six of his fellow Democrats joined the Whig opposition to reject his nominee for the Supreme Court, and one of the deserting Democrats in the

Senate, James Westcott from Florida, explained his defiance of his President thus: "The only way to treat an ugly negro who was unruly, was to give him a d———d drubbing at the start, and he would learn to behave himself." [52] Eight years after this, it was the Republicans' turn to "drub" their own President, Abraham Lincoln, with the Congress' insolent Wade-Davis Manifesto of 1864, proclaiming the legislature's sovereign right to lay down the terms of Reconstruction, as the two Congressmen declaimed: "The President . . . must understand that the authority of Congress is paramount . . . and if he wishes our support he must confine himself to his executive duties—to obey and execute, not make the laws—to suppress by arms armed rebellion, and leave political reorganization to Congress." [53] Belligerent as were these words of the Republican Radicals, they caught the political spirit that would prevail for decades, from Ulysses Grant to William McKinley, at the end of the century. In the 1880's, the reigning temper was accurately reflected in Woodrow Wilson's depiction of the President, in the sight of Congress, as "merely the executor of the sovereign legislative will," and in James Bryce's judgment on *The American Commonwealth:* "The President's wishes conveyed in a message have not necessarily any more effect on Congress than an article in a prominent party newspaper . . . and, in fact, the suggestions which he makes, year after year, are usually neglected, even when his party has a majority in both houses." [54] There had indeed been a prophecy of this whole era in the biting words of Emerson:

> The President has paid dearly for his White House. It has commonly cost him all his peace and the best of his manly attributes. To preserve, for so short a time, so conspicuous an appearance before the world, he is compelled to eat dirt before the real masters behind the throne.[55]

Nor did the end of the nineteenth century bring any end to Congressional delight in humbling the Presidency. Even after both Theodore Roosevelt and Woodrow Wilson had shown what a liberated Presidency might achieve, there came the degrading "normalcy" of 1920. This proved an ugly political spectacle, with the spotlight on the cabal of Republican Senators whom the New York *Times* dubbed the "Senate Soviet." These legislators bent upon putting the Presidency back in a modest place included the aristocratic and tenacious Henry Cabot Lodge from Massachusetts and the ambitious and gluttonous boss of Pennsylvania, Senator Boies Penrose. Standing between these two improbable figures appeared the more conventional shapes of such Senators as Charles Curtis from Kansas, who would serve as Hoover's Vice President, and Reed Smoot from Utah, who would help force the Smoot-Hawley tariff upon the hapless Hoover. The immediate Senatorial task at hand in 1920 was to lead the Republican Convention to break as sharply as possible with the past: since the start of the new century, these Senators had spent fifteen out of twenty years suffering the Presidential presumptions of a Roosevelt and a Wilson. Now fresh from their bracing triumph over Wilson and his Treaty of Versailles—and assured of control of nearly one-third of the Republican Convention's delegates—they proceeded to dominate their party's gathering in Chicago with such arrogance that one Republican governor announced his angry doubt "if this was a Republican Convention or just a Senatorial caucus." [56] Wholly undeterred, the Senators were guided by one political certainty: they knew, as William Allen White wrote, that "a hero in the White House was a bad thing for their party and their country." [57] Ultimately, they needed no further clue. To shun a hero was to seek a Harding.

The mentality of this Congressional coup was no new product of the political scene after World War I. All that was new was the opportunity to put old prejudices to fresh work. In the inviting circumstances, the war between the branches did not have to be waged as a defensive encounter to hold off Presidential advances on Capitol Hill: on the offense, the White House itself could be taken. Only a few weeks prior to the convention, Boies Penrose had shown how the whole exercise was a quite impersonal application of Senatorial logic. At a time when he had not yet focused on Harding, Penrose had tried to persuade his Senatorial colleague from Pennsylvania, Philander C. Knox, to consider his own prospects. "Knox," Penrose asked, "how would you like to be President?" When an incredulous Knox pleaded both old age and failing health,

Penrose blandly replied: "You won't need to do much work. We'll get a good hard-working Cabinet for you, and you can sit at the head of the table and run the show." [58] It would be hard to find a more frank expression of a Senator's visceral feeling that an ideal President must also be idle.*

The need and the clamor for Executive leadership during both the Great Depression and World War II naturally dampened such talk on Capitol Hill, but these historic crises did less than might have been expected to enlarge the outlook of most legislators. Even in the weeks of electrifying White House initiative immediately after FDR's inauguration, his urgent measure for government economies, sent to Congress on March 10, 1933, was spurned by enough Democratic leaders so that it passed the House only with the support of Republican votes. As for the course of Presidential-Congressional relations in the wake of the New Deal, the record from 1936 to 1963—more than a quarter of a century—was dominated by the obstinate resistance of the Congressional alliance between Republicans and Southern Democrats. So largely barren of creative legislation was this period that it could later be remembered only for two notable acts in the realm of domestic affairs: the Fair Labor Standards Act of 1938 and the Taft-Hartley Act of 1947.

These random instances suggest the rather continuing success with which a belligerent Congress has been able to harass—or harness—bold Presidential leadership. The Presidents have sought to return the fire, of course, at least with words. Slyly, Franklin Roosevelt more than once instructed a White House aide, "Give me a bill that I can veto": he meant to remind Senators and Representatives that he did not intend suffering Congressional foolishness gladly.[60] Combatively, Harry Truman repeated himself in 1954: "I've always said that the President who didn't have a fight with the Congress wasn't any good anyhow." [61] With wry humor, John Kennedy confessed, after less than two years in the

* The attitude of Penrose was restated in a conversation between the hesitant candidate, Warren Harding, and his political mentor from Ohio, Harry Dougherty, who later would be disgraced as Harding's acquisitive Attorney General. "Come down to brass tacks," Harding pleaded. "Am I big enough man . . . ?" To this, Dougherty snapped: "Don't make me laugh! The days of giants in the Presidential chair is passed [sic]. Our so-called Great Presidents were all made by the conditions of war under which they administered the office. Greatness in the presidential chair is largely an illusion of the people." [59]

White House, in a speech to the Economic Club of New York: "When I was a Congressman, I never realized how important Congress was. But now I do." [62] With reflective nostalgia, Lyndon Johnson—after he had left behind both the Congress and the White House—looked back to remember:

> For twenty-nine years Capitol Hill was my home. In all those years I thought I knew Congress fairly well. . . . But like other Presidents with previous experience on Capitol Hill, I found that once I reached the White House, the Congress appeared far less familiar. . . . Our relationship could never be the same. . . .
>
> No brief account can fully capture the complexity of this relationship, in which each partner contributes his own share of stubbornness, pride, hostility, warmth, suspicion, skill, and affection.[63]

The lasting tension of this conflict has required, as Hamilton foresaw, more than the "mere parchment" of constitutional scroll. The scheme of the Founding Fathers, no matter how carefully planned, has needed the help of both history and chance. And this has come in several ways.

A basic fact about the political lives of both Presidency and Congress—only partially determined by the Constitution—has been their representation of, and dependence on, altogether different constituencies. Each Senator speaks for some one of 50 states, all with interests by no means identical with the overriding interest of the Federal Union, and each Representative serves some one of 435 Congressional districts, all with power far greater than the President's in the overriding question of the next campaign.* Beside this throng, the President looms, as Truman said, as "the only lobbyist that all the 160 million people in this country have." [65] This role of the President as national tribune would have astonished many Constitution makers of 1787. But they opened the way for it by providing different terms of office for all involved: six years for Senators, four for Presidents, and two for Representatives. Since only one-third of the Senate is chosen in any election—and Repre-

---

* The crisp warning to any President from Lyndon Johnson reads: "It is daydreaming to assume that any experienced Congressman would ignore his basic instincts or his constituents' deepest concerns in quaking fear of the White House." [64]

sentatives rise or fall by largely provincial issues—the gears of the system almost lock against any movement toward a national majority speaking with one voice from both ends of Pennsylvania Avenue.

There have been other factors conspiring to give the Congress a character not only distinct and independent but also, most often, circumspect and conservative. The very size of the legislature— and the galaxy of regions and interests for which it stands—disposes it to be a critical rather than a creative body. Whereas such an assembly can find it hard to concur on a new initiative to resolve an old problem, it can find it easy to agree, for quite motley reasons, that a President's proposal is *not* a solution. At the same time, the operative principle of seniority in Congress has conferred the greatest power on Senators or Representatives from those areas, usually rural, where seats are safest, challenge tamest, and Presidential influence most irrelevant.

The political consequences of all this have often looked quite literally petrifying. In 1961, when the forty-three-year-old John Kennedy moved into the White House, his administration confronted the following array on Capitol Hill: in the House, a seventy-six-year-old chairman of the Rules Committee, a seventy-six-year-old chairman of the Armed Services Committee, an eighty-year-old chairman of the Appropriations Committee, and an eighty-five-year-old chairman of the Committee on Banking and Currency; and in the Senate, the head of the Banking and Currency Committee was seventy-two, the head of the Finance Committee was also seventy-two, and the head of the Appropriations Committee was eighty-two.[66] For any of the young men enlisted in the cause of the New Frontier, there appeared nothing here to allow much hope for a responsive Congress. And indeed, a full decade later— in 1971—the Congressional scene appeared much the same, but with one almost bizarre new accent. At this point in time, the sovereign state of Louisiana ranked twenty-ninth in population among all states in the Union, thirty-first in size, but clearly first in influence within the Ninety-second Congress. In the upper house, Senator Allen J. Ellender at seventy-nine years of age not only served as chairman of the Appropriations Committee but also as president pro tempore of the Senate—a position making him, too, third in the order of succession to the Presidency itself. The second Senator from Louisiana, Russell Long, served as chairman of the Finance Committee. In the lower house, the representation of the Pelican State included Hale Boggs, who had attained, by this thirtieth anniversary of his Congressional service, the post of Majority Leader; F. Edward Hébert, who had recently become chairman of the House Armed Services Committee; and Otto Passman, who had to be content, after twenty-five consecutive years in the House, with heading the subcommittee on foreign aid appropriations, which he viewed as a lamentable waste. Meanwhile, all the three largest states in the Republic—California, New York, and Pennsylvania—could claim the chairmanship of not a single Senate committee.[67]

These facts of Congressional life were not the passing signs of some political aberration in the life of the Republic. Instead, they marked a division between the Presidency and the Congress, ever since the Civil War, almost faithfully following the Mason-Dixon line. With respect to the Presidency, the eleven states of the Confederacy had produced no less than seven Chief Executives before their secession from the Union, but after Appomattox, the former slaveholding states sent no one to the White House until the administration of Harry Truman. Up to that time, furthermore, there had been eight Democrats elected President since the Civil War, but the vote of the supposedly solid South provided a crucial margin in only three of these elections. With respect to the Congress, however, the geographic equation has been entirely different. Ever since Reconstruction times, the monotonously solid Democratic delegations from the South assured these states seniority and eminence in Congress. When Woodrow Wilson was in the White House, for example, Southern legislators in the House headed forty-two of fifty-nine committees, while their chairmen in the Senate presided over all of the ten most important committees of the upper chamber. And this regional contrast between the Executive and the legislature has further accented their temperamental and ideological differences.

From the viewpoint of the White House, the theoretical device for muting these differences—the President's control of his own party—usually has proved unreal, of course. On the Republican side, the first year of the Eisenhower Presidency provided a study in the ir-relevance of this power. The new Chief Executive had won the White House in 1952 with the largest popular vote ever cast, a victory margin of more than 6,500,000 votes, and his party's capture of both houses of Congress. In a matter of months, however, "his" Senate partisans on Capitol Hill had chosen as their leader William F. Knowland of California, who had fought against Eisenhower at the 1952 nominating convention with enough fervor to declare: "We don't want any credit or any responsibility for *that* nomination." [68] The Presidential mandate did nothing to deter most Republican leaders in both Congressional chambers, moreover, from shaping party policies to respect Knowland's sentiments. In the Senate, there was Ohio's John Bricker, pressing his nearly successful amendment to strip the President of power to make executive agreements with other nations, and there was Wisconsin's Joseph McCarthy, pursuing his assault on the Department of State in particular and the executive branch in general, quite as venomously as when a Democrat had occupied the White House. In the House, there was New York's John Taber, leading his Appropriations Committee to cut the President's mutual security program by almost a billion dollars, and there was New York's Daniel Reed, scorning "his" administration's fiscal policies to urge a reduction in income taxes with such obstinacy that he came to be called "the Syngman Rhee of Capitol Hill." [69] . . . On the Democratic side, the legislative scene did not look any more disciplined under the two Presidents to follow Eisenhower. The Kennedy administration, beset by the familiar alliance of conservative Republicans and Southern Democrats, found itself depending on liberal Republican votes for victories on such basic matters as raising the minimum wage and enlarging the Rules Committee. And the Johnson administration—despite this President's 1964 election by the largest victory margin ever recorded—had to treat the Senate's most powerful Republican legislator, Illinois' Everett Dirksen, "almost as if the Republican leader were the Democratic leader in the Senate." [70]

From the viewpoint of Capitol Hill, of course, the abyss between Executive intention and legislative action has been hailed as sacred rather than vacant ground. Almost all that strikes a President as a sorry display of obstruction has been likely to strike the Congress as a heroic show of restraint. Individually, these Representatives and Senators enjoy more power than the members of any other legislative assemblage in the world. And collectively, they have learned, over many decades, various methods—some ingenious, some tedious —for elaborating their constitutional privileges.

They have largely perfected what Lyndon Johnson called "the art of delay." This power to do nothing at all, whenever they so will, has been applied with sometimes devastating effect—since the founding of the Republic. It was an apt omen that the first election of George Washington was deferred a month while legislators took their time meandering toward the capital city of Philadelphia to witness the electoral count. Even though the authors of the Constitution presumed the prompt need for executive departments to aid Presidential conduct of business, the first Congress procrastinated almost two months before allowing the first such creation, a Department of Foreign Affairs. And if the Father of His Country could be treated in such unfilial fashion, there could not be much surprise in the way the Congress—a couple of generations later—turned its back while the hapless James Buchanan fretted and implored as the Republic edged toward the precipice of civil war. During this fifteenth President's miserable last months in the White House, Congress effectively refused to equip him to govern, as it slashed his requests for military funds despite the fact that the Southern states were mobilizing for secession. The legislators also declined to give the President authority to call out militia or volunteers to cope with the insurrection in Charleston. Not until two months after South Carolina had left the Union, and the Confederacy itself had been proclaimed, was a bill for a limited call-up of militia even introduced. This bill was buried by a resolution—characteristically —to postpone.

Such events may seem remote in time or extreme in tenor, but they emphasize an enduring power of the Congress—to avoid and to evade—that rises from its very structure. A bicameral system itself compounds the problems of Presidential leadership. At certain times, a Chief Executive may be unsure which legislative chamber will prove more or less responsive. While the programs of both Roosevelts drew heavier fire from the Senate than the House, the Senate of the 1960's proved more sympathetic than the lower

chamber to the initiatives of John Kennedy and Lyndon Johnson.*
At all times, the devices of delay or opposition are quite different in each chamber. The Senate rejoices in the privilege of almost
unlimited debate and discussion, and the "windy satisfaction of the
tongue" can cause this body to take almost twice the time con-
sumed by the House to discharge the same amount of business.†
But while the House procedures make its floor debate more germane,
the delaying tactics here have become woven into the procedures
and controls of its three principal committees: Rules, Appropriations, and Ways and Means. The chairman of any one of these
House committees may frustrate a President so thoroughly as to be
the envy of all but the most powerful Senators. And the impatient
President who waits upon all this legislative babel and scuffle is
likely to share the judgment of Speaker Thomas Brackett Reed,
once pronounced upon a couple of his fellow legislators: "They
never open their mouths without subtracting from the sum of human knowledge."

All the artistry of Congressional delay is made easier by another
complicating fact of life on Capitol Hill. A President does not face
anything so simple as *the* Congress: such a cohesive assembly does
not exist. Instead, he must confront a confounding array of Senate
and House committees and subcommittees—each clutching its
proud prerogatives and special responsibilities, all responding to
chairmen as personally varied as the nation's Congressional districts
in their presumptions and procedures. The essentials of this committee system have been operative since the 1820's. And any President who has aggressively tried to override or outmaneuver it usually has learned the point of a favored Congressional maxim of

---

* There are several plausible explanations for this change toward a President's
greater rapport with the Senate. A White House with an organized system of
liaison with the Congress naturally finds it easier to work on a personal and individual basis with Senators than with the larger host of Representatives. To the
extent that foreign affairs dominate Executive-legislative relations, moreover, the
Senate is more likely than the House to scan such issues from a national viewpoint. And to the extent that a President's domestic program tends to be geared
to urban problems, the Senators, by virtue of their statewide constituency, are
more likely than the Representatives to be responsive.

† The House managed in the Eightieth Congress to get its business done in
1,226 hours and 30 minutes. But the Senate in 20 more legislative days took
2,164 hours and 30 minutes to accomplish virtually the same tasks. [71]

Lyndon Johnson: "You can *tell* a man to go to hell, but you can't *make* him go." [72]

To appreciate the full complexity of a twentieth-century President's ordeal with Congress' committees and leaders, it may serve to recall the relative simplicity of the methods of Thomas Jefferson, as he proved himself the first masterful manipulator of Congressional opinion. Courting the small legislative body of his day, before the Congress had found ways to seal its powers with precedent and tradition, Jefferson perfected, as never before or since, the custom of small legislative dinners at the White House. They were held almost nightly during the sessions of Congress. And as one historian has described these most effective of rituals:

> In the judgment of observant diplomats from abroad . . . they were the secret of Jefferson's influence. Political purpose pervaded the conception. . . . Rarely more than a manageable dozen guests were invited at the same time. . . . Guests received invitations penned in the President's own hand, often with a personal note. . . . All legislators were invited, most more than once during the course of a session. . . .
>
> The dinners could not have been better staged. A round table was used, thus avoiding a place of precedence for the President and putting him among peers, at the same time that it prevented separate, private conversations. The risk of distraction and eavesdropping by waiting servants was averted by Jefferson's installation of a dumbwaiter. . . . "You see we are alone," he announced, "and our walls have no ears" . . . "You drink as you please and converse at your ease," a bedazzled Senator wrote home. . . . Politics seemed somehow the one subject never discussed, talked around but not about. . . . To farmers he talked of agriculture; to classicists, of philosophy; to geographers, of Humboldt; to lawyers, of Blackstone; for naturalists he brought out his elegantly illustrated bird books from Europe.[73]

The frenetic world of the more modern Presidents leaves no time, of course, for such leisurely exercises in political seduction. Instead, the Chief Executive has had to contend with a Capitol Hill where—decade after decade—even a single legislator can rise and dare a President to prevail . . . a Sam Rayburn from Texas, first elected in 1913 along with Woodrow Wilson, who stayed to watch seven Presidents come and go; or a William E. Borah from Idaho, whose capacity for independence and caprice, over a period of a generation, gave him an influence extravagantly greater than the importance of any constituency he represented; or a Clarence Cannon from Missouri, whose political role in the House, beginning in 1911 as an aide to Speaker Champ Clark, found fulfillment as "the little President" dominating the Appropriations Committee for nearly twenty years, from before World War II until death relaxed his grip in 1964; or a Robert S. Kerr from Oklahoma, who managed to be rated the most powerful member of the Senate in the early 1960's, by virtue of his adroit use of the chairmanship of the Rivers and Harbors Subcommittee of the Public Works Committee, an obscure post from which he could dispense valuable favors to all his Senatorial colleagues. And the President adroit enough to steer a legislative course avoiding direct collision with such potential antagonists must still find his way past the snares that committees of lesser men constantly devise: a weighting of any bill with a rider designed to challenge the White House, a badgering inquiry into executive procedures planned to prove official incompetence, or a public hearing calculated to disparage Presidential policies, at home or abroad.

Any of these Congressional activities at any given time may, of course, help protect the best interests of the Republic against the worst instincts of a President. But whatever their nature and intent, craven or courageous, a President can do little to spare the executive branch many such tormentings. For him personally, moreover, the distress can become most acute when some official of the executive branch may journey to Capitol Hill to conspire as a slyly willing witness in the sabotage of White House policy. Thus, a by no means unusual exchange, at a House subcommittee's hearings on a specific appropriation, can read like this actual transcript:

> *Official:* If I go into those questions my personal opinions might conflict with the Budget Report. . . . But I want to make it clear to the committee that I have acquiesced in the limiting figure of the Budget.
>
> *Congressman:* You want this committee not to increase the amount of this Budget?

> *Official:* Oh, no. I recognize in Congress the power to do what it wants with this Budget.[74]

The moments made dreary by such a dialogue can be counted upon to set any President to pacing the Oval Office, pondering the majesty of his power, and echoing the plaint of John Kennedy: "There is no joy in it." One observant witness to this distraction of Presidents has been Bryce N. Harlow, who had the unusual experience of serving two Republican Presidents, whose lives in the White House were eight years apart. For all the years of the Eisenhower Presidency, and for the first two years of the Nixon Presidency, he served as the principal director of liaison with the Congress. And midway through the Nixon Presidency, Harlow looked back on both administrations and reflected:

> I suspect that there may be nothing about the White House less generally understood than the ease with which a Congress can drive a President quite out of his mind and up the wall. . . . He *expects* hostility or contradiction from *some* sources—like the leaders of the other party, or the fanatics in his own party, or the commentators from press or television. But what he is *not* prepared for is the readiness of Congress as a whole to cross him—or doublecross him.
>
> Perhaps strangely, a President subjected to this—as he always is—becomes more frustrated if he himself has served in the House or the Senate. An Eisenhower, for example, could be exasperated by Congressional stubbornness, but he could take it in stride, rather as the mischievous work of a few misguided individuals. But it has been much harder for a Nixon, because he was trained to think of House and Congress (when he was there) as institutions—and responsible ones. He finds their intransigence incredible. So he ends up almost crying out loud: "How can *they* be doing this to *me?*" And all this may be one more reason why an exposure to the legislative branch may not necessarily be the best preparation for presiding over the executive branch.[75]

Along with the chance of a President's previous Congressional experience, there are some other variables, often affecting the temper of White House relations with Capitol Hill. Thus, the onset of crisis, national or international, has found Congress—not always but usually—in a more docile mood toward the Chief Executive: the sense of need for personal leadership by a President, at such a time, becomes quickened by a collective desire, unarticulated but unmistakable, for as small a share as possible of the responsibility. A rather shrewd instinct for timing also tends to adjust Congressional responses during the course of even a rather uneventful administration: at the outset, a moratorium on acrimony has seemed prudent, until a Chief Executive risks commitment to controversy, but "it is usually toward the close of the first Congressional session that the buttons are taken off the foils." [76] All the while—and whether or not the President's own party represents a majority in the Congress—there may intrude matters of ideology and accidents of personality to change the pattern of relations. With a Warren Harding or Calvin Coolidge in the White House of the 1920's—and a George Norris and a Robert La Follette in the Senate—the Presidency scarcely loomed as the more innovative or progressive of the two branches. And the Republican inheritance of Whig distrust of Presidential leadership—as shown by the trials of Abraham Lincoln and Theodore Roosevelt—has meant a particular softness of Congressional support for almost any Republican in the White House.

A last, and sometimes decisive, variable turns on the wholly personal question of the patience and the persuasiveness that each President brings to his relations with the Congress. Here partisan tradition matters not at all, and individual disposition counts for everything. The Republican Theodore Roosevelt managed, for a considerable while, to court Speaker of the House Joseph Cannon with a man-to-man intimacy almost reminiscent of Jefferson's White House legislative dinners. As Cannon later wrote:

> After I became Speaker of the House, my conferences with President Roosevelt were frequent, two or three times a week when Congress was in session, and sometimes daily. The President would write a note . . . "Come up some evening for a long talk, Tuesday or Wednesday or Thursday evening about 9:30, if you can, so that we shall be free from interruption . . ." . . . We found it more convenient to meet in the evening . . . and it was then, sitting about the fire or later in his study, we talked things over until midnight.[77]

*   *   *

It strains the imagination to conceive of a Dwight Eisenhower, a half century later, gladly devoting even one evening a month to this kind of proselytizing. He would have found it a needless burden and bore. Accordingly, he became the first President to set up within the White House an office formally charged with Congressional affairs. This he did less because of his concern with them than because of his distaste for them.

The relative efficacy of these two Presidential styles for dealing with Congress may be judged by the contrast between the legislative achievements of these two Presidents. These records followed less from any constitutional ordinance, or from any Congressional obstinance, than from each man's personal preference and private decision. And when he authoritatively resolves at least this much, the man in the White House—as he bleakly surveys all the great powers and petty interests entrenched on Capitol Hill—may still go on seeing himself as something of a sovereign.

Seven

The Range of Presidential Power

The greatest difficulty lies in this: you must enable the government to control the governed; and in the next place oblige it to control itself.[1]

—JAMES MADISON

The year 1832 and the state of South Carolina confronted the seventh President, Andrew Jackson, with an ugly sort of challenge. The "fire-and-brimstone eaters" leading the local zealots of states' rights had summoned and dominated a state convention in Charleston to denounce an obnoxious tariff act, passed by the Congress in Washington, as "null, void, and no law." When the President replied with a proclamation reminding the citizenry that the Constitution "forms a government, not a league," the South Carolina legislature shouted its defiance of "King Andrew" and summoned volunteers to repel any federal "invasion." Raising the uproar to a new pitch, the governor of Virginia wrote the President to warn that any national troops dispatched to the South would have to march over his dead body. Although both Washington and Charleston managed to make some mutual concessions to blur for a spell the fateful issue of nullification, this truce was not reached before the President had made vividly clear his response to the threat of the Virginia governor. "If it becomes necessary for the United States troops to go to South Carolina," Andrew Jackson was said to have avowed, "I, as Commander-in-Chief of the army, will be at their head. I will march them by the shortest route. They may pass through Virginia. But if the Governor makes it necessary to pass over his dead body, it will be found that I have previously taken off both ears." [2]

There was more than the humor of the frontiersman in these possibly legendary words—and more, too, than the omen of a sundered national union. There was the gruff reminder that any President often will, occasionally must—and almost always can—effectively assert his powers in ways nowhere to be read in the articles of the Constitution or the debates of its authors. Whether the ghosts of the Founding Fathers shuddered or cheered over the militance of Jackson, they had only themselves to thank for such Presidential performances, since they had bequeathed a charter of power no more indisputably explicit about the nullification of national laws than about the mutilation of state governors. They had seemed to share, it is true, a general intuition that the integrity of the Union was intimately related to the authority of the Presidency. But the truth of this was left to be proved in real life by the very few men in the White House as resolute as a Lincoln.

Thanks to these slack terms, the nation-leading and nation-saving powers of the President have proved no more constant than clear. The President—*any* President—has some power to do almost anything, absolute power to do a few things, but never full power to do all things. From these obvious facts, there have followed some less obvious anomalies. In any political season, the President—*any* President—may discover that he can make a hostile nation politically tremble, while he can make a hostile Senator merely sneer. He may find his relations with American industry more exasperating than his relations with the Soviet Politburo. He might even launch a foreign war with more success than a party purge. And all through the span of his Presidential life—even as he brandishes his powers to appoint justices, assign ambassadors, veto laws, dispatch armies, lower tariffs, raise taxes, test bombs, or bully colleagues—he may feel most distraught in his ceaseless search for the secret to the trust of the ordinary, sovereign citizen, with no fame but one vote.

The Founding Fathers matched their reluctance to grant the Chief Executive many absolute prerogatives, of course, with their refusal to shackle him with many absolute restraints. For this reason, a Woodrow Wilson could plausibly talk of the President as enjoying "liberty" to be "as big a man as he can." The Presidential charter could be read, in fact, as even more sweeping: so far as constitutional writ is concerned, a President can be—short of treason or "other high Crimes"—not only the size, but also the character and manner of man he chooses to be. Rudely stated, he possesses the freedom to be "as big" a deceiver or demagogue, aggrandizer or sloth as the politics of the times may tolerate.

Yet for all the concern and caution of the men of 1787, the dynamic growth of the Republic has allowed no holding of a nice or near balance between frustration and freedom in the Presidency. Relentlessly, the authority of the office has come to swell with an array of resources quite beyond the more fearful imaginings of a Madison or a Jefferson. Even a Hamilton might grimace at some modern ways which Presidents have chosen to prove their "energy" and "despatch." And yet all the actions of even the most assertive and ambitious Presidents have had less to do with the final result than a few historical forces, beyond the cunning or control of any man.

The most decisive of these impersonal forces have been four in number.

First: the emergence of the once-small Republic as a world giant did not merely transform the range of Presidential power in quantitative terms. It almost redefined the office by compelling the man in the White House to accept as his supreme roles the Guardian of National Security and Maker of World Peace. And this radical change has largely come to pass because the very nature of modern warfare bears so little resemblance to any military concepts envisioned by the Founding Fathers.

From the Constitutional Convention to the First World War— and except for the convulsion of the Civil War—the habit of both the Republic's scholars and its leaders was to conceive of war as an enterprise of governments specifically, not of citizens generally. When the contributors to *The Federalist* wrote about Presidential authority over "the common defense," they were thinking about executive or administrative command of armed forces that consisted of volunteers or mercenaries and fought in an arena quite remote from the marketplace or the public forum. The modern experience of "total" or "general" war was wholly unknown, of course, and its complex challenges and dilemmas did not have to be faced until the year 1917, when all the *nation* truly went to war. This confrontation with the unprecedented was met—as so often it would be—by new delegation of extraordinary power to the

President. The endowment was conveyed, following the declaration of war, by a series of sweeping enactments that included the Lever Fuel and Fuel Control Act, the Selective Service Act, the Espionage Act, the Priority Shipment Act, and the Trading with the Enemy Act. These statutes spelled out the swift and general assumption that the President was the only citizen who could lead "a citizens' war." Accordingly, he was armed with powers broad and varied enough to regulate manufacturing and mining; or requisition foods and fuels; or take over factories or rail, water, telephone, or telegraph systems; or raise an army or control exports; or fix wheat prices or reorganize executive agencies; or license trade or censor mail or control enemy aliens or regulate the foreign-language press.

These were the first stark signs of what the advent of modern war meant for the modern Presidency. After the Second World War, the successive tricks and duels with Communist powers made this meaning ever more plain. Even without the pressures and passions of total war, the President came to be accepted—ever more unquestioningly—as the sovereign sage to define the nation's role in the world, to determine troop levels and weapons systems, to discern danger and to proclaim crisis, and—in the awesome process—to set peacetime defense spending at levels that made annual expenditures of $70 billion or $80 billion come to seem commonplace. So profoundly did all this ramify through America's society and economy that the general-President, Dwight Eisenhower, devoted his final Presidential address in 1960 to a grave warning against the insistent growth and threat of what he christened "the military-industrial complex"—whose final master must be, of course, the modern Commander in Chief.*

* The historian Henry Steele Commager has brought this long history up to date with this biting summation: "We had written into our Constitution the principle of the supremacy of the civilian over the military authority. The constitutional provision still stands, but has been in large part circumvented by the willing acquiescence of two successive commanders-in-chief [i.e., Lyndon Johnson and Richard Nixon] in the exercise of independent authority by the Pentagon and the CIA. . . . Much of the emergence of military power has been the consequence of drift rather than of calculation. When Washington became President, the United States Army consisted of fewer than 1,000 men and officers. Now ours is the largest and most powerful military establishment in the world. . . . We delude ourselves if we think the principle [of civilian supremacy] means what the Founding Fathers supposed it to mean." (*The New York Review*, October 5, 1972, p. 7.)

Second: the evolution of the Republic's original thirteen states into the world's industrial marvel has decreed the role of the President as the ultimate Protector of National Prosperity. From the first years of the New Deal, the guardian against Aggression has been no less expected to be the savior from Depression. Such grand expectation undoubtedly burdens and complicates modern Presidential life.* Nonetheless, the unavoidable responsibilities have brought with them unparalleled powers. These have been legislatively enshrined in such statutes as the Emergency Banking Act of 1933 and the Securities Exchange Act of 1934, whose sum of powers was accurately assessed by Clinton Rossiter as a call upon the President to prevent any future economic collapse "by declaring a state of financial martial law." [3] Lest this not suffice, the Employment Act of 1946 defined the Presidential role in the economic arena with memorable clarity and breadth:

> The Congress hereby declares that it is the continuing policy and responsibility of the Federal Government to use all practicable means . . . to coordinate and utilize all its plans, functions, and resources for the purpose of creating and maintaining in a manner calculated to foster and promote free competitive enterprise and the general welfare, conditions under which there will be afforded useful employment opportunities, including self-employment, for those able and willing to seek work, and to promote maximum employment, production, and purchasing power.

Throughout this statute, the President was expressly designated the key federal officer "to avoid economic fluctuations" and to promote prosperous times for all. He not only was called upon to make annual economic reports but also was provided with a Council of Economic Advisers—to give a uniquely authoritative ring to any of his economic pronouncements.

The steady movement of these powers toward the White House, moreover, has been a process that has cut across partisan and ideological lines. Thus, the Taft-Hartley Act of 1947, dedicated to fostering a "sound and stable industrial peace," came out of a Congress dominated by Republican leaders, notably the House's Joseph W.

* Cf. above, pp. 162–63.

Martin and the Senate's Robert A. Taft. This was a legislature eager to curtail rather than enlarge Presidential power. Yet the only *method* that the law's authors could find to achieve their ends was to endow the *President* with new authority to move against major strikes. While Harry Truman deplored the law's intent, he went on to invoke its powers no less than ten times.[4] When a Republican President next came to office—with a clear commitment to restrain federal trespassing on the private sector—he turned out to be Dwight Eisenhower. He was an economic conservative, indeed. But he was also the Presidential author of a message to Congress that accompanied his 1953 Economic Report and conveyed these assurances:

> The arsenal of weapons at the disposal of Government for maintaining economic stability is formidable. It includes credit controls administered by the Federal Reserve System; the debt-management policies of the Treasury; authority of the President to vary the terms of mortgages carrying Federal insurance; flexibility in administration of the budget; agricultural supports; modification of the tax structure; and public works. We shall not hesitate to use any or all of these weapons as the situation may require.

Third: a couple of events in the early part of the twentieth century contrived a fiscal revolution which—again, by no one's design or desire—made the old White House a new sort of citadel.

In the year 1913, the passage of the Sixteenth Amendment allowed Congress to institute a graduated income tax. This would prove to be the most lucrative source of revenue known to modern democratic government. Rather ironically, the innovation had not been pressed upon Congress by venturesome Presidents like Theodore Roosevelt or Woodrow Wilson but by the circumspect William Howard Taft—as unaware as any member of Congress of the amendment's ultimate political impact. The first such tax imposed, during the Wilson years, amounted to a meager 1 percent of net income up to $20,000. But the principle was established and ready for lavish use by future Presidents to meet future needs or crises. And without such a reservoir of funds, there hardly could have followed any grand dreams of Presidential programs in the realms of welfare, education, health, housing, and transport.

Eight years later the Congress passed the Budget and Accounting Act of 1921. Far from being any attempt to enlarge the powers of the Presidency, this had evolved merely from a long-overdue Congressional effort to bring order to chaotic fiscal procedures. As an earlier House committee study had made clear, the traditional budgetary procedures were so haphazard that expenditures were not rationally geared to revenues, the requests of agencies and departments of the executive branch were not subjected to coherent review, and the constellation of Congressional committees could not possibly bring discipline to a process so vagrant. Accordingly, the 1921 act established a new agency, the Bureau of the Budget—directly responsible to the President—with the power "to assemble, correlate, revise, reduce, or increase the estimates of the several departments or establishments." The principal *purpose* of this act was an uncontroversial quest for "efficiency and economy" in federal fiscal planning. The principal *effect* of it, however, was wholly different. It offered a Congressional confession of inability to assume responsibility for preparing a national budget, and it assigned this task to the Presidency, thereby arming the office with new and commanding power for both its struggle with Congress and its control over executive departments and agencies.

With the passage of a little time, the consequences of such events as these reached even further. The familiar balances within the federal system, throughout the fifty states, were upset. More and more, the governments of states and of major cities found the demands upon their services—from schools and police to garbage and transport—far exceeding their sources of revenue. As these sources were drawn off by the federal government, the search for local solvency almost inevitably had to turn toward some scheme of federal revenue sharing. And once more, all political paths pointed toward the White House—without anyone having intended any such thing.

Fourth: there may have unfolded no sequence of developments to change the Presidency so effectively as the politically neutral— and relentless—force of modern technology. And of this force, there appear three major examples.

The character of *nuclear weaponry* drastically recast the nature of the Republic's strategic planning and decision. Even as this sophisticated armament made a President dependent on the expertise of scientists and soldiers, it also made the Congress and the nation singularly dependent on *him* and *his* final judgment. Accordingly, the age of atomic weaponry was inaugurated in 1945 by President Harry Truman's decision to let the atomic bombs fall on Hiroshima and Nagasaki, and his right to make such a wartime decision met virtually no immediate challenge. The following year brought peace, along with the Atomic Energy Act of 1946—and its laconic words outlining a new and awesome Presidential power:

> The President from time to time may direct the Commission (1) to deliver such quantities of fissionable materials or weapons to the armed forces for such use as he deems necessary in the interest of the national defense or (2) to authorize the armed forces to manufacture, produce, or acquire any equipment or device utilizing fissionable material or atomic energy as a military weapon.

Against the background of such events and laws, there remained few citizens—by 1950—ready to question whether it should be the President's prerogative alone to order forthwith the development of the hydrogen bomb. For as it could most plausibly be asked: where else in the constitutional system might such a decision be weighed and made—reflectively, discreetly, and swiftly?

The modern network of *mass media* has given the Presidency an almost revolutionary opportunity to create, to control, to distort, or to suppress the news. As the cases of Lyndon Johnson and Richard Nixon have shown, a President's manipulative use of television by no means can guarantee his personal popularity or credibility.* But there was no earlier time in the Republic's history when a President could stage for all the nation such a drama as Richard Nixon's pilgrimage to Peking—with more than 120 television correspondents, producers, technicians, and engineers enlisted to report to the citizenry every Presidential act or word, frown or smile. And still more awesome is the *kind* of Presidential power underlying

* Cf. above, pp. 160–61.

and provoking such an impassioned indictment of the Nixon Presidency as these words of Henry Steele Commager:

> Even more dangerous than secrecy and deception . . . is the deliberate effort of the Administration to intimidate the press and the television networks. . . . Never before in our history has government employed so many methods for manipulating and distorting the truth as during the past decade, not even during the First and Second World Wars. . . . No other administration in our history has practiced deception . . . as has the Nixon Administration. Where totalitarian regimes invented the technique of the Big Lie, this Administration has developed a more effective technique, that of lies so innumerable that no one can keep up with them.[5]

Whether or not this particular indictment of one Presidency be wholly true or fair, the critical fact is that it *could* be true of *any* Presidency—precisely because of the nature and power of the national media. Such a network of communications, so rich in facilities for the widest circulation of "innumerable lies," alone makes possible any Presidential "technique" for massive misleading. Such a network—precisely because of its own vaunted power and its own vested interests—must also be sensitive and vulnerable to the variety of attacks that any administration may launch: through public critiques of its professionalism or through private threats to its employees, through antitrust actions against television networks or through statutory control over their licenses to exist. And quite possibly there can never be a man in the White House certain to reject at all times any temptation to bring such weapons into play.

The advent of *jet transport,* finally, has done more to enlarge life—and excite ego—in the Presidency than in any other office in the land. It was not until 1960 that a Presidential candidate could campaign on the nation's Atlantic coast *and* its Pacific coast—on the same day. With this, there came the ease of even longer flights that any President could take to distant governments and peoples, on all continents and for any motives. On such occasions, all the White House may seem airborne to attend the Chief Executive: Cabinet members and personal staff, counselors and cooks, generals and secretaries, Secret Service and press corps. At his will and call, he may fly around the globe on a path quite his own: first to the helicopter outside his doors on the White House lawn, next to the military base where Air Force One waits, then into the air lanes cleared for his flight, and onward to the meeting with the statesman—or the throng—of his choice who await his arrival, his waving arms, and his resolving words. In such a world, what President any longer greatly needs a Department of State—or its far-flung ambassadors and ministers—for the supreme moments of negotiation or exhortation? These moments become *his*. For it is both expedient and exhilarating for *him* to play the heroic role in the historic act.

*   *   *

There has been another set of twists and turns in the Republic's life to help a President appear "as big a man" as he can. These have been matters of historical luck. For they amount to the various reasons why the other two branches of the federal government—for all their own imposing and separate powers—so often have *not* challenged or restrained the Presidency.

The case of the Supreme Court approaches something of a study in institutional timidity. There have been occasional confrontations with the modern Presidency, to be sure, when the Justices have known moments of bravura—as when they enraged Franklin Roosevelt, by striking down early New Deal statutes, or when they dismayed Dwight Eisenhower, by striking down school traditions of segregation. But these have been rare exceptions to what one student of the Presidency has called a "lesson of history"—namely:

> Where exercises of extraordinary power are involved, the Court restrains itself and not the President. . . . The Court's primary function in checking a strong President is to act as a symbol of restraint, a moral force, and a constant reminder of established principle—a function which is by no means unimportant—but with regard to executive power, Article II of the Constitution is what the President, and not what the Court, says it is.[6]

The proofs of this have appeared in a couple of ways. In the first place, the pertinent decisions of the Supreme Court, over the generations, have tended to enlarge rather than to narrow the range of Presidential power. Among the more notable of these have been the Prize Cases (1863), approving Lincoln's blockade of the Southern states; *Myers v. U.S.* (1926), assuring full Presidential removal power over the executive branch; and *U.S. v. Curtiss-Wright Export Corp.* (1936), emphasizing Presidential authority in foreign relations. In the second place, the Court has shied, almost embarrassingly, from any serious challenge to the wartime powers of the Commander in Chief, whether brandished by Abraham Lincoln or Woodrow Wilson or Franklin Roosevelt. It is probably not too harsh to say that the judiciary's retreats have been most abject precisely when the Executive's actions have been most arrogant—from Lincoln's suspension of habeas corpus to Roosevelt's consignment of more than 110,000 Japanese-Americans to their "relocation centers" during World War II.* Or as Professor Edward S. Corwin unhappily concluded: "It is the lesson of these cases that in the war crucible the more general principles of constitutional law and theory . . . become highly malleable, and that even the more specific provisions of the Bill of Rights take on an unaccustomed flexibility." [7]

As with the principles of law, so also with the practices of Congress: they have proved, quite often, unpredictable and unreliable as constraints upon Presidential initiative and power. If the Republic's highest court has left even the Bill of Rights to operate sometimes with "an unaccustomed flexibility," the Senate and the House have displayed what might be called an unusual perversity in asserting themselves most slackly when they might have been expected to act most sternly.

This has been the case with even the venerable Congressional power of the purse. From the first—indeed, from the earliest of Hamilton's polemics—this authority was conceived to be critical and irresistible. It should "be regarded," as Hamilton wrote in *The Federalist,* to be "the most complete and effectual weapon with which any constitution can arm the immediate representatives of the people. . . ." [8] But it has proved to be no such thing. Instead, there have arisen remarkably few occasions since the year 1789 when a stubborn denial of funds by Congress has frustrated a major program or purpose urgently pressed by any President.

The historical pattern has been that the times of internal or international stress—which are also those times when some check upon frantic spending has most been needed—generally have found Congress racing the President to spend a little faster to resolve the

* Cf. below, pp. 232–33.

crisis a little sooner. In terms of the national economy, as the federal responsibility has steadily grown, the prevailing Congressional habit has been not so much to limit the full sum of public largesse as to assure each Congressman's own constituency a fair share in the general dispensation. In terms of international commitments and military budgets, the House of Representatives, especially after the Second World War, has been ready, more often than not, to inflate rather than reduce appropriations sought by the Executive. Any programs plausibly related to "national security" or "national prestige" have found the House almost eagerly responsive—as befitting its rural and conservative political temper, with its preoccupation with the virtues of patriotism and the vices of Communism.

The Senate also has shown a capacity for a sort of discreet subservience, whenever its withholding of money might thwart Presidential policy. In the case of the Vietnam War, the upper House almost classically demonstrated its preference for disputing Presidential policy with rhetoric rather than action. In 1967 an Associated Press survey reported forty out of eighty-four responding Senators opposed to President Lyndon Johnson's Southeast Asia policy, but the same year found only three of these Senators actually voting against a $12 billion supplemental appropriation to carry on the war in Vietnam.[9] As one Washington reporter of Senate ways observed:

> While opposition to any other legislation is within the rights of a senator, voting against any defense bills is like civil disobedience, a congressional version of not paying taxes. . . . It is part of the whole confusion between President as Executive and as Commander-In-Chief that has resulted in the logic that even if a war was started wrongly, it is unpatriotic to force a President to stop it before he is ready.[10]

Such surrender of "the power of the purse," moreover, marks nothing new in the ways of the legislature. During the Second World War, the Congress appropriated billions of dollars for a wholly unknown project, which turned out to be the development of the atomic bomb. Almost a half century earlier, it had found itself acquiescing in underwriting the famous dispatch by Theodore

Roosevelt of the Great White Fleet on its journey around the world. And still another half century before, Lincoln had spent some $2,000,000 of public funds, as the Civil War began, wholly without prior Congressional authority or subsequent reproach.[11] *

The failure of "the power of the purse" to prove reliably effective has been only one of several of the Founding Fathers' expectations about Congress that went awry. The whole Senate had been envisioned, for example, as a kind of Presidential council of wise men in the general formulation and direction of foreign policy. As one of the authors of the Constitution, Rufus King, assured the Senate itself, some thirty years after the Philadelphia convention: "The Senate are the Constitutional and the only responsible counsellors of the President. And in this capacity the Senate may, and ought to, look into and watch over every branch of the foreign affairs of the nation." [12] But long before these sentiments were sounded, they had realistically been overrun by events—not least among them, the simple growth in the Senate's size. Just from 1789 to 1795, the Senate membership had risen from twenty-two to thirty-two, an increase already sufficient to make unworkable any notion of the body serving as a confidential and coherent council. Meanwhile, the same years had seen the genesis of what would be known as a "Cabinet"—a logical usurper of the special place earlier planned for a small Senate. Eventually, the growing population of the upper house made more and more impracticable its sharing in the substantive development of foreign policy, so that its role in treaty-making became essentially not a creative power but a veto power, with the President left largely free to negotiate as he wished with other nations. At the same time, the whole of the Congress tended to dilute specifically Senatorial authority in an-

---

* Over the generations, the Presidency also has helped further to blur "the power of the purse" by the simple refusal to spend certain funds appropriated by the Congress. This practice has dated at least from Thomas Jefferson's refusal to spend money authorized for Mississippi River gunboats at the turn of the nineteenth century. Of the modern Presidents, almost all have impounded or frozen a percentage of his annual budget. By the end of the thirty-seventh President's first term, however, Richard Nixon had pressed this strategy to unprecedented lengths, with the impounding of sums estimated to exceed $12 billion. Despite much predictable outrage on Capitol Hill, the White House insisted, through its Director of Management and Budget, that the authority to withhold funds amounted to "an absolutely essential right for every President to have." (New York *Times,* January 22, 1973.)

other way: by substituting for treaty ratification the looser process of Congressional resolution. In 1845, Texas was formally annexed by such a simple resolution (after the Senate had rejected a treaty drafted to the same end). And in 1921, after the bitter struggle over the Treaty of Versailles and the League of Nations, it was not a Senate action but a Congressional resolution that officially terminated the First World War.[13]

Both the size of the Senate and its devotion to unreined oratory help somewhat to explain its frequent failure to dispute or rebuff a President, much less anticipate him. With respect to the Vietnam War, again, it could be said that—while the Senate almost surely would not have started this war—its hundred members proved equally incapable of forcing an end to it. The hazy character of any effort to do so once was rather sadly suggested by an aide to one of the war's more vocal critics, Senator Edward Kennedy, who summarized Senatorial striving thus: "The best way is to *persuade* the President. We don't make executive decisions; it is not the nature of the legislative branch. The Senate never does anything clear-cut or definitive." [14] In the light of such philosophizing, it becomes easy to understand how Lyndon Johnson could tease one of the three Senators actually challenging funds for the Vietnam War, by saying to a Senator from Alaska, Ernest Gruening: "I don't care what kind of speeches you make as long as you don't vote against the appropriations." [15]

Whatever its institutional reasons, the recurrently reticent temperament of Congress—always more apparent when problems look more awkward—can encourage any President to seize the chance to set his own course in most spheres of policy. One aspect of this accommodating spirit in the legislature was summed up in 1972 by the Senate's Democratic majority leader, Mike Mansfield: "There are members of Congress who are called 'the President's men.' In their view, everything a President recommends is right. Everything a President does is right." [16] This allusion to "the President's men" on Capitol Hill was not confined to members of the President's own party, for there always are Senators and Representatives of both parties sensitive to the pleasures of knowing a President's favor— be it personal, social, or political. At the same time, the Senate's own grave and courtly regard for itself, as a group and as an institution, can serve to muffle the kind of debate that might too rudely challenge a President or his apologists within the chamber. Thus, even during the sometimes passionate discussion of the Vietnam War, the fraternal amenities commonly prevailed over the ideological differences—as when Oregon's Senator Mark Hatfield could punctuate a speech, on behalf of his amendment to end the Indochina war, with his tribute to one of the amendment's most dedicated opponents, Mississippi's Senator John Stennis:

> Mr. President, I have listened carefully to the comments and the presentation made by the Senator from Mississippi, the chairman of our Armed Services Committee. I am grateful for the relationship that we have here as colleagues on this floor. . . . Often, people from outside the Senate organization cannot understand how men can deeply, vociferously, and intensely differ on issues and still maintain mutual respect and personal friendship. I think of all the men and one lady with whom I have served in this body, this is always one of my most reiterated thoughts as it relates to my personal relationship with the Senator from Mississippi.[17]

When the voices of Senate critics rise no more "vociferously" than this, the Presidents at the far end of Pennsylvania Avenue have no cause to quake at the sound of forensic thunder on Capitol Hill.

The sum of all these habits of Congress—as it braces or bows before the force of any Presidency—points toward a concluding paradox. There is no doubt that the members of this Senate and House belong to a body whose leaders can exercise, indeed, more political influence than those of any other legislature in the world. But there also is probably no other Republic in the world where one national party, year after year, may commandingly control the legislature—but not the Executive—and be known quite simply as the party *out* of power.

I I

We elect a king for four years, and give him absolute power within certain limits, which after all he can interpret for himself.
—SECRETARY OF STATE WILLIAM H. SEWARD

A vital part of the history of the Presidency has been written in almost invisible ink. All the while that the carelessly conspiring forces of change have so constantly enlarged the office, the newest acquisitions of the greatest powers have gone frequently unrecorded or largely unobserved. These powers merely have come to *be,* ready and waiting for use by leaders with keen enough eye to see them. And perhaps the greatest of these nameless, but matchless, resources have been three: the power to *focus* issues, the power to *blur* issues, and the power to *make* issues.

There may be no authority more subtle or more sovereign in any democracy than the power to bring into focus those matters of state that the citizenry must think about and care about. Such a capacity verges on a mastery of the currents of public opinion, and the opportunity to fill such a role has increasingly become, through the Republic's history, a President's great chance and hope. This hope did not have to wait for radio or television. Even before the age of a mass circulation press, whose impact was so quickly understood by Theodore Roosevelt, the intrinsic power of the President in this area had been clearly stated by Henry Jones Ford:

> The evidence which our history affords seems conclusive of the fact that the only power which can end party duplicity and *define issues* in such a way that *public opinion can pass upon them decisively*, is that which emanates from presidential authority. It is the rule of our policies that no vexed question is settled except by executive policy. Whatever may be the feeling of Congress towards the President, *it cannot avoid an issue which he insists upon making.* [18]

The other edge to this same truth is equally important: there arises only rarely an issue that can summon legislative attention, much less action, if the President does *not* want to make the issue *his.* With a rather different perspective, some learned studies have argued that the technical origins of much "Presidential" legislation really can be found in germinal laws first proposed in Senate or House.† Some such legal lineage can often be traced, in fact,

* Italics added.
† For example: "The President, Congress, and Legislation," by Lawrence H. Chamberlain, *Political Science Quarterly* (March, 1946).

through many realms of national policy—from reciprocal trade agreements to farm price supports, from restrictions on child labor to restrictions on public utilities. Yet the very venerability of much of this legislation shows how long it can languish in one or another legislative chamber, until a Presidential initiative moves it toward living law. Indeed, any new President might find it hard to discover a legislative formula so pristine that it had not been at least even slightly foreshadowed by some forgotten statute or some unremembered speech in Senate or House, months or years earlier. But the telling point is the certainty that once such legislation becomes *his*, publicly and forcefully, it no longer *can* be forgotten.

All that a President can do to *blur* issues appears scarcely less impressive. This faculty can be politically priceless for the obvious reason that so many Presidential dilemmas may be promptly resolved only at high personal cost. In any arena, from civil disturbance to foreign crisis, these challenges may suddenly arise to test a President's capacity to decide and to act. Thus pressed, the Chief Executive may need and want nothing so much as a chance to buy time. And there has unfolded more than one way for him to do this.

In the realm of foreign policy, a Presidential appeal to the virtues of bipartisanship, real or contrived, has proved almost consistently effective. In 1940, a year before the nation's full involvement in World War II, Franklin Roosevelt gave the Republican Party a stunning lesson in this exercise. Just four days before the opening in Philadelphia of the Republican National Convention, FDR announced the appointment to his Cabinet of two of the nation's eminent Republicans. Henry L. Stimson, named to be Secretary of War, had held the same post under William Howard Taft and had been Secretary of State under Herbert Hoover; and Frank Knox, the new Secretary of the Navy, had been the GOP Vice Presidential candidate in the last Presidential election. These nominations to the nation's highest military offices were not only designed to convey a White House vision of national unity—a unity benignly transcending all partisan politics. They were also calculated to stifle any Republican charges against administration military policies as too drastic or too sluggish—an immunity thoroughly pleasurable for the White House.

After World War II, the anesthetizing appeal of bipartisanship did not need the contrivance of coalition Cabinets to dull debate and discourage dissent. It sufficed to summon a generally enthralled citizenry to behold the specter of world Communism. The cliché that national politics and all their conflicts ended "at the water's edge" became a sacrosanct axiom, before which Republicans and Democrats alike duly genuflected. A free society had to prove itself (so it was seriously argued) as capable of concert and unity as any totalitarian society. And from this proposition, it was a short and easy step to the dogma that only the Presidential judgment upon these matters was surely to be respected and probably to be revered.

In the realm of domestic affairs, the tactics of Presidents striving to obscure great issues have been somewhat different but comparably successful. Here a favored recourse has been the creation of Presidential commissions. Whether the pressing matter has been drug abuse or national defense or campus unrest or population growth, the modern Presidents of both parties have found the device of a Presidential study group to be a safe way to gain time and dampen criticism. Politically, the advantages of this action are several: it immediately dramatizes Presidential concern; it indefinitely defers Presidential decision; and it inevitably leaves a President free, in the end, either to applaud heartily the judgment he always wanted or to reject bravely the conclusion he never would have accepted from the outset. In Senate subcommittee hearings on Presidential commissions, presided over by Edward Kennedy in 1971, the Massachusetts Senator tartly summed up the familiar Presidential routine as "a new Commission, a new report, and a new round of lethargy." This would not seem exaggerated, in view of the evidence that, from 1965 to 1970, four Presidential commissions—on crime, violence, riots, and unrest—had produced massive reports that excited minimal response from any source, least of all from the White House. Under Richard Nixon, a couple of Presidential commissions, on Population Growth and Drug Abuse, did evoke response of a sort: the Chief Executive publicly lamented their conclusions. And the history of such Presidential blunting of issues would apparently confirm Senator Kennedy's conclusion: "It seems as though most Presidential commissions are merely so many Jiminy Crickets chirping in the ears of deaf Presidents, deaf officials, deaf Congressmen, and perhaps a deaf public." [19]

As further evidence of the diversity of Presidential powers, there is much important, but not much new, in all this. Even a President with as little adroitness as Herbert Hoover understood these particular stratagems. As he wrote in his *Memoirs:*

> There is no more dangerous citizen than the person with a gift of gab, a crusading complex and a determination "to pass a law" as the antidote for all human ills. The most effective diversion of such an individual . . . is to associate him on research committees with a few persons who have a passion for truth. . . . I can now disclose the secret that I created a dozen committees for that precise purpose.[20]

Or as a verse in *Punch* many years ago suggested, with regard to administrations in London as well as in Washington:

> If you're pestered by critics and
>   hounded by faction,
> To take some precipitate, positive
>   action,
> The proper procedure, to take my
>   advice, is
> Appoint a commission and stave off
>   the crisis.[21]

The third of a President's more distinctive and less discerned powers amounts to his ability not merely to focus, nor clearly to obscure, but plainly to *make* critical issues. This could as well be called the power to make the Republic face the accomplished fact. Once again, there is nothing strikingly modern here: the reality was conceded as long ago as the rationales of Alexander Hamilton. "The legislature is still free to perform its duties, according to its own sense of them," Hamilton vigorously professed, only to admit softly: "The executive . . . may establish an antecedent state of things, which ought to weigh in the legislative decision." [22]

A serious commentary on Presidential power may never have been stated more laconically than this bland acknowledgment of the

Chief Executive's capacity to bring about, on almost any front, "an antecedent state of things." As a kind of political tradition, the readiness to accept a Presidentially arranged order of "things" may carry back as far as the young Republic's acquiescence in George Washington's quiet conversion of the "ceremony" of receiving foreign emissaries (as Madison modestly defined the matter) into the sovereign prerogative of giving or withholding diplomatic recognition to any government on earth. Once the rite was made a right, the President could decree the Republic's posture toward all world upheavals, from the French Revolution through the Russian Revolution and onward. In terms of military commitment, the long trail of Presidentially accomplished facts has run almost unbroken from Thomas Jefferson's dispatch of American war vessels against the Barbary pirates in 1804 through Lyndon Johnson's dispatch of armed forces to the Dominican Republic or into the quagmire of Vietnam. And as for proclamations of national policy, the same freedom to "establish" the Republic's destiny has been indulged, decade after decade, from the purchase of Louisiana in 1803 to the devaluation of the dollar in 1972.

The Executive art of confronting the nation, and more particularly the Congress, with thoroughly accomplished facts has taken on at least two modern refinements, particularly favored since World War II. The first of these—designed to vitiate the *substance* of Senatorial authority in treaty-making—has been the Presidential recourse to negotiating its own executive agreements. And the second —designed to honor the *form* of the legislature's role in foreign policy—has been the Presidential ritual of inviting Congressional resolutions in support of Executive decisions.

The Presidency's relish for executive agreement with foreign powers, as a way to evade the test of Senate approval of formal treaties, has grown into a kind of institutional addiction. In all the 150 years of the Republic prior to the start of World War II in 1939, the nation entered into 799 treaties and 1,182 executive agreements —a ratio of roughly 1½ to 1. In just the 25 years following World War II, the records of the Department of State show the comparable figures to be 368 treaties and 5,590 executive agreements— a ratio of some 15 to 1. In addition, there appear to be more than 400 wholly secret agreements whose substance the State Department has refused to reveal.[23] Nor can it be doubted that these agreements commonly entail military commitments that could lead to war as readily as any formal treaty. Such accords have ranged from the original agreement with Spain in 1953, for the construction and use of air and naval bases, to the series of undertakings throughout the 1960's that amounted to the prosecution of undeclared war in Laos. In the latter case, the American public had virtually no knowledge of the matter until a Senate Foreign Relations subcommittee, defying the wishes of the State Department, revealed in detail how American planes based in Thailand were bombing northern Laos, the Central Intelligence Agency was directing military campaigns by Meo tribesmen, and the nation was spending millions of dollars for military assistance to Prince Souvanna Phouma—all actions which clearly violated the formal accords on Laotian neutrality set forth at the Geneva Conference of 1962.[24]

As if to atone for this systematic undermining of Congressional responsibility, the executive branch has increasingly used a quite different procedure to show a harmless sort of concern for legislative pride. It was this rather quaint concern that inspired a Republican administration to present the legislature with its Formosa Resolution in 1953 and a Democratic administration to contrive the Tonkin Gulf Resolution in 1965. The authorizations of military action, predictably and overwhelmingly voted in both instances, had no substantive effect beyond allowing the executive branch to profess a sense of constitutional virtue—and proclaim a spirit of national union—as it proceeded with its own previously fixed intent. The personal hazard, as well as the political unlikelihood, of valiant Congressional resistance to Presidential will, at a moment of alleged threat to the Republic's security, were highlighted by one postscript to the Tonkin Gulf action. Six years later, a repentent Congress came to feel sufficient grief over its uncritical acceptance of this resolution to revoke formally the authority given. But by this date there was no redress from another kind of judgment: the only two Senators voting against the original 1965 resolution had been promptly voted out of office at the next election.

The historic strengthening of Presidential power thus can be traced, again and again, to the impact—or the exploitation—of political crisis, be it wholly real or largely exaggerated. This particular method of aggrandizement also dramatically quickened its pace in the years following World War II. For the newly grand role of the Republic in world affairs stirred and spread the popular and emotional belief that the nation had to learn to "live with" crisis; and this seemed inescapably to mean that it also had to "live with" a Presidency of steadily swelling power. Or in the mordant words of Professor Alfred de Grazia, an emphatic critic of Presidential presumption:

> To expand the domain of the presidency further, the whole area of governmental powers has been opened up by the doctrine of the age of crisis. The "age of crisis," the "permanent crisis," the "cold war," the "critical times"—all demand mobilization of the country for decisiveness, speed and dispatch. Again occurs the premise that these abilities are incorporated in the presidency. . . .
>
> The problems of today are perhaps grave and critical, but none of them are likely to be solved by collapsing the decision-making process by some months to save time. The French had a decade to save the whole of Indochina from the Communists; the United States had another decade to save South Viet Nam. Never during this period could it be said that the executives of either government revealed some intrinsic advantage over the legislature, or were compelled to act urgently and without recourse to deliberative councils. . . .
>
> In this age . . . it is a growing practice to create crisis. And at creating crisis the presidency has no peer. It has the instruments. It can stir up the press, call White House conferences, begin "crash programs," point with alarm to underprivileged people of different sorts, and altogether discover innumerable pockets of crisis in the world. . . . [And with respect to] the executive establishment, the crises of today are the programs of tomorrow.[25]

Even before the general popularity of the notion of "permanent crisis," however, such a President as Franklin Roosevelt had often proved how the White House could seize the instant of crisis like a sword. Two occasions in 1942, the first year of forthright involvement in the Second World War, may serve to illustrate. In February, Roosevelt issued Executive Order No. 9066 to meet the imagined danger of sabotage on the West Coast by colonies of Japanese-Americans. By the terms of this order, the lives of these residents, overwhelmingly native-born citizens, were declared subject to "whatever restrictions the Secretary of War or the appropriate military commander may impose in his discretion," and the "discretion" thus authorized by the Commander in Chief peremptorily removed more than 110,000 of these people from their homes and farms to the confinement of what were euphemistically called "relocation centers." With characteristic alacrity, the Congress hastened to pass a supporting resolution, while the Supreme Court dismissed two challenges to the executive order on the grounds that its consequences fell within the proper authority of President and Congress "acting in cooperation." And there were some constitutional scholars who viewed these events as probably the most ugly and unprincipled display of deference to the power of the Commander in Chief in all the life of the Republic.* [26]

The second Rooseveltian brandishing of "crisis" followed less than seven months later. This came in the form of a summons to Congress whose demanding tone and argument were perhaps without precedent. To counter spiraling inflation, FDR called for prompt repeal of an objectionable provision of the Emergency Price Control Act. But the Presidential threat—and doctrine—were proclaimed thus:

> I ask the Congress to take this action by the first of October. Inaction on your part by that date will leave me with an inescapable responsibility to the people of this country. . . .
> The American people can be sure that I will use my powers with a full sense of my responsibility to the Constitution and to my country. The American people can also be sure that I shall not hesitate to use every power vested in me to accomplish the defeat of our enemies in any part of the world where our own safety demands such defeat.
> When the war is won, *the powers under which I act automatically revert to the people—to whom they belong.*† [27]

In terms of political philosophy, this preachment faithfully expressed John Locke's concept of "prerogative" as "the power to act

---

* The supporting statute by Congress, with its contempt for civil rights, was termed by Edward S. Corwin "just about the most heartless measure ever enacted by the American Congress." (*Total War and the Constitution*, p. 98—cited by Binkley, p. 240.)

† Italics added.

according to discretion for the public good, without the prescription of the law and sometimes even against it." In the less lofty terms of Presidential presumption, it insinuated the largely baseless fable that powers assumed by a President have *ever* reverted "automatically" to the people.

The almost excited vehemence of Roosevelt's language flowed (quite naturally, by Rooseveltian logic) from an almost serene certainty of the uniquely sensitive bonds between the people and the President: for him, this was the central nerve of the whole Presidential scheme of politics. But this very kinship, with all its intensity and intimacy, has been precisely the mark of the Presidential office that has probably aroused in all witnesses—generation after generation—either their highest delight *or* their deepest fear. Thus, a sanguine Henry Jones Ford in 1898 had been able thoroughly to rejoice: "The greatness of the Presidency is the work of the people breaking through the constitutional form." [28] Yet a no less concerned observer of Presidential life, Henry C. Lockwood, some fifteen years earlier had viewed the same popular "breaking through" with anxiety and alarm. Lockwood had watched the Presidency under Andrew Johnson escape the humiliation of impeachment by a single vote—and then suddenly leap to the enjoyment of its spell of superficial glamor under Ulysses S. Grant. In *The Abolition of the Presidency,* he could foresee no safe hope for the American idea of personal liberty short of an end to the Presidency itself, in favor of such an executive council as the Swiss people had chosen. And he pressed his argument with some historical insight:

> The tendency of all people is to elevate a single person to the position of ruler. The idea is simple. It appeals to all orders of intellects. It can be understood by all. Around this centre all nationality and patriotism are grouped. A nation comes to know the characteristics and nature of an individual. It learns to believe in the man. . . .
>
> Under these circumstances, let a person be chosen to an office, with power conferred upon it equal to that of the Presidency of the United States, and it will make but little difference whether the law actually gives him the right to act in a particular direction or not. He determines a policy. He acts. . . . He is the chief officer of the nation. He stands alone. He is a separate power in himself. The lines with

which we attempt to mark the limits of his power are shadowy and ill-defined. . . .

The sentiment of hero-worship, which to a great extent prevails among the American people, will endorse him. Under our form of government, we do not think so much of what Congress may do. A great multitude declared: "Give us President Grant! We know him. He is strong! He will rule!" [29]

The unappeased spirits of Patrick Henry and George Mason, and James Monroe and George Clinton, could almost be heard still sighing their grave amens.

III

> The war powers of the President are in fact so great and so indefinite that their nature will not be fully known until our Republic has passed through all its trials and ceased to be. Then some historian will be able to tell you just what they *were*—not are—under the Constitution. The President's war power is the unexplored and dark continent of American government.
> —CHARLES A. BEARD, *The Republic*, 1943

The Vietnam War—and all the lives and years, the resources and debates squandered upon it—eventually forced most citizens of the Republic to see this conflict by itself as a kind of "dark continent" of American folly. By the test of military progress, this was a war from the outset condemned to compute and report success by nothing more serious or civilized than "body counts" or unfriendly corpses. By the jargon of official vocabulary, it was a $20-billion-a-year enterprise to bring "pacification" to South Vietnam, but a full decade of warring could be said to have assured a sort of peace, after all, only for the military and civilian dead. And by the measure of political consequences for both nations, a temperate judgment might be that the brutal conflict did as little for American unity as for Vietnamese democracy, all the while that Indochina suffered through its terrible tutoring in what American policy meant by moral and military "commitment" to a cause. By 1972 the weekly newsmagazine *Time*—which had greeted the seasons of most years of the previous decade with editorial salutes to imminent "victory" in Vietnam—could cheer the coming of yet another bloody spring only by resignedly calling the lament of William Butler Yeats: "What was left for massacre to save?" [30]

For the history and the power of the Presidency, the lessons of Vietnam were harsh, but they also could be easily simplified and misread. The very grossness of the tragedy almost insistently implied a weird political aberration—a scarcely believable breakdown in normally rational and prudent processes for making foreign policy or prosecuting foreign war. But to imagine this was to ignore a great part of what there was to be learned. For the appalling *consequences*—but not the underlying *processes* of decision-making —were what made this conflict seem like no other in the life of the Republic. The hazards in those Presidential processes, far from being without precedent or parallel, were old risks and recurrent dilemmas, only newly dramatized. And the historic questions raised by the Vietnam story ultimately concerned not so much *a* President and *his* methods as *the* Presidency and *its* methods.

There happens to be a quite graphic illustration of this truth worth remembrance. It is to be found in the striking parallel between the ways in which two Presidents of the twentieth century used two minor incidents at sea to make each of them a major milestone on the paths to two wars almost a quarter of a century apart. The Presidents were as different as Franklin Roosevelt and Lyndon Johnson, and the wars were as different as World War II and the Vietnam War. The crucial event in both cases involved nothing more apparently ominous than the course set by a Navy destroyer; but the first instance served to provoke a decisive Presidential speech, while the second served to elicit a decisive Congressional resolution. Specifically. . . .

In August of 1964, the destroyer USS *Maddox,* along with an accompanying destroyer in the Gulf of Tonkin, a disputed number of miles off the coast of North Vietnam, exchanged fire with "unidentified surface vessels" officially charged with unleashing torpedoes at the American craft. The attack was described by the Secretary of Defense as so "deliberate and unprovoked" as to demand "a prompt and firm military response." [31] This specifically took the form of more than sixty bombing attacks ordered by the President against North Vietnam. The larger political response came with the Tonkin Gulf Resolution extracted from Congress, authorizing President Johnson "to take all necessary measures . . . to prevent further aggression" and avowing that the Republic viewed "the maintenance of international peace and security in Southeast Asia" as manifestly "vital to its national interest." As the President elicited this Congressional license for what he called "supporting freedom" and "protecting peace" in Southeast Asia, he described the import of the incident in Tonkin Gulf with the hyperbole of almost any President at all such times: "The issue is the future of Southeast Asia as a whole." [32]

From the volume of subsequent testimony, remorse, and recrimination over the Tonkin Gulf Resolution, there seems no need to cite more than a few points. *One:* the American reprisals by air strikes were taken despite the *Maddox* commander's cabled concession that "no actual visual sightings" had been made of the supposedly attacking craft, while the Secretary of Defense acknowledged that "the statements of eye witnesses . . . had not reached Washington at the time the reprisal air strikes were ordered executed." [33] *Two:* only at Senate hearings more than three years after the event did witnesses from the executive branch concede (as they had previously concealed or denied) that the destroyer suffering "unprovoked" attack had been a spy ship collecting military intelligence and collaborating operationally with South Vietnamese patrol boats shelling the northern coast. *Three:* the substance of the resolution of August, 1964, had been formulated by the Department of State in alternative drafts—as what was later conceded to be "normal contingency planning"—months before any incident, large or small, ever occurred in the Gulf of Tonkin.[34] *Four:* the President had seriously asserted "the future of Southeast Asia as a whole" to be at immediate stake following an incident in which no American vessel had been appreciably damaged and no American sailor even slightly injured. And the extravagance of both the military and political response to such an "attack" may be seen in its contrast to the American retort in 1968 when North Korean vessels actually seized the spy ship *Pueblo* and held its crew captive for almost a year—a venture which provoked no retaliation more stern than protests and pleas.

These facts were enough to make the months and years

following upon the Tonkin Gulf Resolution a time for Congressional contrition. The legislators' remorse may have reached a kind of peak when backward-looking hearings before the Senate Foreign Relations Committee in the summer of 1967 brought forth the blunt assertion by the administration's Undersecretary of State that, in the context of the Vietnam conflict, "I think the expression of declaring a war is one that has become outmoded." To complete this declaration of the obsolescence of Congressional authority, the witness for the Chief Executive went on to declare the Tonkin Gulf Resolution to be "an authorization to the President . . . as broad an authorization of war so-called as could be." [35] When these Foreign Relations Committee hearings were done, a unanimous 16 to 0 report on "National Commitments" voiced this alarm:

> Already possessing vast power over the country's foreign relations, the executive, by acquiring the authority to commit the country to war, now exercises something approaching absolute power over the life or death of every living American. . . . The concentration in the hands of the President of virtually unlimited authority over matters of war and peace has all but removed the limits to executive power in the most important single area of our national life. Until they are restored, the American people will be threatened with tyranny or disaster.[36]

The Senatorial warning was surely understandable. But it could have been sounded no less rightly over Presidential practices and tactics by no means so novel or recent as the indictment implied. For there had been that other President, maneuvering along the edges of that earlier war, and scheming in the wake of that other destroyer. . . .

In September of 1941, the USS *Greer,* cruising the waters off Iceland, suffered the indignity of two torpedoes fired by a German submarine. While the American Navy for some time had been convoying as far as Iceland supplies en route to Great Britain under the Lend-Lease Act, President Roosevelt elected to view this incident as radically changing the terms of American nonbelligerence. One week after the event, he went on nationwide radio to excoriate the "piracy" of the submarine attack, to announce that "henceforth

American patrols would defend the freedom of the seas by striking first at all Axis raiders," and to proclaim the bellicose principle that "when you see a rattlesnake poised to strike, you do not wait until he has struck before you crush him." [37] The meaning of this rhetoric for national policy was later cogently summarized by the historian Samuel Eliot Morison: "From the date of the *Greer* incident, 4 September 1941, the United States was engaged in a *de facto* naval war with Germany on the Atlantic Ocean." [38] And this came to pass almost fully three months before the attack on Pearl Harbor.

What actually happened to the *Greer* in the waters off Iceland—and the Presidential use made of the occasion—amounted to an eerie foreshadowing of the story of the *Maddox* off the coast of Vietnam twenty years later. *First:* the indignant President neglected to mention that the American destroyer had been systematically trailing the Nazi submarine and broadcasting its position to a British warplane overhead. *Second:* there was almost as little notice taken of the fact that the "piracy" of two torpedoes had resulted in the damage of nothing and the injury of no one. And *third:* altogether like the Tonkin Gulf Resolution, the Roosevelt declaration of policy had been substantially ready for months, awaiting only a conveniently provocative occasion to rationalize it. As Harry Hopkins later explained the long-standing plan to give the Navy its orders to "shoot on sight":

> The genesis of this speech began as far back as the first of July after the President had initiated his first patrol of the North Atlantic. . . . The President determined upon a far more important patrol before I went to England late in July. . . . At the Roosevelt-Churchill conference in August the President reiterated that he was going to speak early in September on the implications of his new policy. . . . He had not set a date for the speech, although he had discussed it with me from time to time after our return from the conference. But with the attack on the *Greer,* he determined to make his speech at once.[39]

By the principles of the Senate Foreign Relations Committee's 1967 lament upon Lyndon Johnson's "virtually unlimited authority," the plaguing question from this earlier time cannot be answered or dismissed on grounds of the presumed virtue or wisdom of Franklin Roosevelt's intentions, as he led the Republic toward its full role in World War II. The question revolves around those methods of his that *any* astute President could pursue to bring about the Republic's commitment to *any* war. And as further examples of these methods, a few other performances by the Commander in Chief of those years stay particularly memorable.

In September of 1940, after the fall of France, the President's "Fifty Destroyer Deal" changed by executive fiat the status of the nation, with respect to the war in Europe, from technical neutrality to barely camouflaged belligerence. This announcement of September 3 simply reported an executive agreement with Great Britain exchanging the receipt of long-term leases, on certain sites for naval bases on British territory in the West Atlantic, for the tender to Britain of fifty renovated overage destroyers. Such a transaction not only entailed Presidential exercise of powers unmistakably assigned by the Constitution to Congress. It also was defended and excused by the Attorney General with the kind of argument that a less tense nation might have found merely laughable: since the Commander in Chief had authority to "dispose" the Republic's armed forces, he must equally enjoy the right to dispose *of* them. And these Rooseveltian maneuvers were executed less than three months after a Presidential message, even as it had extended "utmost sympathy" to France, had professed a solemn sense of the limits to Presidential prerogative: "These statements carry with them no implication of military commitments. Only Congress can make such commitments." [40]

A half year after the Presidential "deal" of destroyers, the 1941 enactment of H.R. 1776 as the Lend-Lease Act signified even more than Congressional approval of the ambiguously aggressive role of the Republic in the world struggle. For from this, there would gradually be woven a web of mutual aid agreements to furnish the nation's allies more than $40 billion worth of munitions and supplies. Although this Congressional action occurred nine months before formal American entry into World War II, it has been judged by Edward S. Corwin that "no more sweeping delegation of legislative power has ever been made to an American President." [41] The act's terms directed the President to assure the manufacture, procurement, and delivery of whatever he adjudged to be "defense articles"—by sale, loan, or disposal—to the "government of any country whose defense the President deems vital to the defense of the United States." Or in the phrase of Professor Corwin, the law effectively assigned to the President "the power to fight wars by deputy." [42]

The months of 1941 before Pearl Harbor abounded with other displays, less historic but no less symbolic, of the Presidential power to chart the path to war. Thus: in April, there came an executive agreement with the Danish minister allowing the American Republic to take over a "defensive" occupation of Greenland, undeterred by protests from a Nazi regime in Copenhagen. In May, there came the President's personal appeal to the French people to withhold support from a Vichy regime collaborating with the Nazis. In July, the President told Congress of his agreement to take over from Great Britain the task of the defense of Iceland. In August, a meeting with Winston Churchill proceeded beyond agreements on immediate "problems of common defense" to prescriptions for a new and peaceful world under the Atlantic Charter—a kind of *de facto* alliance-for-the-future composed without help from Senate or Congress. In September, the *Greer* episode set the stage for the Presidential vow to strike first at the "rattlesnakes of the Atlantic." In October, the Chief Executive chose Navy Day to observe that "the shooting had started." And in November, with the determination that the defense of Russia was vital to the defense of America, the President pledged the Soviet Union lend-lease aid of $1 billion.[43]

These were some of the signs on a road to war a quarter of a century before Americans would come painfully to know a battleground called Vietnam. They pointed toward an arena of absolutely different historic meaning. And yet they plainly marked for remembering the elaborate arts—and the granite resolves—with which a President always may set forth to make up not only the Republic's mind, but also its fate.

*　　　　*　　　　*

The entry into the Korean War in 1950, as determined by Harry S. Truman and Secretary of State Dean Acheson, came with a thrust of Presidential power so swift as to make the Rooseveltian

devices of a decade earlier seem comparatively sluggish. The enterprise was distinguished equally by its manipulation of the machinery of the United Nations and its disdain for the machinery of
Congress, which was denied even the charade of anything like a
Tonkin Gulf Resolution. This time the will of the Chief Executive
was to be both instant and incontrovertible. And the result was a
new lesson in what the old virtues of "energy" and "dispatch"
might stir in the modern Presidency.

After the arrival in Washington on the night of June 24, 1950, of
a cable from the American ambassador in South Korea, which re-
layed reports of North Korean attacks across the frontier of the
thirty-eighth parallel, the Presidential response came with the quickness of physical reflex. More than all else, the full retort reflected a
particular state of mind in the Presidency, partly shared by the mind
of the nation. This Presidential *Weltanschauung* was suffused with a
grandeur of vision, about the Republic's role in the world, which
was matched only by a passion for simplification. The spirit of this
view of the planet had been voiced by President Truman three years
earlier—with his call to Congress to raise the shield of "the Truman
doctrine" in defense of Greece and Turkey against Communist
adventures. Then he had proclaimed, as he still believed, these
propositions: "Totalitarian regimes imposed on free people, by direct or indirect aggression, undermine . . . the security of the United
States. . . . It must be the policy of the United States to support free
peoples who are resisting attempted subjugation by armed minorities
or outside pressure." [44] A President so globally committed could
hardly react casually to the outbreak of hostilities in Korea—as
Truman later explained in his *Memoirs:*

> I recalled some earlier instances: Manchuria, Ethiopia, Austria . . .
> Communism was acting in Korea just as Hitler, Mussolini, and the
> Japanese had acted. . . . If this was allowed to go unchallenged it
> would mean a third world war. [45]

Such a view of the world of nations, at once apocalyptic and
messianic, virtually commanded the executive branch to tell the
Congress and the nation what was the path of righteousness. So
exalted, Secretary of State Acheson soon tried to sedate the Senate

Foreign Relations Committee with his rationale for forgetting all debate over constitutional processes. "We are in a position in the world today where the argument as to who has the power to do this, that, or the other thing," the Secretary intoned, "is not exactly what is called for from America in this very critical hour." [46] And the pious inference was clear: the historic moment "called for" full freedom for the Chief Executive to lead the way toward the war of his choice.

This is precisely how the Truman Presidency proceeded to act—over a startlingly short span of days. On the night of Saturday, June 24, 1950, the President was at his home in Independence, Missouri, when Secretary Acheson telephoned to announce flatly: "The North Koreans have invaded South Korea." [47] Truman immediately concurred with his Secretary's suggestion that the Security Council of the United Nations be called to deplore such an act of aggression. By the night of Sunday, June 25, the President had flown back to Washington for a dinner conference with his Secretary of State and departmental aides, the highest officials of the Department of Defense, and the Joint Chiefs of Staff. (Although Acheson could then report a Security Council resolution only declaring a breach of the peace and urging a North Korean withdrawal, the President had already decided for himself, as he later wrote in his *Memoirs:* "This was the test of all the talk of the last five years of collective security." [48]) By the night of Monday, June 26, after another meeting with his chief advisers, the President proceeded to (1) direct General Douglas MacArthur "to use air and naval forces to support the Republic of Korea"; (2) dispatch the Seventh Fleet to the Formosa Strait; (3) command "the strengthening of our forces in the Philippines"; and (4) order "increased aid to the French in Indo-China." [49] * On the morning of Tuesday, June 27—finally—the President paid his delayed respect to Constitutional process, as his *Memoirs* later noted: "I asked a group of congressional leaders to meet with me so that I might inform them on the events and the decisions of the past few days." [51] The con-

---

* The "increased aid" to Indochina included the dispatch of a thirty-five-man military assistance group to give training in the use of American weapons. This marked the first American gesture to "save" Vietnam from the fate of Communist dominion.[50]

descension of a militant Commander in Chief could not be expressed more crisply.

The record of those three days gives only a rough suggestion of the audacity of the executive action. For these events were both preceded and attended by a few other circumstances that made this an almost spectacular show of Presidential presumption. And the most relevant circumstances were these:

\# The prior commitment of American policy to South Korea itself could at best be called uncertain. The President was not acting expeditiously to fulfill the terms of a defense treaty: there existed at the time no mutual defense pact binding the Republic to South Korea's defense, and the military orders to General MacArthur were actually issued even before any South Korean request for military aid.[52] Throughout the months preceding the start of war, moreover, the White House had seemed to show sustained indifference to intelligence reports of a military buildup along the thirty-eighth parallel. Whereas past indications of a Communist military threat in other areas, such as Iran and Greece and Turkey, had brought strong warning statements from the White House, the President had nothing to say in this instance until war had started. At the same time, his Secretary of State *had* said something quite pertinent early in the year. In a speech before the National Press Club, he had unmistakably left Korea *outside* the Pacific "defense perimeter" deemed vital to American security. So widely known was this political judgment, indeed, that it guided the response soon thereafter of the chairman of the Senate Foreign Relations Committee, Tom Connally, when the Senator was asked whether Korea was not "an essential part" of American strategy in the Pacific. "No," the chairman answered. "Of course any position like that is of some strategic importance. But I don't think it is very greatly important." [53] And there was no public word from the administration affirming anything to the contrary.

\# The abrupt definition of policy and commitment of forces came as responses to a single cable from the American ambassador in Seoul whose text (1) was not immediately made available to the Security Council or the press and (2) did *not* flatly assert—as Mr. Acheson had informed Mr. Truman—that "the North Koreans have invaded South Korea." The President's own subsequent account contains no evidence, furthermore, that he even knew the precise content of the cable until his return to Washington—a full day after the first moves toward military intervention. For a cable inspiring such decisiveness, the language was, in fact, notably ambiguous. Essentially, it cited South Korean "army reports" described as no more than "partly confirmed." It acknowledged "details of fighting" in a key area to be "unclear." And it cautiously used the qualifying adverb "reportedly" no less than three times in its brief relation of unwitnessed events.[54] None of these ambiguities either tempered the tone of Washington's appeal to the Security Council or slackened the speed of the President's own military decisions.

\# The exploitation by Washington of the initial response from the United Nations was disingenuous and deceptive. When the military orders of June 26 were issued, the only resolution of the Security Council had charged North Korean forces with breaching the peace and urged their withdrawal, a policy to which all United Nations members were asked to render assistance. There appeared in this resolution no call whatsoever for military intervention by the American Republic or any other nation in Korea—much less any allusion to the further military measures that the President chose to order with respect to the Formosa Strait, the Philippines, and Indochina. Nonetheless, Harry Truman's formal public statement, announcing his orders to American air and sea forces to support the South Korean regime, directly cited the actions of the Security Council as "these circumstances" dictating his decision. There seems no way to describe this Presidential explanation as anything less than a deliberate distortion.[55]

\# The disrespect for Congress and its leader went even beyond the White House view that it was necessary to "inform them of the decisions of the past few days" only comfortably after the fact. And the use of the United Nations, as an excuse for military decision, amounted to more than a scheme to avoid a call upon Congress for a declaration of war. All this was a strategy of evasion that—under the law—really evaded nothing at all. For the United Nations Participation Act, approved by the Congress in December, 1945, had expressly forbidden any such devious procedures. The terms of this act implementing the United Nations Charter had specified: (1) any "special agreement or agreements with the Security Council" concerning armed forces "made available to the Security Council" must be "subject to the approval of the Congress by appropriate Act or joint resolution," and (2) lest this seem the least unclear, "nothing herein contained shall be construed as an authorization to the President by the Congress to make available to the Security Council" either armed forces or military assistance except as expressly "provided for in such special agreement or agreements" approved by the Congress.[56] In short, the Congress' original resolve was as unmistakable as the President's eventual contempt for it.

\# Both the magnitude and the hazard of the Presidential decisions of these days—finally—were entirely clear to the participants. It was not possible, and it was not attempted, to condone the peremptory nature of executive action as a relatively minor matter of quick redress of a local and limited crisis. Quite to the contrary, the gravest implications were understood and accepted. As the President's *Memoirs* later recalled: "Secretary Acheson pointed out that . . . what had been done in the last three days might ultimately involve us in all-out war." [57]

The ensuing war would not be mourned as "all-out." Yet it brought suffering and stress that might be called sufficient. The armies of Communist China were finally drawn into the battle, and they threatened, for a while, to drive American forces into the sea. In the end, the human cost for Americans alone surpassed 33,000 deaths along with nearly 160,000 casualties.

The political price could not be computed so exactly. This price involved both constitutional processes within the nation and international consequences around the world. With respect to the first kind of damage, this was lucidly surveyed in a few phrases from a long speech on the floor of the Senate by Ohio's Robert A. Taft, a half year after the Korean War had begun. They were phrases that would take on even sharper meaning for a decade—and another Asian war—soon to come:

During recent years a theory has developed that there shall be no criticism of the foreign policy of the administration, that any such criticism is an attack on the unity of the Nation, that it gives aid and comfort to the enemy. . . .

I venture to state that this proposition is . . . a very dangerous fallacy threatening the very existence of the Nation. . . . If we permit appeals to unity to bring an end to . . . criticism, we endanger not only the constitutional liberties of the country, but even its future existence. . . .

It is part of our American system that basic elements of foreign policy shall be openly debated. . . . Whatever the value of unity, it is also true that unity carried to unreasonable extremes can destroy a country. . . . The best safeguard against fatal error lies in continuous criticism and discussion to bring out the truth. . . .

As a matter of fact, [the President] had no authority whatever to commit American troops to Korea without consulting Congress and without congressional approval. . . . The President simply usurped authority, in violation of the laws and the Constitution.[58]

As for global rather than constitutional matter, the decisions taken at this time and in this manner largely determined the relations that would prevail for twenty years between the American Republic and the People's Republic of China. This diplomatic pattern was forecast—and even welcomed—by a speech in May, 1951, by an Assistant Secretary of State, Dean Rusk. The speech brusquely dismissed the government of mainland China as a "tyranny." And the Assistant Secretary extolled American attachment to the Chiang Kai-shek regime, huddled on the island of Formosa, with the assurance that it "more authentically represents the views of the great body of the people of China." [59]

These were declarations of consequence, both for the moment and the future. For the moment, they posed the riddle of how an American President could possibly negotiate any settlement of the Korean conflict with a Peking regime so categorically denied recognition. For the future, the underlying views pointed toward the time —a decade hence—when the same Dean Rusk would be Secretary of State in another administration. By then the arena of battle would be, of course, not Korea but Indochina. But the aggressive intent of the "tyranny" in Peking would be judged as no less malevolent in this new conflict. And the course of American foreign policy would be inspired, once again, by an oracular certitude about the political life "authentically" wanted—this time—by "the great body of the people" of Vietnam.

*   *   *

The decade of the 1960's brought, perhaps as swiftly as ever in the Republic's history, a true overturning of the familiar political and ideological premises that had shaped and directed, year after year, all partisan debate over the rightful role of America in the world. Between the Presidency of Harry Truman, confronting a Senatorial critic like Robert Taft, and the Presidency of Lyndon Johnson, confronting a Senatorial critic like J. W. Fulbright, the more or less liberal-Democratic and the more or less conservative-Republican beliefs and attitudes on national policy managed to achieve an almost complete reversal. From the first years of the 1950's, the dominant themes of national debate had been set by the strivings of "liberal" internationalists to persuade "conservative" nationalists of the need for generous commitment to the ideals of the United Nations and "the cause of freedom" around the globe. By the latter years of the 1960's, however, the reticent nationalists had become the unrestrained champions of "commitment" to anti-revolutionary causes—from Southeast Asia to Latin America—while the zealous internationalists of the earlier time now had largely become the anxious critics of any grandiose American role as a "global policeman." And these general changes in political temper implied specific changes of view upon a range of related issues: the exact nature and threat of world Communism, the sensible reach and limit of American power, the moral and political implications for the Republic of revolutionary change in distant lands, and the moral and political imperatives of meeting the Republic's own problems of mass poverty, racial strife, and urban decay.

All these redirections of political thought and bias affected no matter of national moment more profoundly than the question of the role of the President himself. For here the new attitudes struck at partisan images of the Presidency that had been cherished for a generation, since the first bold initiatives of Franklin Roosevelt's New Deal. Thereafter—through one national election after another —the promise or the menace of Presidential power had come to be argued, by Democrats and Republicans alike, as virtually immutable articles of faith: the former hailed all enhancement of the office as the nation's best hope for progressive and imaginative statesmanship, of course, while the latter lamented each new Executive prerogative as another sign of the Republic's worst risk of repressive and arbitrary government.

The way these Presidential images of the past were broken, by the political events and emotions of the 1960's, can be seen by a glance at a striking pair of public utterances by Senator J. W. Fulbright. By the end of the decade, this chairman of the Senate Foreign Relations Committee had become a most vigorous critic of Presidential presumption in foreign policy. The warnings he voiced, moreover, could not be discounted as partisan Democratic rhetoric aimed at the Republican presidency of Richard Nixon: he had earlier voiced no less distress, of course, over the use of the war powers by Lyndon Johnson. And a few sentences from one speech of 1971 sum up this new kind of Democratic critique of Presidential power:

Thirty years of war, cold war, and crisis have propelled the American political system far along the road to an Executive despotism, at least in the conduct of foreign relations and the making of war. So far has the process of expanding Presidential power advanced, that, in the publicly recorded view of the Senate Committee on Foreign Relations, ". . . it is no longer accurate to characterize our government, in matters of foreign relations, as one of separated powers checked and balanced against each other." . . .

"Flexibility" has become a euphemism for unchecked Executive power in the making and conduct of foreign policy. . . . Executive incursions upon Congress' foreign policy powers have had three main results. The war power, which the Constitution vested exclusively in the Congress, has to all intents and purposes passed entirely into the hands of the Executive. The treaty power [of the Senate] . . . has been reduced to a near nullity by the frequent use of executive agreements . . . and by the extravagant interpretation of the terms of treaties . . . Finally, the "advise and consent" function . . . has been so diminished that the Executive now feels free to take little or no cognizance of the Senate's counsel, while the term "consultation" is commonly used to refer to ceremonial briefings regarding decisions which have already been made.[60]

The archinternational Fulbright of the past thus found himself in 1971 sounding remarkably like the archnationalist Taft of 1951. He even took the occasion of this same speech to show a sensitivity toward the Founding Fathers' fears of Executive power which would have made Taft smile appreciatively, as he cited Thomas Jefferson's words to James Madison in 1789: "We have already given in example one effectual check to the Dog of war by transferring the power of letting him loose from the Executive to the Legislative body." But the ironic quality of this appeal to constitutional prudence could only be appreciated with the remembrance of a vastly different Fulbright speech of a decade before—exactly ten years before these professions of anxiety, exactly ten years after Taft's decrial of Presidential power. Then, a 1961 university address by the Arkansas Senator, appraising the prerogatives of the White House in the realm of foreign policy, still rang with the familiar Democratic confidence in Presidential initiative. And the firmness of this faith seemed all the more remarkable for the fact that the disaster of the Cuban Bay of Pigs was but a few weeks old —as the Senator insisted:

> My question . . . is whether we have any choice but *to modify and perhaps overhaul the eighteenth century procedures* that govern the formulation and conduct of American foreign policy. . . . I wonder whether the time has not arrived, or indeed already passed, when *we must give the Executive a measure of power in the conduct of our foreign affairs that we have hitherto* jealously withheld.* [61]

The full surrender of such political preconceptions had to have truly grave cause. By the end of the 1960's the new attitudes of old liberals toward the direction of foreign policy could only marginally be related to some changing appraisals of the world of nations: a lessening fear of nuclear collision between the American Republic and the Soviet Union, a growing awareness of the moderation of ideological conflict in both Europe and Asia, and a speeding decline

---

* Italics added.

in the belief that the Republic was specially endowed with the right to counsel all other nations in their wisest governance. Although these were significant shifts of accent in American foreign policy, they alone could not have precipitated the most critical change of all —a new distrust of the Presidency itself as the inspiring source of any foreign policy, be its accents new or old. This crisis of confidence required a profound political shock. It required, in a word, Vietnam.

While there are many criteria, political and moral, for counting the cost of the Vietnam War, there is perhaps one measure that suffices for the Presidency: the disenchantment of those political forces for so long most eloquent in its defense and most eager for its leadership. Almost certainly, no other war in the Republic's history forced so sharp a change in national attitude, or so great a surge of popular doubt, about the range of Presidential power and the reliability of Presidential decision. Such a penalty to the office could not be considered historically unjust. For as much as any conflict could be, this was a Presidential war.

A series of quite specific devices and artifices of Presidential leadership made this so. These were propositions that inspired, and stratagems that traced, the Republic's course toward and through this war. It may fairly be said that only a searching history from some distant time can discover all causes that mingled to make the tragedy. But it may as reasonably be said that such remote judgment need not be awaited in order to discern the more obvious lapses and follies. From the very beginning, these signs stood forth along the way. And they may be described, perhaps not too arbitrarily, as these:

The Abuse of History

Even a great power cannot sensibly expect to win a war that it cannot intelligently define. The Johnson Presidency showed scarcely any awareness of the fact, and it was plagued by this political problem throughout its years of military escalation. Religiously, it persisted in depicting the intervention in Vietnam as a logical and faithful extension of (1) the resistance to Nazi and Fascist aggression before and during World War II and (2) the resistance after

World War II to Communist pressures against Berlin or Greece or Turkey. This line of argument, snarled from its premises, required a parody of history. It implied some real equation between the mature political structures of Western Europe and the unformed political structures of Southeast Asia. It insinuated that the shielding of stable democratic governments in Western Europe bespoke an American concern and commitment that also must extend similar support to unstable military dictatorships in South Vietnam. It insisted that the same principles of American policy, inspiring alliance with established sovereignties of the West in the pre-World War I world, must apply with equal relevance to revolutionary forces of the East in the post-colonial world. It confused the defense of profound traditions of nationhood in all other arenas (even including Korea) with the profound absence of such traditions in Vietnam (except for such nationalist passion as inspired the Communist forces). With the distortions of history so headlong, the abortions of policy could not lag far behind.

The Extravagance of Purpose

A particularly emotional appeal by President Johnson in 1967 unwittingly attested to an essential flaw in all the political analogies being argued by his administration. On this occasion, he urged patience and understanding for the problems of the Saigon regime—on the grounds that South Vietnam was struggling through a labor of nation building quite as difficult as the creation of the American Republic itself in the years between 1776 and 1789. Clumsy as this analogy might be, it betrayed one crucial truth: the aspirations of American policy in Vietnam had *no* serious precedent in the far different kind of American shows of force in all other confrontations with Communist power since World War II. In all these previous crises, the limit of the full American intent was to *defend* a sovereignty in seeming danger. Here alone the grandiose purpose was to *create* a sovereignty where none truly existed.

The proof of this did not depend upon the implications of one burst of Presidential rhetoric. Through all the tortuous involvement in Vietnam, the purpose of American policy was political-creative and not military-defensive. And this was explicitly conceded in a striking summary passage from the Department of Defense's own Pentagon Papers on the shaping of Vietnam policy:

> Without the threat of U.S. intervention, South Vietnam could not have refused to even discuss the elections called for in 1956 under the Geneva settlement. . . .
>
> Without U.S. aid in the years following, the Diem regime certainly, and an independent South Vietnam almost as certainly, could not have survived. . . .
>
> South Vietnam was essentially the creation of the United States.[62]

An enterprise of American policy that any informed analyst could so define bore no resemblance whatsoever to specific military actions to protect a Berlin or a Greece or a Turkey. This venture required a unique ambition and presumption. Even as the major military involvement was barely beginning in the spring of 1965, the confounding nature of the American goal drove the American ambassador in Saigon, General Maxwell Taylor, to cable a terse plea to Washington: "I badly need a clarification of our purposes and objectives." [63] And this precisely stated the need that the whole Republic was to feel and to bear.

The Arrogance of Decision

The commanding officer of American forces in the Korean War, General Matthew B. Ridgway, wrote one of the more incisive judgments upon the decision-making process in the Vietnam War. A few sentences read thus:

> It should not have taken great vision to perceive that a mountainous, jungled area such as Vietnam, devoid of the . . . communications essential for the operations of a modern army, and with a population bitterly divided . . . would be a morass into which we could endlessly and futilely pour our human and material resources; that you cannot kill an idea with bullet and bomb; that no truly vital U.S. interest was present . . . and that commitment to a major effort there was a monumental blunder.[64]

*   *   *

Such a critique contains no opinions or warnings that were not authoritatively available to the White House all the while it chose its course. The chain of Presidential decisions was not cruelly ordained by events: there was no lack of available alternatives or options, and there was no absence of articulate doubt and dissent. As early as the summer of 1963, the head of a Department of State task force on Vietnam urged withdrawal from a politically hopeless situation, but this appraisal was rejected in favor of the dictum of Secretary of State Rusk: "It would be far better for us to start on the firm basis . . . that we will not pull out of Vietnam until the war is won." [65] Over the following years, the judgments of the Central Intelligence Agency again and again questioned excessive military commitment, as well as sanguine estimates on the impact of the bombing of North Vietnam. But the sum of both persistent cautions and possible choices added up to no real deterrent to Presidential will. This unbroken pattern led directly on to the decision by Richard Nixon in May, 1972, to order the mining of the harbors and waterways of North Vietnam. The resolve of this President, too, to come to his own conclusions, with the least possible distraction from contrary views, was made wholly clear by his summoning of eighteen Congressional leaders to the White House—scarcely an hour before announcing his decision. As he then declared, with no pretense of desire for advice or response: "Let me come directly to the point and tell you of a decision I have had to make." [66]

The point beyond Richard Nixon's point was the vividness with which this incident reflected the personal intensity—as it had steadily mounted through the years—of Presidential command over Vietnam decisions. On the eve of the President's announcement, when its substance was still unknown, a single headline on a New York *Times* report of speculations from Washington stated the reality. The headline simply read: NO ONE KNOWS WHAT HE MIGHT DO. And this seriously applied neither to one decision nor to one President, but to the pattern of Presidential action and leadership throughout the Vietnam War.

The Seduction of Optimism

The forming and voicing of Vietnam policy for most of a decade were accompanied by a litany of baseless promises and prophecies, both private and public. These could be heard as far back as John Kennedy's 1963 State of the Union message: "The spearpoint of aggression has been blunted in South Vietnam." They continued to warp military appraisals of the intentions and the capabilities of both Vietcong guerrillas and North Vietnamese armies. They nourished the kind of self-delusion within the White House that could inspire a memorandum of February 7, 1965, from Presidential Assistant McGeorge Bundy—urging the "policy of sustained reprisal" (the air strikes of Operation Rolling Thunder) against North Vietnam and anticipating the rewards: "Once such a policy is put in force, we shall be able to speak in Vietnam on many topics and in many ways, with growing force and effectiveness." [67] And the impulses toward fantasy stayed strong enough to bring forth, seven years later, the assurance of Richard Nixon's 1972 State of the World message: "Vietnam no longer distracts our attention from the fundamental issues of global diplomacy or diverts our energies from priorities at home." *

The record of such oratory could not fail to affect the place of the Presidency in the minds of the citizenry. On the side of harm, this had to cloud with doubt the sobriety of Presidential judgment and the accuracy of Presidential pronouncement. On the side of good, however, all this also served as a rude reminder, for the Republic at large, that Presidential decisions have *never* been the unblemished products of a unique mastery and monopoly of secret, sovereign information. And the lesson might attune the ears of citizens for sharper listening to the speech of Chief Executives, whenever they sounded like the aristocratic gentleman of *The Merchant of Venice:* "I am Sir Oracle, And when I ope my lips, let no dog bark!"

The Faith in Quantity

A prime accent of the Presidency of Lyndon Johnson was his grave reliance on the persuasive force of arithmetic. To many observers, this faith seemed a habit of mind formed by his long life

* The contagion of optimism actually reached Richard Nixon some while before he reached the White House. Visiting Saigon in April, 1967, the then former Vice President publicly declared: "It can be said now that the defeat of the Communist forces in South Vietnam is inevitable. The only question is: how soon?" [68]

on Capitol Hill, where major decisions turned, indeed, upon head counts and roll calls. For whatever reason, no modern President was so given to both the waving of opinion polls to prove his popular support and the counting of Congressional statutes to prove his legislative leadership. And the same trust in sheer numbers clearly appeared to color his strategic decisions with regard to the Vietnam War. Inevitably, the Joint Chiefs of Staff could be counted upon to assure the President that only a larger commitment of ground forces—or a higher level of aerial bombardment—was needed to secure the ever-elusive preponderance of power. Vulnerably, this President listened and believed.

The illusions of Richard Nixon in the mid-1960's, however, were not notably different. On his visit to Saigon in August, 1966, he insisted that the shortest road to victory and peace was "not just to have a marginal number" of ground forces "but more than enough." Accordingly, he urged speeding past an expected administration increase of American troops, up to a total of 400,000, on to the higher level of 500,000—so that "this war can be brought to a conclusion." [69] Only three years later, however, the same strategist —as President—would salute his own withdrawal of the same 500,000 as the most direct road to the same "conclusion" of the same war.

The Deceit of Policy

The military commitment of the nation, as it was covertly escalated year after year, provided a step-by-step study in the Presidential art of camouflage. There appears never to have been any major decision with regard to Vietnam which the White House chose to announce with full candor. And while the specific instances to the contrary abound, it seems enough to recall the general spirit of Lyndon Johnson's pacific assurances to the electorate, throughout his 1964 election campaign:

There are those who say, you ought to go north and drop bombs, to try to wipe out the supply lines, and they think that would escalate the war. We don't want our American boys to do the fighting for

Asian boys. We don't want to . . . get tied down in a land war in Asia.[70]

All the secrecy veiling military action could scarcely surpass, however, the duplicity of the professions of political virtue and purpose. Through the years of destruction, the justifying incantation of American policy stayed the same: a devotion to the right of the Vietnamese people "to decide their own destiny" and "to live under a government of their own choice." Yet ever since the Geneva Conference of 1954, providing for only a temporary partition of Vietnam, the essential aim of American policy had been quite different. In the curt words of instruction cabled by Secretary of State John Foster Dulles to his Undersecretary at the Geneva Conference: "Since undoubtedly true that elections might eventually mean unification Vietnam under Ho Chi Minh this makes it all more important they should be only held as long after cease-fire agreement as possible." [71] From the date of these instructions, and through more than fifteen years of coups and crises in the life of South Vietnam, the overriding concern in Presidential decision-making had little to do with "a government of their own choice" for the Vietnamese people. Indeed, the mere suggestion of a coalition government in Saigon—no matter how realistically representative of the political forces present—was wholly repugnant to American policy. The supreme concern of this policy was not the saving of the Vietnamese people for "their own destiny," of course, but the enlisting of them in the "destiny" that American policy had assigned to itself: the containment of Chinese Communist power.

The Disdain of Congress

A Presidential policy fashioned with such disregard for the citizen's right to know could not fail to show the same disrespect for the Congress' right to share. By its very nature, the surreptitious strategy of the executive branch decreed the exclusion of the legislative branch: the pursuit of undefined purposes through an undeclared war was hardly the hidden kind of enterprise that the men on Capitol Hill could be invited to join—without a risk of their wholly spoiling the secret. This made inevitable the later judgment of Senator

Fulbright that "the great tragedy of the Johnson Administration was its subversion of the constitutional war-making responsibility of the Congress by false information and deception." As the Senator went on to say of the Tonkin Gulf Resolution, this statement of national policy had been disguised by the President's spokesmen as "a proposal which they asserted was necessary to prevent a war, not to prosecute a much greater one." [72] But by way of retort to all such suggestions of political fault, President Johnson had formulated his own doctrine of full absolution, which he announced in June, 1966: "There are many, many who can recommend, advise, and sometimes a few of them consent. But there is only one that has been chosen by the American people to decide." [73]

It remained for Lyndon Johnson's successor in the White House, however, to demonstrate that a Presidential indifference toward Congress, with respect to the Vietnam War, could be a privilege above party. Despite a generation of Republican rhetoric deploring Executive usurpation and extolling Congressional consultation, Richard Nixon proceeded to make and declare his decisions altogether in the well-established White House way. The whole structure of his policy for Indochina, from the formulas for "Vietnamization" to the invasions of Cambodia and Laos, owed nothing to an idea or a word—much less advice or consent—from Congressional leaders. In 1971, an increasingly restive Congress attached an amendment to its Military Procurement Authorization bill asserting national policy to call for an end to all military operations "at the earliest practicable date," but an undaunted President, as he signed the measure, dismissed the amendment as "without binding force or effect," since "it does not reflect my judgment." [74] In 1972, after Richard Nixon had briskly told Congressional leaders of "a decision I have had to make" on the mining of North Vietnamese harbors, a veteran Republican legislator, Leslie Arends, the House Republican whip for almost twenty years, offered the lament: "There's no change in the pattern. I've yet to sit in on one of these conferences and hear the President say: 'What do you think we ought to do?' " And a White House aide's response to this comment caught the prevailing Presidential mood: "Well, what the hell, I think they're used to it by now." [75]

The Vietnam War indeed had made the ritual familiar.

The Twisting of Patriotism

The progress of any war has always tended to measure the patience of any Presidency: the more slow and painful the path toward victory, the more quick and snappish the administration's judgment of the motives of its critics, even including their patriotism. Of all the Republic's foreign conflicts, the Vietnam War became both the most prolonged and the most divisive. Under this pressure, the White House came to lash back at critics with rebuttals whose recipes usually seemed to call for equal measures of sentiment and slander. By Presidential innuendo, all skeptics so safe on the home front were contrasted with all heroes so brave on the battlefront. And there followed from this the insidious illogic of Presidential *ex cathedra* pronouncement upon such situations: since martial victory depended upon national unity, all citizens most critical of the war also must be judged most responsible for the lives lost in it.

The Nixon Presidency strove with some success to surpass the Johnson Presidency in its crusade against dissent. A typical Presidential address to the nation, at a tense military moment in April, 1972, explained the sinister strategy of the North Vietnamese: "Their one remaining hope is to win in the Congress of the United States and among the people of the United States the victory they cannot win among the people of South Vietnam or on the battlefield in South Vietnam." And with this oblique caricature of all critics from Capitol Hill to Main Street as potential creatures of a foreign foe, the President proceeded to link his view of the Vietnam War with the integrity of life in the Oval Office:

> Any man who sits here in this office feels a profound sense of obligation to future generations. No man who sits here has the right to take any action which would abdicate America's great tradition of world leadership or weaken respect for the office of President of the United States.[76]

The unspoken insinuation here was truly remarkable. For it warned that unbelievers might be recklessly subverting the future as well as the present authority of the great office. And the destiny of the American Presidency was depicted, by easy inference, as turning on the fate of the Saigon dictatorship.

The Misjudgment of Communism

The careless Presidential reading of the very causes of the upheaval in Indochina inspired almost spectacular confusion of thought. Over many years, the official gospel obscured the obvious elements of civil war, of course, in favor of the odious images of international war. It came close to presuming a sinister equation of anticolonial traditions with anti-American emotions. It then proceeded to identify anti-American feeling with pro-Communist loyalty. And invoking almost all the ideological simplifications of the generation following World War II, it largely concluded that—by the very nature of world Communism—the behavior of Hanoi could be understood as scarcely anything but the scheming of Moscow or the cunning of Peking.

The shallowness of such propositions could hardly be denied by 1972, for all of them then were effectively overthrown and abandoned by a stunning new version of Presidential diplomacy. This came with the journeys of Richard Nixon first to Peking, then to Moscow, and the pursuit of serious negotiation with both Communist China and the Soviet Union—at a time when no such political communication, much less concord, was yet possible with North Vietnam. Such a diplomatic sequence raised some inescapable questions. How could all this unfold if the two major Communist powers were themselves the real and malevolent authors—the threats behind the threat—of the "aggression" of North Vietnam? What was left, after these events, of the notion of Hanoi as little more than a mercenary power armed and hired by "the Communist world" to banish the American presence from the Far East and convert the Pacific Ocean into "a Red Sea"? What could remain of the specter of a Communist China whose lust for adventure and conquest had to be denied in the mountains and jungles of Southeast Asia, lest it have to be met and fought, at some later date in history, on the shores of the Hawaiian Islands or the Western Hemisphere itself? Yet all these had been the essential threads in the geopolitical fable, propagated by the White House for a full decade, to prove the Republic's vital interest in the fate of Vietnam.

The Blindness to Cost

An American officer in South Vietnam, explaining his strategy for one town under attack in 1968 by the Vietcong, stated simply that there had been no way to "save" it except to "destroy" it. This philosophy came close to describing the general effect of the American "commitment" to South Vietnam: the obliteration of towns and villages, the destruction of farmland and forests, along with the hundreds of thousands of civilians, almost beyond counting, left to be casualties or refugees. From 1965 through 1971 the American forces unleashed some 26 billion pounds of explosives in Indochina—a sum twice as great as they had used in all the theaters of World War II. Along with the incalculable cost in human life, the country of South Vietnam, as "defended" by American bombing and shelling, became a land with some 21,000,000 craters.[77] A sober summary of this carnage was offered in 1971, not by any long-outraged critic of the war, but by a veteran American diplomat, Charles W. Yost, who served for two years as the Nixon Presidency's own ambassador to the United Nations:

> Neither the administration nor the public has faced up to the role, present and future, of U.S. airpower in Southeast Asia. . . . The massive way in which it has been used in South Vietnam since 1965 . . . is so undiscriminating between combatant and noncombatant, so devastating to the lives and livelihood of friends more than of foes, so cruel and inhuman in its scale and consequences that it is unjustifiable under either the laws of war or the laws of humanity.[78]

If the moral damage of all this to the Republic was hard to measure, so also was a kind of political price rarely exacted in the nation's history. This amounted to a faltering of faith in the very processes for weighing the values and the risks of a major national commitment. These processes could hardly escape blame for at least a few terrible misjudgments. As early as the spring of 1966, for example, the Secretary of Defense, Robert McNamara, was looking back upon five years of his own counsel to two Presidents, and he was privately conceding: "If I had ever thought that the Vietnamese on either side could have fought on this long and this tenaciously, I might well have had different thoughts about our involvement in years past." [79] The confession was frank, but it could hardly be called timely. For such basic miscalculation from the beginning, when it decisively mattered, had set Presidential policy on its course.

A fatefully confused sense of timing alone could explain, indeed, the Presidency's whole misjudgment of the political temper of the nation. The initial political question that had never been faced was as old as the Gospel of St. Luke: "Which of you, intending to build a tower, sitteth not down first, and counteth the cost, whether he have sufficient to finish it?" Over the years, the White House unconsciously admitted its own failure to do precisely this—by its very insistence that "victory" or "defeat" could critically depend on whether the citizenry of the Republic, undismayed and undivided, *would* sustain Presidential policy. The contingency amounted to a confession. For the time to have ascertained this was before venturing on so long and cruel a course. It was vain for the White House to decry the lack of unified public support—after the fact. For it was of the essence of Presidential judgment to gauge and foresee the measure of this support—before the fact. The ultimate fault, therefore, could not be pushed upon a disenchanted citizenry. It belonged to a self-enchanted Presidency.

I V

Your Daddy may go down in history as having started World War III.

—PRESIDENT LYNDON JOHNSON,
to his daughter, 1966

There has been one special and striking aspect to the ascendancy of Presidents in the realm of foreign affairs. This has not been simply a political story of the executive branch neutralizing or seizing the powers of the legislative branch. It has also been a personal study in the Presidential assertion of power *within* the executive branch—an aggrandizement without parallel in any other sphere or department of the Republic's government.

Over several decades, the political pattern has developed gradually but relentlessly. It has been shaped by two converging purposes: the general desire for political-military coordination of judgment and the Presidential desire for personal command of foreign policy. The results have likewise been twofold: the eclipsing of the Department of State's traditional responsibility for the conduct of foreign policy and the emerging within the White House of staff and organization to assume this control.

The trajectory of change may be seen with a glance back to the notions and the practices of Franklin Roosevelt. Acting as Secretary of the Navy, Roosevelt in 1919 outlined the first of many modern proposals for fuller coordination of policy between the military departments and the Department of State. Even so, his memorandum to the Secretary of State began with the traditional premise: "It is a fundamental principle that the foreign policy of our government is in the hands of the State Department." [80]

While Roosevelt stayed mindful of the general intent of his 1919 analysis, this "fundamental principle" would find little place in his own handling of foreign affairs. His choice of Cordell Hull to be Secretary of State reflected ample respect for Hull's personal influence on Capitol Hill but no respect for his counsel on world affairs. As Europe's war clouds grew darker in the 1930's, it was Hull who initiated a system of regular consultation between the State, War, and Navy departments in the form of a Standing Liaison Committee—the first agency in the nation's history designed to assure political-military consultation. But the approach of war found the President paying ever less attention to the committee, consulting directly with his Chiefs of Staff, and shying from the counsel of his Secretary of State.* With the progress of World War II, the Secretary found himself left out of the meetings of the War Council, he was left behind when the President journeyed abroad to meet with British or Soviet leaders, and the State Department was left to lan-

---

* The Roosevelt "shoot on sight" speech of September 11, 1940, was delivered over Hull's vehement objections. (Cf. Robert Sherwood, *The White House Papers of Harry Hopkins,* Vol. I, p. 373.)

guish as "almost an auxiliary arm of the military services." [81] Nor did the last year of the war and the prospect of peace change matters, despite establishment of a new State-War-Navy Coordinating Committee, the direct father of the National Security Council. Again and again, the military arguments prevailed over the diplomatic. With respect to Asia—even while disclaiming any role in political decisions—the Joint Chiefs of Staff insisted that all other political considerations should be subordinated to inducing the Soviet Union to enter the war against Japan. With respect to Europe—even though the State Department urged early discussion of postwar boundaries—the Joint Chiefs blocked any such anticipation of future problems, lest their mere mention set the Allies to quarreling.

In spirit and in fact, the development of these processes under Roosevelt served as prologue and model for the decades ahead. While the place of Harry Hopkins in the Roosevelt councils of the 1930's and 1940's foreshadowed the personal role of successive Presidential assistants—Messrs. McGeorge Bundy, Walt Rostow, and Henry Kissinger—in the White House of the 1960's and 1970's, the wartime prevalence of military over civilian counsel set the institutional tone that would dominate most deliberations of the National Security Council after its creation in 1947. Significantly, the council was established by a Congressional act whose primary concern was unification of the armed services. Quite sweepingly, however, it was construed by President Truman to be the "one top-level permanent setup in the government to concern itself with advising the President on high policy decisions" and to provide nothing less than "a running balance and a perpetual inventory of where we stood and where we were going." [82] Such a Presidential concept of the council left a scarcely visible franchise to the Department of State or its Policy Planning Staff. At the same time, as Charles W. Yost has pointed out, "the military orientation of the Council . . . almost inevitably accords undue weight in military factors in assessing foreign policy problems, many of which in other contexts would be seen to be overwhelmingly political or economic." [83]

The full effects of this orientation of the President's "one top-level permanent setup" could be seen in the mid-1960's—with the council's deliberations on the Vietnam War. In the earlier stages of these deliberations, Vice President Hubert Humphrey—quite contrary to his later public declarations—argued strenuously against military escalation, especially massive aerial bombardment of North Vietnam. But by the summer of 1965, his private admission of the futility of his efforts revealed the council's prevailing temper:

> It is a vain exercise—and an unequal struggle between the State Department and the Defense Department. The boys from State come into the NSC supposedly representing the *political* viewpoint; but the bulk of their arguments in favor of caution are generalities or theories. The fellows from Defense come in armed to the teeth. They have charts and graphs and maps and neat flags to plant all over them. Everything is concrete and specific. "Attack here, bomb there, and we promise this exact result." It is all confident and brisk and overwhelming. And it overwhelms any President looking for hard data to support a decision.[84]

From the viewpoint of the Department of State, the question might be asked: why could it not more effectively resist the militarization and centralization of the policy-making process by the White House? The answer largely lies in the paradoxical nature of the department itself. Although it has been the most important and prestigious of all Cabinet offices, it is also the most politically vulnerable and defenseless. For this, there are two basic reasons. In the first place—unlike such departments as Labor or Agriculture or Commerce—it serves and represents no specific constituency to give it a political weight of its own with which even a President must reckon. While farm leaders or union leaders or business leaders may rally to to the defense of their departments of direct concern, there is no community in the nation moved to denounce Presidential trespassing upon the functions of *its* Department of State. In the second place— as the outrage of McCarthyism proved in the early 1950's—almost any decrial of the nation's foreign policy tends to veer away from a frontal attack upon the White House in favor of a denunciation of the State Department. For any President is obviously protected by such allegiances, myths, and powers as shield no Secretary of State.

From the viewpoint of the White House, the question might be asked: why has this assertion of personal command been so much desired? The answer lies in the hope of keeping at a distance the two forces within the government most likely to challenge or to complicate Presidential prerogative: an independent bureaucracy and an inquisitive Congress. The empowering of a personal staff in the White House assures the President of defenses against both. Freed from reliance upon career officials, whose principles and interests can stay independent of any particular administration, the Chief Executive can surround himself with counselors who can be relied on to take ample account of his own political fortunes. And thanks to the protection of executive privilege, these same personal advisers—unlike a mere Secretary of State—can stay mute and safe, when Congressional committees are in a mood for probing or protesting.

From the viewpoint of the Republic itself, the serious effects of all this have appeared vastly less welcome. While the political presence of a powerful Secretary of State—presiding over a confident and independent department—offers no automatic assurance of the rule of wisdom, the centering of power within the White House poses risks that are virtually certain. These are at least five in number. (1) It encourages the direction of diplomacy for the sake of both political and theatrical effect, as exemplified by the secrecy of the Nixon Presidency's planning of the Chief Executive's 1972 journey to Peking, in order to achieve what Nixon proudly hailed as "the biggest surprise in history." (2) It threatens, with the President's ever more frequent recourse to "summit" meetings with other heads of state, the exposure of the Presidential office itself to all the chances of haste or blunder in such encounters. Or as Dean Acheson was given to warning: "When the President fumbles, the whole goal line is wide open." [85] (3) It encumbers the decision-making process by establishing within the White House an elaborate machinery often sure to duplicate and repeat reviews and analyses of major issues already exhaustively studied within the State Department. (4) It assures an eventual decline in the energy and the capacity of all officials, both in the State Department and in overseas missions, who feel shut out from the council making the Republic's policies. (5) It widens the gap—and increases the distrust—between the executive and legislative branches, by vesting policy-making responsibility in a staff that need have no acquaintance, much less conflict, with the views of Senate or House.*

These modern developments in the making of foreign policy oddly suggest a return to diplomatic ways abandoned long before the birth of the Republic itself. In the Western world's history, the growth of modern diplomatic practice—and the evolving of an orderly and systematic machinery for the conduct of foreign business—dates only from the Italian city-states of the fifteenth century. Prior to that age, the dynasts and their courts dealt, personally and autocratically, with all such affairs. This was only logical: as with most else in their realms, emperors and kings could attend to foreign relations as they saw fit. But with no necessary logic at all, the Presidential command over foreign policy has reverted toward that remote time. It has done so with its accent upon the President's personal role and presence, with its disregard for the use of ambassadors and serious negotiators, and with its designation of the White House "court" as the source for all great decisions. And the full consequence would seem to be, as former Undersecretary of State George Ball has written, that "toward the end of the 20th Century, the United States is moving back toward the medieval dynastic practice." * [86]

An arresting kind of confirmation of this appeared late in 1972 with the post-election martial diplomacy of President Richard Nixon with respect to the Vietnam War. The protracted negotiations that allegedly had brought "peace at hand" by October were punctuated, so to speak, by the Presidential order in December to punish North Vietnam with probably the most massive bombings in military history. There were at least two notable aspects to this exercise of Presidential prerogative. First: the Chief Executive felt no need or duty to speak a public word of explanation to the citizenry. Second: the President had made his policy in almost absolutely solitary confidence. He did not consult the Joint Chiefs of Staff. He had not called a Cabinet meeting in two months. He had not held a press conference in two and a half months. He had not called a

---

* In the words of Senator J. W. Fulbright: "The shift of responsibility from the Secretary of State to the National Security Council . . . insulates the makers of foreign policy from consultation. . . . You get the impression that what we have now is a kind of intuitive policy-making system." (New York *Times*, April 28, 1972.)

meeting of the National Security Council in more than six months.

The ultimate danger in all this has hardly been hidden from view. It would have alarmed any of the Founding Fathers, of course, who shared Jefferson's faith that they had empowered the legislature to give "effectual check to the Dog of war." And the shape of the peril was perfectly clear to such an observer of the Presidency as Edward S. Corwin even before World War II. Writing in 1941, he might have been writing of the tragedy of Vietnam—still a quarter of a century distant:

> Contrary to a common, but quite mistaken impression, no President has a mandate from the Constitution to conduct our foreign relations according to his own sweet will. . . . There is no field where Presidential whim has been more rampant or its solicitations for popular support more misleading and dangerous. But why not a foreign policy based on candor and a real attempt at securing popular understanding of its motivation, rather than on bamboozlement and hysteria? [87]

The question would hover in the political air, and haunt the Republic, for decades to come.

Eight

Some Thoughts by Way of Conclusion: The Destiny of the Presidency

I

Shall we have a King?

—JOHN JAY to GEORGE WASHINGTON, 1787

We have begun obscurely to recognize that things do not go of themselves, and that popular government is not in itself a panacea, is no better than any other form except as the virtue and wisdom of the people make it so, and that when men undertake to do their own kingship, they enter upon the dangers and responsibilities as well as the privileges of the function.

—JAMES RUSSELL LOWELL, 1869
"On A Certain Condescension in Foreigners"

I can only believe that after a citizen searches out all the ways for Presidents to lead or to mislead—and all the proofs of Presidential power to dignify or to demean the Republic—the mystery of the Presidency still stays something of a mystery. The end of this inquiry leads, therefore, not to many ringing answers but perhaps to some lasting clues. A favored way for Harry Truman to define his office was: "The buck stops here." A wise way for any watcher of the White House to look upon the Presidency, I think, must be with a like awareness: the *theory* stops here. And the unruly paradoxes take over.

It could hardly be otherwise. For the office was made from the first to taunt its students—or its Presidents—who covet the simple answer. "It is a melancholy reflection that liberty should be equally exposed to danger," James Madison wrote to Thomas Jefferson in 1788, "whether the Government have too much or too little power." [1] The comment applied particularly to the Presidency. But since there could be no way of prescribing "too much" or "too little" for generations yet unborn, there was no recourse but to leave it to them to seek out the balance, and grapple with the contradictions, as the need of the time and the mood of the nation—and the character of a President—might decree.

So it has tensely and unpredictably stayed with the office. To one President, its constraints have ordained scrupulous reticence. To another, its powers have roused sheer exuberance. For one spell of history, it has loomed as a vibrant study in aggrandizement; for another, it has looked like a tame study in appeasement. It has exhilarated the progressives of one decade, and it has exasperated those of the next.

The subtlest tests that the office has imposed upon each President, moreover, have been exercises in political contradiction. He has been the Chief Executive whom the politics of the twentieth century made into the Chief Legislator: the one leader in the Republic always capable of focusing public concern and compelling Congressional action. He has been the hero figure who has been required, by the demands of popular imagery, to be at once the master of politics, who gets great things done, and the disdainer of politics, who leaves great illusions intact. And by the nature of his commission, he has been forced to be two human beings in one: the man who courageously stands alone to make his ultimate decision and the man who intelligently fears his own isolation as his ultimate peril.

By logic or by chance, the abiding paradoxes of the political office often have seemed to be mirrored in the living qualities of the most famous Presidents. This appeared true even from the first, with Washington: the Virginian patrician who chose to lead a revolutionary rabble; the chronic pessimist who made his countrymen stout optimists; and the surveyor of the political scene most distrustful of the role of personality, whose own personality decisively shaped the powers and set the precedents of the Presidency itself. . . . Nor were the contradictory ways any less apparent in a Lincoln: the critic of Presidential power who brandished this power as never before; the pragmatic Great Emancipator who was far more concerned about union than emancipation; and the rough-hewn and self-taught citizen who could speak of his office and his country in language never surpassed for beauty and insight.

As personal proofs of Presidential ambivalence, a Washington or a Lincoln might be discounted, perhaps, as figures from folklore blurred by myth. But there are modern witnesses to similar anomalies. The character of Franklin Roosevelt, for example, was subjected to the close scrutiny of an observer as sophisticated as Robert E. Sherwood. And the conclusions of Sherwood were these:

> I tried continuously to study him . . . but I could never really understand what was going on in there. His character was . . . contradictory to a bewildering degree. He was hard and he was soft. At times he displayed a capacity for vindictiveness which could be described as petty, and at other times he demonstrated the Christian spirit of forgiveness and charity in its purest form. . . .
>
> He could appear to be utterly cynical, worldly, illusionless, and yet his religious faith was the strongest and most mysterious force that was in him.
>
> Although he was progressive enough and liberal enough to be condemned as a "traitor to his class" and "that Red in the White House," he was in truth a profoundly old-fashioned person with an incurable nostalgia for the very "horse-and-buggy era" on which he publicly heaped so much scorn. . . .
>
> He liked to fancy himself as a practical, down-to-earth, horse-sense realist—he often used to say "Winston and Uncle Joe and I get along well together because we're all *realists*"—and yet his idealism was actually no less empyrean than Woodrow Wilson's.[2]

To this appraisal, Roosevelt himself had written a kind of prefatory note, with a "Memorandum on Leadership" that dated from the year 1928. At that time, he had felt two special bonds: a family kinship to Theodore Roosevelt and a party kinship to Woodrow Wilson. But the difference between these two Presidents had not escaped him. "Theodore Roosevelt lacked Woodrow Wilson's appeal to the fundamental and failed to stir, as Wilson did, the truly profound moral and social convictions," FDR judged. "Wilson, on the other hand, failed where Theodore Roosevelt succeeded in stirring people to enthusiasm over specific individual events, even though these specific events may have been superficial in comparison with the fundamentals." [3] And I think it reasonable to believe that this shrewd sense of distinct values stayed with Franklin Roosevelt five years later, when he inaugurated his own ambivalent Presidency.

There followed, of course, the Truman Presidency. The background, personality, and style of this Chief Executive provided an almost absolute contrast to his predecessor. And yet—precisely what Robert Sherwood discerned in Roosevelt was what Dean Acheson later wrote of Truman:

> As only those close to him knew, Harry S. Truman was two men. One was the public figure—peppery, sometimes belligerent, often didactic, the "give-'em-hell" Harry. The other was the patient, modest, considerate and appreciative boss, helpful and understanding in all official matters, affectionate and sympathic in any private worry or sorrow. This was the "Mr. President" we knew and loved. [4]

This particular vignette hints at one more disconcerting mark of the office: the tenuous connection—and the frequent conflict—between personal virtues and Presidential virtues. In simple terms, the "belligerent" Truman would not have been a "considerate" companion, the "understanding" Truman would not have been a lusty partisan, and the "modest" Truman that "we knew and loved" was surely not the campaigner who defeated Thomas E. Dewey in the 1948 election. In broad terms, a quality as estimable as humility in a man can seem no more than timidity in a President. And the steely sense of purpose surely wanted in a national leader is hardly welcomed in a town neighbor.

A remembrance of the deeply different Presidential methods of Franklin Roosevelt and Dwight Eisenhower underscores the same truth. The *effectiveness* of Roosevelt's leadership turned on several intellectually unattractive devices: an appeal to political melodrama, an indifference to philosophic principles, and a deceptive manipulation of his closest counselors. The *ineffectiveness* of Eisenhower's leadership revolved around some undeniably decent dispositions: a distaste for political theatrics, a loyalty to theoretical precepts, and a sincere deference to those around him, whether in the Cabinet or in the Congress. And a perception of these very traits in Eisenhower led a veteran watcher of Presidents, Speaker of the House Sam Rayburn, to his incisive judgment of 1952: "No, won't do. Good man. Wrong profession."

I I

The President is not merely an administrative office. That is the least part of it. It is more than an engineering job, efficient or inefficient. It is preeminently a place of moral leadership. All our great Presidents were leaders of thought at times when certain historic ideas in the life of the nation had to be clarified.[5]

—FRANKLIN ROOSEVELT, 1932

The elusive essence of the Presidency is to be sought in a very few key questions. As befits a mystery, the questions seem reasonably clear, while the answers are surely imperfect. And the probing may go along such lines as these:

Through the history of the Republic, has the quality of Presidential leadership been more truly set by personal character or by political climate?

The advocates of a sort of Presidential determinism, who have scanned each Presidency as a creation of the age rather than the man, can advance at least a couple of plausible arguments. For one thing, there is no doubt that the great increments of Presidential power most often can be associated with great events. These political changes in the office have come under the spur of national crisis, not any plan of Presidential conquest. So it was with Washington's firm show of authority over foreign affairs, or Lincoln's dictatorial posture in the face of civil war, or Wilson's sweeping elaboration of Presidential wartime powers, or Roosevelt's massive legislative retort to the Great Depression. Moreover, it can be contended that Presidents, like most powerful national leaders, seem to wear the circumstances of their particular times so much like robes that it becomes hard to imagine them in any other historic clothing. Can one conceive of even a liberal-minded John F. Kennedy zestfully spreading the gospel of the "New Frontier" to the politically deaf and complacent Republic of the 1920's? Or can one envision even so tough-minded a Chief Executive as Harry S. Truman inventively concocting the brew of the New Deal or artfully maneuvering the nation toward its military commitment in World War II?

Yet all these propositions, reasonable though they are, do not seem the real keys to the life of the Presidency. The quickest proof of this can be seen in the futility of any attempt to re-create the Republic's history with the personalities of even a few Presidents radically changed. One need only ponder how profoundly different would be the story of both the nation and the Presidency *if* Washington had learned from his soldier's life only a passion for militarism, or *if* Jefferson had stayed loyal to his own preachment about strict construction of Presidential powers, or *if* Wilson had been a stubborn pacifist in world affairs *or* a skilled diplomat in Congressional affairs, or *if* Franklin Roosevelt had been . . . a Warren Harding. As for the behavior of a Lincoln in a time of crisis, there is a striking profile of him drawn by the historians Samuel Eliot Morison and Henry Steele Commager, as they saw him after the Seven Days' Battles of the summer of 1862 had ended with the failure of his Army of the Potomac to take Richmond:

> If the situation had changed for the worse, Lincoln had attained new stature. . . . From those anxious vigils at the White House during the Seven Days the perplexed, over-advised and humble Lincoln emerged humble only before God, but the master of men. He seemed to have captured all the greater qualities of the great Americans who preceded him, without their defects: the poise of Washington without his aloofness, the astuteness of Jefferson without his indirection, the conscience of J. Q. Adams without his harshness, the forthrightness of Jackson without his ignorance, the magnetism of Clay without his vanity, the lucidity of Webster without his ponderousness; and fused them with a magnanimity peculiarly his own.[6]

Such a portrait of a Presidency on trial leaves rather little space for the faceless forces of history. There have been times in the life of the Presidency, of course, that would move any citizen to mourn with Emerson that "things are in the saddle, and ride mankind," but it remained for the men in the White House to prove, by their own bearing of "things" and events, whether they were strong enough horses for the burden of such history. The fact that the Republic's trials can be so closely related to the President's powers suggests occasion rather than cause. For might not the pressure of these same times of stress have exhausted, rather than enlarged, the political resources of the Presidency? There is little in the modern fate of Western democracies—from Germany's Weimar Republic to France's Fourth Republic—to argue that political crisis naturally helps fortify executive power.

Nor is it at all a fact of American history that the onset of crisis has found the Presidency, by some wondrous dispensation, always rising strong in mastery of the moment. In the first testing of the young Republic in 1812, James Madison, as President, proved a painfully feeble leader. Throughout the years of mounting tension before the Civil War, a succession of four Presidents—Millard Fillmore, Zachary Taylor, James Buchanan, and Franklin Pierce—contributed nothing historically helpful to the avoidance of national tragedy. And the advent of the Great Depression did not bring on the unveiling of hidden faculties for leadership in Herbert Hoover.

The truth would seem to be that all the historic circumstances working toward an enrichment of Presidential power, at any grave moment in the nation's life, could never assure the *presence* of a man waiting and wanting to claim the legacy. Between the chance and the fact, there had to intervene a creative and persuasive President. Thus, a Woodrow Wilson who led the Republic for the first time to the center of the world stage was not enabled—even by such dramatic circumstance—to avoid an end to his Presidential life that shattered his global dream. Yet a Franklin Roosevelt, who knew so much less than Wilson about the world of nations, could forge a Grand Alliance and die mourned as a hero by all the West. And a John Kennedy, who gave nothing of himself or of his nation to the people or governments of Southeast Asia, could somehow project a political aura and a Presidential style that could make the time of his death an occasion for nearly as much sorrow in Malaya as in Massachusetts.

Among all the Presidencies, can a fair and reasoned judgment single out some for superiority and greatness?

The balancing of this question requires the touching of almost the same scales: the weight of personality against the weight of history. And it is easy to understand those students of politics who challenge any ranking of the Presidents as a specious exercise. There appear no serious and constant historical standards. By what criteria can one compare the regime of a Calvin Coolidge in the apathetic mid-1920's and the administration of a Lyndon Johnson in the turbulent mid-1960's? Or how can the performance of any Chief Executive in peacetime be measured against the leadership of any Chief Executive in wartime? And what is the meaning of "greatness" itself? If the essential test be *intent*—all the goodness of will and purpose that may have been mauled by cruel circumstance— the resulting verdict really deals with the person, not the President. If the test be *impact,* however, a courageous but limited Andrew Johnson, who narrowly averted impeachment for his fight against the Reconstruction Radicals in Congress, would have to be rated "greater" than at least a half dozen Presidents of conspicuously larger talents, from John Quincy Adams to William Howard Taft.

All this is sensible caution, and yet—all historians of the Republic have agreed upon the names of eight to ten Presidents who seem to tower above all the rest. In 1948, for example, the distinguished Harvard University scholar Arthur M. Schlesinger conducted a "Presidential poll" of fifty-five other students of American history and government. The results gave the accolade of "great" or "near great" to ten Presidents: Lincoln, Washington, Franklin Roosevelt, Wilson, Jefferson, Jackson, Theodore Roosevelt, Cleveland, John Adams, and Polk.* The poll was repeated by Professor Schlesinger in 1962, now with seventy-five historians, and as he reported: "The longer perspective adds weight to the previous judgment." [7] For fourteen years later, there was no significant change in the earlier verdict but for the addition of the name of Harry S. Truman.

There always could be thoughtful argument about the order of preference in such a listing, of course. The 1962 survey provoked just such dissent from John Kennedy. As his reactions have been summarized by his aide, Arthur M. Schlesinger, Jr., the President had this to say:

* This may be compared with the list of Harold Laski on p. 76.

He was greatly pleased that Truman made the "near great" class. He was also interested that Eisenhower rated only twenty-eighth, near the bottom of the "average" category. . . . What surprised him particularly in the poll was the high rating given to Wilson—fourth in the list and in the "great" category. . . . Why did the professors admire him so much? . . . He also wondered about Theodore Roosevelt. . . . Why should either Wilson or Theodore Roosevelt rate ahead of Polk (number eight) or Truman (number nine)? It seemed evident that his measure of presidential success was concrete achievement; thus people who educated the nation without necessarily accomplishing their particular purposes rated, in his judgment, below those, like Polk and Truman, who accomplished their purposes without necessarily bringing the nation along with them. The best, of course, were those who did both, and he agreed with the panel's choice of the top three—Lincoln, Washington and Franklin Roosevelt.[8]

The issue of precedence matters less than a larger question: what common qualities of character, mind, and temperament have united and distinguished so select a group? There immediately appears one rather disconcerting fact: a clearly superior intellect has not been a decisive trait. The Presidential elite does not include, for example, two of the most intellectually gifted men ever to live in the White House: John Quincy Adams, who has been appraised by some historians as the Republic's greatest Secretary of State, and James Madison, who has been remembered as the principal architect of the Constitution itself.* Instead, the honorary roll includes the name of a rather pedestrian man whom even a sympathetic biographer has called "Polk the Mediocre." Yet this Polk proved to be the only effective President between Jackson and Lincoln. As the historian George Bancroft, who served in Polk's Cabinet as Secretary of the Navy, could write of him fifty years later:

* There may belong here, too, the more modern case of Lyndon Johnson. After serving in the Johnson White House, Professor Eric Goldman wrote a sensitive but critical assessment under the title of *The Tragedy of Lyndon Johnson* (New York, Dell Publishing Co., 1969). Its closing pages of judgment observe: "After years of meeting first-rate minds in and out of universities, I am sure I have never met a more intelligent person than Lyndon Johnson—intelligent in terms of sheer IQ, a clear, swift, penetrating mind, with an abundance of its own type of imagination and subtleties" (p. 622).

His administration, viewed from the standpoint of results, was perhaps the greatest in our history, certainly one of the greatest. He succeeded because he insisted on being its center and in overruling and guiding all his secretaries to act so as to produce unity and harmony.[9]

And nearly a century later, there came on the Presidential stage a Franklin Roosevelt who earned the famous backhanded tribute of Justice Oliver Wendell Holmes as "a second-class intellect, but a first-class temperament."

The quip of Holmes amounts to an explaining clue. For a President can always hire brains. But there is no way for him to lease fortitude or borrow intuition. Indeed, the history of the Presidency in the twentieth century sharply suggests a related truth: there can follow real harm from an Executive temperament too dedicated to imposing rationality on all the workings of the office. Precisely this temperament set the style of the administrations of Taft and Hoover and Eisenhower. The lawyer, the engineer, and the soldier—all three shared, by virtue of their training and their careers, a stubborn sense of the Presidency as essentially a place for the reign of order and reason and system. And this illusion helped create the air of rigidity —and placidity—so oppressive in the White House of each man.

As for the more positive qualities of the "greater" Chief Executives, there appears none more striking and insistent than a near passion for pragmatism. The habit was seemingly set by a Jefferson who, with all his fondness for purist constitutional theory, could still, as Chief Executive, serenely philosophize: "What is practical must often control what is pure theory." [10] Almost as one, the most assertive Presidents seemed to know what James Russell Lowell meant by the warning that "there is nothing so pitilessly and unconsciously cruel as sincerity formulated into dogma." And by all their more important acts and policies, they seemed as clearly to concur with Lowell's major precepts, inferred from the life of Lincoln, on "the course of a great statesman":

It is loyalty to great ends, even though forced to combine the small and opposing motives of selfish men to accomplish them; it is the anchored clinging to solid principles of duty and action, which knows how to swing with the tide, but is never carried away by it,—that we demand in public men, and not obstinacy in prejudice, sameness of policy, or a conscientious persistency in what is impracticable.[11]

These Presidents had several other marks in common—aside from the harsh fact that all were far less respected by contemporary observers than by future generations. Virtually all of them, as Professor Schlesinger noted, "arrived at their forward-looking convictions from aristocratic stations in life."[12] With really no exceptions, these Presidents reached down, from their own more favored places in the society of their times, to shape the future of the Republic. They all were—with the single exception of Washington—unabashedly ambitious for the office they finally won. They all were—even including Washington—zealous partisans, at the very least in demanding loyalty within their own executive branch. They all were, not surprisingly, acquisitive of more power for their office. They all provoked, quite inevitably, bitter opposition from both public and press, so that even the first President could cry out against his own denunciation "in such exaggerated and indecent terms as could scarcely be applied to a Nero, a notorious defaulter, or even to a common pickpocket."[13] And no aggressive successor to Washington, over the next two centuries, felt himself much less slandered or maligned.

It was both logical and revealing, moreover, that all these men in the White House engaged in vigorous battle not only with the Congress but also with the Supreme Court. Jefferson led the House of Representatives to impeach a particularly obnoxious justice of the Court, and he clearly longed to visit the same treatment on Chief Justice John Marshall. Lincoln repeatedly cited military necessity as his grounds for wholly ignoring Court decrees. Wilson deplored the conservatism of the Supreme Court as the "most obvious and immediate danger" to the Republic.[14] Franklin Roosevelt advanced his scheme for "packing" the Court with younger men as an essential corrective to its "horse and buggy" mentality. These were not chance collisions. To the extent that the Republic was to be presided over by a "government of laws," the Supreme Court obviously held the highest commission to guard this trust. But how could judicial strictures be tolerable to the men who—*also* under the constitutional system—forever had to be playing the "wild card" of Presidential power?

The readiness of these Presidents for such constitutional combat has reflected, in turn, a quite elemental matter of personal temper: an instinct and a vigor for action. A strong strain of this appeared in all these men, almost regardless of political or individual circumstance—whether it was the first Roosevelt strutting in his cowboy suit or the second Roosevelt settled in his wheelchair. Here may also be a clue that explains something of the emotional impact of the Kennedy Presidency. Its life was too short for memorable confrontations with the Congress or the Court—or for serious pretenses to "greatness." But a zest for action was a mark of its brief span. As an administration, it seemed to catch the spirit of words that John Kennedy had written, many years earlier, about his older brother, who had died in World War II: "Even when still, there was always a sense of motion forcibly restrained." The simple sentence might have described any of the more effective Presidents. In a relaxed but reflective moment, this same President could watch the inexhaustible activity of a friend's child and observe seriously: "I suppose if you had to choose just one quality to have, that would be it: vitality." [15] And such a Presidential comment from the mid-twentieth century could be heard as a kind of echo of Alexander Hamilton's first call for "energy in the Executive" as essential to "the definition of good government."

A final quality linked these exceptional administrations and elevated their pragmatic methods. Consciously and tenaciously, all of them aspired to be exercises in moral leadership. They did not merely strive to get things done: they clearly sensed what things *should* be done—above all, in the name of humanity. And a warm statement of this sentiment and this commitment came in 1932 from Franklin Roosevelt, perhaps the most dogged pragmatist of all Presidents:

> We have had in our history three men who chiefly stand out for the universality of their interest and their knowledge—Benjamin Franklin, Thomas Jefferson, and Theodore Roosevelt. All three knew at first-hand every cross-current of national and international life. All three were possessed of a profound culture in the best sense

of the word, and yet all three understood the yearnings and the lack of opportunity, the hopes and fears of millions of their fellow beings. All true culture finally comes down to an appreciation of that.[16]

For the future of the Republic, should the powers of the Presidency be redefined and restricted?

The impulse has been powerful for all critics of Presidential power, especially in the wake of the Vietnam tragedy, to seek to banish all risk for all time by grand institutional reform or sweeping Congressional statute. Yet I have come to believe that there is more prudence in the less exhilarating view of James Bryce that "historical development is wiser than the wisest man." As Bryce went on to say: "A succession of small improvements, each made conformably to existing conditions and habits, is more likely to succeed than a large scheme made all at once in what may be called the spirit of conscious experiment." [17] What Bryce's sense of history lacks in political melodrama, it more than makes up for in political memory of the mood and intent of the Founding Fathers with respect to the Presidency. For the heart of their purpose was to leave the office free enough to act "conformably" to ever-changing times and needs. And there could be no more drastic remaking of this slack but deliberate design of the Presidency than any effort to chisel its limits into statutory stone.

If this seems perhaps too traditional a sort of caution against a reforming zeal, there are other facts of history suggesting quite practical reasons for restraint. A lasting mark of the political life of the Republic has been its constantly cyclical rhythm. For spans of sometimes a dozen years, sometimes nearly a score of years, these cycles have witnessed either a Presidential-progressive ascendancy or a Congressional-conservative ascendancy. The times of innovation have alternated with the times of consolidation, as the temper of the nation has variously called for a surge of change or a pause for rest.* And this historic rhythm could hardly be recognized by any rigid reconstruction of Presidential powers, possibly apt for one such cycle but surely alien to the other.

There must also be some account taken of an elusive but real

---

* A scanning of the Presidencies suggests that Harry S. Truman may have been the *only* strongly aggressive President to have followed an equally aggressive predecessor.

aspect of Presidential life: the often instinctive inclination of the Chief Executive toward *self*-restraint. With one President, this may be ascribed to a sense of timidity, and with another, it may be accredited to a sense of history—and the place he covets there. But whatever the motive, this self-discipline figured importantly even in the political conduct of a President as uninhibited as Lincoln. After years of wielding more arbitrary power than any other Chief Executive, Lincoln still could write to a friend, in the last month of his life:

> I am naturally anti-slavery. If slavery is not wrong, nothing is wrong. . . . And yet I have never understood that the Presidency conferred upon me an unrestricted right to act officially upon this judgment and feeling. . . . And I aver that, to this day, I have done no official act in mere deference to my abstract judgment and feeling on slavery.[18]

Although these words came from a President as rare as a Lincoln, there is much history to support the belief that all Presidents almost always place some check on their "abstract judgments," when faced with their gravest decisions.

A fondness for questionable abstractions may appear, in fact, more often a habit of the office's reformers than of its Presidents. This seems particularly true of one theory for redesigning the Presidency that has enjoyed recurrent fashion: the idea of a single Presidential term of six years. The notion is as old as the Constitutional Convention that rejected it, of course, but it retains some beguiling appeal. Apparently, it promises a President two tempting gifts: a longer time to lead his programs toward fulfillment, and a greater freedom from all supposedly sordid concern over his own reelection. But a few questions may suffice to indicate the shallowness of such a scheme for a responsive democracy. Why should a possibly ineffectual or lethargic Chief Executive be assured half again as much time to stultify the life of the Republic? Why would not a one-term President find the summoning of support for his proudest programs ever more difficult, over more years, as the certain surrender of his power neared? And why should any President be completely freed—from the moment of taking his oath—of all anxious concern for public response to his actions, a response that he may weigh in no terms more scrupulously than his chances to win a new mandate?

A great deal of the search for Presidential reform, I believe, often tends to lose sight of a basic distinction. For any realistic proposals for change must recognize two issues as at least somewhat separable. These are: the Presidency empowered to deal with national affairs and the Presidency armed to deal with world affairs.

This distinction between "the two Presidencies" has to be as imperfect as most generalizations about Presidential life. So close a witness of the White House as Clark Clifford, an intimate counselor of all Democratic Presidents since World War II, challenges the notion, and he cites the legislative achievements of Lyndon Johnson as proof of a President's power to act effectively on the domestic front regardless of the fate of his foreign ventures.* The hazards in foreign affairs, moreover, can prove as dizzying as the powers. Or as John Kennedy more than once remarked: "Domestic policy . . . can only defeat us. Foreign policy can kill us." [19]

And yet—the life of the modern Presidency surely reflects a lastingly larger freedom and power to act in the foreign realm. The fact was at once symbolized and dramatized by two of the towering events of the Truman Presidency: all the dispatch and energy with which the thirty-third President led the Republic into the Korean War meant nothing, either to the Congress or the Supreme Court, when he invoked the same war as sovereign reason for his seizure of the steel industry. Nor was that contrast at all untypical of a general pattern prevailing since the 1930's. After 1938, when conservative Democrats and Republicans forged their Congressional alliance, even a Chief Executive as skillful as Franklin Roosevelt could not win passage of one notable piece of domestic legislation. For varying reasons, neither Truman nor Eisenhower nor Kennedy could point to legislative records of much more distinction. But all this while, there occurred not a single occasion in the realm of foreign policy—from entry into the United Nations to entry into the Vietnam War—when a determined President failed to make his will prevail.†

---

* Cf. "The Presidency as I Have Seen It," Statement of Clark Clifford, pp. 314–20.

† The distance between the two spheres of action can be almost mathematically proved. The Congressional Quarterly Service made a statistical survey of legisla-

There is nothing really strange or surprising in this unbalanced state of Presidential affairs. It follows almost inescapably from some of the most sensitive facts of Presidential life: within the executive branch, the encountering of the least bureaucratic resistance when foreign, rather than domestic, decisions are at stake; with regard to the legislative branch, a like freedom from obstruction by massive lobbies or angry constituencies usually stirred to battle only over matters of immediate self-interest; and with respect to the general public, the special acceptance accorded to Presidential opinions and actions directed toward the world beyond the Republic's frontiers. For all these reasons, a President's artful use of crisis works with particular effect in the realm of foreign affairs. A sweeping and masterful control of domestic policy, such as was witnessed through the first hundred days of the New Deal, can come only with a crisis all too visible—and oppressive—to the whole electorate. But the "crisis" vindicating policy in a distant Far Eastern nation or Latin American Republic needs no such popular recognition. The President's alerting word suffices.*

Nor is this special accent in Presidential authority only a logical product of political circumstance: it is also a respected premise of constitutional theory, as expounded by the Supreme Court itself. In the 1936 case of *United States v. Curtiss-Wright Export Corporation,* the Court outlined "the two Presidencies" in these terms:

> The difference between the powers of the federal government in respect of foreign or external affairs and those in respect of domestic or internal affairs . . . are fundamental and may not be doubted.
>
> The two classes of power are different, both in respect of their origin and their nature. The broad statement that the federal government can exercise no powers except those specifically enumerated in

---

tive responses to Presidential initiatives from 1948 to 1964. Summarily, the record shows the President getting his way in some 70 percent of the instances in foreign and defense policy, as against some 40 percent in the domestic realm.[20]

* There might be added to this the testimony of the thirty-seventh President, whose knowledge of the ways of federal government could hardly be denied by even his severest political critics. After three years in the White House, Richard Nixon reported: "In the field of foreign policy, a President can act, and he should act and he should lead and, generally speaking, he can carry the country with him. . . . But in the field of domestic policy, it is a very, very different matter. Here a President can propose, and then Congress does what it pleases." (Cited by editorial in New York *Times,* December 31, 1972.)

the Constitution . . . is categorically true only in respect of our internal affairs. . . .

We are dealing not alone with an authority vested in the President by an exertion of legislative power, but with such an authority plus the very delicate, plenary and exclusive power of the President as the sole organ of the federal government in the field of international relations—a power which does not require as a basis for its exercise an act of Congress. . . . Practically every volume of the United States Statutes contains one or more acts or joint resolutions of Congress authorizing action by the President in respect of subjects affecting foreign relations, which either leave the exercise of the power to his unrestricted judgment, or provide a standard far more general than that which has always been considered requisite with regard to domestic affairs.

All this points toward one reasonable conclusion about the problem of the threat of Presidential power. The peril does not arise from the historic nature or the whole concept of the office. It follows from an extravagance of the specific freedom and authority enjoyed by the Chief Executive to make foreign war and foreign policy.

Yet there assuredly does *not* follow from this a saving corrective in anything so simple as a broad reassertion of Congressional power. The history of the Republic provides no convincing reason to expect Congressional judgment to be superior, in prudence or foresight, to Presidential judgment on the nation's role in the world. Out of eight wars that the Republic has known since its creation, the force of opinion within the walls of Congress may be credited as decisive with respect to two: the War of 1812 and the 1898 War with Spain. These were neither glorious nor rational encounters.

The weight of this evidence, I believe, argues that the seriously binding restraints must be not so much matters of statute as matters of practice. With regard to the Congress, what might be more healthy and welcome than the striking of a balance between its harsh defiance of the Presidency after World War I and its bipartisan obsequiousness toward the Presidency after World War II? But this cannot be decreed or inspired by some new "law of the land." It is an issue of collective mood, will, and courage.

The same point was underscored, even in the case of the Vietnam War, by the Senate's own Foreign Relations Committee's Report on National Commitments:

> If blame is to be apportioned, the greater share probably belongs to the Congress. It is understandable, though not acceptable, that in times of real or seeming emergency, the Executive will be tempted to take shortcuts around Constitutional procedure. It is less understandable that the Congress should acquiesce in these shortcuts, giving away that which is not its to give.[21]

Or as the awkward but critical role of Congress has been well described by Senator Fulbright:

> To those of us who have developed an appreciation of the capacity of people in high places for doing stupid things, there is much to be said for institutional processes which compel people to think things over before plunging into action. . . .
>
> I for one am not distressed by the charge that Congress is not an up-to-date institution. In this age of the SST, the ABM, the MIRV, and the Indochina War, being "behind the times" may indeed be a mark of wisdom. . . .
>
> The greatest single virtue of a strong legislature is not what it can do but what it can prevent.* [22]

This perception of the place of Senators implied an equally realistic understanding of the presumption of Presidents. For the fact is that statutes and rules designed to control Presidential action *after* the fact of decision matter far less than the debate and the data that come *before* any such decision. It can be a nearly impossible task to control a President, once he has made up his mind. But it is not at all impossible to keep him from reaching a conclusion—mindlessly.

In this political spirit, there appears much reason to seek a few of what James Bryce called "small improvements" in the institutional behavior of the Presidency. There may be four such develop-

---

* This echoes the good sense of Justice Louis Brandeis: "The doctrine of separation of powers was adopted by the Constitution in 1787, not to promote efficiency but to preclude the exercise of arbitrary power." [23]

ments, I believe, both practical and wanted. *First:* there appears no statutory restraint, among all the varied formulas proposed, so likely to be workable as clear Congressional control of selective service. This would limit the scope of Presidential military commitments to the size of the armed forces in being, and it would reserve to Congress alone the authority to use the military draft to serve Presidential causes.* *Second:* there is need for faithful observance of some formal liaison with Congressional leaders that allows for private deliberating of any major foreign policy decision. Ultimately, the observance obviously depends on the insistence of the Congress. *Third:* there can evolve, by law or by custom, an arrangement of terms under which the White House would submit to the Congress, or some designated body thereof, the substance of any executive agreement of a military nature that a President proposed to sign with any foreign power. And a similar kind of understanding needs to be achieved with respect to White House invocation of "executive privilege"—even though any such understanding may eventually require enforcement by a Supreme Court ruling. *Fourth:* there might be no reform of procedures so historically important as a return of the Department of State to its traditional place in the forming of foreign policy. Disconcerting or distasteful as this might be to modern Presidential ways, it would give back the day-to-day burden of foreign affairs to men who know they must answer the calls or the critiques of Congress. And it would bring into the Oval Office the voices of some who are likely to care less about the immediate luck of the Presidents than about the long life of the nation.

Yet all these proposals are rather pallid prescriptions, I suspect, beside one powerful fact. What politically matters and historically decides will be what the citizenry, and their chosen representatives, accept or reject, welcome or question, and give or withhold. These are the crucial contingencies: whether they are too distracted to have a will of their own about their own world; whether they are pleased to leave all concern and judgment to supposedly higher authority; and whether they are uncritical enough to ascribe this authority to any man who may happen to be President. There are

* Cf. "The Presidency as I Have Seen It," Abe Fortas, pp. 330–38.

no statutes that can forbid such surrender. And there are no restrictive laws that can take the place of rebellious men.

III

I pray Heaven to bestow the best of Blessings on this House and all that shall hereafter inhabit it. May none but honest and wise men ever rule under this roof.

—JOHN ADAMS, 1800

The prayer thus offered, for himself and his successors, was composed by the first President ever to sleep in the White House, even before the building itself was finished. Long after, its text was carved into the mantel of the State Dining Room, at the direction of Franklin Roosevelt. A bit of its spirit sometimes even flickered in an occasional "fireside chat" by Roosevelt—as when he told the nation in the spring of 1938: "I never forget that I live in a house owned by all the American people and that I have been given their trust." [24] In any case, the prayer has remained, whether read or unread, the most essential and direct of commandments to all Presidents and their lives.

It is not easy, as should be apparent, to summarize these lives. Figuratively, each appears much more like a web than a quilt. Were it the latter, it could be described in patches or pieces: the President as Chief Executive, as Chief Legislator, as Chief of State, as Chief Diplomat, as Chief Economist, as Chief Partisan, and as Commander in Chief. But the actual life of the President acknowledges no firm lines between these roles: he can discharge few duties independently of all other duties. At one time or another, the diplomat able to deal with the problems of India must be the tactician able to deal with the politics of Illinois. The Great Administrator who cannot keep his own executive house in order cannot be the Great Bargainer in tests of strength with another branch of government. The Chief Executive who, for reasons of policy or personality, fails to command the lasting loyalty of leaders of his own party has little chance for larger influence over leaders of great labor unions or great business empires. The President who cannot persuade the Congress to respect his resolve will have a hard time exciting such respect in the Kremlin. And the Maker of World Peace can assure neither the security nor the serenity of the Republic unless he proves also to be the Protector of National Prosperity. This is the tangled web of politics in which the President must live and lead—all the while keeping his sense of direction, his sense of history, and his sense of humor.

The life of the President becomes, in the most serious political sense, his life with the people. Even a Calvin Coolidge, among the least pretentious of the Republic's first thirty-seven Presidents, glimpsed this well enough to say: "It is because in their hours of timidity the Congress becomes subservient to the importunities of organized minorities that the President comes more and more to stand as the champion of the people." [25] Even a William Howard Taft, among the Presidents most respectful of Congressional prerogatives, years earlier concluded: "The truth is that it often happens that the President more truly represents the entire country than does a majority in one or both of the houses." [26] Yet the communion between President and people is at once intimate and strained, for the popular hunger for leadership stays almost beyond satisfying. With the age of television, there has come the common observation that a President, or any aspirant to the office, must possess charisma. Almost always, the word has been taken to mean little more than personal charm. But the dictionary gives quite another primary definition: "an extraordinary power (as of healing) given a Christian by the Holy Spirit for the good of the church." And in American political life, this comes closer to the popular expectation: a longing and a trusting in this one, ultimate power to cure all national woe and secure the national good.

The communion of President and people therefore cannot fail to throb with tension. The ordeal of leadership—in good causes or bad—probably becomes most poignant at those many times when the choice must be made between appeasing and arousing, and soothing or stirring, the citizenry at large. In a way, Lyndon Johnson once described this when talking of the political pressures upon him from opposite sides either to quicken, or to slacken, the pace of the Vietnam War. "What the American people like is action, drama, and a clear conclusion," he declared. "They don't like 'measured' anything. They want all things to be settled, one way or the other. If I went to Hanoi to make peace, my popularity polls would immediately go up 10%—*and* they would do exactly the same if I bombed Peking." [27] Because this so often can be true, the President must stay mildly cynical—or soberly clinical—toward the very public support so vital to him. And the fitting attitude and temper once were well expressed by Theodore Roosevelt. Irritated by extensive public debate over his relative popularity, he snappishly wrote an editor in 1906: "I am not a college freshman . . . and therefore I am not concerned about my 'popularity' save in exactly so far as it is an instrument which will help me to achieve my purposes." [28]

It is not then too fanciful, I think, to see the complex union of President and people as a kind of marriage, with all its vows, conflicts, doubts, and need for patience and hope. It surely can be said of both—the sacrament and the office—that each time the oath is taken, the subsequent story is unique: with Presidencies as with marriages, there are no two altogether alike. Both kinds of union are called upon to sustain and survive the wild buffetings of chance and circumstance, wholly unforeseeable by either partner. Both signify great gambles, with an electoral triumph assuring future Presidential leadership—or enlightenment—no more automatically than a marriage contract promises everlasting personal happiness. And both so decisively depend upon a shared faith that there is no force more certain than mutual distrust to break a marriage—or break a President.

As all the life of the Republic has shown, the full role of the President in this union amounts to an unparalleled and unending act of reconciliation. For he must find and hold a kind of balance between modes of action that seem contradictory and casts of belief that seem alien. Over the years of his magistracy, such a sense of balance alone can give equal weight to political virtues as different as stoic patience and bold initiative. And he will need both. The avoidance of hasty error is no meager feat, and neither nation nor world is going to be remade before sunset. Still, there are few qualities more likely to cloud a Presidency than a habit of making gray and fretful half-decisions. As in his practical politics, so in his personal philosophy: he must know that a lively vision of the future has to be matched—and nourished—by a quiet reverence for the past. Without the first, there can be no binding purpose that lifts national policy above the level of a miscellany of reactions and improvisations. Without the second, there can be no defining purpose that is faithful to the higher values—and the better dreams—of this particular republic. Or as G. K. Chesterton once observed:

> Tradition means giving votes to that obscurest of classes, our ancestors. It is the democracy of the dead. Tradition refuses to surrender to the arrogant oligarchy of those who merely happen to be walking around.[29]

Such a sense of tradition has seemed, once in a while, to bring together, in fact, the most active and innovative of Presidents in a sort of fraternity transcending time and temperament. In 1962, this seemed so with John Kennedy's tribute to Thomas Jefferson, at his White House dinner for 49 Nobel Prize winners. A generation earlier —in 1932—the most modern of Presidents, Franklin Roosevelt, delivered a speech in George Washington's Virginia which was hard to surpass as a tribute to the first of Presidents:

> While he loved best the serene life of a master farmer at Mount Vernon, it was not given him to enjoy such peace for any considerable time. His life was a succession of long, arduous periods of public service. For six years, military duties relating to the conflict with the French and Indians exacted his energies and at times seriously endangered his health. For the next sixteen years his life at Mount Vernon was more and more disturbed by that growing spirit of revolt against the mother country which stirred the colonies. Then followed the eight years of revolution, with interludes of despair and disaster. When peace with England came, the affairs of the young nation were still critical and nearly six years were given to the making of the new nation. Finally, there were eight years of the Presidency—perhaps the most arduous of all. It is difficult to find any parallel in history for this career. . . .
>
> Other lives in other nations and other times have been similarly filled with action and with tasks. America has no Caesar, America has no Charlemagne, America has no Henry the Eighth, America has

no Napoleon, America has no Lenin. America prefers and always will prefer her Washington.[30]

If this be what tradition means, what is the meaning of leadership? I know no simple answer, but I respect—again—a few clues. The plainest of these must be the gift of those Presidents who, as Franklin Roosevelt said, "clarified" at great moments "certain historic ideas in the life of the nation." At its fullest, this means a silent but steely commitment that conveys to all the citizenry these pledges: to prick their conscience in times of repose, to spur their sacrifice in times of stress, and to honor their intelligence always. I think there is true insight, too, in Henry L. Stimson's appreciation of the two Roosevelts as Presidents who "not only understood the *use* of power, they knew the *enjoyment* of power." For as he went on to explain: "Whether a man is burdened by power or enjoys power; whether he is trapped by responsibility or made free by it; whether he is moved by other people and outer forces or moves them—that is the essence of leadership." [31]

A century back in the life of the Republic, I find some symbolic sign of the same truth in an account by James Polk of nothing more historic than a New Year's Day reception at the White House in the year 1849. "The President's mansion was thrown open," Polk recorded, and "a very large crowd called." And as he went on to tell his *Diary:*

> I must have shook hands with several thousand persons. Toward the close of the day some gentlemen asked me if my arm was not sore. . . . I told them that I had found there was great art in shaking hands. . . . They were curious to know what this art was. I told them that if a man surrendered his arm to be shaken, by some horizontally, by others perpendicularly, and by others again with a strong grip, he could not fail to suffer severely from it, but that if he would *shake and not be shaken, grip and not be gripped,* taking care always to squeeze the hand of his adversary as hard as he squeezed him, that he suffered no inconvenience from it. . . . When I observed a strong man approaching I generally took advantage of him by being a little quicker than he was and seizing him by the tip of his fingers, giving him a hearty shake, and thus preventing him from getting a full grip on me. They were much amused. . . . But though I gave my account of the operation playfully, it is all true.[32]

It seems to me also true that the "art" that Polk discovered in shaking hands was altogether like the art of Presidential leadership in meeting issues. The Chief Executive who simply waits for their thrust cannot, indeed, "fail to suffer severely from it." And the question forever before a President is whether to "grip" or "be gripped" . . . and whether to "shake" or "be shaken."

The choice confronts not a President alone, of course, but all political leaders, whatever their time in history or place on earth. Indeed, the spirit of this leadership was well described as long ago as the orations of Demosthenes. "As a general marches at the head of his troops, so ought wise politicians . . . to march at the head of affairs," the Greek philosopher explained. "They ought not to wait the event, to know what measures to take; but the measures which they have taken ought to produce the event." [33] And during the dark days of the American Revolution, these ancient aphorisms were carefully inscribed in the Artillery Company Account Book of Alexander Hamilton, for remembrance along with his other prophecies about a Presidency unborn and unknown.

A Presidency of "honest and wise men," wearing the armor of this confidence, may go on to answer the prayer of Adams and the hope of the Republic.

Notes and Sources

ONE: The Problem of the Presidency

1. *Polk: The Diary of a President*, Allan Nevins, ed. (New York, Capricorn Books, 1968), p. 54.

2. Cf. Charles C. Thach, Jr., *The Creation of the Presidency* (Baltimore, The Johns Hopkins Press, 1969), pp. 20–22.

3. Aaron Wildavsky, ed., *The Presidency* (Boston, Little, Brown & Co., 1969), p. ix.

4. *Memoirs of Harry S. Truman* (Garden City, N.Y., Doubleday & Co., 1955), Vol. I, p. x.

5. Cited by Clinton Rossiter, *The American Presidency* (New York, The New American Library, 1960), p. 112.

6. Harold J. Laski, *The American Presidency: An Interpretation* (New York, Harper & Brothers, 1940), pp. 7 and 11.

7. Richard B. Morris, ed., *Alexander Hamilton and the Founding of the Nation* (New York, Harper Torchbooks, 1969), pp. 143–44.

8. Three articles on "The American Political Scene," *The Nation* (November 16, November 23, and November 30, 1946).

9. Rossiter, *op cit.*, pp. 149 and 151.

10. Woodrow Wilson, *Constitutional Government in the United States* (New York, Columbia University Press, 1908) p. 68.

11. Cited by Wilfred E. Binkley, *The Man in the White House* (Baltimore, The Johns Hopkins Press, 1958), p. 54.

12. James MacGregor Burns, *Presidential Government* (New York, Avon Books, 1965), p. 245.

13. George E. Reedy, *The Twilight of the Presidency* (New York, World Publishing Co., 1970), pp. 30–31.

14. Rexford G. Tugwell, cited by Theodore Sorensen, *Decision-Making in the White House* (New York, Columbia University Press, 1963), p. 9.

15. *Ibid.*, Foreword by John F. Kennedy, p. xi.

16. Arthur M. Schlesinger, Jr., *A Thousand Days* (Boston, Houghton Mifflin, 1965), p. 674.

17. Paul M. Angle, ed., *The Lincoln Reader* (New Brunswick, Rutgers University Press, 1947), p. 412.

TWO: The Idea of the Presidency

1. Harry S. Truman, *Truman Speaks* (New York, Columbia University Press, 1960), pp. 3 and 41.

2. Cited by Thach, *op. cit.*, p. 83.

3. *The Federalist* (New York, Random House Modern Library), No. 67, p. 436.

4. Rossiter, *op. cit.*, p. 72.

5. Cited by Thach, *op. cit.*, p. 21.

6. Cited by James Thomas Flexner, *George Washington and the New Nation* (Boston, Little, Brown & Co., 1970), p. 105.

7. Thach, *op. cit.*, p. 166.

8. James Madison, *Notes of Debates in the Federal Convention of 1787* (Athens, Ohio, Ohio University Press, 1966), pp. 322–23.

9. Thach, *op. cit.*, p. 101.

10. Madison, *Notes, op. cit.*, p. 48.

11. *Ibid.*, p. 599.

12. *The American Heritage History of the Presidency* (New York, American Heritage Publishing Co., 1968), p. 37.

13. *Ibid.*, p. 13.

14. *Ibid.*, pp. 36 and 37.

15. *Ibid.*, p. 35

16. Madison, *Notes,* op. cit., pp. 600–1.

17. *The American Heritage History, op. cit.*, p. 37.

18. *Ibid.*, pp. 46–48.

19. *Ibid.*, p. 24.

20. Morris, *op. cit.*, p. xvii.

21. *The Federalist, op. cit.* No. 70, p. 454.

22. *Ibid.*, Nos. 73 and 77, pp. 476 and 502.

23. Cited by Binkley, *op. cit.*, p. 80.

24. *The Federalist, op. cit.*, No. 69, p. 452.

25. *Ibid.*, pp. 448–49.

26. Speech of June 22, 1787, cited by George Seldes, *The Great Quotations* (New York, Lyle Stuart, 1960), p. 295.

27. *The Federalist,* op. cit. No. 68, p. 444.

28. Cited by Morris, *op. cit.*, p. xii.

29. Cited by Thach, *op. cit.*, p. 169.

30. Cited by Flexner, *op. cit.*, p. 54.

31. Cited *ibid.*, pp. 171–72.

32. Cited by David C. Whitney, *The American Presidents* (Garden City, N.Y., Doubleday & Co., 1967), p. 14.

33. Cf. Flexner, *op. cit.*, pp. 171 and 173.

34. Cited by J. A. Carroll, "George Washington," in *America's Ten Greatest Presidents,* Morton Borden, ed. (Chicago, Rand McNally & Co., 1961), p. 6.

35. Cf. *ibid.*, p. 182.

36. *Ibid.*, p. 191.

37. Saul K. Padover, *The Washington Papers* (New York, Grosset & Dunlap, 1955), p. 102.

38. Cited by Flexner, *op. cit.*, pp. 195–96.

39. *Ibid.*, p. 196.

40. Padover, *op. cit.*, p. 83

41. Carroll, *op cit.*, pp. 29–30.

42. *The Federalist*, op. cit., No. 67, p. 436.

43. James Kent, cited by Edward S. Corwin, *The President: Office and Powers* (New York, New York University Press, 1957), p. 21.

44. Cited *ibid.*, p. 22.

45. Henry Jones Ford, *The Rise and Growth of American Politics* (New York, Macmillan Company, 1898), p. 293.

46. Cited by Corwin, *op. cit.*, pp. 26–27.

47. Cited *ibid.*, pp. 28–29.

THREE: The Mystery of the Presidency

1. James Bryce, *The American Commonwealth* (New York, G. P. Putnam's Sons, 1959), p. 27.

2. New York *Times*, January 15, 1960.

3. Sorensen, *op. cit.*, pp. xi–xiii.

4. New York *Times*, April 30, 1962.

5. Thach, *op. cit.*, p. 138.

6. *Polk Diary*, op. cit., pp. xii–xxii.

7. Dean Acheson, *Present at the Creation* (New York, Norton, 1969), p. 730.

8. *Polk Diary*, op. cit., pp. 326–27.

9. James Schouler, cited by Binkley, *op. cit.*, p. 120.

10. *Polk Diary*, op. cit., p. 197.

11. Cited by Richard E. Neustadt, *Presidential Power* (New York, John Wiley & Sons, Inc., 1961), pp. 9–10.

12. Cf. Emmet John Hughes, *The Ordeal of Power* (New York, Dell Publishing Co., 1964), p. 112.

13. Reedy, *op. cit.*, pp. 57 and 59.

14. Cf. Wildavsky, *The Presidency*, pp. 230–43.

15. Cited by Rossiter, *op. cit.*, p. 25.

16. New York *Times*, July 1, 1971.

17. *Ibid.*, June 13, 1971.

18. *Ibid.*, July 1, 1971.

19. Cited by Frederick Lewis Allen, *Only Yesterday* (New York, Harper & Row, 1964), p. 28.

20. *Ibid.*, pp. 36–37.

21. Seldes, *op. cit.*, p. 268.

22. Cf. Burns, *op. cit.*, p. 113.

23. Cf. *Ibid.*, pp. 113–14.

24. Cf. Fred I. Greenstein, "Popular Images of the Presidency," in Wildavsky, *op. cit.*, p. 290.

25. Louis Harris poll, New York *Post*, June 1, 1971.

26. Gallup poll, New York *Times*, June 6, 1971.

27. Cf. Greenstein, *op. cit.*, p. 291.

28. Laski, *op. cit.*, p. 34.

29. Cited *ibid.*, p. 37.

FOUR: The Man in the White House

1. *The Federalist*, op. cit., No. 68, p. 444.

2. Laski, *op. cit.*, p. 8.

3. Harold J. Laski, *Parliamentary Affairs* (Winter, 1949), p. 18.

4. Jeremy Larner, *Nobody Knows: Reflections on the McCarthy Campaign of 1968* (New York, Macmillan Company, 1970), pp. 56–57.

5. Speech in House of Commons, 1801.

6. Bryce, *op. cit.*, p. 30.

7. Philip Guedalla, *The Hundred Years*, in John Bartlett's *Familiar Quotations* (Boston, Little, Brown & Co., 1955), p. 950.

8. Corwin, *op. cit.*, pp. 324 and 24.

9. Grant Singleton, cited by Seldes, *op. cit.*, p. 640.

10. Cited by Richard F. Fenno, Jr., *The President's Cabinet* (New York, Vintage Books, 1959), p. 125.

11. Cited by Charles E. Jacob, *Leadership in the New Deal* (Englewood Cliffs, N.J., Prentice-Hall, 1967), p. 34.

12. Cited by Rossiter, *op. cit.*, p. 151.

13. Corwin, *op. cit.*, p. 30.

14. Cf. Rossiter, *op. cit.*, p. 79.

15. *Polk Diary, op. cit.*, pp. 194 and 340.

16. Laski, *op. cit.*, p. 64.

17. Reedy, *op. cit.*, p. xv.

18. Laski, *op. cit.*, p. 263.

19. *Selected Letters of William Allen White* (New York, Henry Holt, 1947), p. 311.

20. Cited by Rossiter, *op. cit.*, p. 87.

21. David Jacobs, in *The American Heritage Pictorial History of the Presidents*, (New York, American Heritage Publishing Co., 1968), Vol. I, p. 69.

22. Cited by Stephen G. Kurtz, "John Adams," in *America's Ten Greatest Presidents, op. cit.*, p. 32.

23. Cf. *The American Heritage Pictorial History of the Presidents, op. cit.*, Vol. I, p. 72.

24. Rossiter, *op. cit.*, p. 97.

25. Henry F. Pringle, *Theodore Roosevelt* (New York, Harcourt, Brace and World, 1931), p. 97.

26. Cited by Wilson Sullivan, in *The American Heritage Pictorial History of the Presidents, op. cit.*, Vol. II, p. 632.

27. Samuel Eliot Morison, Henry Steele Commager, and William E. Leuchtenburg, *The Growth of the American Republic* (New York, Oxford University Press, 1969), Vol. II, p. 296.

28. Archie Butt, *The Letters of Archie Butt*, Lawrence F. Abbott, ed., (New York, Doubleday & Co., 1924), p. 233.

29. Theodore Roosevelt, *An Autobiography* (New York, Charles Scribner's Sons, 1929), pp. 357 and 386.

30. *Ibid.*, p. 548.

31. Cited by Sullivan, *op. cit.*, p. 635.

32. Roosevelt, *op. cit.*, p. 548.

33. Cited by Sullivan, *op. cit.*, p. 647.

34. Cited by Erwin C. Hargrove, *Presidential Leadership: Personality and Political Style* (New York, Macmillan Company, 1966), p. 26.

35. Cited by *The American Heritage History of the Presidency*, op. cit., p. 9.

36. Cited by Hargrove, *op. cit.*, p. 83.

37. *Ibid.*, p. 79.

38. *Ibid.*, pp. 84–85.

39. *Ibid.*, p. 85.

40. *Ibid.*, p. 87.

41. *Ibid.*, p. 92.

42. James David Barber, *The Presidential Character* (Englewood Cliffs, N.J., Prentice-Hall, 1972), p. 178.

43. Quotations from Michael Harwood, in *The American Heritage Pictorial History of the Presidents, op. cit.*, Vol. II, p. 668.

44. Hargrove, *op. cit.*, p. 78.

45. Cited by Harwood, *op. cit.*, p. 663.

46. *Ibid.*, p. 668.

47. Frederick Lewis Allen, *op. cit.*, p. 111.

48. *Holmes-Laski Letters,* Mark DeWolfe Howe, ed. (Cambridge, Harvard University Press, 1953), Vol. I, p. 524.

49. *Ibid.*, Vol. I, p. 671.

50. Cited by Arthur M. Schlesinger, Jr., *The Crisis of the Old Order* (Boston, Houghton Mifflin Co., 1958), p. 57.

51. Harwood, *op. cit.*, p. 761.

52. *Ibid.*, p. 746.

53. Cited by Schlesinger, *op. cit*, p. 61.

54. *Ibid.*, pp. 142–43.

55. Cited by Francis Russell, *The Shadow of Blooming Grove* (New York, McGraw-Hill, 1968), p. 350.

56. Cf. Walter Johnson, *1600 Pennsylvania Avenue* (Boston, Little, Brown & Co., 1963), p. 36.

57. *Ibid.*, pp. 25–26.

58. Cf. James David Barber, "Classifying and Predicting Presidential Styles," in *Journal of Social Issues*, XXIV (1968).

59. Cf. Richard Hofstadter, *The American Political Tradition* (New York, Vintage Books, 1948), p. 307.

60. Cited *ibid.*, p. 283.

61. Barber, in *Journal of Social Issues, op. cit.*

62. Hargrove, *op. cit.*, p. 106.

63. Herbert Hoover, *The Challenge to Liberty* (New York, Charles Scribner's Sons, 1934), p. 166.

64. Barber, in *Journal of Social Issues, op. cit.*

65. *Selected Letters of William Allen White, op. cit.*, p. 329.

66. *Ibid.*, p. 331.

67. Robert E. Sherwood, *The White House Papers of Harry L. Hopkins* (London, Eyre & Spottiswoode, 1949), Vol. I, p. 39.

68. Cited by Johnson, *op. cit.*, p. 53.

69. Leo Rosten, "The Washington Correspondents," in Wildavsky, *op. cit.*, p. 322.

70. Cf. Cabell Phillips, *From the Crash to the Blitz: 1929–1939* (New York, Macmillan Company, 1969), p. 264.

71. Schlesinger, *op. cit.*, p. 455.

72. Cited by Hofstadter, *op. cit.*, p. 331.

73. Cf. Johnson, *op. cit.*, p. 46.

74. H. L. Mencken, "Three Years of Dr. Roosevelt," *American Mercury*, (March 1936).

75. Hofstadter, *op. cit.*, p. 315.

76. Frances Perkins, *The Roosevelt I Knew* (New York, Viking Press, 1946), p. 330.

77. Cf. Arthur M. Schlesinger, Jr., *The Politics of Upheaval* (Boston, Houghton Mifflin, 1966), p. 1.

78. Schlesinger, *The Crisis of the Old Order, op. cit.*, p. 436.

79. Laski, *The American Presidency, op. cit.*, pp. 267 and 270.

80. Cited by Max Frankel, *New York Times Magazine*, January 7, 1968.

81. Richard Goodwin, quoted in *Newsweek*, February 1, 1971.

82. *The New York Review*, May 20, 1971.

83. Laski, *The American Presidency, op. cit.*, p. 38.

84. Binkley, *op. cit.*, p. 166.

85. *Ibid.*, p. 135.

86. *Ibid.*, p. 66.

87. Morison, Commager, and Leuchtenburg, *op. cit.*, Vol. II, p. 590.

88. Frankel, *op. cit.*

89. Cited by Padover, *op. cit.*, p. 100.

90. James Russell Lowell, in *Essays, English and American* (New York, P. F. Collier & Son, 1910), Vol. XXVIII, pp. 441–63.

91. Schlesinger, *A Thousand Days, op. cit.*, p. 673.

92. *Ibid.*, p. 674.

93. Frank Kingdon, *As FDR Said* (New York, Duell, Sloan and Pearce, 1950), p. 30.

FIVE: The Gates of the White House

1. Cited by Richard Harris, *The Real Voice* (New York, Macmillan Company, 1964), frontispiece.

2. Bryce, *op. cit.*, pp. 25–26.

3. *Polk Diary, op. cit.*, pp. 140 and 340.

4. Confidential source to EJH, 1971.

5. Frederick Lewis Allen, *op. cit.*, p. 28.

6. *Ibid.*, p. 30.

7. *Ibid.*, p. 29.

8. Lyndon Baines Johnson, *The Vantage Point* (New York, Holt, Rinehart and Winston, 1971), p. 569.

9. Confidential source to EJH, 1971.

10. Cf. John Kenneth Galbraith, *The Great Crash* (London, Hamish Hamilton, 1955), p. 131.

11. Cited by Walter Johnson, *op. cit.*, p. 13.

12. *Ibid.*, p. 37.

13. *Sherwood Anderson's Memoirs* (New York, Harcourt, Brace & Co., 1942), p. 415.

14. Schlesinger, *The Crisis of the Old Order, op. cit.*, p. 57.

15. *Truman Speaks, op. cit.*, p. 93.

16. New York *Times*, November 6, 1958.

17. Robert E. Sherwood, "Inaugural Parade," *Saturday Review of Literature*,

March 4, 1933.

18. Walter Lippmann, *Interpretations: 1931–1932* (New York, Macmillan Company, 1933), p. 261.

19. *Holmes-Laski Letters, op. cit.*, Vol. II, pp. 1416 and 1420.

20. *Ibid*, Vol. II, p. 1470.

21. Cited by William N. Chambers, in *America's Ten Greatest Presidents, op. cit.*, p. 95.

22. Woodrow Wilson, *George Washington* (New York, Schocken Books, 1969), p. xiv.

23. Cf. Binkley, *op. cit.*, pp. 41 and 105.

24. Lyndon Baines Johnson, *op. cit.*, p. 567.

25. Cited by Richard B. Morris, *Great Presidential Decisions* (New York, Fawcett Publications, 1969), p. 16.

26. Cited by Burns, *op. cit.*, p. 50.

27. Corwin, *op. cit.*, p. 309.

28. Cf. Burns, *op. cit.*, p. 52.

29. Morris, *op. cit.*, p. 171.

30. *The Lincoln Reader, op. cit.*, p. 280.

31. Truman, *Memoirs, op. cit.*, Vol. I, p. ix.

32. New York *Times*, January 5, 1971, article by William Safire.

33. Cf. Sorensen, *op. cit.*, p. 4.

34. Safire, *op. cit.*

35. New York *Times*, January 23, 1971.

36. Sorensen, *op. cit.*, p. 3.

37. Interview with EJH, 1971.

38. Lyndon Baines Johnson, *op. cit.*, pp. 327 and 441.

39. Cited by Louis W. Koenig, *The Chief Executive* (New York, Harcourt, Brace, and World, Inc., 1968), p. 367.

40. Cited by Sorensen, *op. cit.*, p. 42.

41. New York *Times*, June 12, 1970.

42. Arthur M. Schlesinger, Jr., *The Age of Jackson* (Boston, Little, Brown & Co., 1945), p. 67.

43. *Ibid.*, p. 67.

44. *Ibid.*, pp. 72–73.

45. Cf. Alex B. Lacy, "The White House Staff Bureaucracy," in *Trans-Action* (January, 1969), p. 50.

46. *Ibid.*, p. 51.

47. Letter to Richard E. Neustadt, *American Political Science Review* (December, 1963), p. 864.

48. Cited by Arthur M. Schlesinger, Jr., *The Coming of the New Deal* (Boston, Houghton Mifflin Company, 1959), p. 525.

49. Letter to Richard E. Neustadt, *op. cit.*, p. 864.

50. Sherwood, *op. cit.*, Vol. I, p. 4.

51. *Ibid.*, p. 6.

52. Lacy, *op. cit.*, p. 51.

53. Clayton Fritchey, interview with EJH, 1971.

54. Cited by Barber, *The Presidential Character, op. cit.*, p. 62.

55. *Foreign Affairs* (January, 1967).

56. Cf. Richard F. Fenno, Jr., *The President's Cabinet* (New York, Vintage

Books, 1959), p. 12; and *The American Heritage History of the Presidency, op. cit.*, p. 43.

57. *The Federalist*, No. 70, *op. cit.*, pp. 462–63.

58. Cf. *Polk Diary, op. cit.*, pp. 21, 114, and 284.

59. Cf. Arthur M. Schlesinger, *Paths to the Present* (New York, Macmillan Company, 1949), p. 132.

60. Schlesinger, *The Coming of the New Deal, op. cit.*, p. 518.

61. Angle, *op. cit.*, p. 411.

62. Cited by Fenno, *op. cit.*, p. 123.

63. *Ibid.*, p. 125.

64. Cf. Pendleton Herring, *Presidential Leadership* (New York, Farrar and Rinehart, 1940), pp. 98–99.

65. Clark Clifford, interview with EJH, 1969.

66. Laski, *The American Presidency, op. cit.*, pp. 252–53.

67. New York *Times*, November 26, 1970.

68. *Polk Diary, op. cit.*, p. 308.

69. George E. Reedy, *The Center Magazine*, Vol. IV, No. 1, pp. 12–13.

70. Cited by Malcolm Moos, *The Republicans* (New York, Random House, 1956), p. 390.

71. Cited by William Howard Taft, *The Presidency* (New York, Charles Scribner's Sons, 1916), p. 33.

72. Woodrow Wilson, *Constitutional Government in the United States* (New York, Columbia University Press, 1908), p. 68.

73. Schlesinger, *Paths to the Present, op. cit.*, p. 110.

74. Cited by Herman Finer, *The Presidency: Crisis and Regeneration* (Chicago, University of Chicago Press, 1960), p. 195.

75. Padover, *op. cit.*, p. 404.

76. *The American Heritage History of the Presidency, op. cit.*, p. 342.

77. New York *Times*, January 21, 1971.

78. New York *Times*, article by Arthur M. Schlesinger, Jr., February 6, 1972.

79. New York *Times*, January 23, 1972.

80. Washington *Post*, June 1, 1971.

81. New York *Times*, cited by Schlesinger, *op. cit.*, February 6, 1972.

82. Anthony Lake, *Foreign Policy* (Spring, 1971).

83. Cited by Sidney Hyman, *New York Times Magazine*, December 1, 1963.

84. Leo Rosten, in Aaron Wildavsky, *op. cit.*, p. 321.

85. Cited by Sidney Warren, *The Saturday Review*, July 21, 1962.

SIX: The Restraint of Presidential Power

1. Theodore Sorensen, *Kennedy* (cited by Murray Kempton, review in *Atlantic Monthly*).

2. Cf. James David Barber, in Wildavsky, *op. cit.*, p. 101.

3. Cited by Finer, *op. cit.*, p. 36.

4. *Truman Memoirs, op. cit.*, Vol. II, p. 508.

5. Cited by Binkley, *op. cit.*, p. 207.

6. *Polk Diary, op. cit.*, p. 374.

7. Cf. Finer, *op. cit.*, p. 35.

8. Lyndon Baines Johnson, *op. cit.*, pp. 441–42.

9. Rossiter, *op. cit.*, p. 52.

10. Sherman Adams, *First-Hand Report* (New York, Harper & Brothers, 1961), p. 355.

11. Pendleton Herring, *Presidential Leadership* (New York, Farrar and Rhinehart, 1940), p. 91.

12. *Democracy in America* (New York, Doubleday Anchor Books, 1969), p. 126.

13. Cited in *Fulbright of Arkansas*, Karl E. Meyer, ed., p. 265.

14. Cf. Binkley, *op. cit.*, p. 261.

15. *The American Heritage Pictorial History of the Presidents, op. cit.*, Vol. II, p. 630.

16. Cited by Rossiter, *op. cit.*, pp. 62–63.

17. Truman, *Memoirs*, Vol. II, p. 477.

18. Cited by Schlesinger, *The Crisis of the Old Order, op. cit.*, p. 57.

19. Cf. Laski, *op. cit.*, p. 131.

20. Rossiter, *op. cit.*, p. 103.

21. *Polk Diary, op. cit.*, p. 184.

22. *Ibid.*, p. 194.

23. *Ibid.*, p. 70.

24. Cited by Rossiter, *op. cit.*, p. 122.

25. *Truman Memoirs, op. cit.*, Vol. II, p. 1.

26. Cited by Charles E. Jacob, *Leadership in the New Deal* (Englewood Cliffs, N.J., Prentice-Hall, 1967), p. 22.

27. Harold Seidman, *Politics, Position, and Power* (New York, Oxford University Press, 1970), p. 75.

28. New York *Times*, January 24, 1971.

29. Cf. Nelson W. Polsby, *Congress and the Presidency* (Englewood Cliffs, N.J., Prentice-Hall, 1964), p. 3.

30. Cf. Burns, *op. cit.*, p. 80.

31. Seidman, *op. cit.*, p. 115.

32. Cited *ibid.*, p. 107.

33. Cf. *ibid.*, p. 22.

34. New York *Times*, December 11, 1971.

35. Cited by Hargrove, *op. cit.*, p. 28.

36. Cf. Binkley, *op. cit.*, p. 185.

37. Cited by Seidman, *op. cit.*, p. 88.

38. *Truman Speaks, op. cit.*, p. 7.

39. Cf. Louis W. Koenig, "More Power to the President (Not Less)," *New York Times Magazine*, January 3, 1965.

40. Cited *ibid.*

41. *Polk Diary, op. cit.*, pp. 195–96.

42. Madison, *op. cit.*, p. 235.

43. Cited by *The American Heritage History of the Presidency, op. cit.*, p. 48.

44. Finer, *op. cit.*, p. 58.

45. Cited by *The American Heritage History of the Presidency, op. cit.*, p. 237.

46. *Polk Diary, op. cit.*, pp. 123 and 184.

47. Cf. Frank Freidel, *Franklin D. Roosevelt: The Apprenticeship* (Boston,

Little, Brown & Co., 1952), p. 86.

48. *The Federalist, op. cit.*, p. 476.

49. *Ibid.*, p. 337.

50. Madison, *op. cit.*, p. 233.

51. Cited by Corwin, *op. cit.*, p. 22.

52. *Polk Diary, op. cit.*, p. 46.

53. Cf. Morison, Commager, and Leuchtenburg, *op. cit.*, Vol. I, p. 737.

54. Cited by Laski, *The American Presidency, op. cit.*, pp. 126–27.

55. Cited by Binkley, *op. cit.*, p. 52.

56. Cf. William Allen White, *A Puritan in Babylon* (New York, Capricorn Books, 1965), p. 208.

57. *Ibid.*, p. 207.

58. *Ibid.*, pp. 204–205.

59. Cited by Russell, *op. cit.*, p. 334.

60. Cf. Louis W. Koenig, *The Chief Executive* (New York, Harcourt, Brace and World, 1968), p. 137.

61. Cited in Robert S. Hirschfield, *The Power of the Presidency* (New York, Atherton Press, 1968), p. 113.

62. New York *Times*, December 24, 1970.

63. Lyndon Baines Johnson, *op. cit.*, p. 438.

64. *Ibid.*, p. 458.

65. *Truman Speaks, op. cit.*, p. 5.

66. Cf. Koenig, *The Chief Executive, op. cit.*, p. 151.

67. Cf. analysis in Philadelphia *Bulletin,* January 28, 1971.

68. Cited by Koenig, *The Chief Executive, op. cit.*, p. 135.

69. *Ibid.*, p. 134.

70. *Ibid.*, p. 147.

71. Polsby, *op. cit.*, p. 77.

72. Lyndon Baines Johnson, *op. cit.*, p. 461.

73. James Sterling Young, *The Washington Community: 1800–1828*, excerpted in Wildavsky, *op. cit.*, pp. 417–18.

74. Cited by Polsby, *op. cit.*, p. 90.

75. Interview with EJH, 1971.

76. Laski, *The American Presidency, op. cit.*, p. 140.

77. Cf. Herring, *op. cit.*, p. 50.

SEVEN: The Range of Presidential Power

1. *The Federalist, op. cit.*, p. 337.

2. Cited by Leon A. Harris, *The Fine Art of Political Wit* (New York, E. P. Dutton, 1964), pp. 63–64.

3. Rossiter, *op. cit.*, p. 33.

4. *Ibid.*, p. 83.

5. *The New York Review*, October 5, 1972, pp. 10–11.

6. Hirschfield, *op. cit.*, p. 246.

7. Corwin, *op. cit.*, p. 236.

8. Cf. Rossiter, *op. cit.*, p. 48.

9. John Rothchild, "Cooling Down the War: The Senate's Lame Doves,"

The Washington Monthly (September, 1971), pp. 7–8.

10. *Ibid.*, p. 13.

11. Cf. Hirschfield, *op. cit.*, p. 248.

12. Cited by Corwin, *op. cit.*, p. 208.

13. Cf. *ibid.*, pp. 211 and 216–17.

14. Rothchild, *op. cit.*, p. 11.

15. *Ibid.*, p. 13.

16. *Time* (May 22, 1972), p. 18.

17. Rothchild, *op. cit.*, p. 11.

18. Cited by Wildavsky, *op. cit.*, p. 435.

19. Quotations from opening statements of Senator Edward M. Kennedy at hearings on Presidential Commissions, May 24 and 26, 1971.

20. Herbert C. Hoover, *The Memoirs of Herbert Hoover, The Cabinet and the Presidency, 1920–1933* (New York, Macmillan Company, 1952), p. 281.

21. Cited by Seidman, *op. cit.*, p. 23.

22. Cited by Corwin, *op. cit.*, p. 179.

23. New York *Times*, May 1, 1972.

24. Cf. *Time* (January 11, 1971), p. 16.

25. Cited by Wildavsky, *op. cit.*, pp. 64–66.

26. Cf. Corwin, *op. cit.*, pp. 255–56.

27. Cf. *ibid.*, pp. 250–52.

28. Wildavsky, *op. cit.*, p. 439.

29. Corwin, *op. cit.*, pp. 25–26.

30. *Time* (May 1, 1972).

31. Cited by Merlo Pusey, *The Way We Go to War* (Boston, Houghton Mifflin, 1969), pp. 118–19.

32. Cited *ibid.*, pp. 134–35.

33. Cited *ibid.*, pp. 130 and 132.

34. *Ibid.*, p. 140.

35. Testimony of Nicholas de B. Katzenbach, August 17, 1967, from *Congressional Record,* August 21, 1967, pp. 11882–84.

36. Senate Report No. 797, "National Commitments," November 20, 1967, pp. 26–27. (Cited by Pusey, *op. cit.*, p. 3.)

37. Cited by Pusey, *op. cit.*, p. 71.

38. Samuel Eliot Morison, *The Battle of the Atlantic, 1939–1943.* Cited by Pusey, *op. cit.*, p. 3.

39. Sherwood, *op. cit.*, Vol. I, p. 371.

40. Cf. Corwin, *op. cit.*, pp. 202 and 238.

41. *Ibid.*, p. 237.

42. *Ibid.*, p. 239.

43. *Ibid.*, pp. 202–204.

44. Thomas A. Bailey, *A Diplomatic History of the American People* (New York, F. S. Crofts and Co., 1968), p. 796.

45. *Truman Memoirs, op. cit.*, Vol. II, p. 333.

46. Cited by Pusey, *op. cit.*, p. 11.

47. *Truman Memoirs, op. cit.*, Vol. II, p. 332.

48. *Ibid.*, p. 334.

49. *Ibid.*, p. 337.

50. *Ibid.*, p. 338.

51. Cf. Pusey, *op. cit.*, p. 116.

52. Cf. *ibid.*, pp. 88 and 89.

53. Cited by I. F. Stone, *The Hidden History of the Korean War* (New York, Monthly Review Press, 1969), p. 12.

54. *Truman Memoirs, op. cit.*, Vol. II, pp. 333–34.

55. Cf. Pusey, *op. cit.*, pp. 91–92.

56. Cf. Corwin, *op. cit.*, p. 221.

57. *Truman Memoirs*, Vol. II, p. 340.

58. *Congressional Record*, Eighty-second Congress, 1st Session, January 5, 1951, pp. 55 and 57.

59. Cited by Stone, *op. cit.*, p. 278.

60. Address to the American Society of Newspaper Editors, April 16, 1971.

61. Cited in *Fulbright of Arkansas, op. cit.*, p. 263.

62. New York *Times*, July 5, 1971.

63. "The Pentagon Papers," Washington *Post*, June 16, 1971.

64. *Foreign Affairs*, July, 1971.

65. *Time* (July 5, 1971).

66. *Ibid.* (May 22, 1972).

67. New York *Times*, June 15, 1971.

68. *Ibid.*, April 18, 1967.

69. *Ibid.*, August 8, 1966.

70. Lyndon Johnson, September 25, 1964, cited in New York *Times*, June 20, 1971.

71. "The Pentagon Papers," quoted in New York *Times*, July 5, 1971.

72. Address to the American Society of Newspaper Editors, April 16, 1971.

73. Cited by Arthur M. Schlesinger, Jr., "The Limits and Excesses of Presidential Power," *Saturday Review* (May 3, 1969).

74. Cited by Tom Wicker, New York *Times*, May 9, 1972.

75. *Time* (May 22, 1972), p. 18.

76. New York *Times*, April 27, 1972.

77. *Scientific American.* Cited by New York *Times*, May 8, 1972.

78. Washington *Post*, April 11, 1971.

79. Interview with EJH, June, 1966.

80. Ernest R. May in Wildavsky, *op. cit.*, p. 660.

81. *Ibid.*, p. 666.

82. Truman, *op. cit.*, Vol II, pp. 58–59.

83. New York *Times*, May 30, 1971.

84. Interview with EJH, August, 1965.

85. Cited by George Ball, "Is This Trip Necessary?," New York *Times*, February 13, 1972.

86. *Ibid.*

87. In Hirschfield, *op. cit.*, p. 226.

EIGHT: The Destiny of the Presidency

1. Cited by Thach, *op. cit.*, p. 24.

2. Sherwood, *op. cit.*, Vol. I, p. 10.

3. Cited by Schlesinger, *The Crisis of the Old Order, op. cit.*, p. 482.

4. Acheson, *op. cit.*, p. 730.

5. New York *Times*, November 13, 1932.

6. Morison, Commager, and Leuchtenburg, *op. cit.*, Vol. I, p. 665.

7. *New York Times Magazine*, "Our Presidents: A Rating by 75 Historians," July 29, 1962.

8. Schlesinger, *A Thousand Days, op. cit.*, pp. 675–76.

9. Cf. Rossiter, *op. cit.*, pp. 100–1.

10. Cited by Schlesinger, *Paths to the Present, op. cit.*, p. 103.

11. Lowell, *op. cit.*, p. 241.

12. Schlesinger, *Paths to the Present, op. cit.*, p. 103.

13. *Ibid.*, p. 106.

14. Cf. Schlesinger, *New York Times Magazine, op. cit.*

15. All quotations from *A Thousand Days, op. cit.*, p. 672.

16. *As FDR Said, op. cit.*, p. 124.

17. Bryce, *op. cit.*

18. Cf. Burns, *op. cit.*, pp. 56–57.

19. Cited by Wildavsky, *op. cit.*, p. 242.

20. Congressional Quarterly Service, "Congress and the Nation: 1945–1964" (Washington, 1965).

21. Cf. Pusey, *op. cit.*, p. 145.

22. Address to American Society of Newspaper Editors, April 16, 1971.

23. Cited by Seidman, *op. cit.*, p. 27.

24. *As FDR Said, op. cit.*, p. 224.

25. Cf. Rossiter, *op. cit.*, p. 250.

26. *The Presidency, op. cit.*, p. 15.

27. Harry Reasoner, 1971 interview with EJH.

28. Cited by Burns, *op. cit.*, p. 76.

29. Cf. W. H. Auden, in New York *Times*, February 2, 1971.

30. *As FDR Said, op. cit.*, p. 109.

31. Cf. Barber, *The Presidential Character, op. cit.*, pp. 11–12.

32. *Polk Diary, op. cit.*, pp. 361–62.

33. Cf. Burns, *op. cit.*, pp. 26–27.

A Special Supplement

The Presidency As I Have Seen It

Sherman Adams

Clark M. Clifford

Benjamin V. Cohen

Ralph A. Dungan

Abe Fortas

Clayton Fritchey

Bryce N. Harlow

W. Averell Harriman

David E. Lilienthal

Nelson A. Rockefeller

Samuel I. Rosenman

Theodore C. Sorensen

A Note of Explanation

The American Presidency is so unique a sovereign office that the judgment of no one man upon it could possibly be sovereign.

I have wished, from the outset of this inquiry, to know some insights and some conclusions of others who have played living roles in the White House. There is no living company of former Presidents to give such a range of views. But there are a number of men who have worked intimately with the Presidents of the past generation, as their White House advisers or personal counselors.

The twelve such men who here give their own perceptions of the Presidency may be said to share, as a group, two distinctions: a true proximity to Presidential labor and a wide diversity of personal background. By partisan political terms, nine may be considered Democrats and three Republicans. Three have had extensive experience in elective politics themselves, while nine have not. They appear equally divided between primary interests in foreign affairs or domestic affairs. They include six who have served abroad as Presidential envoys, three who have been state governors, and one former Supreme Court Justice. And of the twelve, a total of seven have served with two or more Presidents.

All these veterans of White House life addressed themselves to the same set of questions, which were designed to be not so much precise inquiries as rough guides to thought, so that all responses might follow a similar enough form to invite comparison or contrast. Like the questions, the responses cover three broad aspects of the Presidency: the personal qualities most vital to Presidential leadership and decision-making; the personal and professional capacities most necessary in a President's advisers, White House staff, and Cabinet; and the proper range or restrictions of Presidential power, especially in the realm of foreign affairs. The commentaries were prepared in one of two ways: either the respondent wrote his answers at length or he gave an extensive interview, whose final text he fully edited. Whatever the procedure, each man emphasized or minimized—or ignored—whatever phase of the Presidential office he so preferred to treat.

I am grateful to all these witnesses for the seriousness of thought—and the richness of experience—that make their varied testimony authentic and provocative.

I think it inappropriate to intrude with any superfluous summation of the range of judgments of these men. They speak incisively for themselves. And as they do, there emerges at least one striking consensus: after almost two centuries of Presidential government, they plainly believe still that the creation of the Founding Fathers was a work of art and wisdom.

E. J. H.

Sherman Adams

> A veteran of Republican Party politics and a central figure in the
> Eisenhower administration. . . . Assistant to the President
> (1953–1958). . . . Previously member of the New Hampshire
> House of Representatives (1941–1944), Speaker of the House
> (1943–1944), member of U.S. Congress (1945–1947), Governor
> of New Hampshire (1949–1953).

I

Two personal qualities vital to the success of any President are intellectual
receptivity and the instinct to recognize his own prejudice or bias. Intellectual
receptivity is the capacity to absorb and assimilate information, opinion and
conclusion imparted by others; to subject all three to the process of his own
thinking logically; and effectively to reach his own conclusions.

To understand and counterbalance his own bias and prejudice is to enable
the President to approach maximum objectivity in treating an issue upon its
merits. Pure objectivity being a myth, the more a President can detect and
allow for his prejudice, the more likely he will come to correct courses of
action and decisions. Conversely, to misunderstand or fail to sense the motives of a political being is a serious deficiency in the personal qualities of a
President. To be unable to perceive, accept, and relate such motives to the
American political system is to be unable to understand the validity of the
system and accept its implications.

The most helpful experience that a prospective President can have is political exposure in holding elective office. Experience in either the legislative
or executive branch while in a position to assume a large measure of responsibility for decision and action is of great benefit to an incoming President. Conversely, entering the office from a high-ranking corporate position
may prove a handicap in comparison with the varieties of other pre-office
experience.

The immediate decisions which Franklin Roosevelt made upon taking office—the bank holiday and subsequent actions taken to deal with a stagnating
economy—were important and courageous. In a different field of action, the
measures which Eisenhower took to terminate the Korean War, meet the
Quemoy-Matsu crisis, and stabilize, even though temporarily, an incipient
Near East war at the time of the Suez incidents were all acts of courage and
decisiveness.

II

Advisers of substantial value to the President will have an intuitive understanding of the functioning of the Presidential mind, an ability to sense cor-

rectly his course of action, and the capability to carry out an order even though implied and contextual. Competent advisers will provide the President with every important and essential shred of information on which a decision is to be based and, at the same time, will winnow out the nonessentials and be sufficiently alert to know the difference.

As long as the President continues to assume the ultimate responsibility for the variety of decisions and actions entrusted to him today, some growth of the White House staff appears inevitable. A better means of delegating power and responsibility must eventually evolve.

The Cabinet should be an effective screen through which ideas and courses of action can pass or be intercepted. Possessed of the wisdom and experience of men and women of vision and intelligence, the Cabinet can best act in the nature of a general staff to the President to help shape and give direction to his policies and projects. The quality of people who comprise the Cabinet should be such as to command the respect of the President. Thus the views of the Cabinet can have weight in the decisions, but this primary Cabinet function can work only when its members are possessed of great breadth of vision and experience.

I I I

Freedom of the President to act in international affairs has become overextended. Without diluting constitutional prerogatives, the President should find the means of consulting with and obtaining from the Congress sufficient exchanges to enable him fully to appraise the sense of the Congressional leadership. Executive responsibility in foreign affairs must not be compromised, for a weak President can exercise only weak authority. It should be remembered that in respect to domestic questions every member of Congress considers himself an authority; in foreign matters few members can be completely knowledgeable. Never in this generation of international suspicion and rivalry can foreign negotiation be spread upon the Congressional, much less the public, record. The President is the chief architect of foreign policy, but implicit in our system of coordinate government is the fact that the President has the obligation to obtain the advice and consent of the Congress in matters which it has the constitutional power to negate.

The cause of the extension of the use of Presidential power and the change in political attitude toward it stem largely from Asian involvements. The exercise of power has been followed by ex post facto exchanges with the Congress with the result that the liberal has seen the President assuming the role of dictator and therefore become an advocate of limiting Presidential power. The change may be no more permanent than the trend in the process of overextension.

The structure of the organization is likely to exert a considerable influence upon the decision-making process. But this is not an absolute precept. A President of strong will, self-confident in the truth of his knowledge, will assert himself over the influence of organization. The reverse is also a sound assumption.

Rather than tamper with the definition of the Presidential office or restrict its power, the electorate ought to exert greater selectivity in the person chosen for the office.

The following points are relevant to advice offered to a President-elect of whatever party or platform:

In making important decisions, seek out the opinions of a few people for whom you have respect, and who are known to differ with the views of yourself, the Cabinet, or your personal staff.

Reflect upon the opinions holding conflicting points of view. In coming to a decision, be guided by what you believe to be for the best interests of the people you represent, over the longest period of time, doing your best to look into the future for this purpose.

Keep in mind that the government of which you are to become the Chief Executive is a political institution. In your dealings with others within the system, try to understand that they are probably doing their best to represent the people whom they represent. Understand that even though their views are of the minority, this institution called government can only work successfully by compromise, and your ingenuity in seeking out the logical compromise and your ability to make it acceptable to the people will determine your success or failure in the office.

Take no pride in the decision you know to be right. Whatever may be the nature of it, share it to the maximum extent you feel possible and prudent with the people, keeping in mind that most of the secrets of the office are born of pride or fear, either of which has no place in your office.

Clark M. Clifford

A personal and official adviser to three Democratic Presidents. . . . Special Counsel to President Harry S. Truman (1946–1950). . . . Private counselor to Presidents John F. Kennedy and Lyndon Johnson. . . . Secretary of Defense in the Johnson administration (1968–1969).

I

One of the great strengths of the office of the Presidency of the United States is the wide latitude that it gives to the holder of the office. Article II of the United States Constitution says simply that "the executive Power shall be vested in a President of the United States of America." There are only four sections under Article II, and they give no indication of the enormous power of the office. It is clear to me that this is part of the genius evidenced by our forefathers in describing the office simply in such a manner as not to circumscribe for future generations the potential for expansion of the duties and responsibilities of the Presidency.

Even though enormous flexibility is built into the office, and although our Presidents have been men of varied backgrounds, attainments and ability, yet it seems, to me that a study of the holders of that office demonstrates that there are certain qualities that have been present when it is generally agreed that a certain President has had a successful tenure.

In order of importance, I consider those qualities to be character, intellect, decisiveness, political understanding, and awareness of the potential of the office.

Character must come first. With no concern about appearing to be cliché-ridden or a user of the hackneyed phrase, the essential attribute must be character. One is reminded of the comment by Horace Greeley in commenting upon the activities of men prominent in the important issues of his day: "Fame is a vapor, popularity an accident, riches take wings, those who cheer today will curse tomorrow, only one thing endures—character."

The unique facet of our political system is that the character of a President colors his entire administration. I have often felt that the executive branch of our government is like a chameleon. To a startling degree, the Executive Department reflects the character and personality of the President. If there is honesty, ability, and forthrightness at the top, these qualities will be apparent throughout an administration. The success of an administration will depend to a great extent upon whether it engenders confidence among the people in our country. The character of the President is the determining factor.

Intellectual capacity on the part of a President is an asset so apparent that it needs little comment. Some Presidents bring a well-trained intellect to the office, and some develop it during their tenure. The American people are quick to recognize it and respond enthusiastically to its presence. Its lack leads to an unproductive and colorless term in office.

The element of decisiveness is a condition precedent to success in a President. The number of decisions confronting our Chief Executive are legion, and the postponement of the decision-making process will inundate him. I have had the feeling on certain occasions that the American people are rather quick to forgive a President who makes an occasional mistake, but they will not tolerate the deliberate avoidance of meeting the difficulties. You can procrastinate in some branches and areas of our government but not in the White House. So many times the problems confronting a President are inter-related. The lack of decisiveness results in his position becoming intolerable and unmanageable.

Our successful Presidents have understood politics. Politics has been described as the art of the possible. Politics is the lubricating oil that permits the wheels of our government to operate smoothly and with a minimum of friction. For a President to be a successful and commanding figure, he must have a program. At the same time, a program is valueless unless he can get it adopted and put into operation. An understanding of the political equation enables a President to be a leader of his country and to work closely and effectively with the Congress.

The fifth and last quality which is vital to the success of a Presidency is an awareness of the potential of the office. Some of our Presidents have been bold and venturesome in this regard, and, in my opinion, those have been the successful periods in our country's history. Other Presidents have felt restrained and constricted and have refrained from innovation and the exploration of new thinking and new concepts. Some men have been content to accept the status quo. Others have been impatient with conditions as they found them, and they have offered new ideas, new solutions, and new experiments. The opportunities are boundless, and the most fascinating experience associated with our government is to watch a strong President expanding the limits of the office to gain the goals he seeks for our country.

When one directs his attention to the converse of the above discussion, it is not an oversimplification to state that the lack of the above qualities constitutes the major threat to the success of a Presidency. Some of the terms of office of our Chief Executive have been characterized by a lack of intellectual attainment and clear control over the decision-making process. Some well-meaning Presidents have failed because of their lack of understanding of the political ramifications of the office. Others have produced a mediocre record by reason of their misunderstanding of the office. It is not enough for a man to be well meaning. He must have an understanding of the office, a clear concept of the country's goals, and the determination and industry to accomplish them.

The men who have served as President in the twentieth century offer a fascinating variety of qualities that have led both to success and failure. Woodrow Wilson had the character, the intellect, and other important attributes, but his Presidency was adversely affected by his lack of understanding of the political equations involved. The most dramatic illustration of this was the bitter contest he waged with the Congress over the League of Nations. Harry Truman, because of his courage, his doggedness and strength of character, led the nation through one of its most difficult periods and emerged as an outstanding President.

Warren Harding was an amiable man who just never should have been President. Calvin Coolidge apparently was content to drift with the developments of the times. Herbert Hoover was a man of sterling character and intellect who was engulfed in the cataclysm of 1929 and whose administration is conspicuous by reason of his lack of awareness of the importance of the political factors of that day.

Our Presidents have come from varied backgrounds, occupations, and training. At one period during the twentieth century, the electorate looked to governors as the most appropriate candidates for the Presidency. Theodore Roosevelt, Woodrow Wilson, Calvin Coolidge, and Franklin Roosevelt all served as governors. One would have said at the time that this was the proper road to the White House.

However, as our country became inextricably involved in world affairs, the emphasis shifted, and it is interesting to note that Harry Truman, John Kennedy, Lyndon Johnson, and Richard Nixon all came from the United States Senate.

If other factors were even, I would be inclined to believe that training as the chief executive of a state would constitute the right kind of preparation and experience for the office of the Presidency. A governor must work with his staff, he must deal with the legislature, and he must run the affairs of the state in such a manner as to receive the approbation of the citizens. Service in the legislative branch of the federal government does not appear to be the best training ground for President. Such experience does acquaint him with the inner workings of the federal government, but it certainly does not lead to the specialized type of training or experience that is required of a chief executive. However, experience demonstrates that a President who comes from the legislative branch of the government can acquire the skills and expertise necessary to operate as a successful Chief Executive.

I had a close and friendly relationship with Dwight Eisenhower. He served as Chief of Staff of the Army while I was serving as Counsel at the White House. He was a loyal, dedicated American with high ideals and a splendid concept of public service. However, it is my opinion that a military career is the least helpful preparation for the Presidency that exists. A young man leaves high school and goes to the Military Academy, and from that time on, his life is carefully and meticulously structured so as to remove him from the ordinary currents of a man's existence. He doesn't have to go out and find a job, he doesn't join a labor union, he is not concerned with his future security, and he ordinarily takes no part in politics. He spends a great part of his time with other Army personnel at various Army posts, where the matters of interest are mainly concerned with military affairs. To project such a man into the office of the Presidency is a real imposition. Fortunately, the period in which he served helped, and the regard and affection in which he was held by the American people enabled him to serve two terms, and, were it not for the Twenty-second Amendment, the probability is he would have been reelected.

I am aware that I cannot be wholly objective in evaluating our various Presidents who have served in the twentieth century. It seems to me, however, that the period of President Truman's term in office constituted one of the most significant and one of the proudest periods in American history. The enunciation of the Truman Doctrine, the Marshall Plan, and the North Atlantic Treaty Organization demonstrated a prescience and a breadth of vision that are both rare and admirable. This country saved the free world after the conclusion of the Second World War, and President Truman will properly receive the credit when the history of the period is written for the future generations of Americans.

One interesting personal footnote is appropriate here. When the plan for extensive aid to Western Europe was being evolved, I recommended to President Truman that it be characterized as the Truman Plan. He very wisely rejected the suggestion because he had a Republican Congress at the time, and he felt that for the plan to bear his name would constitute a real hindrance. Dean Acheson was the major architect of the plan, and it was President Truman who decided to present it to General Marshall in such a manner that it could be offered to the country as a concept of Marshall's, so that it might become known as the Marshall Plan.

I I

For a man to be a successful White House adviser who operates in close conjunction with the President, the necessary qualities bear some resemblance to those necessary for a President. I would suggest that the ideal White House staff man would be a man of character, intellect, completely loyal to his boss, and a man of modesty, with even some humility. A White House staff man must be careful that he doesn't begin to think of himself as being an important figure, actually making decisions on his own, engaged in running the country and being indispensable to the nation's welfare. There have been many able and competent White House staff men whose names have never become known by the public. Such men would qualify accurately under the Franklin Roosevelt rule that staff members should have a passion for anonymity.

I consider the startling growth in the size and authority of the White House staff in recent years to be a dangerous trend. Obviously, some increase has been necessary as our population increases and as the burdens of the Presidency are enlarged. However, I think it is clearly inimical to the proper operation of the executive branch for operations to be set up in the White House which preempt the proper functions of one of the departments of our government. As a result of this development, which has taken place in the present administration, I believe we are witnessing a serious breakdown in the morale of personnel in important positions throughout the executive branch.

From time to time, there is considerable discussion about the proper role of the Cabinet in our system of government. I have never felt that the Cabinet, as a group, had any function at all. I have never considered that the Cabinet was a policy-making body. It is a collection of individuals each of whom has a personal relationship with the President and whose major function is to run an important department in government. At one time, James Forrestal felt that our Cabinet should be transformed to operate in much the same manner as does the British Cabinet. He recommended the creation of a Cabinet secretariat and a process by which individual members could be informed as to policy decisions that would be considered at meetings of the body. I had the impression that President Eisenhower looked upon his Cabinet to some extent as a policy-making group. It is clear to me that this is not the function of the Cabinet and that it cannot work as a policy-making body.

To some who are new to government, the Cabinet is looked upon in the same light as though it were a corporate board of directors. This is a wholly fallacious concept because, whereas a corporate board of directors is given the power by the stockholders to control and operate the affairs of the company, the Cabinet has no existence under our system of government, nor does it have any power whatsoever. A story, possibly apocryphal, is told about President Lincoln and his Cabinet at the time consideration was being given to the Proclamation of Emancipation. President Lincoln is reputed to have submitted the matter for Cabinet discussion and vote. The vote on the part of the Cabinet was unanimously in opposition to the issuance of the Proclamation. President Lincoln is then reputed to have informed the Cabinet that he appreciated their consideration, but inasmuch as the Constitution provided that he, and he alone, was to make the decision, he was signing the Proclamation forthwith.

III

There has been much discussion regarding Presidential initiative in international affairs as contrasted with alleged restrictions of his freedom to operate in domestic affairs. I do not find the distinction valid. President Johnson's enormous accomplishments in behalf of the less fortunate of our citizens will be a permanent monument to this successful phase of his Presidency. The fact that these accomplishments are temporarily overshadowed by the tragedy of the war in Vietnam should not, and in my opinion will not, detract from the credit due him. I find very little distinction, if any, between his freedom of operation in international and national affairs.

It is my opinion that individuals, groups of individuals, or political parties who are in power invariably seek to enlarge powers of the government, while those who, at the time, are on the outside criticize this effort and raise a clamor for a limitation on governmental power. The reason why it can be asserted that the prevailing "liberal" view since FDR's time has generally favored the enlargement of Presidential powers, is that "liberals" have been in office more of the time than conservatives. Now, with what would ordinarily be described as a "conservative" administration in power, we find this administration is also pressing for an enlargement of Presidential powers even though many of the public statements are phrased in semantics that imply— but do not mean—a cutting back of Presidential powers. In short, those "in" want more; those "out" don't want their opponents to have any more and don't want Presidential powers enlarged until they themselves have become the "ins."

With reference to the recurring debate as to whether the individual or the structure of government ultimately sets Presidential policy, I would suggest that a debate of this sort is academic and oftentimes meaningless. A strong President with weak institutional support is no more likely to succeed than a weak President with strong institutional support. There have been examples of both of the above alternatives in our past history and the country has muddled through. Occasionally, we get a strong President who gets strong institutional support, and we have an outstanding term of office. On at least one occasion we have had a weak individual with weak institutional support, and the result was a tragedy.

When the suggestion is made that there should be a redefinition of the office of the Presidency or certain restrictions placed upon the powers of the President, I rise strongly in opposition. I consider this as inadvisable and inappropriate tinkering with a piece of machinery that has operated well with widely varying individuals in office and under extreme pressures of dissension and division. There are any number of phases of our government's operations that can be improved, but I would leave this one alone.

Every individual I know who has served in government is ready and even anxious to give his advice to a newly elected President. I would suggest to a new President that first he select the ablest men he can find to serve in his Cabinet. Some Presidents have felt that this was unwise, for it might take something away from the main star of the performance. This is incorrect. The honest, intelligent, and efficient operation of the various departments adds to the reputation and luster of a President. I would next advise the President to select a small capable staff, and I would keep the staff small. I would give back to the departments and agencies of government those functions and responsibilities which have been taken from them and incorporated within the White House. I would also counsel a new President not to try to be his own Secretary of State. This is a will-o'-the-wisp that has led to disappointment and despair. The idea that the complex problems existing between nations can be settled by friendly chats between heads of state is an egregious error. A President must exercise a strong influence on foreign policy and must be the innovator and final arbiter of questions in this field. But I believe strongly that he must leave it to his Secretary of State to carry out such policies. And, lastly, I would urge a President to approach new problems with an open mind and not from a standpoint of a previous determination. Flexibility in a President is a quality to be highly prized. Also, one might suggest to a President, with extreme tact of course, that it is possible the President, during his term, might make some mistakes. In this regard, I would suggest to him that perhaps the most dangerous instinct that beats strongly in the human breast is the desire for vindication. This has led our government down more dead-end streets than almost any other one failing. A President who makes a mistake, admits it, and then rectifies it gains the understanding, approval, and affection of his people.

Benjamin V. Cohen

A principal architect of New Deal legislation. . . . Associate General Counsel to the Public Works Administration (1933–1934) and General Counsel to the National Power Policy Committee (1934–1941). . . . Counselor of Department of State (1945–1947). . . . Adviser to or member of U.S. delegations to conferences of Bretton Woods and Dumbarton Oaks (1944), successive UN General Assemblies (1946–1952) . . . U.S. representative before International Court of Justice (1950) and on UN Disarmament Commission (1952).

I

I am convinced that the most important quality and test of the Presidency is its ability to arouse and enlist, in government and without, the energies, the loyalties, and, if need be, the sacrifices of the people. The ultimate role of the President is to give inspiration and outlet to the tremendous forces for good at large in this great nation. To do this, certain qualities of mind and heart are essential.

First, he must sense the need of a healthy mix in the array of his advisers to catch the moods and know the needs of the people. He must have persons about him of varied experience and outlook, some bold and some prudent. He must never become the prisoner of any one school of thought. He is the President of all the people.

Second, he must be conscious of his democratic responsibility to enlighten public opinion, not to manipulate it. He must be conscious that the right to govern depends on his ability to lead and convince, not to dictate and coerce, on his ability to enlist, not to command, the support of an informed Congress and an informed people.

Third, and most important, he himself must have a liking and respect for people, a genuine regard for their lay judgment, a feeling of kinship with them born of the humility and compassion we associate with President Lincoln.

There are other qualities that a great President needs in balanced measure. Some situations call for courage and decisiveness; others call for caution and restraint. It requires great wisdom on the part of a President to decide when and how to respond to a specific challenge.

I remember, when President Roosevelt instituted the Atlantic Patrol after the fall of France in World War II, some eminent journalists inquired of Secretary Stimson why we stopped short of the final and decisive step and hesitated to declare war. Stimson stated that he appreciated their point of view but suggested they address their query to the man in the White House.

They did. Roosevelt reminded them that he served under President Wilson when Wilson was confronted with a similar situation in World War I. Wilson had impressed upon him the awful responsibility it was to bring a divided nation into war. Roosevelt wanted to be sure, very sure, that if we had to enter the war, we would enter it as far as humanly possible as a united nation.

No President should commit himself completely to a specific course of action—whether it is executive action, national legislation, or international engagement—until he has some idea of the support he may expect and the opposition he may encounter. Roosevelt frequently guarded himself against premature or improvident action by encouraging members of his administration to advance controversial proposals, sometimes rival or even conflicting proposals, to test public reaction before he would take a definite position. The one time Roosevelt radically departed from this practice was when— after his sweeping victory in the 1936 election—he committed himself to a detailed plan for the enlargement of the Supreme Court after consulting only the draftsmen of the plan. Woodrow Wilson also lost his fight for the League of Nations by insisting on the acceptance of the Covenant without amendment or reservation.

Lyndon Johnson, when majority leader of the Senate, seldom announced his position before he knew he had the votes. As President, he followed the same practice in regard to domestic legislation. Unfortunately, however, he allowed himself to become so enmeshed in the day-to-day policy decisions in the Vietnam War that it became impossible for him to review his own decisions and consider alternative suggestions of friendly critics.

To succeed in his great office, a President must have intuitive vision and practical judgment. He needs intuitive vision to know not only where he aspires to go but where realistically he can hope to go. He needs to have a practical judgment of men and measures to know how to reach his goals. He should never become so isolated or aloof that he loses touch with realities and fails to observe when things are not working out as planned. Nor should he allow himself to become so personally involved in the minutiae of his plans and the means of implementing them that he is resistant to the need of a change in strategy or substance. A President must have not only the courage to lead, but the wisdom to make reasonable concessions to secure the support and cooperation of the Congress and the people.

I I

The men about the President in the White House are in a sense the eyes and ears of the Presidency. As the tasks of government expand and become more complex, the time the President has to give to some of the most important decisions is unbelievably limited.

The idea that the President always knows more and knows best is comforting but far from true. The President does need about him a trusted group— persons he trusts and persons who trust and respect him—but persons of varied experience, outlook and habits of thought. It is the task of the President's counselors and advisers to ensure that the President is as well prepared and as well informed as possible before he makes his decision.

As the tasks of government have continued to expand, some of the President's counselors and advisers have become more than personal assistants to the President and have been entrusted with the responsibility of acting for the President.

During the war years, President Roosevelt entrusted broad powers to Justice Byrnes to act for him in the handling of domestic problems so that he could concentrate on the war problems. Byrnes' position was not secret but established by executive order. He appeared before Congressional committees and never claimed executive privilege.

It is clear that some Presidential advisers today have in fact been given power to act for the President, but their authority is not defined by executive order or statute. They do not appear before committees of Congress; they claim executive privilege not only for the advice and assistance they give to the President but for the action they take on their own responsibility in relation to others than the President. They have built up their own large staffs which tend to supplant rather than supplement the staffs of the established departments.

With the great expansion and increased complexity of government operations, the President needs some personal assistants and counselors to assist and advise him, but without authority to act for him on their own responsibility. He needs, in addition, a limited number of surrogates to share his responsibility and to act for him on their own responsibility within limits prescribed and guidelines set by him. Such surrogates individually or collectively should have adequate authority to monitor, approve, and coordinate the policies and programs of the various departments and agencies to keep them within and abreast of the Presidential guidelines, but they should scrupulously avoid involvement in the minutiae of departmental and agency operations. The surrogates should be persons of high and independent public standing and should be confirmed by the Senate; they should form a small inner or super Cabinet that can share with the President his gravest responsibilities. This cannot be done by a large Cabinet composed of the heads of many departments and agencies with widely different and specialized interests.

There are times when the President very much needs unbiased judgment and moral support from persons he can regard as his peers. This would not diminish his position, since he would have the power of decision and the last word. The position of other Cabinet members would be enhanced because they would have a far more meaningful relation with the President through the members of his inner Cabinet who could give much more time to an adequate understanding of their problems than a President difficult to reach and heavily overburdened.

III

I do not accept the doctrine that the powers of the President are more limited in domestic affairs than in foreign affairs. I think the Constitution divided power in both areas between the President and the Congress and did not intend the President as a general principle to be less accountable to Congress and the people in one area than in the other. I do not believe the Founding Fathers accepted the idea that the waging of war or the management of foreign affairs is an esoteric art or science beyond the ken of the experience and judgment of the people who must bear the costs with their lives and treasure.

There have been instances when the President has acted to repel armed attack without awaiting formal action of the Congress. There have also been instances, from Jefferson's Louisiana Purchase to Roosevelt's transfer of destroyers for bases, when the President, without awaiting formal Congressional action, has entered into important international agreements necessary to protect the national interests in a pressing emergency. In such situations the President should be conscious of his accountability to the Congress and the people and should, so far as circumstances permit, satisfy himself beforehand that the Congress is willing to accept or acquiesce in his action.

In the destroyers for bases agreement, Roosevelt hesitated to proceed without formal Congressional action, but concluded that Congressional debate on the eve of the 1940 election would divide rather than unite the country. The William Allen White Committee reported that sentiment in the country supported the transfer, and Willkie, the Republican nominee, also favored it, although he had not indicated his view as to the need for Congressional action. Before going ahead with the agreement, Roosevelt was informed by Senator Pepper that Senator McNary, the minority leader, had advised him that his past commitments would make it difficult for him to support the transfer if it would require formal Senate approval before the election, but he, McNary, would make no objection if plausible grounds were found for proceeding without Senate action. Roosevelt decided to proceed. Willkie then vigorously protested Roosevelt acting without formal Congressional approval. But after the election Willkie told me that it was the one act of his campaign that he deeply regretted.

In April, 1941, Roosevelt issued an executive order establishing an Office of Price Administration and Civilian Supply. Under the order—which had no specific statutory base—the administrator was authorized and directed, among other things, to fix maximum prices, prevent speculation, and stimulate the increased supply of materials and commodities required for civilian use. The authority thus granted was used sparingly, because enforcement powers were limited.

It was not until nearly a year and a half later that Roosevelt asked for price and wage control legislation. By then inflation was beginning to get out of control, and Congress was reluctant to take action. Some of Roosevelt's advisers urged executive action on the basis of his war powers. Others urged him to insist on Congressional action because the legislation would affect many little people and small business, and he was entitled to have Congress on record. He sent another message to the Congress and made a fireside chat, and the bill was passed. Some Congressmen complained he was putting too much heat on them. They would have preferred to have him act on his own responsibility so that they would not have to take a stand and alienate some of their constituents whether they voted one way or another.

I doubt whether it is practical or wise to try to define with precision the emergencies in which the President may act without Congressional action. The important thing is that the President recognize his accountability to the Congress and the people and his duty to keep the Congress and the people currently and fully informed of developments in matters that vitally affect their lives and well-being. Congress should assert by legislation its rights to terminate hostilities commenced without a declaration of war by a resolution of either house. Congress should also, by legislation, set up a commission on which the Congress and the executive branch are equally represented, to devise ways and means that will ensure the free flow to Congress of intelligence reports and other information pertinent to its legislative work and constitutional responsibility. The only information which should be withheld is that which is objectively determined to be a clear and imminent threat to the security of the United States.

A President who recognizes his accountability to the Congress and the people and his responsibility to give leadership to an informed Congress and an informed people is a strong President. A President who relies on naked power is a dictatorial President, ill-equipped to lead a great democratic nation.

The President should be the leader not only of his own party but of the nation. In a country as large and diversified as ours, the two-party system can exist only by allowing party members to be responsible to their constituents, rather than subjecting them to strict party discipline which would lead to the formation of splinter parties. To give leadership to the Congress and to obtain its support, the President must be able to work with members of both parties. Seldom can an important measure get through the Congress without the support of some members from both parties. Roosevelt was able to get his New Deal legislation through Congress without serious amendment only with the assistance of the progressive wing of the Republican Party. When war threatened in Europe and Roosevelt perceived the need to strengthen our defenses, modify the neutrality laws, and resort to the draft, a number of the Democratic New Dealers were intransigent isolationists; Roosevelt then sought and secured support from the conservative wing of the Republican Party.

The President must also be able to secure the cooperation and to tap the great and often hidden resources of the great federal bureaucracies. He must see that the bureaucracies follow his policies, and not their own, when they conflict. That is not easy. He must appoint able men to head the departments who can gain the confidence of the bureau chiefs without giving them the impression that the only task of a department head is to give unquestioning support to bureau views and recommendations. Department heads must keep the experts on tap, not on top, and they must not assume that career men are all of one mind. In most departments there are some independent thinkers whose views are often muted or discarded before they reach the Secretary. Not infrequently their innovative ideas appear without attribution in a Senator's speech or the testimony of a witness at a Congressional committee hearing. Oddly enough, the dominant groups in the bureaucracy are often as scornful of "political intermeddling" by the President as a dictatorial President is of "political intermeddling" by the Congress.

My own observations persuade me the nation fares best under strong and effective Presidential leadership. Such leadership, I believe, is best judged by a President's ability to utilize the resources of the executive establishment, secure the cooperation of an informed Congress, and enlist the support of an informed electorate.

Ralph A. Dungan

> An aide to John F. Kennedy both in the Senate and the White House. . . . Special Assistant to Presidents John F. Kennedy (1961–1963) and Lyndon Johnson (1963–1964). . . . Previously legislative assistant to Senator Kennedy (1956–1957). . . . Subsequently U.S. Ambassador to Chile (1964–1967) and (from 1967) Chancellor of Higher Education, State of New Jersey.

I

Anyone who has given much thought to the Presidency and its critical position in the American system of government could specify those characteristics and qualities they would prefer in a President. But whatever one believes important—courage, intelligence, and the like—a key characteristic, in my opinion, is the capacity to bring all qualities to bear on particular problems and in the correct proportion. This integrative capacity—the ability to see things whole, to measure long as well as short-term effects, and to make decisions with compassion as well as technical or logical precision—this capacity is perhaps the most essential and the least susceptible of prior evaluation or assessment.

This quality in any man, it seems to me, distinguishes the superior human being. It is the quality which permits rejection of the advice of one's collaborators, when to take the advice would pose an uncertain risk for the nation and perhaps the world. While no one can say what exactly motivated it, it is my opinion that John F. Kennedy's decision to reject the advice of senior officials to commit U.S. forces at the Bay of Pigs—or even more pertinently to defer air strikes against the SAM sites in Cuba during the missile crisis—illustrated the integrative principle at work most dramatically.

In addition to this fundamental quality, there are other characteristics which mark an effective President. A person who lacks knowledge of a broad range of public issues and the processes (governmental, financial, and others) by which society runs—or who lacks a substantial measure of intellectual curiosity and acuity—is seriously impaired in terms of Presidential performance. Closely linked to a concern with public questions and intellectual capacity is possession of a sensitive knowledge of the social condition and aspirations of major elements of the population. The importance of this knowledge is probably the only good argument for the maintenance of the current Presidential primary system—which presents an unparalleled opportunity for the fast learner.

Although it is difficult to single out any quality in a President which is of overriding importance, I would certainly give the nod to knowing (other than intellectually) a good deal about the conditions, the problems, the frustrations, and the aspirations of the citizenry. While this certainly should be the aim of every public official, the President has a special responsibility to force himself to place his actions and thoughts in the perspective of the concerns of ordinary citizens. For some this is easier than for others; some I believe have to work at it. But if history has any lesson to teach us about politics and government, it is the decline of societies whose leaders permitted themselves to lose perspective on the needs of the governed.

The importance of Presidential knowledge of, and respect for, the legitimate constitutional rights of the other two branches of government—along with a jealous concern for the protection of Executive rights—cannot be overlooked. From this constitutional commitment should flow, especially with regard to the Congress, a capacity to compromise and negotiate. In recent years, I believe that this important balance of constitutional power has not been maintained because of a lack of respect for the constitutional principles involved or, perhaps more accurately, a subordination of constitutional principle to the demands of Presidential ego and, correspondingly, to the lack of strong leadership in the legislative branch.

I believe that the interplay of power between the executive and legislative branches is essential to social harmony and constitutes as sensible a way as men have devised to insure representative and responsive government. In order for the system to work well, both branches must respect the legitimate rights of the other, *and* never lose the capacity for independent initiative and judgment. There are many in the Congress who are sensitive to the principle and who regularly polish and enshrine it rhetorically. There are few, however, who seem willing to make the commitment of time and effort necessary to sustain a serious independent initiative. Congress tends to be passive and generally to respond only to the Presidency. Under contemporary circumstances, technology, especially in the field of communications, has tended to strengthen the position of the Presidency in the American system. This factor, together with the proclivities of some recent Presidents and the seeming inability of the Congress to cope with the complexity of contemporary governmental problems has, I believe, made the question of sensitivity to constitutional principles an important consideration in qualifying a President.

On the other hand, not all blame for the shift in power to the Executive is attributable to Presidential aggressiveness. The unwillingness of Congress to face up to the fact that it has failed in fulfilling its proper constitutional role —primarily because of an archaic organizational structure and a defective seniority system—is both reprehensible and dangerous. No more dramatic example of Congressional failure to exercise its constitutional powers exists than its abandonment of responsibility with respect to the power to wage war. Less dramatic but equally portentous is the cumbersome appropriations process, which by and large takes place with little or no reference to the total economic situation. Congressional abandonment of responsibility in these and other crucial areas has strengthened the tendency toward concentration of power in the Presidency.

Finally, any President to be successful must have a capacity to communicate with assurance and credibility to the public a sense that major issues are being faced and resolved rationally—and that drift, indecision, and injustice do not characterize Presidential decision-making. The ability to so communicate is not by any means limited to the explicit use of the media or to formal speeches or press conferences. This art of communication results from a totality of actions and statements which together constitute the message.

A vital part of this communication, of course, is with the Congress. While each President employs those devices to communicate with Congress with which he feels comfortable, there are few in my opinion who have performed well in recent years. John Kennedy's Congressional relations were marked by a formality and stiffness which, I believe, stemmed from the fact that he had never really felt comfortable as a member of the legislature, nor did he personally identify with it. He was unwilling to pay the dues, so to speak, and felt something of an aloofness, if not a disdain, for the legislative body. Moreover, his struggle for the Presidency was marked by cool relations with a number of prominent members, some of whom had very good reason to feel cool.

President Johnson, on the other hand, acted toward the Congress as if he were still majority leader in the Senate—with all of the gusto he employed in that office. This smothering, all-pervasive, totally intimate style—combined with the powers and prerequisites of the Presidency—was, to put it mildly, most effective. History will judge whether the Johnson approach to Congressional relations, in addition to obvious short-term effectiveness, had any long-term adverse effects on the institutional relationships between the two branches of government. I am inclined to believe that when Congress finally reasserts its constitutional powers, we are likely to witness a more severe swing than is desirable, as a result of the "heavy hand of the White House" which characterized the Johnson Presidency.

I I

Since the latter days of the Roosevelt administration, at least partly due to the exigencies imposed by World War II, the Executive Office of the President with its various elements and the immediate Presidential or White House staff have expanded greatly and taken on increasing importance in the U.S. governmental system. To some considerable degree, the necessity for these Presidential staff services have been dictated by events and a shift in power to the Office of the President.

Given the differing views on centralization of power held by the several incumbents since Roosevelt, one must conclude that there are some not wholly controllable centripetal forces at work which tend toward strengthening and increasing the authority of the Office of the President. I believe that on the whole this tendency should be resisted, for the basic reasons which caused the Founding Fathers to resist concentration of political power and to establish systems of checks.

I hasten to say that I do not believe that the *de facto* growth in the power of the Presidency is the result of a deliberate effort of any modern President to grab power for its own sake. But it is disingenuous to expect a President to resist power thrust on him or not to exercise whatever power is available and useful in the solution of a problem. In the circumstances, the only feasible counterforce to continued accretions of Presidential power is the Congress. What is needed is a good deal more creative tension which does not diminish Presidential power or initiative but places limits on its exercise.

The implication of this analysis is that Presidential staff will continue to grow in size and importance. How much depends on the personality of the President and his attitude toward his Cabinet. While there is not much recent history to support the thesis, I believe it is possible to have responsible Cabinet government with a strong Presidency. Not very much in the U.S. political system, including the professions from which we typically draw our political leaders, facilitates the development, the skills, and attitudes which appear necessary to the working of a "strong President-strong Cabinet" type of government.

I I I

Most recent Presidents, with the exception of Eisenhower, came to the office from a set of experiences where the premium was on individual rather than team effort, where trust and confidence was not widely shared, and where success was measured largely in personal terms. Given such characteristics, it is not surprising that recent Presidents had difficulty identifying persons whose competence they respected or in whom they reposed much confidence to take the principal posts in government. Yielding substantial power and autonomy to Cabinet officers or other subordinates, without rather close Presidential staff review and oversight, requires of the President, at least (1) a confidence in the capacity of the subordinate; (2) a sense or feeling of unity of purpose; and (3) a trust that the subordinate's actions are consistent with Presidential interests, as distinguished from personal, agency, or interest-group objectives.

The dilemma and problem are well illustrated by a conversation I overheard as a young staffer between a Cabinet officer very closely identified with President Eisenhower and a senior official in the Executive Office at the beginning of that administration. One said to the other: "We have to get them [other members of the Cabinet] under control early because in six months they will be captured by their bureaucracies or the interests."

Despite these and other formidable obstacles, I believe that a greater diffusion of power within the executive branch, rather than centralization in a Presidential staff, is far preferable to what we have today. Indeed, if Presidential staff continues to grow in numbers and power, the important and necessary role of the Presidential adviser will, paradoxically, be diminished, and the Presidential staff will become another vested-interest group with whom the President must contend. No doubt the President needs a personal staff; what he does not need is a command-post bunker where large numbers of operational decisions are made.

Probably the simplest and truest statement which can be made about the Presidency is that the office depends greatly on the intelligence, sensitivity, and capacity of the incumbent. If he or she has a sound appreciation of the Constitution, a sense of restraint about the use of the power of the office, and a deep concern with the welfare of the mass of the people, then the administrative arrangements of the office and even the intellectual limits of the incumbent are not critical. Powerful and demanding as the office most certainly is, a sense of humor and the constant awareness of human limitations, including mortality, should assist an incumbent in bearing the burden.

Abe Fortas

A jurist and personal counselor to President Lyndon Johnson. . . . Previously retained as counsel or administrator by Agricultural Adjustment Administration (1933–1934), Securities and Exchange Commission (1934–1937), and Public Works Administration (1939–1950). . . . Undersecretary of the Interior (1942–1946). . . . Adviser to U.S. delegation to the United Nations Conference in San Francisco (1945). . . . Associate Justice of the U.S. Supreme Court (1965–1969).

I

Generalizations about the Presidency—and all the presumed requirements for so-called success in that office—are difficult. They are likely to be out of focus because the historical reference is the heart of the matter. The requirements for a successful or great Presidency are different depending upon the context of the times—the point in history—in which the particular President is functioning.

The case of Dwight Eisenhower, for example, illustrates this. There are some reasons for saying he was a successful Chief Executive. He certainly was such in terms of popular esteem and support. Perhaps he deserves acclaim because no disaster occurred during his eight years in the White House. Perhaps he was the sort of President that the times required—a prudent, cautious, and low-keyed national leader. . . . But there are other times in history when a President with his qualities and with his approach to the office would have been a catastrophe. Even this leads to a further speculation: that different times might have induced Dwight Eisenhower himself to be different. The fact seems to be that one point in history calls for a kind of patient time server, while another calls for a bold and venturesome spirit.

You find a quite different example in the case of Harry Truman. I doubt that anyone could have said, before he entered the White House, that he had manifested the outstanding qualities one tends to associate with the Presidency. But after a surprisingly short time, he showed the key qualities needed for the office: decisiveness, leadership, courage, and an insistence upon protecting and performing the constitutional functions of the Presidency coupled with a sound, if perhaps limited, comprehension of the constitutional and historic role of that great office. And perhaps above all, he had a clear conception of *the point in history* at which he operated.

It can be endlessly debated, of course, whether a President makes the times or the times make a President. In turbulent or critical times, one looks to the Presidency for the vigorous and affirmative qualities necessary to serve the needs of the nation at such a moment. In such a time, the Presidency requires a capacity for courage, a comprehension of the nature of the present challenge, a perception of the alternatives that are available, and a sense of national direction compatible with and sensitive to the genius of the nation and the thrust of history. Another quality that it seems to me a President must have at a time of crisis is *a sense of the extent and limitations* of the feasible. This demands political sensitivity in the largest sense—an awareness of what he can or cannot do, with respect to the Congress and with respect to the people. The challenge has two dimensions. The crisis President must not only know and respect the outer limits of the feasible, he must also have the courage and resourcefulness to exploit the range of feasible action in the national interest and not to undershoot it. And if he is a very great leader, he can shape and expand the dimensions of the feasible.

The master in this area was Franklin Roosevelt, and if you compare him with Lyndon Johnson, you find an interesting study in contrast of techniques for testing the limits of the feasible. Both were careful analysts of the limits upon their actions, both were skillful at shaping and expanding those limits, and neither fell far short of exploiting the possibilities available to him for constructive leadership. But their methods were quite different. Roosevelt was very articulate about his methods, very clear in his own mind about techniques and their use and very deliberate in the whole exercise. His reference point always was the public—rather than the Congress or a select group of counselors. The Johnson technique was altogether different. I think he, too, was a very great President, but his reference point was not the people so much as it was Congress and a highly diversified group of advisers.

With FDR, the prime example of his leadership genius was his carefully paced direction of the nation leading to our participation in World War II. It was a study in step-by-step leadership. Throughout the process, he showed that testing the limits of the feasible can also mean fashioning and shaping them. As a characteristic instance, I recall more than one occasion, when I was Undersecretary of the Interior, watching FDR quite deliberately use Harold Ickes (then Secretary of the Interior) by encouraging him to make a speech outlining a position that was considerably in front of where the nation stood at the time. The speech given, Roosevelt would sit back—his antennae waving in the air and his cigarette holder pointing toward heaven—and wait for the playback from the country. Or to change the figure of speech: he would see if an Ickes could open a hole in the defensive line of public opinion. If so, Roosevelt would take the ball and run through it. If not, he would toss his head and deplore Ickes' rashness. He was a bold leader of people, but he was usually careful to test and prepare public opinion. And when he had prepared and aroused opinion, he could usually get Congress to come along and accept the public decision.

With Johnson, a decision to move in a particular direction meant that he would test its feasibility directly with the representatives of the people. It is fascinating to speculate why these two men—both great, powerful, and successful Presidents—operated so differently. Their wholly contrasting techniques had to reflect profoundly different psychological preparation and emotional makeup. Roosevelt had no background in Congress, of course, while Johnson's was predominately there. Roosevelt was a man whose birth and home and life had given him no reason for self-doubt, and with such a heritage he had no cause to be afraid of verbally launching bold or grand conceptions—which is one of the techniques of leadership.

To go on from these thoughts to John Kennedy: he was an extraordinarily complex man, and his was a clearly different kind of Presidency. His was a Presidency of ideas rather than accomplishments—or more precisely, it was a Presidency of accomplishments in terms of ideas and ideals, rather than explicit and concrete programs. There are men and Presidents who can exercise leadership by dramatizing ideas and gaining their acceptance, while not immediately getting men to act. There are points in history where this special type of man can make a great contribution—a record of *verba non facta*—ideas but not accomplishments. And it is interesting, once again, to wonder: were the psychology and character of this Presidency rooted in Kennedy's personal background—or was the determining factor the time in history when he became President? Like other men, Presidents frequently delude themselves that the things they do, or the positions they espouse, are entirely products of themselves, rather than largely the fruit of the mysterious forces of history.

To me, the process of program formulation in the Presidency is not materially different from the process of constitutional decision-making in a body like the Supreme Court. In a real sense in both cases, the bricks from which any structure is built—the vital ingredients of the decision—are already there. These are the creations of the past that inhabit the present. The problem always is how the man puts them together. Different men do this quite differently. But they often delude themselves that they have made the bricks.

All generalizations about the Presidency are perilous. I suppose that one could say, for example, that an essential quality in a President is the ability to view complex problems with utter simplicity—a simple sense of what are the right and wrong directions. I think this was the secret of Harry Truman. Certainly, in the case of the Supreme Court, this was a secret of Earl Warren's greatness. In the White House, this means the strength to stand in the rushing, turbulent stream of events, pressures, and advice where each President finds himself, and never to lose sight of the water that flows from the deep springs of our history and our ethics and our values—never to lose sight of our historic mission, if you will, as a people. The challenge to a President is always to be able to lead the nation along this particular part of the stream—never getting too far ahead of it, never falling too far behind. Simplification—a genius for the essence—is the priceless ingredient of leadership.

And yet all great Presidents do not fit this pattern of essential simplicity. I think Lyndon Johnson was one of our most powerful and effective Presidents, but he had one of the most complex minds—and one of the most complex emotional and psychological personalities—of any Chief Executive in our history. This complexity applies, too, to Richard Nixon, whom I regard as the most radical President in my lifetime. The proofs of this observation about President Nixon seem to me obvious—from the use of wage and price controls on the domestic scene to his rapprochement with China and the Soviet Union and the interruption in international affairs of 'thirty-five years of multilateralism, both monetary and political. In the first few weeks since his reelection, President Nixon has given further evidence of this surprising, powerful readiness to break with the past. The bothersome question to me, which is still to be resolved, is whether this particular kind of radicalism will go on to depart from what I believe to be the main roots of American life: the commitment to personal rights, humane justice, and equal opportunity for all.

I I

The qualities most requisite in a Presidential adviser are the courage to assert one's views and the capacity for humility. An adviser must be able and willing to subordinate himself to the role—most obviously, with a discretion that assures the absolute confidentiality of the relationship. At the same time, he must be steadfast in stating his own views forthrightly and willing to accept decisions contrary to those views. He must be willing sometimes to accept public blame for decisions which he did not make and to go on functioning in the context of policies with which he did not agree. As for specific skills, the most important is not only a broad background of experience and the ability clearly and neatly to express his views, but also the ability to listen, to distill the statements of others, and to summarize facts and opinions with an objectivity undistorted by his own personal views. Since the President has to act on a distillate of data and opinion, an essential advisory task is to aid the process by making sure that the distillate is true to the ingredients.

I stress humility in all this for one reason. A Presidential adviser always has to realize that a President, if he does his job, makes his decision on the basis of a huge variety of factors and values. No single adviser can possibly be in a position to evaluate the totality of the factors that a President should consider or to receive the total input that a President should and must get. By the definition of his particular role, an adviser is disqualified to take the initiative in obtaining this kind of input. He must therefore realize that his own conclusions are based on data far more limited than what is available to the President and on less than all of the value factors that a President must consider. He must also realize that he is the adviser—the helper—that he is not the President.

One thing I regret very much is our country's tendency—with its premium on controversy and inside information—to incite or seduce an adviser to betray his trust, to undermine a President's confidence that he can have advisers to whom he can trust his inmost thoughts. A President has to have this, just as a citizen can go to a doctor or a lawyer, a priest or a psychiatrist, to discuss his problems, without fear of disclosure of his confidences. I would place a premium on the kind of man as President who consciously and insistently works, as Lyndon Johnson did, to get a constant diversity of views, freely expressed, from which to distill his own judgment. As for most disclosures that are made by trusted advisers, including memoirs after the fact, they are generally worth no more than a boy's account of a football game which he has seen through a knothole in the fence. Advisers, however close, don't and can't see all of the action.

The matter of the proper structure and size of the White House staff is a far from simple question. It is necessary, of course, to distinguish between "staff" and "advisers." Their roles are wholly distinct and different. The White House staff can be important or relatively inconsequential, depending on a number of factors which have little to do with the ability or experience of its members. It can be appraised only in the context of the President's working style and in terms of the Presidency's relations to three other groups: the Congress, the Cabinet, and the independent regulatory agencies.

In the case of the Congress, it is now recognized that drastic reform and reorganization are necessary if we are to avoid centralization of power in the White House staff. Without such reorganization, I think we face the real danger that the power of Congress may be largely confined to negative functions, rather than serious participation in policy formulation. Congress may become critic rather than policy-maker. Personally, I deplore this downgrading of the Congress because I believe in a pluralistic society and a pluralistic government.

With regard to the Cabinet as an institution, as differentiated from the individuals who compose it, as I have seen it operate under three Presidents, it is a joke. As a collegium, it doesn't exist. Its members, sitting as a Cabinet, neither advise the President nor engage in any meaningful consideration of serious problems or issues. I remember Harold Ickes describing Cabinet meetings as "dormitory sessions." Of the sessions that I took part in under Roosevelt and Truman, I am sure that nothing of importance, beyond mere reporting, was ever said.

When you consider the Executive departments themselves, I believe they should be responsive to the President in a broad policy sense. We have developed no techniques for assuring this other than the White House staff. But this does not mean that the staff should run or supervise the various departments. A part of the reason why a Kennedy and now Nixon are tempted to run the executive agencies from the White House is the fact that the lines of communication and control run from the President and his staff to a department head who sometimes doesn't control his own department and who most often is a temporary appointee without much knowledge of his job or experience. There is a constant temptation for a President to seek control through the use of his White House staff rather than through the head of the department. I think this is unfortunate. It can be demoralizing to the agencies, and it leads to excessive centralization of power in the White House, exercised in a faceless, "under-the-table" sort of way. I think it advisable to try some merging of departments and establishing some new procedures with direct, recognized responsibilities to the President from the top professional level of a department as well as from its political head.

As for independent agencies of a quasi-judicial character—such agencies as the SEC or CAB—I think it is entirely wrong to allow the President or the White House staff to interfere at all in their decisions or procedures. Such intervention is only one step removed—if that much—from interfering in court decisions. This is unthinkable. Or it ought to be.

III

There is obviously a broad difference between the range of Presidential power and initiative in domestic and in foreign affairs. We need, however, to take account of a further distinction. This is the distinction between international-political and international-economic affairs. While the two obviously overlap and interact in certain ways, Congress should have and exercise greater direction over international-economic affairs. There are two reasons for this: First, it has become more and more apparent that it is an illusion to suppose that Congress can deal competently with domestic economics without also dealing with international economics. Second, the President must necessarily have a great deal of authority in international-political matters. The Constitution merely recognizes a reality in giving the President his authority over international affairs. This is inevitable, as in such areas as the treaty-making power. But this should be understood as referring to international-*political* affairs, despite the obvious difficulty in separating economic and political affairs. This arena of action calls for procedures which are impossible for the Congress. Congress has and must have a role, but it is largely that of consultant and critic, with an ultimate power of veto which, however, is and can be of only limited effectiveness.

In the international-political field, I believe the President has to be given use of the armed forces. I see no alternative to a recognition that the President must have such power and that Congressional control over its use is bound to be restricted. The question is whether we must rely merely on the President's willingness to consult the Congress or whether his power to use the armed forces can be subjected to really effective checks. I like the idea of Justice William O. Douglas to provide a measure of effective check upon the President through control of Selective Service. This is to say: let the power of the President to make a military commitment be limited to the professional Army, Navy, and Air Force in being, but provide that no persons subsequently recruited by Selective Service may be required to bear arms unless and until the Congress has expressly so authorized by a declaration of war. It does not seem to me reasonable or possible to limit the President in terms of *situations* in which he may or may not use armed forces, which are hardly foreseeable, but it is possible to limit him in terms of resources, by insistence that he can commit only standing forces without a formal declaration of war by Congress. Such a constraint would have a salutary effect on the military establishment, as well as the Presidency. And I believe it would restrain the President more effectively than would be accomplished by attempting to require concurrence of Congressional committees or similar devices that have been suggested.

On the general question of the powers of the Presidency, these have certainly vastly increased as the years have brought a vast increase in the powers and roles of the federal government in general. Such disproportion—such overshadowing of the Congress—as we have seen should, I think, be traced to default by Congress as much as to the power drives of the Presidents. On the whole, I should say that the danger we confront is less a matter of the increase in Executive power than the lack of an effective Congress. There are good people in the Congress, but the machinery is not working. As the nation and its concerns have become larger, the work product of the Congress has become smaller—more and more directed to minutiae, sometimes petty, instead of to the great issues of program and policy. Congress has become more and more the national plumber and tinkerer, instead of the policy-making body which our Constitution—and perhaps our survival as a democracy—requires. The *reductio ad absurdum* is the Congressional handling of revenue and appropriation bills, the ultimate Congressional instruments. Congress, like the Executive, should formulate a program at the beginning of each session. It should have its own State of the Union message to the people, its own agenda for the session, which should sympathetically take into account the President's program. This program should constitute, in effect, a pledge by the Congress that it will devote a majority of its time and effort to the great issues confronting the nation. It should legislate and appropriate in broad strokes, so that policy and program values will not be buried by attention to detail. Congress must be willing to delegate detail to the Executive establishment, subject only to the scrutiny of special investigative committees of the Congress. To do this, reforms are essential, reforms that involve staffing, seniority, procedure, and—above all—Congress seriously defining its own role. The members of Congress simply have to locate the bones and nerves and heart of their own job and to confine themselves to these essentials. They have to choose between policy-formulating and nit-picking. They have to move toward a greater reliance on the Executive to execute and the administrative agencies to administer.

Until this branch of the government works as it should, I believe, it is idle to talk of curtailment of the powers of the Presidency. The federal government has powers and functions that have to be exercised. We cannot have a national vacuum. It will be filled by the President—indeed, at some phases of the cycles of history, even by the courts—unless Congress acts. Only after Congressional reform can we talk of Presidential reform.

As to any advice or counsel that I might offer a newly elected President, I am, of course, hesitant to speak. I would suggest to any President that he should never forget the fundamental referent of his task, which is the historic genius and direction of this country. Although we have sometimes acted immorally, the referent postulated by our background, history, and tradition is essentially moral. Our ideals and our ideology, our wealth, and our strength have led us to stand for the great principles of humanity, domestically and internationally. We still have the strength, the ability, and the freedom to do this. If we abandon this position, we shall, I think, first lose our soul and then our strength. You find these moral principles well set forth in the Constitution itself: the dedication to personal rights, the embracing of

Judeo-Christian ethics, and the thrust toward equality. Specifically, in domestic terms, I would say that the President who tries to turn his back on the revolutionary Kennedy-Johnson programs of the 1960's—the affirmation of civil rights and racial justice and equal opportunity—runs the risk that history will remember him as a violator of America's past and future and as an architect of chaos.

I have enough faith in the future of our country to believe that no President insensitive to these principles will be regarded as having fulfilled his mission. These are fundamental. All else is detail.

Clayton Fritchey

> A veteran of Democratic Party politics and aide to President Harry S. Truman and Adlai E. Stevenson. . . . Assistant to President Truman (1952). . . . Previously Assistant to Secretary of Defense George Marshall. . . . Subsequently deputy chairman of the Democratic National Committee (1953–1957), Presidential campaign adviser to Stevenson (1952 and 1956) and special assistant to Ambassador Stevenson at the United Nations (1961–1965).

I

In a democracy, where the will of the people is supposedly paramount, all —or nearly all—depends on whether the leader, the man in the White House, wants to make the best or the worst of his fellow Americans. His power to do either is incalculable. If it is agreed that a nation is at its best when its finest instincts are flourishing, then we must seek for the Presidency a man who is capable of arousing these instincts and directing them toward benign ends. This would seem to suggest that in a President the most important "personal" qualities are the ones which add up to moral leadership.

In practice, as well as theory, this is so. The Presidents that Americans revere most are all associated with exalted undertakings: Lincoln (Emancipation), Wilson (League of Nations), Franklin Roosevelt (New Deal), Truman (Marshall Plan). And hindsight demonstrates that such undertakings usually turn out to be not only right, but rewarding as well, which may explain why the most admirable Presidents have generally been the most successful ones.

Conversely, it can be seen that the more grubby administrations—the ones headed by Presidents with a mean, if not cynical, view of the electorate— have seldom left the country any legacy worth mentioning, although during their incumbency they invariably have been hailed as "practical," "pragmatic," "no-nonsense" leaders. This is especially true of the laissez-faire Presidents, who pride themselves on leaving the people (and, above all, their exploiters) alone. The more idealistic Presidents have shown that the people can be prodded into making sacrifices and risking changes to advance the common weal, but the more mundane Chief Executives have also demonstrated that the people are quite happy to concentrate on their own narrow interests if encouraged to do so.

It is worth noting that the principal economic disturbances of the twentieth century have occurred in the wake of dollar-minded, do-nothing administrations—notably Herbert Hoover's great depression, Dwight Eisenhower's series of small recessions, and Richard Nixon's severe recession of 1970–71. In contrast, the years of the people-minded Presidents have consistently been distinguished by rising prosperity.

All of this is by way of arguing that we should particularly look for positive qualities in choosing a President, which is another way of saying we should favor comparatively optimistic, sympathetic, courageous, decent, humane, sensitive, and open men. Along with this, they should be worldly and not wholly without guile or humor. This sounds like Franklin D. Roosevelt, who, with all his very human shortcomings, is about the maximum that can be hoped for in a democratic society.

There is much to be learned about the American Presidency, I believe, by studying the administrations of FDR and Richard Nixon. Roosevelt was a master politician, as is Nixon. Both knew how to reach the public directly and intimately—Roosevelt by radio, Nixon by television. Both knew how to create new and winning political coalitions. Neither was handicapped by illusions that the American people are much different than they really are. Yet Roosevelt was elected four times by betting that Americans were ready for a cooperative, fraternal, social-minded state, while Nixon has been reelected overwhelmingly by catering to all that is divisive in our society.

So one President proved that the appeal to hope and trust is an unbeatable political formula, and a later one has just shown that the appeal to fear is apparently equally effective. Franklin Roosevelt carried all but two states by telling the people they had nothing to fear but fear itself. Richard Nixon carried all but one state by making them fear everything, especially each other: blacks against whites, young against old, hawks against doves, AFL against CIO, educated against uneducated, fundamentalists against freethinkers.

Out of the politics of hope came the greatest nonviolent democratic revolution in history. Out of fear there may come apartheid in America. This would seem to answer the question: which Presidents of the twentieth century most clearly personify both the qualities most wanted and the failings least wanted?

As compared with character, heart, and courage, previous political preparation is a lesser consideration in choosing a President. In the last fifty years, five of our Chief Executives have been Senators—Harding, Truman, Kennedy, Johnson, and Nixon—all of whom were comparatively familiar with the federal government before they began running it. Yet both their successes and failures can be traced to personal rather than professional qualities. This is overwhelmingly true of Mr. Truman, who seems assured of a high place among American Presidents not so much because of brains, knowledge, sophistication, and previous experience, but because of simple integrity.

In the final analysis, Truman was always ready, if necessary, to sacrifice personal popularity to advance the long-range interests of the United States. The dismissal of General Douglas MacArthur is the supreme example of this. It was clear to all of Truman's chief advisers that firing General MacArthur at the height of his heroic career would fatally injure the President politically, and to a man they told him so. He, of course, knew this, too, but what would become of the American principle of civilian control over the military if a general could defy the President and get away with it? So the general was fired. It was a decision which finished MacArthur, as every later general will keep in mind, but it also grievously hurt Mr. Truman politically. He never regained his old popular standing until long after leaving office.

In all my years in government, including the White House, the MacArthur episode has become in my mind the best example of how to put a President to the supreme test: will he knowingly risk his own future for the country's?

II

A President's advisers unquestionably play some part in his decisions, but in the long run a President gets the advisers he deserves or at least wants around him. Our Chief Executives never lack for advice—including good advice. It's a question of what advice they take. The Pentagon Papers, along with the White House papers exposed by columnist Jack Anderson, show that both Lyndon Johnson and Richard Nixon had a wide range of advice and intelligence on Vietnam, but, predictably, they chose to ignore the information and recommendations that ran counter to their war policy.

In a collective sense, the Cabinet has almost ceased to function as a policy-making body, although individual members may exert considerable influence on the President in a personal way. The Nixon administration is more and more centering power in the White House. George Shultz, for instance, has not only been made Secretary of the Treasury, but Special Assistant to the President, as well—which raises a nice question. As Treasury chief, Shultz is accountable to Congress. He can be summoned to Capitol Hill and interrogated. But what can Congress do if he wears his White House hat and claims executive privilege? Shultz would then enjoy the same sanctuary as Henry Kissinger, who, unlike Secretary of State William Rogers, is beyond the reach of Congress. The trend toward concentration of power in the White House has gone on under both Democratic and Republican administrations. The only thing new is the length to which it has now been carried.

III

The debate and battle over Presidential powers go on interminably. Having pressured Congress into giving the executive branch blank checks for war-making (the Formosa and Tonkin Gulf Resolutions), the White House is now demanding similar power over the budget. Mr. Nixon has not hesitated to tell Congress that it must delegate to the President its constitutional power over appropriations and expenditures. The House (in 1972) actually voted Mr. Nixon authority to impound funds it had already appropriated, and the Senate almost followed suit. The battle will be renewed in the Ninety-third Congress.

So, in 1973, the Republic is back where it started, so far as the Presidency is concerned. The office must have enough day-to-day power to be effective, plus special powers to deal with emergencies, particularly threats to peace. Yet there must be checks on the President if the government is to be kept in balance, as contemplated by the Constitution. The responsibility devolves on Congress, the courts, and the press, but none of them alone is capable of reining in an ambitious President.

There are encouraging signs, however, that each is beginning to respond to the challenge. Congress, for instance, has repealed the Tonkin Gulf Resolution, and it is now taking a hard look at all executive agreements. The Supreme Court, even with four Nixon appointees voting, has stood against the President's efforts to weaken the desegregation of schools. And the media, although supporting Mr. Nixon for reelection, are beginning to perceive that the First Amendment is in danger.

Against this background, what might be the most useful counsel to give any newly elected President? I think it would be a strong note of caution: never overplay your hand. The impulse to do this has seemed almost irresistible to twentieth-century Presidents of the most different styles and temperaments. After the 1936 election, Franklin Roosevelt thought he had a mandate to "pack" the Supreme Court. After the 1964 election, Lyndon Johnson thought he could do what he wanted in Southeast Asia. And after the 1972 election, Richard Nixon thought he had a license to devastate the urban areas of North Vietnam.

These Presidents, and all who react like them on such occasions, have been wrong. They have failed to sense and respect, at these times, a mechanism of resistance in the American people—a historic resistance against a President who tries to go too far. The people really never quite forgive—or trust—the President who dares this. They want strength in the office of the Chief Executive, but they also have a built-in alarm system that warns against Caesarism. Between strength and Caesarism, there intervenes an almost invisible boundary line, and the President who ventures across it never returns with his power intact. And any future President should know and remember this, for the sake of himself and of the Republic.

Bryce N. Harlow

An expert on relations between the executive and legislative branches. . . . Administrative Assistant and Special Assistant to President Dwight D. Eisenhower (1953–1961) . . . Assistant to President Richard Nixon for Legislative and Congressional Affairs. . . . Previously served on staff of House Armed Services Committee (1947–1951).

I

The truly critical qualities in any President are, by all odds, integrity and candor and honesty. There is a basic and rather fateful reason for this. The power for good in the White House is equaled only by the power for evil. Paradoxically, I learned this through my eight years of service with Dwight Eisenhower. For even with so scrupulous a man—and such a strict constitutionalist as a President—I left the White House awed by, more than all else, the potential power of the man, *any* man there, to do great good or great harm.

Along with these decent and humane qualities, however, a President has to possess a will and a readiness to lead and to force, to press and to compel. The great office involves a far more brutal sort of business than most citizens imagine. Politics and politicians are tough and hard, and a President has to have *his* toughness. He has to do more than try to arouse the willingness and desire of other people to go along with him: he has to find ways to get them to go along whether they desire to or *not*. This ultimately calls for a very rare mixture and balance: one part compassionate and understanding, one part stern and relentless.

The fatal flaws or lacks in Presidential leadership seem to me just as clear. The gravest of these is simple political expediency: an addiction to the facile, plausible, short-range answer to a problem. This habit will assure that a President will find himself politically hanged about a year later. But in both domestic and foreign affairs, the temptation stays constant to reach for the seemingly quick and easy solution. A President always finds himself surrounded by politicians whose whole lives have encouraged and trained them to slide past or around hard decisions. Because he was so aware of this, an Eisenhower would say: "The worst place to go looking for a future President is in the halls of Congress." For the veterans of Congress—session after session, and election after election—have been taught to slide.

A second menace almost as serious for any Presidency is the danger of getting nibbled to death by the guppies of minor or marginal issues. The President has to budget his time with an eye—and a mind—on the *big* decisions. This is the motive and the reason for a Richard Nixon having the

largest Presidential staff in our history. Such a staff is anything but an indulgence or an extravagance. It is what lets him, as President, focus most on
the things that matter most.

How does one best prepare for the ordeal of the Presidency? The best mixture, it seems to me, is a blend of both executive and political experience,
bringing as broad as possible a living contact with the problems of mankind at
large. I think that practical, and specifically administrative, experience *does*
matter. Such direct and explicit experience can even be decisive. I do not
doubt, for example, that if Eisenhower, with all his sophistication in military
affairs, had been President instead of Lincoln, Grant would have been in
Richmond years sooner than he was.

As for displays of courage and decisiveness, these have taken different
forms in the history of the modern Presidency. Perhaps what first comes to
mind is the courage of Franklin Roosevelt in facing the Great Depression.
In essence, he showed this courage by ignoring or abandoning all the rhetoric
and posturing of his 1932 campaign, and he proceeded to be the kind of
opportunist activist who could hearten and inspire the Republic. This must
be rated one of the most remarkable of all Presidential achievements—quite
like Winston Churchill steadying the morale of Great Britain to endure the
Nazi blitz. And FDR showed the same Presidential capacity later in other
ways. He had to reach down into the ranks of the military, for example, to
raise up General George Marshall to his post of wartime leadership. This
took both nerve and brains to do.

With Harry Truman, there followed repeated shows of courage and boldness, from his decision to drop the atomic bomb on Japan to his decision to
defend South Korea. Along the way, there came the Marshall Plan for
Western Europe, the airlift to save West Berlin, and the firing of General
Douglas MacArthur—which made clear that the Commander in Chief was
still exactly that. The same kind of courage made possible the fervor and
dash of his own 1948 campaign for reelection, against odds that all political
wise men dismissed as hopeless.

With Dwight Eisenhower, there appeared courage of yet another tone and
temper. This was a quiet courage: a sober, assuring, and steadying influence
from the White House. It was not sporadic or dramatic or flashy. It was not
highlighted by terrible crisis. But I think it was the steadfast sort of courage
that conveyed a strength and sureness of purpose that made even the Soviet
Union move cautiously in all such arenas of possible conflict as Berlin or the
Middle East or Southeast Asia.

II

The men around the President need, above all else, a capacity for personal
loyalty and selflessness. This counts for much more than all technical competence. For there can be nothing more dangerous to a President than a
supremely skilled egoist in his employ.

There are other qualities, of course, that matter a great deal. Ideally, a Presidential adviser should be a generalist with breadth of view and sensitivity of feeling. He should have some seasoning in public service. He should possess a certain humility of personal opinion. He needs, too, the special stamina to take the inevitable hammering of critics always ready to aim their fire at him or at the White House. But he must also—along with these respectful and deferential qualities—have and express an integrity of his own. He must accept the risk of being fired for the sake of talking up forthrightly to the President. He has to live with the awareness that the life of the White House can be all too insulated and incestuous. And he must therefore stay receptive to outside views, especially those least welcome to his President.

As for the size of the White House staff, I think this is something always to watch, but without undue alarm. Just now, this is a fact less of federal life than of the life of the Nixon administration. Richard Nixon is *running* the whole government from the White House. The National Security Council now finds its match in the Domestic Council, and the old Bureau of the Budget is now the Office of Management and Budget. The whole White House staff has become institutionalized. But all this could be a passing phenomenon, and the next President might well revert to a Truman-type staff—a small gathering of personal cronies.

I worry about the concentration of power in the White House and the potential abuse of executive privilege, but I also doubt that these dangers are likely to go too far. After all, the Congress retains full power to check these tendencies. It can politically crucify the Secretaries of State or Defense and ultimately force the White House to be more open about its policies. And it still controls all funds to support a White House staff of any size. It is also a little misleading to talk too broadly about the White House staff usurping the functions, for example, of the Department of State. Put a man as tough as John Connally into the role of Secretary of State and see what happens! All legends aside, the truth is that we do not have a government of laws or procedures or protocols, of course, but of *men*.

This especially applies to the Cabinet. We tend to talk or think of it *institutionally*. But the Cabinet is some twelve or fourteen human beings, all quite different personally and politically. At any given moment under any given administration, some feel elated, some feel emasculated; and some are apathetic, and some are arrogant. Thus, it is easy to generalize about the usual feebleness of a Cabinet's resistance to a President's policy or wish. But it is necessary then quickly to make major exceptions for a Dean Acheson under Truman, or a John Foster Dulles under Eisenhower, or a John Connally under Nixon.

It is equally easy to simplify and exaggerate the distance between a President and the members of his Cabinet. They may have different interests, obviously. But any perceptive President knows that each member of the Cabinet presides over a sprawling bureaucracy that must be made to work effectively—lest the whole administration suffer, including the Presidency.

Here there follows another paradox about the executive branch. The best officers of the Cabinet may be those of whom the citizen hears least. And this is simply because they are running their operations with such quiet effectiveness that they do not make news or provoke controversy.

I I I

Perhaps it is an oversimplification to say that we have "two Presidencies," but it is incontestably true that, under the Constitution, the President has far more power as Chief of State or Commander in Chief than as Chief Administrator or Chief Partisan or Chief Legislator. This helps to explain why Presidents like Eisenhower and Nixon have been more immersed in foreign than domestic affairs: they have felt they could *do* more. And yet the two roles are obviously interrelated, and every President has to guard against any notion that he can really separate them.

Still, it often happens that Presidents tend to be versed and expert in either foreign or domestic policy, but not both. This surely was so, for example, with Dwight Eisenhower and Lyndon Johnson. In the first instance, the man might have been called almost "acting President of the world" before he became President of the United States, but even then, he probably had only the vaguest idea of what Social Security was. In the second instance, Lyndon Johnson knew next to nothing about international affairs, but even so, he knew every detail and trick about labor laws or farm programs or welfare plans or education bills.

As for the right range of Presidential power, and its proper restraint, this is not essentially a matter of "liberal" or "conservative" judgment. This is a matter of pure politics. It is not unlike the issue of foreign aid: if you are in power, you are for it, and if you are out of power, you are free to rail against it. These questions have very little to do with partisan ideologies. Over the decades, there have been Congressional leaders—from a Republican Borah to a Democratic Fulbright—who have made their political living by opposition to Presidents. To be sure, there are some underlying differences between a Republican tendency to see the Congress as the center of political decision and a Democratic tendency to look toward the Presidency as the source of political activism. But the prevailing partisan attitude at any given moment generally turns on the simple question: *who* is in the White House?

The same question transcends all discussion of "structure" inside 1600 Pennsylvania or throughout the executive branch. The nature of the *man* is absolutely crucial and decisive, altogether overriding the issue of organization. From Theodore Roosevelt to Richard Nixon, each President has had his own way of getting things done and decisions made. And this has largely been the case not just in or around the Oval Office but in the Cabinet departments as well. A Dulles as Secretary of State, a McNamara as Secretary of Defense, or a Connally as Secretary of the Treasury: the very selection of such men as these revealed, in each instance, a great deal of the intensely individual character and special temperament of each President and each administration.

I think it is precisely this great liberty of each President to make of the office almost what he wants of it which causes so much worry and concern over its future. I have spent many years working at *both* ends of Pennsylvania Avenue, and this meant, for much of the time, working toward exactly opposite purposes. On Capitol Hill, you strive mightily, of course, to limit Presidential power, and in the White House, you labor equally hard to free it. This constant tension is vital to our system of government. Generally, when a President has asserted too much power, I think it will be found that this has been possible only because Congress has been slack and delinquent. I doubt that any statutory reform can prevent such Congressional lapses or supplant the need for Congressional vigilance and courage. Nor can any redefinition or restriction of Presidential power possibly fit all the unforeseeable political circumstances of the future. And yet I must concede that my overwhelming feeling about the office—bred by those years of watching it from totally different perspectives—amounts to an almost fearful awe of its power. For you cannot look closely at this power without a painful awareness that, if it ever were to fall into the hands of a bad man, it could spell total disaster.

What private counsel would I most urge a President-elect to heed? Here, too, all depends on *who* the man is. If he is prone to be impulsive, I would urge caution. If he tends to be reticent, I would urge some boldness. And any such counsel also has to take full account of the temper of the times and the state of the nation. If the country were exhausted from the kind of "legislative indigestion" that came with the volume of laws of the Lyndon Johnson years, I would hope for a spell of political rest and quiet. If the society were being wracked by massive problems, however, we might need to try to match the furious creativity of the New Deal's first hundred days. But whatever the wildly varying circumstances or conflicting possibilities, there is one fact that stays firm and central: the office always *is* the man.

W. Averell Harriman

A Presidential aide or ambassador under four Democratic Presidents. . . . Under Franklin Roosevelt, administrator in National Recovery Administration (1934–1935), Special Representative of the President to Great Britain and to Soviet Union (1941), Ambassador to the Soviet Union (1943–1946). . . . Under Harry S. Truman, Secretary of Commerce (1946–1948) and Special Assistant to the President (1950–1951). . . . Governor of State of

New York (1955–1958). . . . Under John F. Kennedy, Assistant Secretary of State for Far Eastern Affairs (1961–1963). . . . Under Lyndon Johnson, Undersecretary of State for Political Affairs (1963–1965) and personal representative of the President to Vietnam peace talks in Paris (1968–1969).

I

There is nothing more essential to Presidential leadership, I believe, than a deep understanding of the historical development of the United States—all the forces that have made this country what it is. Only with this understanding of the past can a President have the vision to project the nation's course into the future. And only with the combination of this understanding and this vision can the Chief Executive be ready and able to meet his central and constant responsibility: the analyzing of specific situations and the making of firm decisions.

Precisely these qualities and capacities, I believe, described the administration of Harry Truman. Though he had limited formal education, he was enormously well read and versed in the history of the nation generally and the history of the Presidency particularly. This sureness of historical perception helped inspire the decisiveness of judgment that may have been the outstanding mark of his years in the White House. You could go into his office with a question and come out with a decision from him, more swiftly than from any man I have ever known. Because he so clearly saw the President to be what he called "the only lobbyist" for the whole people, he saw with equal clarity the proper relationship of his office to the Congress. There was nothing more obvious to him than the fact that Congress, with its vast army of special interests, could not dominate the Presidency without producing chaos.

To produce coherence rather than chaos, the modern Presidents have had to make a series of historic decisions, largely on their own. These have included Roosevelt's quiet resolve to stand by Great Britain in World War II, Truman's quick commitment to come to the aid of Greece and Turkey in 1947, and Kennedy's adroit handling of the Cuban missile crisis of 1962. The last of these may have been the most skillful handling of a major crisis in our modern history, certainly in my lifetime. This was one of those situations in which a President had to override a lot of strictly military and other advice. He had to find a way to lead the Soviet Union's Nikita Khrushchev to withdraw along a politically acceptable path of retreat. He found this way. And the handling of this confrontation made possible the later turning point of the limited test-ban treaty of 1963, which was the first agreement between these superpowers in the whole field of nuclear weaponry.

II

The most indispensable quality in any White House adviser is a selfless and steadfast devotion to the President and to what he is trying to achieve. Of the many Presidential advisers I have known, over forty years, I would rate Harry Hopkins as the most remarkable and effective. During World War II, it was a delight—and a lesson—to see his recognition of the importance of close working relations between FDR and Winston Churchill. He dealt with both men with equal skill, and he became the catalyst of their personal alliance. In his meetings with Churchill, he could be brutally frank without ever being personally offensive, and in his reports to Roosevelt, he always had the courage to stand up to him to make a Churchillian point of view perfectly clear. At the same time, in all Hopkins' work, he never got in the way of relations between the President and his Cabinet officers. In fact, I was at times present when he insisted that the President consult by telephone his Secretary of State, Mr. Hull, or his Secretary of Defense, Mr. Stimson, before making a decision. And this example of Hopkins helped me years later, when I was in the position of Special Assistant to President Truman during the Korean War.

I have watched the growth of the White House staff, with mounting concern, from its modern beginning under Franklin Roosevelt to its full burgeoning under Richard Nixon. The two principal forces making for this growth, of course, are well known: the proliferation of independent agencies of the New Deal, coping with the problems of the Great Depression and reporting directly to the White House; and the expansion of the President's prerogatives, as Commander in Chief, throughout World War II. Understandable as these historic pressures have been, I have always believed in a small White House staff. Odd though it may seem, a large staff around a President can waste, rather than save, his time, and its simple existence can lessen, rather than increase, the hours he has for quiet thought and independent work. And I recall—by way of analogy on a lower level—that when I served as Ambassador at Large to Lyndon Johnson, with the particular responsibility for getting the Vietnam negotiations started, I had only one assistant working directly with me and for the rest used existing departments.

It seems to me imperative that the White House should not become a breeding ground for activities and operations that merely duplicate the labors of the regular federal departments. Admittedly, it is a fact of federal life that an ever larger bureaucratic establishment tends to encourage an ever larger White House to oversee its performance or its nonperformance. But the professional machinery of the Department of State, or the Department of Defense, or the Central Intelligence Agency is there to be thoughtfully used, not thoughtlessly re-created.

Beyond this, it seems to me extremely dangerous to leave critical decisions on foreign policy to Presidential assistants in the White House who are not accountable to the Congress and who are not liable, in most cases, to have direct access to the more detailed reports from our embassies around the world. In the case of President Nixon's decision to make his pilgrimage to Peking in 1971, for example, any Third Secretary in our embassy in Tokyo —or any desk officer on Japanese affairs in the Department of State—could have told the White House that any such sudden and spectacular approach to Communist China, without prior consultation, could only do irreparable harm to our relations to Japan.

All this points up the potentially greater role that our Cabinet could and should play in the making of major national decisions. The men in this Cabinet are not only accountable to the Congress; they also should be better informed, with broader experience, and more effective with the President. And they should be of high enough caliber, individually and collectively, to make any President listen.

I learned the sense and importance of a group of this responsibility when I was President Roosevelt's Special Representative in London during World War II. The British Cabinet was then kept well informed and took a serious part in all important decisions on what really were life-or-death matters for the future of Great Britain. The executive committee of the Cabinet—known as the War Cabinet—in those anxious years included the head of no armed service, but the real *political* leaders of the country. This is what a Cabinet is for—even under a Churchill. And something of this spirit and structure of shared responsibility could spare the American Republic much of the hazards of decision-making by one man.

III

There is only one Presidency, and all talk of "two Presidencies"—one foreign and one domestic—is nonsense. All policies *within* and *beyond* our national frontiers have to be concerted and integrated. They can only be different aspects of the same national purpose.

As for the issue of whether Presidential power generally is too great or too small, I believe this is not an ideological question at all. It is just a matter of whose ox is getting gored: who is in or out of power, and what actions either side may want. Even the traditionally "conservative" hostility to excessive federal intervention is aimed at national action in general, not White House action in particular. And the beneficiaries of Presidential largesse, whether "liberal" or "conservative," will always prove quite receptive to their good fortune.

I feel quite vehemently that all definition of the Presidency in terms of "structure" of the office is rubbish. It is the person of the President that is vital and controlling. Each President has his own working habits and needs, and he will accordingly organize himself, and those around him, to handle his affairs as he sees fit. In any case, you cannot "organize" wise decisions.

There is no realistic way to talk of the procedures or the powers of the Presidency, moreover, without also talking of the other branches, especially the Congress. I believe that both the Presidency and the Supreme Court have assumed more power than was contemplated by the Founding Fathers, because the Congress has assumed less. There have been at least two historic factors limiting the Congress' potency. Its archaic rules of procedure have generally weakened, and sometimes destroyed, its capacity to work effectively. And the preoccupation of its members with the demands and opinions and prejudices of particular constituencies limits it in developing a clear vision of the needs of the nation as a whole. The short two-year term of the House members accentuates this. There have been and are individual leaders of outstanding quality on Capitol Hill, of course, and there will always be a need for a President to lead the way in shaping national policy in the future. But I strongly believe that the Congress as an institution must profoundly improve its working methods and procedures, so that it can assert—and meet —a greater responsibility in setting the nation's course. To this end the term of office of the members of the House of Representatives might well be extended to perhaps four years. Only as it becomes more effective can a President consult with, and confide in, the Congress in such a way that the relationship between them becomes essentially constructive, not combative, and creative, not hostile.

The question of what advice one might most want to urge upon a new President reminds me of my own seeking of advice when I first entered the Cabinet in 1946 as Secretary of Commerce. I asked Justice Felix Frankfurter for his general counsel on meeting my new responsibilities. He promptly recalled the response of Oliver Wendell Holmes to the same inquiry from Woodrow Wilson, which was simply: "Read every paper before you sign it." Understood and applied in its broadest sense, this proposition reminds any President that, perhaps above all else, he must get a full understanding of any major problem before he brings himself to a decision or commits the nation to a policy. Only with the confidence based on such a thorough understanding can he then follow through as he must—clearly and vigorously— by his every word and every action, with the Congress and with the people.

David E. Lilienthal

An adviser or administrator in the administrations of Franklin Roosevelt, Harry S. Truman, and Lyndon Johnson. . . . Director of Tennessee Valley Authority since 1933, Chairman of Authority (1941–1946). . . . Chairman of Atomic Energy Commission (1946–1950). . . . Co-chairman of Joint Postwar Development Group, Vietnam (1967–1969).

I

There is an obvious range of qualities to be hoped for in any President—like integrity of character, or breadth of vision, or courage of decision. But I would rate above all else (and perhaps the source of all others) the man's inner strength and self-confidence. To be a leader, he has to be resolute, and to be resolute, he has to be at peace with himself. Ultimately, this is a matter of steadiness and serenity of spirit.

The two Presidents whom I knew best and longest—Franklin Roosevelt and Harry Truman—were different enough, of course, to be almost a study in contrast. Yet each of them, in his own way, had the capacity to be at once confident, determined, and even relaxed in the midst of all the pressures (and all the pomp) around them. In the case of FDR, I remember noting more than once in my *Journals* of the late 1930's what struck me as this President's "amazing assurance and nonchalance and complete lack of self-consciousness." The instances of this abounded. I remember one early-morning conference with him when I was taken into his bedroom to discuss some serious business with him—which he conducted efficiently while still in his BVD's and his valet was strapping the braces on his shriveled legs. Again, a few years later, I recall a long luncheon in the spring of 1942 when we spent much time discussing forestry problems (from the Tennessee Valley region to Hyde Park) in a way that would have made one think that this most harassed and responsible of men in all the world hardly could *also* be worrying about the war in the South Pacific, the ruckus over war profits, or the events on the Russian front. Surrounded by all this, a Roosevelt could still stay himself—and be relaxedly confident.

Harry Truman, too, knew how to be *himself*. For those of us who knew him well, he always retained a sweet kind of humility unchanged by all the terrible trappings of power around him. I remember the end to one of my first meetings with him in the Oval Office, when we had quite seriously reviewed the current state of TVA. As he took me to the door, his words were: "Enjoyed talking to you. Come back again when you haven't anything better to do." Could one imagine the equivalent of that kind of wry Midwestern humor from the ruler of any other country on the globe? Of course, no. But more than this, it could not be imagined from any President of the United States who was not essentially at ease with himself, his office, and his responsibilities.

The unself-consciousness or humility of either of these Presidents—both of whom I would rank among the strongest Chief Executives of this century—was accompanied, of course, by a lusty readiness to fight for principles and policies they held vital for the country. I remember a meeting with Truman in late 1945 when I warned him that his stand on my own reappointment to TVA meant a fight—and his laconic reply: "I never run away from a fight—don't invite 'em, but don't run away from them." This had been the ruling spirit, of course, of FDR's Presidential leadership through twelve grueling years. And I recall the time in late 1949 when I advised Truman that the Senate committee under Brien McMahon was likely to "put on a blitz" to force a decision their way—and the President grinned tightly as he said: "I don't blitz easily." At critical times, that is the way Presidents should grin and talk.

All these qualities—the confidence, the humility, the unpretentiousness, and the combativeness—are not quite enough, ideally speaking, without one thing more. A President has to have a capacity for a kind of historic purposefulness. This seemed almost bred into Franklin Roosevelt, as he faced the Great Depression: he knew the needs and values and ethics that had to be served. As for Harry Truman, I shall always remember a day in 1949 when he talked to me about the Tennessee Valley Authority—not in terms of the United States—but in terms of what a TVA could mean for the Euphrates or the Yangtze or the Danube. He described himself as having "been dreaming" of what such projects could mean to millions of humans no longer hungry or harassed or frightened—and to the future peace of the world. And I believe that such dreams are the stuff that memorable Presidents are made of.

This suggests, too, what weak Presidents are made of. They may suffer from self-doubt. They may be too logical to dream. They may be defensive in spirit or negative in thought. They may be oversensitive to contradiction or criticism. And if they are these things, they will fail.

What prepares a President—best or worst—for what he will have to face? The best preparation, I believe, is the trial of running for and serving in *elective* office. For this is the experience that forces him to know people and all the not-at-all-logical motives and purposes that sway them. On the other hand, I think the *worst* preparation has to be strictly managerial or business experience. There is almost nothing here to prepare a man for the complexities and subtleties of national leadership. When I was an ardent propagandist for atomic energy and its creative uses back in the late 1940's, I remember a sharp conflict of opinion with one of the leading figures in the automobile industry—and my unhappy conclusion in my *Journals* of that time: "Life is pretty simple to a man whose great talent is in finding ingenious ways of repeating the same operation millions of times." Unfortunately, this simplistic view of life has very little to do with what makes up national politics—or what makes for great Presidents.

The effectiveness and success of the leadership of both Franklin Roosevelt and Harry Truman seem striking to me precisely because they were so radically unalike in background, temperament, method, speech, and manner. Roosevelt, of course, was always the cultivated patrician from Hyde Park; he welcomed the presence and service of intellectuals; he embraced and refined ideas that he believed profoundly liberal; and he loved to spell them out in elegant rhetoric. Who could be more different than his rough-hewn and little-educated successor from Missouri? I remember more than once talking with Clark Clifford, who figured so importantly in Truman's White

House, of our common awareness of Truman's deep reaction *against* the ideas, the mood, and the very words of the New Deal period. He was a populist son of the Middle West and its Populism, a political descendant of Norris and Bryan and La Follette. As such, he had no use for the notions or the vocabulary of a Leon Henderson or a Chester Bowles. He found their very language simply highfalutin. And he once told Clifford he thought that FDR had surrounded himself with "crackpots and the lunatic fringe."

What makes this contrast interesting historically is that it narrows the area in which to look for the key to the common success of both Presidents. In the face of such differences, what did these Chief Executives share, so much that the second seemed in some ways a most fitting successor to the first? What they shared was a sense of serenity—the gift of confidence.

I I

The important qualities and talents in White House advisers, in general, have to be as varied as the Presidents they serve. Their essential role is serving *him,* and since the working methods of each President differ sharply, so should their staffs. Only one thing is vital for all: a passion for anonymity.

The *modus operandi* of a Franklin Roosevelt was a good example of how special and personal a President's methods are. Roosevelt's administrative manner, as I observed in my *Journals* repeatedly, was "so gentle as to be vague," but it was also, of course, immensely shrewd. He liked overlapping assignments to his principal aides and department heads, to stimulate competition in ideas and performances. He sensitively knew how to handle prima donnas like Harold Ickes. He was almost a genius, too, at waiting to take a controversial position, letting contrary pressures build up—to give him time to make a decision or allow him finally to avoid it altogether. All this suggests how a Presidential staff must be selected and geared to the particular administrative ways of any given President.

The extraordinary growth in the size of the White House staff in modern times raises a wholly different problem. I regard this development as highly undesirable—even potentially disastrous. The reason is that this reflects, and is part of, an obsessive centralizing of administration in Washington that burdens and strains the Cabinet structure and the whole federal government.

I believe strongly that, if the executive branch is to perform as it should, there must be a wholly new concept of the function of the Cabinet. This concept can become a reality only with a broad-scale decentralization, out of Washington, of the *administration* of the national government in the field of natural and human resources. This would bring a radical change in the functions of the Cabinet. That is what TVA was created to do and has done. For, as I have written elsewhere, it amounted to "a major experiment in the reorganization of the Federal government . . . a demonstration that greater and greater centralization in the Washington bureaus and departments was not inevitable, that a practical way could be worked out for regional decentralization."

The effect of such a redirection of national policy would be to make the Cabinet a more manageable instrument. It could assume a far more thoughtful and creative role as an advisory body aiding the Chief Executive in formulating broad policy. The Presidency itself would thereby be strengthened to function more effectively.

III

I see the Presidency, generally speaking, as too personal an office to be seriously defined in terms of "structure" or substantially changed by designs for reform. The latter usually deal with structure, but the history of the office shows that a similar or identical structure in the White House produces, with different administrations, quite different results. These variables include such things as popular support, bureaucratic support, and press support. But these are only in the smallest measure affected by administrative methods. Consequently, I rather downgrade the importance of the "operational" aspect of the office, its efficiency or organization. The attempts at theoretical redefinition of the Presidential role are interesting exercises, but I fear they are largely futile.

The question of what advice one might most urge upon a new President reminds me of Professor John Chipman Gray's answer to the question "Is it constitutional?" As he replied: "It depends." In the case of a President, it depends on what inner strength he brings to his leadership—and what particular weaknesses he must control or overcome. Certainly, I would urge any new President at a minimum to decentralize and therefore humanize the federal establishment.

The rest is really a matter of the man—and his steadiness and serenity of purpose. I think this was well illustrated in one meeting I had with President Truman in the spring of 1949. As Chairman of the Atomic Energy Commission, I restated to him, on this occasion, the commission's determination to carry out his policy of an entirely civilian administration of atomic energy in all of its aspects. But I had to add: "I want to be frank to say that there are elements in the military establishment . . . that don't agree with you and are pretty outspoken about it and are causing some difficulties." Mr. Truman drew himself up and practically stuck his chin in my face, and said in a way that was unmistakably impressive: "Well, I'm the Commander in Chief." I added that we didn't want to "come running to Papa" all the time with all the troubles or obstacles we might run into. But he concluded: "Well, Papa won't hesitate to use the strap if that's what it takes."

And *that* is the sort of spirit it takes to be a strong President.

Nelson A. Rockefeller

An executive or adviser in both Republican and Democratic administrations. . . . Under Franklin Roosevelt, Coordinator of Inter-American Affairs (1940–1944) and Assistant Secretary of State (1944–1945). . . . Under Harry Truman, Chairman of International Development Advisory Board (Point 4 Program, 1950–1951). . . . Under Dwight D. Eisenhower, Undersecretary of Health, Education and Welfare (1953–1954) and Special Assistant to the President (1954–1955). . . . Since 1958, Governor of State of New York.

I

The President is the unifying force in American life. He alone of all our elected officials has the entire people as his constituency, the entire nation as his charge. He must, in a large sense, embody the national will and the national purpose.

Every man who occupies the office will bring to it the special stamp of his own character. Yet fundamentally, there are but two approaches to the Presidency. To Theodore Roosevelt, the President's duty was "to do anything that the needs of the Nation demand, unless such action is forbidden by the Constitution or the laws." William Howard Taft, in sharp contrast, believed the President possessed "no undefined residuum of power which he can exercise because it seems to him to be in the public interest." Where Roosevelt elected leadership, Taft chose stewardship. My own preference is clearly for the President who leads.

My preference for active executive leadership is a product of thirty-five years of experience in government, embracing service to three Presidents and fourteen years as governor of a populous, complex industrial state whose problems reflect—and often foretell—those of the nation as a whole.

I would sum up the most important Presidential qualities as the courage to lead, the capacity to inspire trust, the ability to persuade, the personal stature that will draw men of talent to his side, the emotional strength to remain cool and compassionate under grueling pressure, a sense of America's historical meaning, and, most crucial in our time, the personal quality that will unite and not divide the people.

Few nations can match America in sheer diversity. Whether we speak of the land itself or the people who inhabit it, there is a limitless richness, an infinite variety, to America. Out of this diversity grows our strength and vitality. But some force must bring a unifying sense of national direction to it. That force is the office of the President.

Traditionally, in overviews of the Presidency, one recites the many roles the President plays simultaneously—Chief of State, Commander in Chief, leader of his party, and the like. But with all this, the President is first and foremost an executive. His capacity to administer creatively the vast enterprise of the government of the United States is clearly his strongest claim to the office.

An executive must be able to sort out the pertinent information affecting a given issue—then make the firm, lonely decision so essential to effective leadership. Executive style based on executive experience often contrasts sharply with the "consensus politics" of those with a legislative background. It is not surprising, then, that those who have discharged the office of President with distinction, even greatness, were often men who came to it with broad experience as public executives.

In giving the nation direction, the President also is inescapably cast as lawmaker as well as administrator. This Presidential role in no way controverts the inherent power of the Congress to originate and enact our laws. Yet true leadership cannot rest with a President saying: "Tell me where to lead the nation." Rather, it calls upon him to say: "If I am to lead the nation, here is the policy, the power or the program that I need to lead it effectively."

Of course, the President of so diverse a nation must be flexible in accommodating legitimate objections to his programs that will improve them or increase their odds of acceptance. But he must have the capacity to distinguish between concession and capitulation. There is an irreducible core in any proposition that cannot honestly be compromised. The President must know where this core lies and fight for his convictions along its perimeter.

The political process and our political parties are not something alien to national leadership. They are the pathway to it. The President first must be the choice of his party if he is to be the choice of the people. His party is also one of the two main suppliers of representatives with whom the approval of his program rests. If he believes in his own leadership, then, logically and only humanly, he must care deeply about the kinds of men his party is producing—and he must exercise his own party leadership.

I I

The President faces a critical and recurring test of leadership in the caliber of men and women he attracts to his Cabinet and personal staff.

Cabinet officers must have great administrative force. They must possess the capacity to affect the administration's intentions down into the deepest layers of the bureaucracy. This is not easily done. An agency of government can be like a mountain on casters—technically capable of movement, but not easily moved. It is not going too far to say that the best Cabinet officers will themselves display qualities of Presidental stature.

As for members of the President's personal staff, they must be his eyes, his ears, and often an extension of his mind—but never his crutch. He must not shrink from immersing himself, when necessary, in the details and issues of a particular problem before his administration. It is this kind of absorption that usually creates a genuine "feel" for a problem. Neither should the President fear to violate the administrative symmetry of even the most carefully laid-out White House organization when necessary. To respect a formal structure too rigidly is to lock oneself into the position of being last-to-know—becoming a prisoner of the predilections and prejudices of even the ablest, best intentioned, and most loyal subordinates.

The President should not seek the deceiving comfort of total compatibility in his official family. There is nothing wrong with a touch of conflict, as long as someone is in a position to resolve conflicting views. Nor should the President allow himself to be cut off by staff from open communication with the diverse minority groups in our society who have a dissent to record. The quality of that communication is crucial not alone to Presidential wisdom but to the morale of the American people.

III

The President's leadership is measured in the quality of the decisions he makes. These judgments are inevitably influenced by highly subjective factors—the President's own experiences in the past, his intuitive feeling as to the best course to take, his personal rating of one adviser's wisdom as against another's, and, above all, his capacity for conceptual thinking and planning. Nonetheless, Presidential decisions can be little better than the information on which they are based; the important consideration is that the information be as complete as may be essential to prudent judgment, and as objective as humanly possible.

The computer today performs a remarkable job of informing the businessman of what he needs to know about economic trends and market prospects in order to make decisions affecting his private business. We have yet to enlist the computer's enormous potential for informing our highest civilian leadership of the complex, swift-changing status of world conditions that affect the infinitely more fateful decisions governing the conduct of the public's business. Modern technology can offer powerful tools for strengthening Presidential leadership in four vital areas: in briefing, in giving early warning, in organized correlation of information, and in improving decision-making by laying out the options open to the President and the consequences of each option for any given situation.

The information available to the White House is susceptible to rational organization and digestion by data-processing systems. Seemingly disjointed facts can be computer-analyzed to divine an emerging pattern. Jumbled bits of data can be fitted into a mosaic that reveals their overall meaning. The computer does not supplant human judgment, but serves it. This modern technology can give the President the time edge and information edge to make sound decisions before crisis conditions narrow and harden his area of choice.

The Future of Federalism

The federal idea of multiple centers of initiative and responsibility is the genius of American democracy. The President has a deep responsibility to respect and to nurture the values of genuine federalism. This means stimulating vigorous leadership at state and local levels of government—not seeking to dominate such leadership.

By providing states and cities with more federal aid and less federal dictation, by working with all levels of government to achieve a more rational division of responsibility, Washington can stimulate initiative instead of stifle it, nourish creativity rather than starve it, restore local responsibility rather than replace it.

The World Role of the President

The man who ascends to the American Presidency walks, at once, into a position, unwritten yet undenied, as a leader of the Western world and chief protagonist of democratic freedom.

President Richard Nixon, for example, has conducted an extremely successful foreign policy during the past four years. Many of the problems which faced the President when he assumed office have been dealt with:

\# U.S.-Allied relationships have improved.

\# Inter-NATO relationships are emerging on a new basis.

\# U.S.-USSR relations have been relaxed, and we are in a new era of détente.

\# The opportunity for increased Asian and world stability has been improved by the President's opening to China.

\# The agonizing problem of South Vietnam is finally approaching a solution, and,

\# Stability—if tenuous—has been established in the Middle East and South Asia.

In my view, the President has been successful because he has had the courage not only to assume a new posture and try new approaches but also because he has had the ability to implement his policies. He has had a flexible approach to international relations. He has used a wide variety of diplomatic tools from Presidential missions and personal diplomacy to the threat of military intervention. Most important, he has designed policies so that their scope is broad enough to insure their success. He has placed the United States in a position in which it had a wide range of options available to it. Finally, the President has conducted his policies so that they reinforce each other.

President Nixon has had the courage, in short, to reorient the international posture of the United States, so this nation can cope with the realities of international politics. By his broadly based approach to negotiations, his expansion of this country's contacts, his insistence on honoring commitments, and his ability to readjust relations within alliances, the President has resolved a number of troublesome issues. He has given this nation a breadth of movement which it lacked and which, in the final analysis, is necessary if constant confrontation is to be avoided.

I believe history will record that President Nixon has conducted a most successful foreign policy—one which exemplifies rare qualities of Presidential leadership and extraordinary staff support. His second term offers a unique opportunity—despite the unfavorable political outlook in the Congress—for comparable progress, just as real if possibly less spectacular, in the conduct of our domestic affairs.

Samuel I. Rosenman

A jurist and long-time adviser to Franklin Roosevelt. . . . Special Counsel to President Roosevelt (1943–1945) and to Harry Truman (1945–1946). . . . Previously member of New York State legislature (1922–1926), counsel to Governor Roosevelt (1929–1932), and Justice of New York Supreme Court, first appointed in 1932. . . . Subsequently member of steel industry fact-finding board (1949) and chairman of Railway Labor Emergency Board (1963).

I

The most important requisite for a President is the kind of political experience typified by both Roosevelts—along with the quality that Franklin Roosevelt called moral leadership. The strength of all Presidential leadership rises from education and persuasion, rather than from arbitrary action or dictation. To achieve this, a President must understand both the history of his office and the sentiment of his country, for he always has to know how far and fast he can go. As FDR said right after his first inauguration, the ultimate challenge for a President was to apply old values to new conditions, and he referred to both Theodore Roosevelt and Woodrow Wilson to explain what he meant. As he saw the difference between them, Woodrow Wilson had the basic idealism without being able to get popular opinion to rally to it, whereas Teddy Roosevelt was most skillful at arousing public enthusiasm behind him, even though he did not really attack the fundamentals. To FDR, an effective moral leadership in the White House meant a combining of these approaches and an application of historic principles to contemporary problems.

A President has to apply this sense of leadership to the Congress, in particular, recognizing them as the chosen representatives of the people. Here again, he must strive not to dictate but to persuade. And again, a Franklin

Roosevelt recognized this in almost every important instance, except for his major failure in attempting to remake the Supreme Court. In that case, in 1937, he just sprang his plan, in effect saying: "I've just won an overwhelming mandate, and this is the way I've chosen to put it into effect." He consulted almost no one, least of all the Congress, and he spurned compromise. This was a most uncharacteristic design for defeat.

A President—any President—has to learn to compromise. When Franklin Roosevelt forgot this in his fight over the Supreme Court, he was repeating the mistake of Wilson over the proposed Senate reservation to the League Covenant. Nothing could have been more uncharacteristic of the man. In fact, the readiness of this Roosevelt to compromise in order to get his ends was one recurrent source of friction between him and his famous, and often zealous, wife. With all her idealism, she had never had to run for office or face a legislature, so she could barely understand it when he said: "You *have* to compromise, either to win elections or get laws passed."

Close to this capacity for compromise is another vital Presidential quality: a sense of timing. When does one act with decisiveness, and when does one act with restraint? This question tests all Presidents. FDR was a master in answering it throughout his years in the White House. I think this was especially true in 1934 and 1935, when the whole New Deal program was under fire from the lunatic fringes on both the political left and the political right. These were the years when the harshest fire came from the left, from Senator Huey Long and Dr. Francis Townsend, and, from the right, Father Charles Coughlin, the American Liberty League, and others. At such a time, it would have been a great temptation for any President to compete with the demagogic appeals of a Huey Long, and many people urged Roosevelt to do this. He steadfastly refused, however, and said that the people would sooner or later recognize the folly of all these specious schemes to help the poor or the aged. But at the same time—and with his special sense of timing—he was getting the country ready for his own program of Social Security that he set forth in 1935 and for the Second Hundred Days of that year. In all this, the timing could not have been better, as it related to (1) the demagoguery of Huey Long at the height of his power and (2) the forthcoming Presidential election in 1936.

The same skill impressed me just as much through all of the months of 1940 and 1941, as Roosevelt was shaping the role the nation would play during World War II. All during this period, a number of people close to him—including Henry Stimson and Harold Ickes—kept pressing him to go to Congress for a declaration of war. He refused, for he had his own method toward the same end. Month after month, he gradually increased escorts and convoys across the Atlantic carrying the steady shipments of supplies and munitions to Great Britain and the Soviet Union. All this was a perfect display of his keen sense of just how much the American people would stand for and support, as well as the Congress. For he knew that if he suffered any major defeat on Capitol Hill during this crucial time, it could wreck his whole policy.

In setting this patient pace, he was profiting from an earlier experience when, conversely, his sense of timing had been poor. This had occurred in 1937, with his speech calling for a "quarantine" of international aggressors. The speech received no support anywhere. He simply had gotten too far ahead of public opinion. And this was his reminder that a mastery of public opinion always entails two things: first, knowing what it *is*, and second, educating it toward what you *want* it to be.

Out of my experience and observation of these same times, I would stress the need always for a President to recognize his accountability to Congress. This recognition was a mark of even as vigorous a Presidential leadership as Roosevelt's. An important example of this came in 1942, when the nation was in a dangerous inflationary spiral and many people were urging the President to act by executive order to establish wage and price controls. (He actually had no statutory authority to do this, but a President as strong as Roosevelt always believes he possesses all necessary authority to act for the good of the nation in any way not expressly prohibited by the Constitution.) Once again, Roosevelt refused to be stampeded. Rather than act summarily, he sent Congress his vigorous but balanced message of September 7 that effectively put before it two propositions: first, the President himself would institute controls if Congress failed to do so by a given deadline, but second, out of respect for the democratic process, he preferred, even in a time of crisis, to act *through* the Congress.

The same spirit prevailed with him, too, all through the protracted debate on the Lend-Lease Act that finally became law in March, 1941. That debate dragged on for some three months, and many of the people around Roosevelt urged him to do something to cut it short. But he always replied that this would be a departure from the American tradition and that he *preferred* a full and exhaustive debate, so that its conclusion with the passage of the law by Congress could be seen as a democratic sign of real national unity. In those months, I marveled at his patience. But he was also using the time to work up a complete list of all things that Great Britain would need. The result was that almost the same day he signed the act he could issue orders to have the goods moving. During the long weeks of waiting before that day, I had often felt exasperated, and so had Churchill. But Roosevelt was right.

I I

The great recent growth of the White House staff around the President has been, I think, very undesirable. The primary objection is the fact that the larger such a staff gets, the more clumsy and inefficient it becomes. It demands more and more time from the President, whereas a staff's basic function should be to leave him more, rather than less, time to concentrate on major policy decisions. When I served as Special Counsel to FDR after 1943, I had no assistants at all. The man in that position today has at least four or five. I cannot imagine what they all do.

A further great objection to an inflated staff is its inevitable tendency, as it takes on more and more functional duties, to become an operational rather than an advisory body. The process has two very bad results. First: it duplicates and conflicts with the action and responsibility of the departments, thus impeding the efficiency of Cabinet officers. Second: it seriously impairs the chance of responsible relations with Congress, since it increases the number of staff officials empowered to act behind the shield of executive privilege. Under President Nixon, for example, a Henry Kissinger can enjoy this immunity from any kind of Congressional inquiry even though his decisions and opinions profoundly affect the whole foreign policy of the nation, while Secretary of State William Rogers—who should be doing the things that Kissinger is doing—can claim no such privilege. The consequence is a drastic loss in the accountability to Congress that any Presidency should respect.

The limit to which a White House staff should go with functional duties competing with the departments was set, I believe, by the role of Jimmy Byrnes during World War II. When disputes then arose *between* departments, he had the authority to settle them, simply to save the President's time. Even this, however, was done pursuant to statute: the Congress had set up the office, had given the President the rights to delegate this specific authority, and Roosevelt had delegated it to Byrnes.

There is one particular development in the White House staff that Bernard Baruch and I tried to urge upon both Presidents Roosevelt and Truman—unsuccessfully, in both cases. We believed it essential to set up in the White House what we called a "Think Board." Our reasoning was simple. The life of any President is so incredibly busy, on any given day, that he is likely to be happy if he has managed to sign every paper put before him by the time he goes to bed at night. This leaves him very little time to think—about next week or next month. To be sure, he already has specialized advisory groups around him like the Economic Council. But there are two problems with them: (1) they are occupied with functional duties of their own, and (2) they do not have free, direct access to the President. With respect to the Cabinet as a "Think Board," there also arise two problems: (1) their administrative functions consume their time, and (2) their breadth of view is not wide enough to help shape national policy. Also, they do not have the necessary immediate access to the President at all times.

There are no officials close to the President—even with the huge White House staff of today—whose sole duty is to fill this need. There is no one commissioned to consider the future, travel the country, and come back to the White House to say: "There is this or that situation. I think it is serious or critical. You should consider taking some action." If there had been any such thoughtful advice reaching the White House, I doubt that President

Nixon, for example, would have had to rush, so belatedly and so hastily, to invoke wage and price controls, as he did in 1972.

The role and the requirements for a "Think Board" in the White House seem to me clear. Its members should have no staff other than personal secretaries. They should have no functional duties whatsoever. They should have authority to walk into any department or agency in quest of information on any problem. They should have easy access to the President at any time, as well as his full confidence. They would then be able, in short, to help a President to think seriously about next month and next year.

III

How should one counsel a new President? I do not know any magic secrets to success in the office. But I would naturally encourage him to weigh the thoughts I have put down here. They could help him, I believe, to be a good President.

I do not believe in substantial reform of the office itself, and I do not fear that the President has too many powers. I probably believe in more powers to the President, but subject always to his respecting his accountability to Congress. In general, he needs full authority to be an effective Chief Executive, in both domestic and foreign affairs.

With respect to his war-making powers, it is the duty of Congress to act whenever they may think action is called for. If they have the courage, they have the power. If they believe Presidential action in Vietnam should be curbed, for example, they should act accordingly, through legislation or appropriations. They might also well consider placing a time limit—perhaps of ninety or a hundred and twenty days—on a President's commitment of military forces without prior Congressional approval. But it would be dangerous and foolish to try to tell a President that he cannot take any military action without prior authorization. I would never want to see the office so limited.

The more zealous reformers put their arguments about the Presidency in terms of the Vietnam War, of course. But it is unwise to take a particular and special experience as a basis for talking generically about the office. We have already had one modern example of this unwisdom with the Twenty-second Amendment's limitation of a Presidency to two terms. This appealed to Republicans who were aiming at Franklin Roosevelt in the 1940's, but it very shortly frustrated Republicans who would have objected not at all to Dwight Eisenhower running for a third term in 1960. We have to remember, as a nation, that the Constitution should not be amended by emotion.

Theodore C. Sorensen

A principal aide and speech writer for John F. Kennedy for a decade. . . . Special Counsel to Presidents Kennedy and Lyndon Johnson (1961–1964). . . . Previously attorney for Federal Security Agency (1951–1952), secretary to New England Senators' Conference (1953–1959), and assistant to Senator John F. Kennedy (1953–1961).

I

Without recounting all of the personal qualities most wanted in any President that are rather obvious, there are two that I would rank above all others: judgment and leadership. A President does not have to be a great creative or innovative thinker, as helpful as that may be. For an almost endless flow of new ideas will almost certainly come to him, and his real task is to discriminate and choose among them. Similarly, he does not personally have to be a great administrator, but he has to choose and guide those who are. He has to be as discriminating in his judgment of men as of ideas.

Leadership also requires a profound understanding of both the public pulse and the political process. Otherwise, a President's capacity for judgment would be essentially passive and mean relatively little. This calls for a kind of Presidential presence—an equipment of spirit and energy and intellect with which to animate the President's own team of advisers, convey his will to Congress, and impress the foreign nations with which he must deal. It requires a vigorous will, an articulate voice, and a willingness to fight for what he believes and wants. Within this framework, I would place these two qualities, judgment and leadership, above all other desirable attributes—more important than intellect or idealism or imagination.

Conversely, of course, the lack of these same qualities can be fatal. A President is in desperate trouble if he does not understand the political process and cannot effectively communicate both what he wants and why it is important—with his own staff, with the executive branch, with the Congress, with the public, and with the world. To "communicate," in this sense, means much more than rhetoric. By deed and by posture, as well as by word, he has to show that he has done his homework, he has studied the problems, he has defined the solutions, he has set his aims—and he has the vitality and determination to reach them.

As for the presence or absence of these qualities in the modern Presidents, I naturally believe John Kennedy to have had them in abundance, and I think this would have become clear to all, had he lived. Franklin Roosevelt, too, had much the same gifts. Theodore Roosevelt certainly displayed qualities of leadership, though at times his judgment could be questioned. I once thought Woodrow Wilson had all the right talents, but now I am not so sure he properly understood the political process.

The great failures lacked both judgment and leadership. This must include all three Presidents of the 1920's: Warren Harding, Calvin Coolidge, and Herbert Hoover. Harding had considerable political experience, but he understood neither the tools of political power nor the currents of public opinion. (Lyndon Johnson, incidentally, well understood the former but had difficulty with the latter.)

The case of Harry Truman seems to me rather ambivalent, even though I know it has become fashionable to mark him for greatness. He had much of the forcefulness essential for *leadership*. But he could be uncertain and unwise in his *judgment*. He could make poor appointments to the Supreme Court. He could be easily led by Dean Acheson into accelerating the cold war. He could be intemperate in his encouragement of the loyalty-security system within the federal government. On the other hand, he had the courage to assert the supremacy of civilian over military authority when facing the political ordeal of recalling General Douglas MacArthur from Korea. In the final analysis, I am not sure that Mr. Truman, as admirable and outspoken as he was, had the necessary ability to communicate in the sense that I have defined it. Accordingly, it was harder for him to earn and hold the respect of leaders of national and international opinion, and he was handicapped by that fact.

Looking at these successive administrations, as well as earlier ones, I find it difficult to single out any particular experience as preparing one for the Presidency. The Vice Presidency is a training ground for nothing at all. Having served with John Kennedy both in the Senate and the White House, I also seriously doubt that the first is adequate preparation for the second. The pertinent and valuable feats that mark one's success in the Senate—the ringing oration, the pointing-with-alarm, the cloakroom dealing, the fiery critique, the stubborn obstruction—these matter very little in the White House. Much the same may be said for the political experience of governors. The administering they do is hardly on the scale of Presidents, and the thinking they do may be even less broad than that of Senators. There may be something to be said for the old tradition of looking toward experience in such places as the Department of State or the Department of Defense. Today it might be experience in the White House itself if it produced a cross between a Kissinger and an Ehrlichman. A Secretary of Health, Education and Welfare might also effectively combine national political experience with direct knowledge of the life and problems of the White House. What ultimately matters is the breadth of experience joined by an understanding of the political process.

When one examines the major Presidential decisions of recent times that signify true courage and leadership, a few come to mind immediately. With Truman, one remembers his confrontation with MacArthur and his sponsorship of the Marshall Plan—a bold and historic stroke. With Eisenhower, the ordering of federal troops into Little Rock, Arkansas, was both important and courageous. In the case of Kennedy, I would cite three major packages of decisions: those resolving the Cuban missile crisis, those assuming leadership in the arena of civil rights, and those symbolized by the test-ban treaty that sought general détente with the Soviet Union. With Johnson, I mention first the package of decisions by which he withdrew himself from candidacy for reelection, halted the bombing of most of North Vietnam, and initiated the peace talks in Paris. All this took courage. In the case of Richard Nixon, there should be cited his journey to China and his acceptance (if this comes to pass) of the peace planks of the North Vietnamese in settling the Vietnam War. For these actions also required a kind of courage, if only by their reversal of all the rhetoric of his political past.

I I

To list the attributes required in an effective Presidential adviser is a paradoxical undertaking. On the one hand: he must serve with an absolute and undivided loyalty. He must represent no other constituency—neither farmers nor blacks, neither business nor labor, no region and no class—nothing but the interests and needs of the President and *his* views and purposes. On the other hand: he cannot be a merely sycophantic servant. He must be willing at all times to tell the President, if need be, the kind of facts that the Chief Executive least wants to hear, and an adviser who is shrewd and sensitive will know how and when to bring the bad news and report the harsh criticisms. He must know, in short, the terrible danger of isolation facing every President—a threat that the White House staff must not increase but positively try to counter.

This complex relationship demands certain things of both White House advisers and the President himself. Of the advisers, it requires a raw intelligence and judgment about political as well as substantive affairs. This does not mean that they have to be politicians or political figures, but they must have a sense for both the political process and public opinion. As for the President, he has to choose advisers talented enough to fill these special roles. He should not be swayed by any appeal or clamor to appoint men who represent important factions or regions or interests. He has to choose his men on the basis of their merit and capacity—to serve him as he needs and wants.

I think the growth in size and influence of the White House staff is largely inevitable and—to a point—desirable. Any President needs people around him who can readily see a problem as the White House must see it, not in the narrower terms of any Cabinet Department and its particular constituency. More than one recent President has summoned a member of his Cabinet for private consultation and exhorted him: "I want your personal and independent judgment on this, not your department's opinion." But this is basically unrealistic: the member of the Cabinet almost inevitably must speak for the great bureaucracy over which he has to preside. This is what makes it so necessary for a President to have as well an advisory staff that is truly his own.

But the White House staff may now be too large numerically. There is no need to duplicate the entire machinery of the State Department in the White House basement. Nor is there any need to shift the important functions of the Bureau of the Budget (now the OMB) to within the White House walls.

Yet in all these matters, I strongly feel that each President has to be, and should be, free to find and choose his own *modus operandi*. This is not something to be frozen by formula or legislated by Congress. With respect to the Cabinet, for example, John Kennedy very rarely found much use in full meetings of all the heads of the various departments. After all, how many matters were there for a Secretary of State and a Secretary of Agriculture to discuss with equal competence? But a President like Dwight Eisenhower, with much less direct political experience, might well have gained from listening to a cross section of views of varying merit.

Whatever the limits to the collective role of the Cabinet, however, there should be no downgrading of the continuing importance of the individual roles of its members. Each of them has to run a huge bureaucratic establishment. Here, as on the Presidential level, a gift for leadership weighs more importantly than special expertise. These men, too, have to be commanding, convincing, and articulate. They inevitably have to spend a vast amount of their time being persuasive with the divisions within their own departments and explaining their policies to committees on Capitol Hill. In all of this, like the President, they have to know how to *communicate*.

III

There is a clear difference between the range of Presidential power and discretion in foreign affairs as compared with domestic affairs. There are at least three basic reasons for this. In the first place, the Founding Fathers wanted it this way, and the Constitution gives the Chief Executive a freer hand in the foreign arena than in the domestic. In the second place, the speed and complexity of modern weaponry and diplomacy confirm this distinction, making almost inevitable Presidential actions in crisis situations without the benefit of prolonged Congressional debate. In the third place, the general public seems to accept and welcome this distinction, sometimes too much so. There prevails a general presumption in foreign affairs that "*he* knows best": he alone can read all the cables, and he alone may authoritatively know what is happening anywhere in the world. But no such sentiment rules in domestic affairs, where every citizen, like every Congressman, feels sufficiently expert to have his or her own opinion on income taxes or civil rights.

With respect to these Presidential powers in foreign affairs, I suspect that the pendulum may have swung too far in his favor. But my preference is not to lower Presidential discretion and flexibility but to raise Congressional authority in order to achieve a proper balance. This will require reform, not at the White House end of Pennsylvania Avenue, but on Capitol Hill. Such reform means better staff, better procedures—and greater courage and independence. Thus I am not among the new revisionists who now favor strictly limiting the President's powers.

There have been two causes for this revision of liberal opinion on the Presidency. First: the Presidents since 1963, Lyndon Johnson and Richard Nixon, have been unpopular with liberals who felt that Congress as a whole was both more liberal and more dovish than the White House. I doubt that this was consistently true, and I doubt even more strongly the wisdom of deciding long-range institutional questions in terms of passing Presidential personalities. Second: there has arisen an altogether understandable concern about excessive secrecy in Presidential decision-making and the practice of executive privilege that seals off Presidential advisers from Congressional inquiry. Under the Nixon administration, for example, it is meaningless for a Senate committee to cross-examine Secretary of State William Rogers on policies being set by Henry Kissinger in the White House. I deplore this. But this kind of abuse of Presidential power does not mean that the power of the office itself should be redefined by statute. It simply means that it should be more properly used by Presidents.

The summary advice to be given any newly elected President is not easy to state, but two points come quickly to mind. Above all, I would urge him to try always to take the long view. Obvious as this may seem, it is not easy. Throughout his term of office, the political pressures of this week or next week tend to seem inexorable. The special interests demand action, the national press demands answers, and the nervous advisers urge responses. A President has to resist all this. He has to know that the most seemingly urgent pressures of today may mean little or nothing two years or four years hence—not to mention in the view of future generations or historians. To stay steadfast, he has to hold onto values and purposes of his own, despite the din around him. This is hard, because he is a politician who is sensitive to public and media demands, or else he would not be President. But he has to reach for something other than the politician's quick reward.

I would say, secondly, that he should know that the most important of all his decisions are likely to come before he even takes office. For it is then that he makes his appointments and selects his advisers. Throughout the Presidency, he will have to rely on them to help do his work and spread his word. Any one of them may fatally mislead him or stain his administration. As the head man in the White House, he obviously must have confidence in his own character and his own intelligence. But he needs more than this. He will have to have all the brains and talents he can enlist, if he aspires to be a great President.

Index